# THE EARLY HISTORY

OF THE

# OLD SOUTH WALES IRON WORKS

(1760 TO 1840).

[FROM ORIGINAL DOCUMENTS.]

BY

**JOHN LLOYD,**

AUTHOR OF "HISTORICAL MEMORANDA OF BRECONSHIRE,"
VOLS. I AND II; AND OF
"THE HISTORY OF THE GREAT FOREST OF BRECKNOCK."

LONDON:
PRINTED BY THE BEDFORD PRESS, 20 & 21, BEDFORDBURY, W.C.
1906.

BODLEIAN
20 3 1907
LIBRARY

# PREFACE.

THE great period of the first formation of the South Wales Iron Works dates from 1760 to 1810.

The eminent firm of solicitors of that time, Messrs. Walter and John Powell, of Brecon, had the privilege of being largely employed and trusted by the chief Ironmasters, with the result that in the course of years a mass of documents relating to the South Wales Iron Works accumulated in their offices, and passed on to successive members of the firm; but what they consisted of, and to what they precisely related, had been in course of time forgotten. Eventually, in 1860, every member of the firm having retired or died, the contents of the office became the property of Mr. A. Maybery by descent, and finding a stable convenient in the yard of the office, he placed the whole of the papers (a heterogeneous mass of all kinds, tens of thousands in number) into this impromptu storehouse.

There they lay for forty years, undisturbed by anyone, except a casual old stamp collector; but rust, damp, and dirt were not idle, and the condition of the papers was such as to make it a risk to health to make among them even a search of a few hours' duration.

Thus came the papers to Mr. Maybery, the present owner; and, by his permission, I have been able to examine and reduce them to some kind of order, though at what risk to my own health and at what trouble I leave unsaid.

The history now presented to the reader has thus its genesis, and the papers are authentic, and safely to be trusted; and at a later stage, after they had been indexed and sweetened by exposure to air, with the assistance of a clerk placed at my service, I examined the Iron Works' papers one by one, and when of importance, careful summaries were prepared. These summaries or abstracts I have since woven into what I hope may be considered a readable, orderly, and connected history.

Whether the play is worth the candle is another matter. I think it has been, because the introduction of a great chain of Iron Works into South Wales in barely more than a generation, and their rapid development to a great height of prosperity, and subsequently their equally sudden decadence, is too important a factor in South Wales history, and in the history of our country, to be ignored: and if dealt with at all by the historian, it then becomes of first importance that the knowledge obtained should be accurate, so that the conclusions he may draw shall rest on solid facts, and not upon hearsay evidence, which otherwise is certain to abound in romance and fiction.

---

This survey of the Old South Wales Iron Works is based on the following plan:—

Brecon Furnace and Pipton Forge first claim notice, both being established as early as 1720, and alike dependent solely on charcoal for fuel, and on water for motive power.

From Brecon we drive across the Beacon range of Old Red Sandstone mountains to Penderin, and then turning sharply eastward proceed down the Aberdare Valley, along the northern border of the great South Wales coal basin; describing, more or less in order, the Old Hirwain Works, and those of Aberdare, Abernant, Gadlys, Aberaman, etc.

Crossing the Aberdare Mountain, we deal with the group of great Iron Works adjacent to the River Taff, at Merthyr Tydfil, consisting of the Dowlais, Cyfarthfa, Plymouth, and Penydarran Furnaces and Forges, and these conclude the Western Division.

We commence the Eastern Division on the Rumney River, with the Bute and Union Works, taking next the Tredegar and Sirhowy Works in the Sirhowy Valley. Thence we cross into the Ebbw Fawr Valley, describing the Ebbw Vale Works, and so on to Blaenafon and Garnddyris, at the extreme east of the mineral basin.

Retracing our steps, we describe the great Nantyglo Works (an offshoot of Blaenafon), in the Ebbw Fach Valley, and those close by of Beaufort (though on the Ebbw Fawr River).

Leaving then the high plateau land (1,250 ft. above O. D.), we descend rapidly down by the Clydach stream, describing the Clydach Furnaces (an offshoot of Beaufort) and Clydach Forge (very old), and then cross the Valley of the Usk to Llangrwyney Forge.

We then follow the course of the Usk to Trostre Forge, and make our way to Abbey Tintern Works on the Wye, and thence to Monmouth Forge on the Monnow. Lastly, we conclude our survey with a notice of the old Forge at

New Wear on Wye, which is, perhaps, the oldest of all the Works described, and which George White, an ancestor of mine, built in 1684.

---

Dealing more particularly with the Blast Furnaces, apart from the Forges, it will be seen by the map accompanying this book that they are studded at intervals along a band of mountain land extending from Hirwain to Blaenafon, some eighteen miles in length, and a little over a mile in width. This strip or band of land was just where the Millstone Grit is overlaid by the outcrop of the Coal Measures of the Great South Wales Coal Basin, and was the *raison d'être* of the Iron Works, the ironstone being found there in abundance, and worked at slight expense in patches by turning over, like a garden, the open mountain slopes. The ironstone was good in quality, although not rich in iron, and the coal for smelting purposes was closely adjacent, and of unsurpassable quality.

The limestone for fluxing was also near at hand to the north, and that being inexhaustible, and the coal also of immense extent, it may be said that had the ironstone continued to be obtainable from patches, these very Iron Works we are describing to-day would have all been still in full work, and probably by this time larger than ever they had been in the zenith of their power, from 1800 to 1840. But the ironstone became deep and too expensive for profitable working; and with that failure, and the invention of Bessemer steel, the great decadence of the South Wales Works set in. Nature gave limestone and coal profusely, but of cheap ironstone her gift was scanty.

We have marked the Brecon and Abergavenny Canal and the Monmouthshire Canals, but not those in the Neath and Swansea Valleys, nor have we marked on the map the old lines of tram-roads. We allude to these here and there in the course of the volume, but are unable to add the tramways to the map, as their course generally followed the mountain streams very closely, and if marked thereon, as well as the streams, would much confuse the details of the plan. Our readers must be good enough to imagine that each little mountain valley had its own tram-road leading down to the Canal head, or to join the Canals at some point: such being made under the well-known eight-mile clause of the Canal Acts, either by the Canal Companies or the owners of the Works.

Before these tramways and canals were made—say 1792—the pig-iron and manufactured iron were carried on pack-saddles on the backs of horses and mules across the mountains to certain customary loading-places, and thence by waggon for shipment at the seaports.

How far the power of our pen may succeed we cannot tell, but it has been our aim to try in these pages to depict the scenes and actors of the past, as if they existed and passed before our view to-day.

---

The Author's thanks are due, first, to Mr. A. Maybery, of The Priory, Brecon, for permitting the use of his great collection of old papers; and, secondly, to Sir William Thomas Lewis, Bart., who placed at my disposal a clerk for a couple of months in 1904, to assist in the examination of these papers, and who has given material assistance in addition in other ways.

I have also to thank many others too numerous to mention for their kind assistance, which has been readily given whenever asked for.

JOHN LLOYD.

15, Chepstow Place, London, W.,
February 1st, 1906.

# CONTENTS.

## WESTERN DIVISION.



## EASTERN DIVISION.

## ERRATA.

Page 2, *for* brother-in-law *read* father-in-law.

Pages 33 and 41, *for* Josiah John Guest *read* John Josiah Guest.

Page 105, *for* tons cwt. qrs. *read* cwt. qrs. lbs.

Page 161, *for* Harvey, Partridge and Co. *read* Harford, Partridge and Co.

PAGE 1

THE OLD FURNACE AT BRECKNOCK ON THE HONDDU RIVER.

I.

# Brecon Furnace and Forge, and Aberllonvey Forge.

COUNTY OF BRECON. *CIRCA* 1720.

OUR History commences with the account of the furnace and forge at Brecon, and of the forge at Pipton, near Glasbury, both of which appear to have been founded by Benjamin Tanner, of the town of Brecon, ironmonger, and Richard Wellington, of the town of Hay, in the county of Brecon, gentleman, in 1720-23, as co-partners.

The leases date respectively, in the case of Pipton Forge, from 1722, and in that of the Brecon Furnace from 1723; but the latter was erected a few years previously—if the date cast on the massive lintels of cast iron supporting the stonework of the two outlets is trustworthy—for in several places the date of 1720 is cast, as may be seen to-day, and so pictured in the accompanying photograph.

It was usual thus to mark such massive castings; and in a recent number of the *Illustrated London News* a photograph is given of a broken cast-iron lintel at the great Carron Works in Scotland, on which is cast

CAR$^{N}$ C$^{O}$ 1760.

Our little Furnace at Brecon had, therefore, been forty years in existence before the Carron Works were begun.

From where these massive castings were brought to Brecon we have no certain knowledge. They may have been brought up the Wye by barge to Hay, and thence by land carriage; or they may have come from either of the old works at Yniscedwin, Llangrwney, or Clydach. In any case, it must have been a memorable event: not only the casting of such heavy pieces of iron, but their transport over a long distance on bad roads to their destination.

The Brecon Furnace is situate on the Honddu brook, about a mile distant from the county town of that name, and being comparatively uninjured by the ravages of time or the hand of man, presents to view to-day its original appearance, and is well worth a visit. An old corn-mill had previously stood there, and the site of it, with mill-pond and leat were ready to hand for conversion to their purposes by the new lessees.

Of course, both works were so placed—the Furnace on the Honddu and the Forge (Pipton) on the Llynfi stream—in order to utilise the water-power in driving the large bellows necessary to produce a strong blast of air, without the aid of which a sufficiently intense heat could not be produced to melt the iron ore, or pig-iron, as the case may be. The Honddu is a brook of fair size, equal to driving two pairs of millstones; and the Llynfi, which issues from Llangorse lake, has a trifle less—though more equal—volume of water through the year.

We give a photograph of the Honddu Furnace as it stands to-day.

To this furnace the iron ore (and the limestone required for fluxing) were conveyed in sacks on the backs of horses and mules from the open patch workings at Hirwain, eighteen miles distant, and elsewhere; and the abundant oak and other woods of the district—first burnt into charcoal—supplied the fuel. No coal was used; "coales," or "coals," being a very different article! The consumption of cordwood for charking into cordwood was large, and formed the main item of expense. The coppice woods in the Cwmdwr Valley, beyond Llywell, and far away up the Wye Valley and across Epynt mountain at Llangammarch and Llanwrtid had to be requisitioned: both the furnace at Brecon and the forge at Pipton being almost insatiable in their demands.

It would almost seem that a forge was added at a later period to the Brecon furnace, but of that no trace exists to-day. Pipton was, however, a forge and nothing more, and it may be assumed was fed by a supply of pig-iron from the Honddu furnace; until a time came when the Honddu furnace fell into disuse, and the pig-iron for the use of all their forges was brought from the Hirwain furnace.

How the manufactured iron was conveyed to market we do not know, but the Wye being navigable to Hay, some six miles distant from Pipton, it may have been taken in barges down the river to Chepstow, and thence to the merchants at Bristol. In any case, whether by water or overland, the cost of carriage was great, but the price of the best merchant iron was high also, exceeding probably £20 a ton.

The original lease of the Brecon premises had been granted by Edward Jeffreys, of the Priory (the Camden family), and that of the Pipton property jointly by Henry Williams, of Gwernefed (now Wood family), and Charles Williams, of Trevithel, both being riparian owners, one on either side the stream, and interested in the water rights of the Llynfi river.

In 1750, it appears that William Tanner, son of the previously-named Benjamin Tanner, with his father's consent and that of Richard Wellington, assigned all their interests in the works, including, it is said, "the recently-built furnace for running iron," to Thomas Daniel and Richard Reynolds, merchants and dealers in iron at Bristol.

And in 1753 the same Messrs. Daniel and Reynolds sold all their interests in the works so acquired to Thomas Maybery for £400; whereupon immediately the latter, in consideration of natural love and affection, and of 10*s.* paid, conveys to his son, John Maybery, all his interests in the said leasehold property, held for the remainder of ninety-nine and fifty years respectively.

This is our first introduction to the Maybery family, who came from Powick Forge, on the Teme, in Worcestershire; but we shall hear more of them later in connection with the first formation of the iron-works at both Tredegar and Hirwain.

It may be interesting here to mention that it is recorded in the Breconshire Quarter Sessions books that a man was indicted for stealing a piece of iron at Pipton, the property of Richard Wellington; also, that among the entries in the Parish Register of Glasbury the name of Maybery several times occurs about 1750. We also find that among the Volunteers enrolling themselves "in defence of King and Country" in the perilous times of 1798, the names of several men are given as living "att the Foarge." This is, however, no proof that the Forge existed as late as that, for the so-called "Forge dwellings" might be tenanted, though the forge had ceased to exist.

But we must now introduce the important Wilkins family, who, being attorneys, had for several generations held the office of Deputy Prothonotary (or Deputy Clerk) of the Crown for the Brecknock Circuit (Counties of Brecknock, Glamorgan, and Radnor) of the Great Sessions.

In 1757, John Maybery, who we have seen had become the lessee of the Brecon and Pipton Ironworks, took a lease from Lord Windsor of his mineral property at Hirwain; and immediately afterwards, on marrying Annie, a daughter of John Wilkins, the then Deputy Prothonotary, joined with his brother-in-law in taking a fresh lease, dated 1760, of the same property from the Dowager Lady Windsor.

In 1764, the same John Maybery took a lease of the Tredegar Forge from the Hon. Thomas Morgan, of Ruperra, and a Mr. Thomas Wilkins became his partner, though it is said no articles of partnership were actually signed between them. In 1777 he appears also, in conjunction with his father-in-law, John Wilkins, to have been tenant of the Iron-works at Machen.

We find that in 1760 the following letter was addressed to the firm of Wilkins and Maybery at Brecon :—

"Navy Office, 19 Nov., 1760.

"Messrs. Wilkins and Co.,
"At Brecon, South Wales.

"In return to your letter offering to suply (obliterated) hundred Tons of Iron Ballast for His Majesty's Navy,

"We acquaint you the Service is not in want thereof, and are
"Your Affectionate Friends,
"THOS. STEELE, SAML. BRETT."

Our opinion is—though no record confirming it is to be found among our papers—that after the partnership in the Hirwain Iron-works between John Maybery and John Wilkins commenced in 1760, the Brecon Furnace and Forge and the Pipton Forge were worked by them as part of the common partnership. Also, that being able to procure pig-iron from their iron furnace at Hirwain, the Brecon Furnace fell into disuse. If this surmise is correct, it is probable that when the firm fell into difficulties in 1777, and the sons of John Wilkins, Walter and Jeffreys, who founded with others "Wilkins' Old Bank at Brecon" in 1778, took over the liabilities, the works at Brecon and Pipton gradually fell into disuse, and were finally abandoned several years before 1800, but as to the exact date of the closing of these works, our papers are silent.

John Wilkins, the Attorney and Prothonotary, and who probably financed the firm, died in 1784, and John Maybery, the practical, skilled, and enterprising ironmaster, died about the same time, both leaving vigorous descendants in the Town of Brecon, either as lawyers or bankers. One of the sons of John Maybery, named Charles, is said to have gone to America into an iron-foundry, but his subsequent history is entirely unknown.

We add copies of the various documents referred to in connection with the Brecon and Pipton Iron Works.

## BRECON FORGE AND FURNACE, AND ABERLONVEY FORGE, COUNTY BRECON, 1755.

### THOMAS MAYBERY TO JOHN MAYBERY (INCLUDING ASSIGNMENT OF LEASES DATED 1723 AND 1722).

[Maybery Papers, Bundle D.]

THIS INDENTURE made the 22nd day of May in the 28th year of the Reign of King George the 2nd by etc., etc., and in the year 1755.

Between

THOMAS MAYBERY, of Powicks Forge, in the County of Worcester, Ironmaster, of the one part,

And

JOHN MAYBERY, of Aberlonvey, in the County of Brecon, Ironmaster, Son of the said Thomas Maybery, of the other part.

WHEREAS Edward Jeffreys, late of the Inner Temple, London, Esquire, now deceased, did by his Indenture of Lease, bearing date the 8th day of November, 1723, and made between the said Edward Jeffreys, Esq., of the one part, and Benjamin Tanner, of the town of Brecon, Ironmonger, and Richard Wellington, the Younger, of the Town of the

Hay in the said County, Gentleman, of the other part, DEMISE, GRANT, SET, and to FARM LET unto the said Benjamin Tanner and Richard Wellington,

ALL THAT Mansion House and Garden commonly called Tuy Watkin or felin, otherwise Tafern y Trap, and the Parcel of land thereto belonging or adjoining, commonly called or known by the name of Cwm y Velin, in as large and ample a manner as Catherine Morgan, Widow, then or then lately held the same.

TOGETHER with one Fulling or Tucking Mill to the said House or parcel of land belonging then or then lately in the occupation of Thomas Watkin, Tucker, all which said House, Garden, Parcel of land, and Tucking Mill, with their appurtenances, are situate lying and being in the several Parishes of St. John Evangelist and Llanthew in the said County of Brecon, TOGETHER with all ways, Waters, Watercourses, Floodgates, Wears, Stanks, Liberties, Priviledges, and Advantages, whatsoever thereto belonging, with liberty for the said Benjamin Tanner and Richard Wellington, their exors., admors., or assigns, during the Term therein and hereinafter mentioned, to make, Erect, and Build One Iron Forge and Furnace for making and Running of Iron, and unto that end and purpose to Dig up and raise Wallstone or other stone and to Dig one or more Ponds, and to make Buildings, Wears, Stanks, Floodgates, and Sluices, on any part of the said Premises that shall and will be necessary to carry on the said Works.

TO HOLD all and singular the said premises with the Appurtenances unto the said Benjamin Tanner and Richard Wellington, their exors., admors., and assns., from the Feast day of Saint Michael, the Arch Angel, then last past, for the term of 99 years then next ensuing, at and under the Yearly Rent of £7 at Lady day and Michaelmas, by equal portions, exclusive of all Taxes, then or thereafter to be rated or assessed upon the said premises or any part thereof.

AND WHEREAS by one other Indenture of Lease, bearing date the seventh day of March, 1722, and made or mentioned to be made Between Henry Williams of Gwernevatt, in the County of Brecon, Esq., of the 1st part, Charles Williams of Trevithell, in the same County, Esq., of the 2nd part, and the said Benjamin Tanner, by the name of Benjamin Tanner, of the Town of Brecon, in the County of Brecon aforesaid, Ironmonger, and the said Richard Wellington, of the 3rd part. The said Henry Williams did thereby demise, Set, and to Farm Let unto the said Benjamin Tanner and Richard Wellington,

ALL THAT Messuage, Workhouse, or Building called the Forge, then lately erected upon a Parcel of Ground called Maes y Wern Ysse, situate, lying and being in the Parish of Aberlonvey, in the said County of Brecon, then or then lately in the possession of the said Benjamin Tanner and Richard Wellington, or their assigns; and also a certain Wear, made across the river Llonvey, the one end thereof being fixed on the lands of the said Charles Williams, which conveys the Water of the said River to the said Forge. AND ALSO one certain Water-course that leadeth from the said Wear through a Field called Ywern Degge, then or then late in the Possession of Charles Baker, and through another Field thereto adjoining, then in the Possession of John Williams, called by the name of Maes y wern Ysha, towards the Pound of the said Forge, with all Wears and Sluices, and also the benefit and advantage of another small River that Runs through the Park of the said Henry Williams a Cross the Highway, and from thence through part of the said Field called maes y wern yssa into the said Pound, when it can be spared from the Mill called Aberlonvey Mill, with free liberty of Ingress, Egress, and Regress to and for the said Benjamin Tanner and Richard Wellington, their exors., admors., and assigns, and their Servants and Agents, to Amend and Repair, Scour, Cleanse, and enlarge the said Wears, Water-courses, as often and whensoever occasion should Require; with liberty for the said Benjamin Tanner and Richard Wellington, their exors., admors., and assigns, to dig and raise Wallstone and Tyle Stone on the most Convenient Place or places, on any of the Lands and Tenements of the said Henry Williams, for Repairing the same Premises, and with free liberty of Ingress, Egress, and Regress for them, their servants and Agents, Cattle and Carriages, to carry away the same without the Lett or Disturbance of the said Henry Williams, his heirs or assigns, or his or their Undertenants, together with all Workhouses, Outhouses, Yards, Gardens, Stanks, Wears, Sluices, Floodgates, Ways, Waters, Watercourses, Liberties, and Appurtenances to the said Forge belonging, and in as large and ample manner as the same then were or at any time theretofore were used and enjoyed by the said Benjamin Tanner and Richard Wellington, or either of them (Liberty of Fishing with Angleing Rods and Netts in the said Watercourses and Ponds at all times and seasons to the said Henry Williams, his heirs and Assigns, Excepted and reserved).

To HAVE AND TO HOLD all and singular the said Demised Premises, with the appurtenances (Except before Excepted) unto the said Benjamin Tanner and Richard Wellington, their exors., admors., and assigns, from the Feast day of St. Michael the Arch Angel then last past, for the term of 50 years, at and under the Yearly Rent of £30, payable Half-yearly (that is to say) upon the 25th day of March and the 29th day of September, by equal portions without any Deductions whatsoever.

AND WHEREAS by one Indenture of Assignment, bearing date the 26th day of December, 1750, and made between the said Benjamin Tanner and William Tanner, of Brecon aforesaid, Gentleman, Eldest Son and Heir of the said Benjamin Tanner, and the said Richard Wellington of the one part, and Thomas Daniel and Richard Reynolds, both of the City of Bristol, Merchants and Dealers in Iron, of the other part, After reciting to the effect hereinbefore recited, and that since the granting of the first lease therein and herein in part recited, a Furnace for Running of Iron had by virtue thereof been erected and Built on part of the premises thereby Granted by the said Benjamin Tanner and Richard Wellington, or one of them; and that the said Premises, together with the several Indentures of Lease and Terms therein respectively mentioned, were then vested in the said William Tanner, who did for the Consideration therein mentioned, by and with the consent and approbation of the said Benjamin Tanner and Richard Wellington, testified as therein expressed, Give, Grant, Bargain, Sell, Assign, Transfer, and Set over, and the said Benjamin Tanner and Richard Wellington did Ratify and confirm unto the said Thomas Daniel and Richard Reynolds the said in part recited Indentures of Lease and the premises thereby demised.

TOGETHER with the said then new Erected Furnace and all the Buildings thereto belonging, and the Terms therein then to come and unexpired, and all their Right, Title, and interest in and to the same.

To HOLD the same to the said Thomas Daniel and Richard Reynolds, their exors., admors., and assigns, for and during all the Rest, Residue, and Remainder of the said several Terms of years thereby severally granted and then to come, unexpired, subject unto the Rents and conditions therein expressed.

AND WHEREAS the said Thos. Daniel and Richard Reynolds did by an Indre. of Assignment, bearing date the 30th day of March, 1753, in consideration of £400 to them in hand paid by the said Thos. Maybery, Grant, Bargain, Sell, Assign, Transfer and Set over unto the said Thos. Maybery

ALL and singular the said Messuages, Houses, Mills, Furnace, Workhouse, Buildings, Parcels of Land, Wears, Watercourses, Liberties, and other the premises above mentioned and Recited, and by the said several in part recited Indentures Granted unto the said Benj. Tanner and Richd. Wellington;

AND ALL THE ESTATE, Right, Title, and Interest, Term of years then to come, etc., of them the said Thomas Daniel and Richard Reynolds,

To HOLD to the said Thos. Maybery, his exors., ads. and assigns, for and during the remainder of the said sevl. recited terms of 99 years, and 50 years then to come and unexpired, in as large and ample manner to all intents and purposes, as they the said Thos. Daniel and Richard Reynolds, their exors., or admors., might, could, or ought to have held or enjoyed the same by virtue of the said in part recited Indentures of Assignment, subject nevertheless to the payment of the Rent and performance of the Covenants as therein mentioned, as in and by the said several in part recited Indentures, relation being thereunto had more fully and at large it doth and may appear.

AND WHEREAS the said Thomas Maybery hath agreed to assign over all and singular the said Premises to the said John Maybery, his Son,

NOW THIS INDENTURE WITNESSETH that the said Thos. Maybery, as well for and in consideration of the natural love and affection which he hath and beareth for or towards the said John Maybery, as also of 10s. of lawful money paid, etc., the receipt, etc., and for other good Causes and cons'ons, Hath granted, bargained, Sold, Assigned, Transferred, and set over, and by these Presents did grant, Bargain, Sell, Assign, Transfer, and set over unto the said John Maybery,

ALL AND SINGULAR the said Messuages, Houses, Mill, Furnaces, Forge, Workhouse, Buildings, Garden, parcels of land, Wears, Watercourses, Liberties, Priviledges and Advantages, and Premises above mentioned and recited; and by the said several in part recited Indentures of Lease Demised and Granted to the said Benjamin Tanner and Richd. Wellington, and by the said last in part recited Indenture, Assigned, Transferred, and set over to the said Thomas Maybery, his exors., admors., and assigns as aforesaid, and every part and parcel thereof, with their and every of their appurtenances, AND ALL the Estate, Right, Title, etc., of him the said Thomas Maybery,

TOGETHER with the said in part recited Indres. of Lease and Assignments, and all other Deeds or Writings relating thereto,

TO HAVE AND TO HOLD all and sing'r the said Messuages, Houses, Mill, Furnaces, Workhouse, Buildings, Gardens, Parcels of Land, Wear, Watercourses, Liberties, Priviledges, Advantages and Premises in the said several in part recited Indentures of Lease and Assignment, Demised, granted and transferred, or intended to be hereby granted, Transferred, assigned, or Set over, with their and every of their appurtenances, unto the said John Maybery, his exors., admors., and assns., for and during all the Rest, Residue, and remainder of the said several Recited Terms of 99 years and 50 years, in and by the said several in part recited Indentures of Lease respectively granted, as are yet to come and unexpired, in as large and ample a manner as the said Thos. Maybery, his exs., might or could do if these Presents were not made Subject to the payment and performance of the several Yearly Rents, Covenants, Conditions, and agreements reserved and contained, which as well in the said several in part recited Indentures of Lease on the Lessees' part, and behalf of their exors., admors., and assns., as in the said last in part recited Indenture of Assignment on the part and behalf of the said Thos. Maybery, his exors., ads., and assigns is, are, or ought to be paid, done, and performed.

COVENANTS by said Thomas Maybery with said John Maybery: That he had good right to assign, free from all incumbs., and for quiet enjoyment by John Maybery on payt. of rent.

COVENANT by sd. John Maybery with sd. Thos. Maybery: To pay rents and keep indemnified in regard to performance of Covenants.

THOMAS (L. S.) MAYBERY.

Sealed and Delivered (being first duly Stamp'd)
in the presence of

(S'd) John Nixon.

(S'd) Benj. Taylor.

## ACCOUNT OF CORDWOOD BOUGHT FOR FURNACE.

| 1753. Short Cords. | Recorded. | Price. s. | d. | Miles to Furnace. | Miles to Forge. |
|---|---|---|---|---|---|
| Coal'd 152¼ | Hugh Pendry, Esqr., at Lanvihangell . | 2 | 9 | 5 | |
| Do. 78½ | Wm. Gwin Vaughan, Esqr., at Lanvathen . . . | 2 | 0 | 10 | 10 |
| Do. 595¼ | Do. at Abberdohono . . | 2 | 0 | 10 | 9 |
| Do. 1137½ | Do. at Skiog . . | 2 | 0 | 10 | 8 |
| Do. 28 | David John's Unisgoverrah, Cutt. . | 3 | 6 | 4 | 4 |
| Do. 25 | Thos. Protherro Do. on ye Stoole . | 2 | 9 | 4 | 4 |
| Do. 64 | Jno. Powells, Bailleyholog . . | 2 | 0 | 7 | 5 |
| Do. 72 | Mr. Goolds, Landavathley . . | 2 | 6 | 5 | 4 |
| Do. 291¼ | Thos. James, Esq., Crickaden . | 3 | 0 | 7 | 4 |
| Do. 21¾ | Thos. James, Crickaden . . | 3 | 0 | 7 | 4 |
| Do. 30¾ | Wm. Williams, Landavathley, Cutt. . | 4 | 0 | 5 | 3 |
| Do. 192½ | Mr. Griffiths, Cutt and Corded . | 2 | 9½ | 8 | |
| Do. 15 | Phill. Brooks, Bruntless, Cutt at . | 4 | 0 | 5 | 1½ |
| Do. 1476 | Caple Hanbury, Esqr., Crickaden, Cutt and Corded . . . | 5 | 4½ | 7 | 4 |
| Do. 53 | Whalter Morgans at Vale, at . | 2 | 9 | 3 | |
| Do. 69½ | Whalter Morgan and Thos. Prothero, wood at Warnvawr, at . . | 2 | 9 | 4 | |
| Do. 45¼ | Thos. Jones, wood at Tinwain . | 2 | 9 | 4 | |
| Do. 155 | David Johns, Unnisgoverrah . | 2 | 9 | 4 | |
| Do. 56½ | Jno. Howell, at Pentuin, Cutt at . | 4 | 3 | 3 | |
| Do. 66¾ | Jno. Williams, wood at Penclyn, at . | 3 | 0 | 3 | |
| 35¾ | Charles Powel, Esqr., Delivered but not Coal'd . . . } | 2 | 6 | 10 | 12 |
| 145 | Do. not delivered . . } | | | | |
| 161 | Mr. Lloyds, of Dinnas, Do. . | | | | |
| 24 | Mr. Samuel Evans at Langam'h . | 2 | 6 | 10 | 12 |
| 128¼ | Mr. Davis, of Gwender's, near Do. . | | | | |
| 136¾ | Mr. Price, of Maseyronn, near Do. . | | | | |
| 141¼ | David Rees Protherah, near Do. . | | | | |
| 169¾ | Thos. Davis, of Langam'h . . | 2 | 6 | | |
| 61 | Charles Powel, Esq., near Castle- | | | | |
| 29 | madock . . . | 3 | 0 | | |
| 69 | Mr. Watkins at Battle . . | | | | |
| | Mr. Jones at Lanvase . . | | | | |
| | Mr. Jeffreys . . . | | | | |
| | Mr. Wilkins . . . | | | | |

[Outside of Old Forge Book endorsed :]

## ACCOUNT OF CORDWOOD BOUGHT, AND WHAT EACH LOADE OF COALS . . . . . . . .

### CORDWOOD BOUGHT FOR FURNACE.

| 1754. Short Cords. | | Supposed. . . . . . . . . . . ou ye stoole. | Price. | | Miles to Furnace. | Miles to Forge. |
|---|---|---|---|---|---|---|
| | | | s. | d. | | |
| Coal'd | 60 | Whalter Morgan on ye stoole | 2 | 9 | 3 | |
| Do. | 18 | Robert Probert, Landavathley, ready Cutt | 3 | 9 | 5 | 3 |
| Do. | 100 | Thos. Price and Wm. Williams, Gwenther | 2 | 0 | 7 | 5 |
| Do. | 100 | Whalter Morgan and Thos. Prothero | 2 | 9 | 3½ | |
| Do. | 50 | Thos. Jones, wood at Tinwain | 2 | 9 | 4 | |
| Do. | 120 | David John, Unisgoverrah | 2 | 9 | 4 | |
| Do. | 100 | Jno. Williams, wood at Penclyn, in ye parish of Llanspythid | 3 | 0 | 3 | |
| Do. | 4000 | M'r Wilkins, wood at Commoredore | 2 | 3 | 9 | |
| Do. | 400 | Do., at Mertha | 2 | 6 | 5 | 8 |
| Do. | 1500 | Do., at Trallwng | 3 | 0 | 4 | 9 |
| Do. | 1000 | Do., at Veney wood | 3 | 6 | 2 | 8 |
| Do. | 600 | Do., at Llandyfaelog | 3 | 6 | 2 | 7 |
| Do. | 200 | Thos. Lloyd, wood at Trallwng | 2 | 9 | 5 | 10 |
| Do. | 300 | David Davies, wood at Gwenther | 2 | 6 | 7 | 5 |
| Do. | 40 | Jno. Howell, at Pentuin. Cutt | 4 | 3 | 2½ | 8 |
| 1756. | | | | | | |
| Coal'd | 200 | Rees Havard, wood at Seney | 2 | 6 | 7 | |
| Do. | 1200 | Revd. John Williams, at Reneglws | 3 | 0 | 4 | 4 |
| Do. | 2000 | Messrs. Powel and Rumsey wood, at Vungless | 3 | 6 | 3 | 5 |
| Do. | 100 | M'r Havard, wood near Vungless | | | 3 | 5 |
| Do. | 20 | Harry Hurgas, wood at Laneglws | 3 | 0 | 5 | 4 |
| Do. | 40 | Walter Williams, do. | 2 | 9 | 5 | 4 |

"Furnace" means the Brecon Furnace; "Forge," the Aberllynfi Forge; "Coals" is the term used for Charcoal. "D" denotes "dozens of sacks"; "S," "sacks."

## ACCOUNT OF WHAT EACH LOADE OF COALS (CHARCOAL) LIES IN (THAT IS, COSTS).

| 1754. Jan. | £ | s. | d. |
|---|---|---|---|
| 35 cords of David John's of Unisgowerach, cutt at 33s. 6d. | 6 | 2 | 6 |
| And 25 Thos. Prothero's Do. on the Stoole at 2s. 9d. | 3 | 8 | 9 |
| Cutting Thos. Prothero's at 9s. | 2 | 10 | 0 |
| Cording of both and Hurdles | 1 | 5 | 0¾ |
| D. S. | | | |
| Coaling 16—1 of Coals at 3s. 6d. | 2 | 16 | 3½ |
| Carredge of Do. at 5s. | 4 | 0 | 5 |
| | 20 | 3 | 0¼ |
| Each Loade Lies in | 1 | 5 | 1 |

| | £ | s. | d. |
|---|---|---|---|
| 152¼ cordes of Wood from Cotydù at 2s. 9d. | 20 | 18 | 8¼ |
| Cutting do. at 2s. 4d. | 17 | 15 | 3 |
| Cording and Hurdles | 2 | 7 | 1½ |
| D. S. | | | |
| Coaling 39—2 of Coals at 3s. 6d. | 6 | 17 | 1 |
| Carredge of Do. at 7s. | 13 | 14 | 2 |
| | 61 | 12 | 3½ |
| Each Loade lies in | 1 | 11 | 6 |

| | £ | s. | d. |
|---|---|---|---|
| 64 cords of woods from Gwenther 2s. | 6 | 8 | 0 |
| Cutting Do. at 1s. 4d. | 4 | 5 | 4 |
| Cording and Hurdles | 1 | 2 | 10 |
| D. S. | | | |
| Coaleing 18—1 of Coals at 3s. 6d. | 3 | 3 | 3½ |
| Carredge of 11—7 to furnace at 7s. | 4 | 1 | 1 |
| Do. 6—6 to forge at Do. | 2 | 6 | 4 |
| | 21 | 6 | 10½ |
| Each Loade Lies in | 1 | 3 | 7 |

| | £ | s. | d. |
|---|---|---|---|
| 72 Cords of Wood at Llanvathly at 2s. 6d | 9 | 0 | 0 |
| Cutting Do. at 2s. 1d. | 7 | 10 | 0 |
| Cording and Hurdles | 1 | 3 | 0 |
| D S. | | | |
| Coaleing 17—5 at 3s. 6d. | 3 | 7 | 0 |
| Carredge of 14—0 to furnace at 6s. | 4 | 4 | 0 |
| Do. of 3—5 to forge at 5s. | | 17 | 1 |
| | 25 | 15 | 1 |
| Each Loade lies in | 1 | 9 | 8 |

| 1756. | £ | s. | d. |
| --- | --- | --- | --- |
| 477¾ Cords of Wood at Trathlwng. Mr. Wilkins wood at 3s. | 71 | 13 | 9 |
| Cutting 430¾ Cords at 2s. | 43 | 01 | 06 |
| Do. 45½ Do. at 1s. 3d. | 2 | 09 | 03 |
| Cording 477¾ cords at 5s. per score | 5 | 19 | 05 |
| Hurdles | | 15 | 0 |
| D. S. | | | |
| Coaling 111—4 at 3s. 6d. | 19 | 09 | 08 |
| Carredge of 111—4 of Coales at 5s. | 27 | 16 | 08 |
| | 171 | 05 | 03 |
| Each Loade Lies in | 1 | 10 | 8 |

| | £ | s. | d. |
| --- | --- | --- | --- |
| 110½ Cords of Wood at Trathlwng. Thos. Floyd's wood at 2s. 9d. | 15 | 03 | 10 |
| Cutting 60½ Cords at 12d. | 3 | 00 | 03 |
| Do. 50½ Cords at 11d. | 3 | 15 | 04½ |
| Cording Do. at 5s. | 1 | 07 | 07 |
| Hurdles | | 07 | 00 |
| D. S. | | | |
| Coaleing 33—3 of Coales at 3s. 6d. | 6 | 05 | 04 |
| Caredge of Do. to furnace at 6s. | 9 | 19 | 06 |
| | 39 | 19 | 00 |
| Each Loade lies in | 1 | 04 | 0 |

| 1756. Octbr. 10th. | £ | s. | d. |
| --- | --- | --- | --- |
| 313¾ of Wood at Mertha. Mr. Wilkins wood at 2s. 6d. | 32 | 04 | 04 |
| Cutting 250 Cords at 2s. | 25 | 00 | |
| Do. 63¾ at 15d. | 3 | 19 | 08 |
| Cording of Do. at 5s. | 3 | 18 | 05 |
| D. S. | | | |
| Coaling 77—5 of Coals at 3s. 9d. | 14 | 10 | 04 |
| Carredge to furnace of Do. at 7s. | 27 | 01 | 11 |
| Hurdles—4 Doz. at 3s. 6d. | | 14 | 0 |
| | 114 | 08 | 08 |
| Each Loade lies in | 1 | 9 | 6¼ |

The Entry :—Coaling, 33 3 (D. S.), denotes that 33 Dozen Sacks and three Sacks over had been coaled and delivered at the Works, the Charcoal-burner being paid by the dozen sacks.

The Merchant Iron turned out, when Charcoal only was used at the Furnace, and in the Forge, must have been, in the hands of a skilled manufacturer, of the purest and finest kind and grade on the market.

When heating the Furnace, the cordwood would first be converted into charcoal, and then mixed, as coke is now being mixed, as fuel with the iron-stone and limestone.

II.

# The Hirwain Iron Works.

[MAYBERY PAPERS, BDLE. E.]

## DEEDS (COPIES) RELATING TO THE HIRWAIN WORKS.

1757. Lease of Minerals.—Lord Windsor to John Maybery.

1760. Lease of Minerals.—Lady Windsor to John Wilkins, John Maybery and Ann Maybery.

1773. Sub-lease.—John Maybery and Thomas Wilkins to John Wasse and William King.

1780. Assignment (Rent reserved).—John Maybery and Thomas Wilkins to Anthony Bacon (the first A.B.)

1786. On A. Bacon's Death: Short Lease granted.—Court of Chancery to Samuel Glover.

1799. Award.—Samuel Glover surrenders his interest to the brothers Anthony and Thomas Bacon, on being paid £13,000.

Sale.—Anthony Bacon sells his interest to his brother Thomas for £3,000.

1803. Lease—Thomas Bacon to Jeremiah Homfray, F. W. Bowzer, Simon Oliver and Lionel Oliver.

Change of Partnership.—Homfray went out, George Overton takes his place.

Shop.—Edward Overton's Agreement.

1808. Fresh Agreement.—Messrs. Walter and Jeffreys Wilkins, now possessed of the John Maybery and John Wilkins' interest, agreed with Lionel Oliver on behalf of himself and partners, to pay an increased rent in lieu of supplying pig-iron.

1814. Bankruptcy of Bowzer, Overton and Co.—Lawsuit between Thomas Bacon and Fry, the Receiver of the Bankrupt Estate.

1816. Lawsuit commenced between Walter and Jeffreys Wilkins, of Brecon, and Thomas Bacon.—The Works had become much dilapidated, and Thomas Bacon had refused to pay the rent reserved under the Deed of 1780. Messrs. Wilkins took the opinion of Counsel (Mr. Taunton) on the case; and eventually, as a settlement, they conveyed all their interest in the Hirwain Works, and also considerable amount of freehold land they were possessed in the Parish of Penderin, and elsewhere adjacent to the Works, to Thomas Bacon for the sum of £3,000.

---

WE HAVE now left the Valleys of the Wye and Usk, and the small Furnace at Brecon, and the Forge at Pipton behind us, and are crossing the ranges of the Brecon Beacons to breathe the fresh air of Penderin parish at the altitude of 1,200 ft. above sea-level. John Maybery, ironmaster, is our pioneer guide, and we find ourselves at Hirwain, on the fringe of the great South Wales mineral basin, surveying the long meadow or open common land, in and under which lay an abundance of minerals, and of which Lord Windsor was the Lord of the Manor.

There had been some patch-working here previously for mine for supplying the Brecon Furnace; but it was now resolved by John Maybery, having ascertained the capabilities of the district, both as regards iron ore, coal, and limestone, to lease from Lord Windsor the minerals, and to erect a furnace on some adjacent land in the Parish of Penderin, which he had been able to secure the freehold of.

Accordingly, in 1757, Mr. John Maybery arranged with Lord Windsor for a lease of his Hirwain mineral property, the terms of which were as follows:—

"By indenture of lease dated November 22nd, 1757, Lord Windsor did demise, grant, and let to John Maybery and his exors. full power, liberty, and authority to dig for, search, raise, and land All mines of iron ore or coal that could or might be found in or upon a certain Common, Tyr wain Wrgan, otherwise Hirwain Wrgan, situate, lying, and being in the several Manors or Lordships (of the said Viscount Windsor) of Miskin and Glynronthoy, in ye County of Glamorgan, with liberty of making ditches, gutters, levels, Drains, Dams, and Ponds for scouring and raising the same, and also part of the Right, interest title and liberty which the said Lord Viscount Windsor had of inclosing 200 acres of Miskin Measure, remainder of 250 acres of the Common aforesaid, the liberty of enclosing of 4 acres of the Measure aforesaid in a certain place there called Godre Bryn y Mairdy, situate near the River Cynon, in the parish of Aberdare, within the Manor or Lordship of Glynronthwy aforesaid; with liberty to and for the said John Maybery, his exors., etc., upon the said 4 acres or any part thereof, to erect and build a Furnace for the making of Pig Iron, or any other Manufacture, and to raise stones and slates for the building and covering the same.

"And also for the making of court yards and other conveniences as to him or any of them should seem meet and requisite (excepting always and reserving free liberty for all Passengers and Travellers to pass through the said Inclosure, where, when, and as often as their occasion should require, excepting also liberty to and for the tenants of the said Lord Viscount Windsor of a certain Hamlet, called Rigoes, in the parish of Ystradyvodock, situate in the Manor or Lordship of Glynronthwy aforesaid, at any time during the term hereby granted to dig for and raise coal and carry away the same; and from a certain place called Nant yr Uchain, upon the Common of Hirwain Wrgan aforesaid, for burning and making of lime to manure the said Lord's lands in their several possessions, and for no other use.)

"And also full liberty and power to and for the said John Maybery, or any person or persons by his order, to make dams, ponds, or pond heads or wears within the Manors aforesaid, for raising the river Cynon aforesaid, and the conveying thereof for the working of the said Furnace, or any other Works or Buildings to be erected upon the said 4 acres, or any part thereof.

"And also full liberty for the said John Maybery and his exors., etc., to dispose of 200 Dozen horse-loads of Iron ore so raised, exclusive of what he should make use of towards the furnace aforesaid, to whom and for what use he or they or any of them might think proper in every year during the term thereby granted.

"To hold for the term of 99 years, subject to the rents, covenants, and conditions therein reserved and contained."

The object, no doubt, of obtaining the permission to take 200 dozen of mine beyond that required for the Hirwain Works was to enable the lessee to send a part of it across the hills on horseback, to supply the Brecon Furnace.

It appears that Mr. Maybery did not build his Furnace at Hirwain on any part of the Windsor property, but outside its boundary in Penderin parish, in the County of Brecon, on the Tyr Gwynbach land, the freehold of which he had purchased from others. This may have been because the site was more favourable in respect of water power, or for other reasons.

Such a step could be scarcely agreeable to his lessor; and when a year or so later, on Lord Windsor's death occurring, it was proposed to add the names of John Wilkins, his father-in-law, and Mary Maybery, his mother, to that of Mr. John Maybery, in the lease of 1757, it was stipulated that this land of Tyr Gwynbach, and the Furnace built thereon, should be transferred to Lady Windsor on granting a new lease, and should thenceforth form an integral part of the Hirwain mineral property of the Windsor family, and this was provided for in the following lease:—

"By Indenture of Lease, dated February, 1760, made between Lady Windsor of the one part, and John Wilkins, John Maybery, and Mary Maybery, of the other part, Lady Windsor, after confirming the lease of 1757, did demise, grant, and to farm, set, and let to John Wilkins, John Maybery, and Mary Maybery, a certain Furnace for Making of Iron, and other works, at a certain place called Tyr Gwynbach, close adjoining to Hirwain Common aforesaid, for the term of 99 years, from June 24th, 1758, by the following description, viz:—

"All that parcel of land lately part and parcel of the land called Tyr Gwyn bach, situate in the parish of Penderin aforesaid, with the Furnace and Works erected, and the Mine Yard and appurtenances thereto belonging, the said premises being bounded with the lands of George Venables Vernon, Esq., in the possession of Rees Daniel, called Gelly Penychall; on the west part, and one other tenement of the said George Venables Vernon, called Tyr Maes y Rhydid, then in the possession of Thomas Lewis, on the east part, having the River Cynon on the south part, and extending from thence to the several fields of the said John Wilkins, John Maybery, and Mary Maybery, called Cae Maes y Ridiau, Cae Tyle Gwennon, Cae Mawr, Cae Tuy dû, the Fold or yard adjoining to the Mansion House and barn of the said John Wilkins, John Maybery, and Mary Maybery, on the north part thereof, containing seven acres and twenty-two perches statute measure, be the same more or less, and particularly mentioned and described in the Plan thereto annexed.

"With free liberty for the said John Wilkins, John Maybery, and Mary Maybery, their exors, etc., at all or any time or times during the term therein mentioned, to set up, erect, and build in or upon any part or parts of the said premises such and so many Furnaces, Blast Furnaces, Forges, Mills, Engines, Store-houses, coal-houses, Yards, Courts, Edifices, and Buildings, for the placing and keeping of ore, coal, coke, and charcoal, and the melting and manufacturing, as they the said John Wilkins, John Maybery, Mary Maybery, their exors., etc., should think fit, proper, and convenient.

"And also full and free liberty of turning and conveying such parts of the River and water called Cynnon, or such other water or water courses as there were near adjacent to the said demised premises, to serve such Works as they the said John Wilkins, John Maybery, and Mary Maybery, their exors, etc., had built and erected, or from time to time should build and erect as aforesaid.

"And for that purpose to have full liberty and power to and for the said John Wilkins, John Maybery, and Mary Maybery, their exors., etc., to make such and so many channels, sluices, dams, ponds, pond heads, stanks, and wears as they shall think fit.

"With full and free liberty, licence, and authority to and for the said John Wilkins, John Maybery, and Mary Maybery, their exors., etc., from time to time and at all times during the term thereinafter mentioned, to bore, dig, search, work for, raise, and land all such coal, culme, kennell, slack, iron mine and Iron ore, Turf, or Peat as should or might be found, or were then opened in or upon or under all that waste or uninclosed land called

"Tyr Wain Wrgan, or Hirwain Wrgan, situate in the several Lordships of Glynronthey and Miskin, in the County of Glamorgan,

"*Exceptions and Reservations.* Unto Lady Windsor all coal, culm, etc., which should be over and above supplying such Works, and the 200 dozen Horse loads of Iron Ore granted by the said Lord Windsor to John Maybery, his exors., etc., to be disposed of as he should think fit.

"*Declaration and Agreement* that £23 only yearly should be the rent payable for both the above recited Property, and the Property and premises comprised in the before recited lease by Lord Windsor."

[Mary Maybery is described as relict of Thomas Maybery, of St. John's, co. Worcester, Ironmaster. The partnership consisted of three equal shares.]

[The Hirwain Works were erected on land in Breconshire outside the Windsor manors, the freehold of a portion of which was, as we have seen, subsequently acquired by Lady Windsor. The boundary between the two properties was the subject of a dispute in 1855, just before the termination of the lease; and after considerable trouble the matter was arranged with Mr. Francis Crawshay, the then owner of what had been the Maybery property in the parish of Penderin, by the settling of an irregular line, leaving the Blast Furnaces and mills on the Bute property, and the Blast Furnace yard and limekilns immediately behind the Furnaces on the Crawshay property, called Tyr Gwyn bach.]

The Works under Mr. John Maybery's management—Mr. John Wilkins and Mary Maybery being only sleeping partners—rapidly developed, and proved profitable. And we find that in 1764 Mr. John Maybery, and with him Mr. Wilkins, extended their operations to Tredegar, where they leased from the Honble. Thomas Morgan, of Ruperra, the Tredegar Forge and furnaces and a large extent of mineral land. Mr. Maybery also appears to have become lessee of a small Iron Works at Machen.

However, a bad time, wholly unforseen, was at hand, occasioned by the disturbances in America in 1774, which greatly affected the Iron business; and, in 1775, the partners were obliged to part with the Tredegar lease; and, being hard-pressed in carrying on their Hirwain Works, it was resolved to grant a lease of them to John Wasse of the town of Stafford, Esqre., and Mr. William King, of Bristol, glassmaker.

The lease is dated August 14th, 1775, and was to run for fourteen years, at the yearly rent of £324, payable half-yearly, the lessors undertaking first to repair the wheel, so as to "make it fit to work the cylinders already fixed for the use of the Furnace, and also to finish the new road leading to the Coal works, known as Bryngwyn Coal Works."

Beyond paying the reserved rent, the lessees bound themselves to supply yearly from the Furnace 300 tons of dark grey pig iron, at £4 per ton; the same to be made with a proper mixture of mine and limestone, so as to make it fit for making bar iron; the same to be delivered weekly *at the half-way place between the Town of Brecon and Machen Forge, in the County of Monmouth.*

The property included the Hirwain Furnace, in the parish of Penderin, the Tyrgwyn-bach lands in the said parish, the Gollen and Bryngwyn Coal Works in the Lordships of Miskin and Glynronthwy, and also the iron mine, and other mineral rights under the Windsor leases; and also the right to raise coal and iron ore on the estates of Edward Matthews, Esqre., paying him the galage agreed upon.

The Works had been carried on for a short time only by the new firm, when Mr. King, who had been the managing partner (a person of the name of Bowzer, of whom Messrs. Maybery and Wilkins had a very bad opinion, having been his agent and clerk), died, his estate being insolvent.

Upon this, the lessors called upon Mr. Wasse, who was a responsible person, to make good the covenants which they alleged had been broken, as to payment of rent, delivery of iron, and repairs.

One of the complaints made by the lessors was that they had been obliged to buy pig iron to carry on their Forge at Brecon, where they could use 200 tons annually; "but it was impossible at present to get such a supply from the neighbouring Iron Works, owing to the great demand for making of cannon for Government"; and that they are obliged to buy at £6 per ton, and cannot even be supplied at that price.

When a distress was put in, Bowzer appears to have removed the pig iron from the furnace yard at night, and sent it to Bristol!

The result of the suit instituted against Mr. Wasse, the remaining solvent partner, was that he had to compensate the lessors to some extent, and the lease was put an end to.

The property then reverted to Messrs. Maybery; but, at that date—1777—the difficulties and complications surrounding them were so great, that they even contemplated making an assignment of the Works for the benefit of the creditors. However, at that crisis, Messrs. Jeffreys Wilkins, of the Priory, Brecon, and Walter Wilkins, of Maesllwch, Radnorshire, who were sons of John Wilkins and brothers-in-law of John Maybery, came to their assistance. [Walter Wilkins, who went to India in 1759, had amassed a considerable fortune there; and he, with his brother, Jeffreys Wilkins, and two other partners, formed in the following year—1778—what was known as Wilkins's Old Bank, Brecon.]

The result of this timely assistance was that it enabled John Maybery (now possessed also of the share of his mother, Mary Maybery, deceased) and his partner Thomas Wilkins (what relation to John Wilkins is not clear), to get out of their difficulties, and to be in a position to grant a lease of the Hirwain Works, to the great Ironmaster, Anthony Bacon, of Cyfarthfa, when he applied to take the same in aid of his own Works at Merthyr.

The deed—which is dated July 1st, 1780—transferring the property is in the nature of an assignment or mortgage, and all the estate of the partners in the leases and property passed to Anthony Bacon, subject, however, to the payment of £133 6*s.* 8*d.* yearly in rent to John Maybery and Thomas Wilkins, or the equivalent in value in pig iron, at their election.

Mr. Bacon, of course, at once put the Works in thorough repair, and carried them on vigorously until his death, in 1786.

By his will, his estate in these Works was left to his natural sons, Anthony and Thomas Bacon, then minors, and the Hirwain property, like the rest of Mr. Bacon's Iron Works, was placed under the Court of Chancery. And the Court granted a lease of the Works now in question to Mr. Samuel Glover, of Abercarne, for a period co-extensive with the minority of the sons, Anthony and Thomas Bacon.

In October, 1799, the Brothers Bacon, being of age, took over the interest of the Messrs. Glover, by an arbitration, in which the most eminent of the South Wales Ironmasters acted as arbitrators: Samuel Homfray, of Penydarran; Wm. Taitt, of Dowlais; and Edward Kendall, of Beaufort.

The following is a copy of their Award, the original of which is among our papers:—

"*By an Award* given at Merthyr Tidfil, October 4th, 1799, £650 per annum to be paid by Messrs. Bacon to Mr. Glover half-yearly, as compensation for giving up contract for 34 years for Supply of Pig Iron, from September, 1799; Glover to make good all engagements at Hirwain furnace to September 29th last, and to indemnify Bacon against all claims during terms he held premises. Bacon to give Glover a Bond for £13,000, to secure s'd £650. Bacon and Glover to give mutual Releases as to above. Powells, of Brecon, to draw same. Expenses of same, borne equally, (sd.) Sam'l Homfray, W. Taitt, Edward Kendall."

It has occurred to me whether the Brothers Anthony and Thomas Bacon are to be properly classed as ironmasters. They evidently had little liking for the business, and we now find that Anthony, having disposed of Cyfarthfa to Mr. Richard Crawshay, and Plymouth to Mr. Hill, divested himself of the remaining Works at Hirwain, selling his interest to his brother Thomas for £3,000. And his next step was, having purchased the Aberaman Estate, to reside there as a private gentleman.

Thomas, again. was no sooner possessed of the entirety of Hirwain Works than he sought out a tenant in Mr. Berkin, but the negotiations, though far advanced, were never completed.

And we find by an Indenture dated 1st March, 1803, between Thomas Bacon, of Oaken, in the parish of Godsall, in the co. of Stafford, of the one part, and Jeremiah Homfray, of Llandaff, in the co. of Glamorgan, ironmaster, Francis William Bowzer, of Highwood, in the parish of Hendon, in the co. of Middlesex, Esq., Simon Oliver, of the city of Bristol, linen merchant, and Lionel Oliver, of the same city, linen merchant, of the other part, the said Thomas Bacon did demise unto the said Homfray Bowzer, Oliver, and Oliver, the Works called the Hirwain Furnace, for the term of 55 years, from the 24th June last, at the rent of £1,500 for the first 20 years, and of the rent of £1,000 for the residue of the said term of 55 years: rent to be paid on the usual quarter days.

It was Mr. Jeremiah Homfray who first arranged the lease with Mr. Thomas Bacon; but he very soon retired from the firm, Mr. George Overton taking his place as partner.

Messrs. Walter Wilkins and Jeffreys Wilkins having become possessed of the interest of Mr. Maybery and Mr. Thomas Wilkins in the Hirwain Works, they entered into an arrangement with Mr. Oliver on behalf of himself and the other partners, Messrs. Bowzer and Overton, to release them from the delivery of the pig-iron reserved in the assignment to Anthony Bacon of 1780, and to accept in lieu as a permanent arrangement £186 13*s.* 4*d.* as a yearly rent, in addition to the fixed rent of £133 6*s.* 8*d.*, making together the yearly rent of £320.

Messrs. Bowzer, Overton, and Oliver continued the Works with varying fortunes, paying the rent stated; but in the year 1814 the firm became bankrupt, when the payment ceased.

Upon this insolvency taking place, Messrs. Fry, the bankers of St. Mildred's Court, London, took possession of the Hirwain Works, and after continuing such possession a very short time, they dismantled the Works, and soon after transferred it to a nominal person —in short, to a beggar.

Upon this, Mr. Thomas Bacon commenced a suit in Chancery against Messrs. Fry, but which was decided before the Master of the Rolls in favour of the latter.

During the progress of the suit, Messrs. Wilkins did not put in their claim, but at the request of Mr. Bacon they awaited the result of the trial. Upon that being ascertained, they applied to Mr. Bacon for the old rent then in arrears, but they received for answer that he was advised he was not liable, in consequence of their having relieved Messrs. Bowzer and Oliver from the payment in its original form.

Some very nice points of law arose upon this, and opinion of Counsel (W. E. Taunton) having been taken by Messrs. Wilkins, which was to the effect that they could not recover any arrears of rent from Mr. Bacon, it was considered advisable by both parties to avoid litigation, and to enter into an agreement for the sale of the works to Mr. Thomas Bacon for the sum of £3,000.

The conveyance is dated November 29th, 1817, and is made between

Walter Wilkins, of Maeslough, in the County of Radnor, Esq., and Jeffreys Wilkins, of Maesyderwen, in the Co. of Brecon, of the 1st part; Richard John Hill, of Plymouth Lodge, in the County of Glamorgan, Esq., of the 2nd part; and Thomas Bacon, of Farnborough, Coy. of Southampton, Esq., of the 3rd part.

Reciting the before-mentioned lease of November 22nd, 1757, by Lord Windsor, and Deed of Confirmation by Lady Windsor, and the Indenture of July 1st, 1780,

It was witnessed that in consideration of the said sum of £3,000 paid to the said W. Wilkins and J. Wilkins, they did grant, bargain, etc., to the said T. Bacon.

All those two several messuages and lands called by the name of Cwmnant y Spittaden, *alias* Wain y Spittaden, and Tyr Gwyn bach; and also all that piece of land called Trepederen, which said lands are commonly called Tyr Gwyn bach, situate, lying and being in the parish of Penderin, in the County of Brecon, and for several years past in the occupation of Thomas Bacon and his undertenants. Together with all Works, Furnaces, etc., to the use of T. Bacon for his life, etc., Mr. Hill being Trustee.

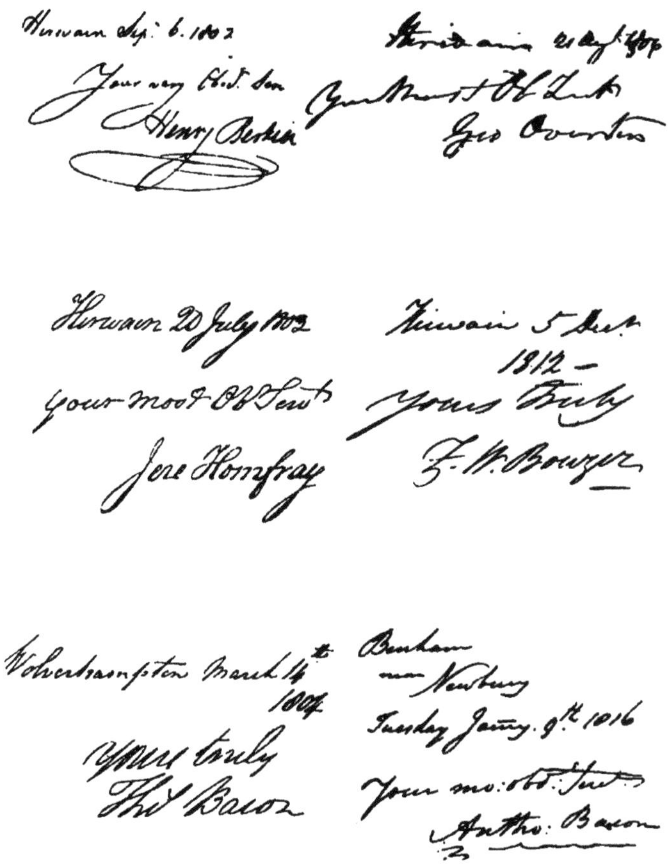


SIGNATURES OF PARTNERS IN THE HIRWAIN IRON WORKS.

And, in consideration of the further sum of 10*s.*, the Messrs. Wilkins granted to the said T. Bacon all their interest in the Assignment of February 1st, 1780, on behalf of themselves, or on behalf of John Wilkins, John Maybery, and Thomas Wilkins, subject nevertheless to the rents, covenants, reservations, contained in the original leases of November 22nd, 1757, and 1760.

We may add here one or two notes :—

Of John Maybery—the date of whose death we have not yet ascertained—we have formed a high opinion of his character and ability. As events proved, he was too sanguine; and it seems now a pity that he extended his business over so wide a field. And it is strange that while the disturbances in America made the fortune of some ironmasters by creating a demand for cannon, these brought to him disaster. Possibly, being of a religious, peace-loving family, he declined this class of business. However, John Maybery must ever rank as one of the very first pioneers of the iron industry of South Wales.

Upon the failure of Bowzer, Overton, and Oliver happening, the deepest regret was felt for Mr. George Overton, the father of the late George Overton, whom we knew so well. No man was more highly respected; and it is probable that had he not been associated with Mr. Bowzer in the firm, Mr. Richard Crawshay would, before he died, have given the firm the material moneyed support that, from the very outset, was deficient.

And what did Thomas Bacon with the Works he had now purchased. We do not think he had much experience in the business, and no very great love for it: and we should not be surprised to find that he soon handed it over to others to carry on.

Our paper history ends, however, at 1817-1818; but from other sources we learn that William Crawshay (II), of Cyfarthfa, became almost immediately the purchaser, and placed one of his sons in charge of the Works.

The old buildings were no doubt antiquated, and had, as we have seen, fallen into disrepair, and a great change was soon made by the new owner. In 1820 (date inscribed on engine-house), four new massive blast-furnaces were erected, with the engine-house adjoining on the right, and the mill-house on the left, close to the river Cynon, and on its left bank, and in the parish of Penderin, in the county of Brecon.

Immediately above these furnaces, at a higher level, a range of calcining furnaces or ovens were built, in order to calcine the ore before being used in the blast-furnaces below. It may be assumed that in the renovation of the Works every expedient and device for perfecting the manufacture of iron were adopted that Cyfarthfa experience could suggest, and that abundant capital could provide.

While the Works were on the left bank of the Cynon brook, the mineral takings lay wholly on its right bank, in Glamorganshire (the old mineral leases of 1757-60 still running), except the limestone quarries used in providing limestone for fluxing purposes. These great quarries were situate very near to Penderin church, and the stone was brought down on a tramway, some two miles long, following the course of the Cynon brook.

On recently visiting the now dismantled Works, we learnt that William Crawshay (II) frequently came over from Cyfarthfa to see how things were getting on under his son's management; and in the Cardiff Arms Inn, close by, the landlord shows with some pride the room the great ironmaster used in "mine Inn," and how the mantel-shelf came to be so loaded with samples of iron, that it was nigh to breaking with the weight. Two beautifully-made pillars of the finest steel were, however, one fine day brought over from Cyfarthfa and fixed, and all danger of a future breakdown averted.

The portraits of Clark of Dowlais, Frank Crawshay, Robert Crawshay, Fothergill, Wayne, and Lord Bute, hanging on the walls, add an interest to what we may call the "steel-pillar room."

We were also shown the "Mansion House," as it is called in our old papers, built and occupied by the first firm of Maybery and Wilkins.

And here must end our notice of the chequered and not too-prosperous life of the Hirwain Iron-works.

## A FEW NOTES OF INTEREST.

### Overton's Shop.

Company's shops were common in the olden days, and were probably necessary at the first start of the Works, before tradesmen could settle in the district.

The following is the agreement made 28th October, 1803—

Between the Hirwain Iron Works Company of the one part, and Edward Overton, late of Dowlais, in the parish of Merthyr Tydfil, of the other part:—

1. Partnership to be formed between the Company and Edward Overton, to carry on trade of Linen Drapers, Grocers, and Shopkeepers, under the name of "Edwd. Overton and Co.," for 14 years, if Overton should so long live.
2. That all workmen employed by the Company should, at the request of one or more of the partners, have credit for Goods of the said Edwd. Overton and Co., not exceeding the wages they should be entitled to for his 1 month's service; and that Overton should be enabled to receive at the Hirwain Co.'s Office on the following monthly pay-day so much and such part of wages as may be due to Edwd. Overton, but that Hirwain Co. not to be responsible for any sum beyond amount of wages of such workmen.
3. The House and Garden late of John Walter to be fitted up as Shop to carry on trade, and as a residence for Overton at Hirwain Co.'s expense, he to pay the Co. the rent of 8*s.* yearly, and pay all taxes, etc.
4. Overton to be allowed coke and firing, that the wages of all assistants in the employment of the Co-partnership to be paid out of trade of Overton and Co.; Overton should accommodate with living and board one assistant. No person to be taken into or continue in the employ of Edward Overton who may be disapproved of by either party.
5. Dissolution clause, and all usual clauses to be inserted in Articles.

Signed by F. W. Bowzer, George Overton, and Jere. Homfray, and Lionel Oliver (on behalf of Simon Oliver and Charles Ridout), and also by the said Edward Overton, and attested as to the execution thereof by F. W. Bowzer, Lionel Oliver, and Jere. Homfray, by Sarah Chiswell.

### Driving a Level.

Agreement for driving forward a certain Level, called by the name of the Graig Vein New Level, until the Coal sought for shall be met with,

Between John Walters of Hirwain Furnace, on behalf of Messrs. A. and T. Bacon and Isaac Davies and Evan Davies, Miners, of the Parish of Hirwain.

Work to be carried on unremittingly, and to be done in a sufficient and workmanlike manner.

Plates to be laid and kept in repair by the workmen.

Payment to be made at the rate of Eighteen shillings for every yard driven forward.

Dated June 1st, 1801, and signed by John Walters, and the marks of Isaac Davies and Evan Davies attached.

### Depredations Committed at Hirwain Works.

"One of the colliers gone off; the other served with a warrant to appear before Mr. Bruce on Monday next. There is no one cutting the coal at present, nor does John Watkins suppose any one will again. The whole of the people have quitted premises—some on Thursday and some by night on Friday.

"A witness speaks to men going to the Engine-house, and using a bar to get the brasses out from under the Rolls; also iron bars from under the puddling furnaces.

"John Watkins has placed a man to live in the Cot facing the Works, by way of guard over them.

"(Sd.) F. G. Sept. 27th, 1817."

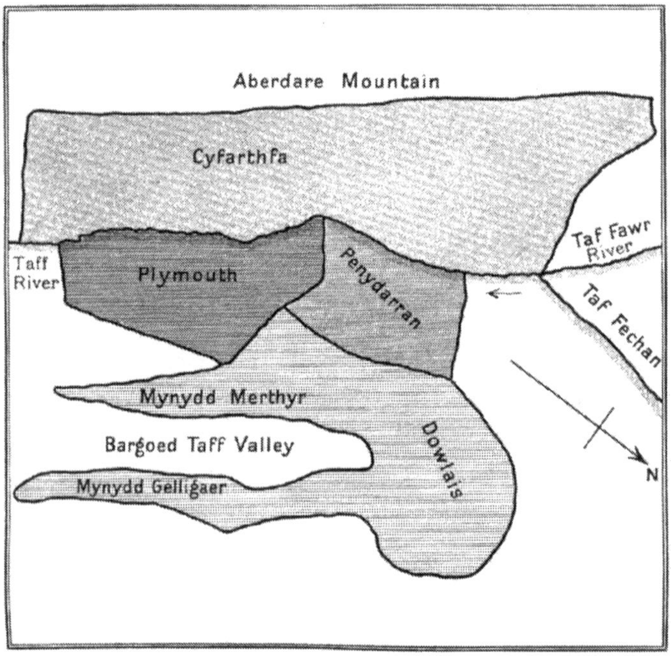


THE MINERAL TAKINGS OF THE FOUR GREAT MERTHYR IRON WORKS.
PAGE 19.

III.

# The Dowlais Iron Works.

---

We have before us, when writing, several large bundles of original papers connected with these great Ironworks, and containing the history of their formation, of the first and successive partners in the undertaking, and of the leases, with the extent of the mineral property; and it has greatly puzzled us how to arrange these papers, so as to enable our readers easily to understand and realise the whole story of these Works from their first formation.

We have come to the conclusion that this can best be done by giving first the earlier and current leases existing before the partnership was entered into in 1757, and for the purpose of securing which leases the partnership was in fact formed. These leases form the groundwork of the whole superstructure, and it will be a safe plan to build up our history on their foundation.

We may first state that the Dowlais Works are known to all the world, ranking as one of the largest in the United Kingdom, and having enjoyed uninterrupted success from their early formation in 1759 down to the present time, or for a period nearly of 150 years, and words fail us to describe the vastness of their operations. And this preliminary observation is made for the information of the uninstructed and casual reader, rather than for those who are the least familiar with the iron industry. To the latter it is sufficient to say we are writing of *The Dowlais Works.*

The first and oldest Lease is that known as Lady Pembroke's Lease to William Edwards, in 1696, in the reign of William and Mary. It is as follows :—

LADY PEMBROKE'S LEASE TO EDWARDS, 1696.

Copy of a Grant from Jeffrey Jeffreys and John Jeffreys, Esqrs., Trustees for Lady Pembroke, of certain Coal Works in the Parish of Merthyr, viz., Sengenith.

At the Audit for the Revenue of Jeffrey Jeffreys and John Jeffreys, Esqres., Trustees for the Right Honoble. Henrietta, Countess Dowager of Pembroke and Montgomery, now wife of Timoleon Gouffier, Marquis De Thois, in the Kingdom of France, held at Cardiff the 24th day of October, 1696.

Granted then by the Auditors and Commissioners of the Trustees aforesaid to William Edward, of Eglwys Silan, in the County of Glamorgan, Gent., All those the Coal works, mines, and veins of Coal lying and being in the Parish of Merthyr and Lordship afsd., in certain places there called

Tyle Dowlais, Toryvan, adjoining on the East to Fynon Gwenlliu and the highway from the heath Market to the Village of Kelligare, on the north to a place called Dowlais, on the South to Sarn Howell and Nanty bwchton, and on the West to Dowlais and Pwllyrhwyaid and Tyr-ton-y-ffald and Gwayne Nanty-bwch, and also all the Water courses thereto belonging, with free liberty, power, and authority to search for, dig, mine, and take up Coal there to his own use, and to dig erect limekilns in and upon the said ground called Tyle Dowlais and Toryvan, or any part thereof, with liberty to Dig Stones in the Quarries for the burning and making of lime there.

To hold and enjoy the said premises unto the said William Edward, his exs. ads. and assigns, for and during the term of 77 years from hence forth next ensuing, and fully to be completed and ended if George William, Thomas William, and Edward William, sons of the said William Edward, or any or either of them shall so long live, at and under the rent of 20*s*., payable at Michaelmas yearly, for the price of £5.

THOS. EDWARDS,
Commiss.
Rowland Hughes.

---

Explanation of the boundaries mentioned in the within Grant, in a Letter from Lewis Edwards, of Ytgwddgwnn, to Mr. Nathl. Webb, 20th April, 1765.

N.B.—Sarn Howell is on the Common near a place now called Twyn-y-poock, a piece of an old Causeway on the highway which leadeth from the ffurnace down to Cardiff.

Nant-y-buchton begins and springs out just by Sarn Howell, and runs down the Common and parteth between Earl Plymouth's Land and Mr. Phillips land called Trebedda.

Pwyll-yr-hwyaid, that is David Rees's land.

Tyr ton y ffald, that is Pen y daren land.

Gwayne Nantybwch is the flat on ye Common against Penydaren land.

Am your humble friend and servt.,
LEWIS EDWARDS.

---

## THE SENGHENITH MANOR (SUPRA AND SUPTUS) LEASE, 1748.

HERBERT, LORD VISCOUNT WINDSOR, TO THOMAS MORGAN OF RUPERRA, IN THE COUNTY OF GLAMORGAN, ESQUIRE.

Having regard to the almost classic character of this early and important Lease, the terms of which are again and again referred to in the history of the Dowlais and adjacent Ironworks, this document is here given *in extenso*, or as nearly so as is necessary to explain its full meaning.

By Indenture dated 10th March, 1748, between

The RIGHT HONBLE. HERBERT, LORD VISCOUNT WINDSOR, of the Kingdom of Ireland, and Baron Montjoy, of the Isle of Wight, in Great Britain, Lord of the Manor of Senghenith, Supra and Suptus, in the County of Glamorgan, one part; and

The HONORABLE THOMAS MORGAN of Ruperra, in the County of Glamorgan, Esquire, other part.

IT WAS WITNESSED that the said Lord Windsor, in consideration of the rents, reservations, covenants, and agreements hereinafter mentioned, expressed, and reserved, which on the part and behalf of the sd. Thos. Morgan, his exors., admors., and assigns, are or ought to be paid, done, and performed, Hath demised, granted, and to farm letten, And by these presents Doth demise, grant, and to farm lett unto the said Thos. Morgan, his exors., ads., and assigns,

All that messuage or dwelling-house, stable, market-house, or toll-house called Marchnad y Wayne, and all buildings, privileges, and advantages thereunto belonging or therewith enjoyed.

And also all the parcell of land containing by estimation 20 acres of Welsh measure (be the same more or less), situate, lying, and being in the Parish of Merthyr Tidvil, in the said Manor of Senghenith Supra, in the County of Glamorgan aforesaid.

And also all the fairs and markets, and all the pickage, stallage, shops, profits of Standings, toll, and tollage, and all other the profits and commodities of fairs or markets growing, accruing, arising, or becoming due, or which at any time shall happen to grow, accrue, arise, or become due, of, from, or out of all and every the fairs and markets hereafter to be holden and kept within the liberties thereof; with full power and free liberty to and for the said Thomas Morgan, his exors., administrators, and assigns, to erect or make any other new or additional building or buildings on any part of the sd. premises, that he, the sd. Thos. Morgan, his exors., etc., should think fit.

Also all those mines and veins of iron and coal, and all quarries of Stones, tyle, and slate arising, growing, or to be found in, upon, or out of the Free Common or Waste called Blaen Rumney, or upon any of the Free Commons or Wastes lying in the several Parishes of Merthyr Tidvill and Kelly gare, or elsewhere within that part of the said Manor of Senghenith Supra and Subtus, in the Coy. of Glamorgan aforesaid, commonly called Supra Cayach, with full power and free liberty to and for the sd. Thos. Morgan, his exors., ads., assns., his and their Servants, Agents, and workmen, to dig for, make, and sink pits, and to make trenches, ditches, gutters, ponds, and levels, and to erect limekilns for burning of lime, engines, banks, stanks, sluices, and all other conveniences for the better scouring for getting, having, and obtaining all such iron mine, coal, and stone, and the earth and rubbish raised out of the said pits, trenches, ditches, gutters, ponds, and levels, and the iron mine, coal, stone, and tile raised out of the said Works, and the lime that shall be burnt to lay on the Ground next the mines, pits, kilns, and other places where the same shall be found, burnt, or raised, or on any other place being waste or common within that part of the said Manor of Senghenith called Supra Cayach convenient for that purpose, and to take, carry away, with horses, carts, or any other carriages, and to dispose of the same at his and their will and pleasure, and to his and their proper use and benefit (except those Coal Works, Mines, and Veins of Coal lying and being in the said Parish of Merthyr Tydvil, in certain places there called Tilla Dowlas and Tory Van, by Mears and bounds, as well known and distinguished which Robert Morrice, of Killvach Vargod, in the Parish of Killigare aforesaid, Gent., claims by vertu of an Assignment of a Grant from William Edward, late of Eglwys-silan, in Coy. Glamorgan afsd., Gent., bearing date 1696, wherein the life of Thomas, the son of the said William Edward, is said to be now in being during his, the said Robert Morice, Estate or Interest therein).

Also except and always reserved unto the said Lord Windsor, his heirs and assigns, All timber trees, and trees likely to make timber, all mines and veins of tin and lead in and upon the sd. premes., or any part thereof, with full liberty of ingress, egress, and regress to and for the said Lord Windsor, his hrs. and assns., his and their servants and workmen, to work, dig, land, load, drive, and carry away the same.

To have and to hold all and singular the said several premises and every part and parcel thereof, with the appurts. (except before excepted) unto the sd. Thos. Morgan, his exs., ads. and assns. from the 1st day of May,[1] then next ensuing, the date thereof for and during and until the full end and term of 99 years thence next ensuing, and fully to be complete and ended.

And also to have and to hold the rest and residue of the said mines and veins of Iron, Coal, and Stone (before excepted and mentioned, to be claimed by Robert Morrice aforesaid. By virtue of the Assignment of the grant from William Edward aforesaid), from the end and expiration of the Term of, or making the said Grant void unto the sd. Thos. Morgan, his exors., admors., and assigns, for the remainder of the sd. term of 99 years, as shall be then to come and unexpired.

[1] Commencement and termination of Term. From 1st May, 1749. Duration, 99 years. Terminates, 1848. The year 1749 being previous to the alteration of the style, the following year ended on March 25th.

Yielding and Paying therefore yearly, and every year during the said term for the premises in the *habendum* first herein contained unto the said Lord Windsor, his hrs. and assigns, the yearly rent of £23, of lawful, etc., on St. Michael the Archangel, and the Annunciation of the Blessed Virgin Mary, by even portions, the first payment to be made on the Feast of St. Michael next ensuing the date hereof, over and above all rates, taxes, etc.

And also Yielding and Paying from and after the end, expiration of the term of, or the making void the grant of the premises in the second *habendum* herein contained for the sd. premises the additional yearly rent, or sum of £3, unto the sd. Lord Windsor, at the two feasts, as above, the then first payment to be made at such of the feast days aforesaid, which should happen next after the determination of, or making void of the grant last mentioned.

Proviso, that if rent in arrear, and unpaid for 15 days after feast day, or sd. Thos. Morgan, his heirs, etc., should violate, break, or not perform any of the covenants and agreements herein contained, power for Lord Windsor to re-enter and expel said Thos. Morgan.

Covenants by T. Morgan, with Lord Windsor for heirs, etc.: To pay rent, to keep premises in repair, and deliver up same in good state of repair.

Covenant by sd. Lord Windsor with Thos. Morgan, That said Thos. Morgan might divert water for scouring and cleansing the said Iron, Coal, or any other Minerals, in most convenient way over wastes or commons to any river, etc. To keep sd. Thos. Morgan indemnified, and his Workmen in respect of scouring or cleansing the said Mines. For quiet enjoyment.

THOS. (L. S.) MORGAN.

Signed, Sealed, etc., by Morgan in presence of—
James Robotham,
Edmund Lloyd.

---

We now give the Lease of Rees and John to Thomas Lewis, of Newhouse, in Llanishen, in Glamorgan, Esq., and Company, dated 20th September, 1757, almost immediately following the formation of the Dowlais Company.

## LEASE OF REES AND JOHN.

By Indenture dated 20th September, 1757.

Between

THOS. REES and DAVID JOHN, both of Merthyr, in the Coy. of Glamorgan, Yeomen, one part; and

THOS. LEWIS, of Newhouse, in Llanishen, in Glamorgan, Esq., and Company, other part.

IT WAS WITNESSED that sd. Rees and John, in conson. of rent and covenants to be paid and performed, Did demise to Thos. Lewis and Co. their exors., etc., All those mines and veins of Ironstone and all Quarry Stone and Coal arising, growing, or to be found in or upon, or out of, the free common or waste called Pantywain; and after the decease of Thos. Williams in, upon, or out of any other Coal pits on the said Common or waste called Tilla Dowlas and Toryvan, by mears and bounds well known and Distinguished with full power and free liberty for the said Thos. Lewis and Co., their exors., etc.; Servants, Agents, and workmen to dig for, make and sink pits, and to make trenches and ditches, Gutters and levels, and to erect Engines, Banks, Stanks, Sluices, and all other conveniences for the better scouring, getting, having, and attaining all such Ironstone and Coal in the places aforesaid; conformable to the priviledges, liberties, clauses, limitations, and restrictions granted in the Original Indre. of Lease, which the said Rees and John hold from the Hon. Thomas Morgan of Ruperra ; And also the said Thos. Rees and David John did further grant unto the sd. Lewis and Coy. full and free liberty and power (with their Servants, etc.) to dig for or raise any Stone whatsoever that shall be found on any part of their Freehold Estate for building a Furnace or Furnaces or any other building whatsoever, or where it is erected by the sd. Thos. Lewis and Co., their exors., etc., or any of them.

And also full power and free liberty of conveying any Water or water courses from the Common or Waste lands through their own freehold in order to turn any Wheels, and to erect or place pipes for carrying air or Water underground through their lands, or Tying of Wase or Wases or any other Works, Arts, or Devices whatsoever in, upon, or through any part or parts of land of the said Thos. Rees and David John for the bringing, carrying, conveying, or diverting the water off and from the said Common for the use and benefit of a certain furnace which is to be erected by the sd. Thos. Lewis and Co., their exs., ads., etc.

To have and to hold all and singular the Iron, Stone, and Coal, together with all libertys, privileges, and Authorities afsd. unto the sd. Thos. Lewis and Co., their exs., ads., and assns., from the 1st day of Novr. next ensuing the date hereof, for the term of 99 years.

Yielding and Paying the yearly rent of £38, on 1st May and 1st Novr., the 1st payt. to be made on the 1st day of May next ensuing, free and clear of all deductions. Proviso, that if sd. rent in arrear for 15 days or on breach of covenants, then usual power of distress and re-entry.

(Stipulation, that Rees and John are to have what pit coal they shall use in their own house Grates, if there shall be any raised out of the said Work.)

And the sd. Thos. Lewis, for himself and Company, covenanted with the sd. Rees and John to pay rent and sufficiently repair and deliver up at end of term. Covenant by Rees and John with Lewis and Co. for quiet enjoyment.

In witness, etc.

THOMAS REES.
DAVID JOHN.

Attested
Hugh Jones.
Richd. Davis.

---

## THE MYRTHY FURNACE, OR DOWLAIS IRON WORKS.

Having given the preceding leases, it is now the proper place to state the terms of partnership of the Proprietors of the Myrthy Furnace, otherwise the Dowlais Iron Works, which was now formed —

[Maybery Papers.]

ARTICLES OF CO-PARTNERSHIP BETWEEN THE PROPRIETORS OF MYRTHY FURNACE, 19TH SEPTEMBER, 1759.

[Taking over Various Leases from other parties.—Establishment of Merthyr Furnace for Making Pig Iron, etc.]

THIS INDENTURE, made the 19th day of September, in the 33rd year of the Reign of Lord George the Second, 1759, between

THOMAS LEWIS, of Newhouse, in the County of Glamorgan, Esq., 1st part.

THOMAS PRICE, of Watford, in the County of Glamorgan, Gentleman, 2nd part.

RICHARD JENKINS, of the Town of Cardiff, in the County aforesaid, Mercer, 3rd part.

THOMAS HARRIS, of the City of Bristol, Esquire, 4th part.

JOHN CURTIS, of the City of Bristol, Esquire, 5th part.

NATHANIEL WEBB, of the City of Bristol, 6th part.

JOHN JONES, of the City of Bristol, Ironmaster, 7th part.

ISAAC WILKINSON, of Place Gronow, in the County of Denbigh, Gentleman, 8th part. And

EDWARD BLAKEWAY, of Shrewsbury, in the County of Salop, Esquire, 9th part.

WHEREAS the said several Parties hereto have agreed with each other to enter into Co-partnership and joint Dealing in the Art, Misterry, Occupation, and Business of an Iron Master and Iron Manufacturer, and for that purpose to build a certain ffurnace or ffurnaces for Smelting of Iron Oar, or Iron Mine or Stone, into Pig Iron, in the Parish of Merthir tidvil, in the County of Glamorgan; and also for the buying and procuring of Materials for the Building and Erecting thereof. And for the selling and uttering of Iron made, wrought, or manufactured in the said ffurnace or ffurnaces, and all other things incident and belonging to the Art, Misterry, or Business of an Iron Master for and during the time and term of 99 years, from hence next ensuing, and fully to be compleat and ended, and that with the Joint Stock of £4,000 which the said Co-partners have agreed to bring in, advance and deliver in and before the 1st day of January, A.D. 1760, in manner hereafter mentioned.

And whereas, in pursuance of the said Agreement of Co-partnership, Herbert Moses, of Langattock, Crickhowell, in the County of Brecon, Yeoman, by a certain Agreement in Writing, dated the first day of July, A.D. 1757, contracted with the said Thomas Price for 200 dozen Bushells of Mine, to be delivered yearly at the Bank at Carno, in the Parish of Gelligare, in the County of Glamorgan, at 2*s*. 10*d*. every Dozen Bushells.

And whereas also, William Moses, of Langattock, Crickhowell, aforesaid, Yeoman, and the said Herbert Moses, by Agreement, dated 25th July, A.D. 1757, did demise and to farm lett to the said Thomas Pryce, All that messuage and tenement with the Appurtenances in the possession of William Thomas, situate in the Parish of Bedwellty, in the County of Monmouth, with certain privileges therein, granted at the rent of £20 for the term they held it from the said Lord Windsor and Henry Burgh, Clerk.

And whereas David John, of the Parish of Merthir afore said, Yeoman, by his Indenture of Lease, dated the 29th day of July, A.D. 1757, Did grant and demise to the said Thomas Lewis, All his Moiety of the Coal and Iron Stone, which he held under the said Lease from Viscount Windsor in Dowlais, and Tor y van, as also Liberty to erect a ffurnace or ffurnaces on his freehold lands, and to raise Stones, Hearth, Lime Stones, clay, or sand, with a court or yard for laying down Ironstone, Limestone, Coal, Sand, and Pig Iron, as should be thought necessary. To hold the privileges granted thereby for 99 years, Paying £4 yearly for Keven Dowlais and Tor y van, and for a Place to build the furnace or furnaces, and to lay the stone and to make watercourses, 40*s*. yearly.

And whereas also John Griffiths, of Abercarne, in the County of Monmouth, Iron Master, by a certain Agreement dated the twenty-ninth day of July, A.D. 1757, did lett and sett unto the said Thomas Price the Coal Work called Bryn Oar, in the Parish of Bedwelty, at the rent of £10 yearly.

And whereas also Thomas Rees, of Merthir aforesaid, and the said David John, by their Indenture of Lease dated the 20th day of September, 1757, Did demise and grant to the said Thomas Lewis and Company All those veins and mines of Iron, Stone, and all Quarry Stones and Coal on Pant yr wayn, and after the disease of Thomas William in and upon the Common called Tilla Dowlass and Tor y Van, with full power of raising Stone and conveying certain Water and Water Courses from the Common or Wast lands through their own freehold, in order to turn any Engine or Wheels or placing Pipes for carrying Air or water under Ground through their Lands, or tying any Wase or Wases, or any other Art or Devise, to hold for 99 years from the 1st of November then next, at the Rent of £38 yearly.

And whereas also George William George, of the Parish of Gelligarre aforesaid, did by his Indenture of Lease, dated the 11th day of October, in the year of our Lord, 1756, grant unto the said Thomas Price All those pieces or parcels of land called Brin Pwllog and Gwayn y Llan, containing 5 acres, situate in the Parish of Gelligarre aforesaid, and all veins and mines of coal, Tin Lead, Iron, and all other Mines, Minerals, and Oars whatsoever, and certain Priviledges therein granted, And also All that messuage or Tenement of land called Koed Kae Brin Pwllog, and the House and Smith's Forge at Carno, with certain priviledges also granted therewith, to hold for 99 years, from the 1st of November aforesaid, if William Moses, son of Evan Moses, of Carno, should so long live, paying for Brin Pwllog, gwain y Llan and the Priviledges granted therewith, £8 yearly; and for the other Premises thereby granted £2 12*s.* 6*d.*, as in and by the said several Leases and Agreements, relation being thereunto had, may more fully and at large appear.

And whereas it is agreed between the said Co-partners and parties to these presents that the several Contracts, Agreements, Leases, and Assignments hereinbefore recited and every part of them are to be and remain from henceforth and at all times hereafter for the mutual benefit and advantage of the said Co-partnership, and the person or persons in whose name or names the same are so taken shall stand possessed thereof in Trust for the said Co-partnership.

Now this Indenture witnesseth, and the said Thomas Lewis, Thomas Price, Richard Jenkins, Thomas Harris, John Curtis, Nathaniel Webb, John Jones, Isaac Wilkinson, and Edward Blakeway, and each and every of them for himself, Doth respectively, and for each and every of their respective exors. and admors., covenant, promise, and agree to and with the other of them, his exors. and admors., that from and after the day of the date of this present Indenture that they, the said Thomas Lewis, Thomas Price, Richard Jenkins, Thomas Harris, John Curtis, Nathaniel Webb, John Jones, Isaac Wilkinson, and Edward Blakeway, shall and will be and continue Co-partners and Joint Dealers together in the said Art, trade, Misterry, and Business of the Iron Trade at the said Ffurnace or Ffurnaces intended to be erected upon any part of the said demised Premises in the several Countys of Glamorgan and Monmouth, or elsewhere in South Wales, for and during the full end and term of 99 years from hence next ensuing, and fully to be compleat and ended, And for the carrying on the said Joint Trade, and for the Building and Erecting of the said furnace or furnaces, each and every of the said parties to these Presents doth for himself respectively, and for each and every of their respective exors. and admors, covenant, promise, Grant, and agree to and with the other of them, his exors. and admors., that they will bring, advance and put together into the said Joint Trade or Stock in Money, Goods, or Materials to be used and had in the said Joint Trade or Stock on or before the 1st day of January, A.D. 1760, the full sum or value of £4,000, to be used and employed in the said Joint Trade upon the Joint Account, in the several shares and proportions following (that is to say): The said Thomas Lewis the sum of £750, being $\frac{3}{16}$th parts of the said £4,000, the whole into 16 parts to be divided; The said Thomas Price the sum of £500, being $\frac{2}{16}$th parts thereof; The said Richard Jenkins the sum of £250, being $\frac{1}{16}$th part thereof; the said Thomas Harris the sum of £750, being $\frac{3}{16}$th parts thereof; The said John Curtis the sum of £500, being $\frac{2}{16}$th parts thereof; The said Nathaniel Webb the sum of £500, being $\frac{2}{16}$th parts thereof; The said John Jones the sum of £250, being $\frac{1}{16}$th part thereof; The said Isaac Wilkinson the sum of £250, being $\frac{1}{16}$ part thereof, and the said Edward Blakeway the sum of £250, being one other $\frac{1}{16}$th part thereof.

And for the orderly proceeding and carrying on of the said Intended Iron Trade and Business, It is mutually covenanted, concluded, and agreed upon by and between the said parties to these presents, and each of them doth hereby for himself respectively, and for each and every of their respective exors. and admors., covenant, promise, Grant, and agree to and with the other of them, his exors. and admors., by these presents in manner and form following (that is to say),

### Covenants and Agreements by Co-partners.

That they, the said Thomas Lewis, Thomas Price, Richard Jenkins, Thomas Harris, John Curtis, Nathaniel Webb, John Jones, Isaac Wilkinson, and Edward Blakeway, shall and will be true, just, and faithful to each other in all their Buyings, Sellings, Contracts, Agreements, Accounts, Reckonings, Disbursements, and Dealings concerning the said Co-partnership, and shall each of them endeavour by all just means, care, and diligence to advance and promote the said Joint Trade and Stock without Fraud or Deceit.

And also that the said Thomas Lewis, his exors., admors., and assigns, shall have the full Interest, Right, and Property of, in, and unto $\frac{3}{16}$th parts, the whole into 16 parts to be divided, of all the said Joint Stock of £4,000, and of all Piggs, Metals, Castings, Iron, Timber, Woods, Coal, Coak, Charcoal, Braisess, Tools, Utensils, and other Stock things and materials that are or shall be hereafter brought into the said Joint Stock, or any part thereof, or that shall be bought, procured, or had for the use or upon Account of the said ffurnace or ffurnaces or other Iron Works hereafter to be erected for or by means of any Contract, Agreements, Leases, or Assignments already had or to be had or taken for, or on Account of or relating to the said Furnace, or other Iron Works so to be erected, And also of, in, and unto all the Gains, profits, and increase which shall arise, happen, accrue, or be made thereby, or in the ordering or employing the same, or by any Creditt or Business to be managed and done as Co-partners in the Stock aforesaid, And also shall and will bear, pay, and sustain $\frac{3}{16}$th parts thereof, the whole into 16 parts to be divided, of all losses, Charges, Costs, Rents, Payments, Expences, and Damages which shall at any time happen, arise, or accrue, or be expended, paid, or laid out in, about, or concerning the Joint Trade or Co-partnership aforesaid in any wise howsoever.

And also the said Thomas Price, his exors., admors., and assigns, shall have the full right, interest, and property of, in, and unto $\frac{2}{16}$th parts, the whole in 16 parts to be divided, of all the said Joint Stock of £4,000, And of all Pigs, Metals, Castings, Iron, Timber, Woods, Coal, Coak, Charcoal, Braises, Tools, Utensils, and other Stock, things, and Materials that are or shall be hereafter Brought into the said Joint Stock, or any part thereof, or that shall be procured, bought, or had for the use or upon account of the said furnace or furnaces, or other Iron Works hereafter to be erected for or by means of any Contracts, Agreements, Leases, or Assignments already had or to be had or taken for or on account of or relating to the said furnace or other Iron Works so to be erected.

And also of, in, and unto all the gains, profits, and increase which shall arise, happen, accrue, or be made thereby, or in the ordering or employing of the same, or by any credit or Business, to be managed and done as Co-partners in the Stock aforesaid ; And also shall and will bear, pay, and sustain $\frac{2}{16}$th parts, the whole into 16 parts to be divided, of all losses, charges, costs, Rents payments, Expences, and Damages, which shall at any time happen, arise, or accrue, or be expended, paid, or laid out, in, about, or concerning the Joint Trade or Co-partnership in anywise howsoever.

And also that the said Richard Jenkins, his exors., admors., and assigns, shall have full right, interest, and property of and in $\frac{1}{16}$th part, the whole into 16 parts to be divided, of all the said Joint Stock of £4,000, and of all Piggs, Metals, Castings, Iron, Timber, Wood, Coal, Coak, Charcoal, Braises, Tools, Utensils, and other Stock, Things, and Materials that are or shall be hereafter Brought into the said Joint Stock or any part thereof, or that shall be bought, procured, or had for the use or upon account of the said furnace or furnaces, or other Iron Works hereafter to be erected for, or by means of any Contracts, Agreements, Leases, or Assignments, already had or to be had, or taken for or on account of the said furnace or furnaces or other works hereafter to be erected ; and also of, in, and unto all the Gains, Profits, Increase, which shall arise, happen, accrue, or be made thereby, or in the ordering or employing of the same, or by any credit or business to be managed and done as Co-partners in the Stock aforesaid. And also shall, and will bear, pay, and sustain $\frac{1}{16}$th part, the whole into 16 parts to be divided, of all losses, Charges, Costs, Rents, Payments Expences, and Damages which shall at any time happen, arise, or accrue, or be expended, paid, or laid out, in, about, or concerning the said Joint Trade or Co-partnership aforesaid in anywise howsoever.

And also that the said Thomas Harris, his exors., admors., and assigns, shall have the full Right, interest, and property of, in, and unto $\frac{3}{16}$th parts, the whole to be divided as aforesaid; of all the said Joint Stock of £4,000, and of all Piggs, Metals, Castings, Iron, Timber, Wood, Coal, Coak, Charcoal, Braises, Tools, Utensils, and other Stock, Things, and materials that are or shall be hereafter brought into the said Joint Stock or any part thereof, or that shall be bought, procured, or had for the use or upon Account of the said furnace or furnaces or other Iron Works hereafter to be erected for, or by means of any Contracts, Agreements, Leases, or Assignments already had or to be had, or taken for or on account of the said furnace or furnaces or other Iron Works, so as aforesaid to be erected. And also of, in, and unto the gains, profits, and increase which shall arise, happen, accrue, or be made thereby or in the ordering or employing of the same or by any Credit or Business to be managed and done as Co-partners in the Stock aforesaid. And also shall and will bear, pay, and sustain $\frac{3}{16}$th parts, the whole into 16 parts to be divided, of all losses, Charges, Costs, Rents, Payments, Expenses, and Damages which shall at any time happen, arise, or accrue, or be expended, paid, or laid out, in, about, or concerning the said Joint Trade or Co-partnership aforesaid in any wise howsoever.

And also that the said John Curtis, his exors., admors., and assigns shall have the full right, interest, and property of, in, and unto $\frac{2}{16}$th parts, the whole to be Divided as aforesaid of all the said Joint Stock of £4,000, and of all Piggs, Metals, Castings, Iron, Timber, Wood, Coal, Coak, Charcoal, Braises, Tools, Utensils, and other Stock things and Materials that are or shall be hereafter brought into the said Joint Stock or any part thereof, or that shall be bought, procured, or had for the use or upon account of the said furnace or furnaces or other iron works hereafter to be erected for or by means of any Contracts, Agreements, Leases, or Assignments already had or to be had, or taken for or on account of the said furnace or furnaces or other Iron Works, so as aforesaid to be erected. And also of, in, and unto all the Gains, profits, and increase which shall happen or accrue or be made thereby or in the ordering or employing of the same, or by any Credit or business to be managed and done as Co-partners in the Stock aforesaid. And also shall and will bear, pay, and sustain $\frac{2}{16}$ parts, the whole in 16 parts to be divided, of all losses, charges, Costs, Rents, Payments, expences, and damage which shall at any time happen, arise, or accrue, or be expended, paid, or laid out, in, about, or concerning the said Joint Trade or Co-partnership aforesaid in anywise howsoever.

Similar covenant and agreement by Nathaniel Webb, as to his $\frac{2}{16}$th parts, as above set out.

Similar covenant and agreement by John Jones, as to his $\frac{1}{16}$th part, as above set out.

Similar covenant and agreement by Isaac Wilkinson, as to his $\frac{1}{16}$th part, as above set out.

Similar covenant and agreement by Edward Blakeway, as to his $\frac{1}{16}$th part, as above set out.

Covenant as to keeping Books.

Covenant and Agreement by the Co-partners with each other to keep Books at the Furnace, or other place to be agreed upon, shewing all Buyings, Sellings, dealings, etc., of the Business, and should both during the continuance and after the expiration of the partnership have free access to inspect and take copies of same.

Joint Liability Only.

All securities to be given and taken in the names of the Co-partners and Company, and that every Bargain, sale, Contract, and Agreement made for Coal Mine, Charcoal, Oar, Wood, Castings, Iron, Timber, or other materials relating to the said Works not made in the names of said Co-partners and Company should be made good by the Party that made the same.

No sum of money to be taken out of the Joint Stock by either partner without consent of major part of said Co-partners, and duly entered in Books.

Agreement by the said Parties that all Pigg Iron, Castings, Metals, Blooms, Authory (*sic*), Wood, Charcoal, Coak, Coal, Iron, Oar, Mine, or Cinders, Drawn, made, Bought, Sold, received, or delivered on Account of the said Furnace, Iron Works, or Co-partnership should be properly entered in a Book kept for that purpose, And that the Clerk or Clerks or other person having management of said Furnace, should upon the 24th of June, 29th Septr., 25th Decr., and 25th March yearly, and every year during said Co-partnership, if demanded by any of the said Co-partners, make a true copy of all and every entry made in said last-mentioned Book, from the quarter-day next preceding the Quarter-day on which the said copy shall be taken, and shall be signed by Stocktakers and Clerks of the works, and within 10 days after such quarter-day be sent to Partner demanding same.

And that said Clerk, or other person having the management of the said furnace and other Iron works, should in every year upon the 24th June, 29th September, 25th December, and 25th March, or within 30 days after, send and deliver to every Partner demanding same a full and true Account of all Iron Sold and money received and paid, etc., relating to said Co-partnership, in the Quarter of the year next preceding such Quarter-day.

Agreement that each partner should have power to apply all or any part of the money he should receive upon the joint Account in Discharge of joint debts, and that every sum of money remaining in hands of said Partners should at the end of every Quarter-day aforesaid after payment of joint debts be paid into hands of Clerk, or others having management of said Iron Works, within 30 days after said Quarter-day, to enable them to carry on said joint trade, And also that said Clerk having management should yearly during said Co-partnership on the 25th of March, or between 25th March and the 1st of June next ensuing, make up a true and perfect Account concerning all the Buyings, Sellings, Exchangings, Trading, etc., of the said Joint Trade, and of the Stock, ready money, Gains, Profits, and Increase thereof, also of the charges, Losses, etc., Debts owing and payable by the said Partners, to shew the state and condition they stand in reference to the said Partnership and Joint Stock, and upon perfecting the said Account to write same in Books to be provided for that purpose, said Books to be signed by said Co-partners before the 1st of August next ensuing the perfecting of same, and one of them to remain with each Partner, and not to be called in question unless some error be discovered in the lifetime of all the Parties subscribing same.

Provided always that if either of the said parties to these Presents should die during Partnership term, yet nevertheless no Benefit of Survivorship shall arise, accrue, or be had or taken by the survivor of them in any wise howsoever, any law, usage, or custom to the contrary notwithstanding.

And the Co-partners did each of them for himself respectively, and for each of his respective Exors. and admors., covenant, promise, grant, and agree to and with the other of them, their exors. and admors., that neither of them had or would during the Partnership term become interested or engaged in any Iron Works in the several Counties of Glamorgan and Monmouth, or elsewhere in South Wales, or erect any Iron works for his own benefit, or make any Contract or Agreement on Account of said Co-partnership, without consent in writing of major part of said Co-partners, save and except such share or part either of the Parties to these presents had in a certain Forge situate at Cardiff aforesaid. And neither of the said parties should grant, Bargain, Assign, or convey their right, title, or Interest in or to the said Furnace or Furnaces, or any of the Premises granted by any of the said recited Contracts, Agreements, Leases, or Assignments, or any part of the said Joint Stock, to any person or persons whatsoever, Except to or in trust for his Wife, Children, or next of kin, without the consent in writing of the major part of the Parties first had and obtained. And in case either of the Parties should die before the end of the said Co-partnership, and thereby more Persons than one should become interested in his share to the said Joint Stock, that then the Persons so entitled to his share should appoint only one person who shall have the care and management of the said works with the other surviving Partners, and not more at one and the same time.

Agreement and Declaration by said Parties that all and singular the several recited Articles, Contracts, etc., hereinbefore recited should be deemed and taken to be for the use and Benefit of the said Joint Trade, and the Persons who took the same should be deemed and taken as trustees thereof to the use and benefit of said Joint Trade, and not otherwise.

Agreement that no Apprentice, or Servant, or workman should be taken or be employed in or about the said Joint Trade during the partnership without the consent of the major part of the said parties, and major part without consent of Others to discharge and turn away any workmen, etc.; and any workmen kept by major part of the said partners, should be paid out of such Joint Stock, and if any part of said Joint Stock should be embezzled, purloined, or stolen, or spoiled by such Apprentice, Workmen, and others, or Agent or servant of the said parties to be taken and kept as aforesaid during the said term, then the loss occasioned shall be equally borne and sustained by the said parties in the shares and proportions which they are entitled to the Capital Stock.

Neither of the said parties, without the consent of the major part, shall release and discharge any debt, Duty, sum or sums of money, or other thing that shall be due or owing to partnership, or any securities for same, but only such sum as shall be actually received and brought into said Account, nor compound for any debt, duty, etc., without the consent, etc., of major portion of Parties as aforesaid.

Covenant by the said parties with each other that neither of them should sell or deliver out upon trust, and without ready money anything belonging to the said Joint trade, or trust, or lend money out of the said Joint Stock, to any person except at the hazard and Peril of him trusting the same, and not by the Joint Stock; and in case either Partner during said term becomes insolvent, etc., then the said furnace and other Iron works, and other the Premises above recited, and all tools, Utensils, Stock in Trade, to be valued by two indifferent persons, to be chosen—one by the Insolvent Partner, and the other by the other Partners; and after such Valuation made the share of said Insolvent Party shall be assigned within 1 calendar month after valuation to the other partners, such Partners paying the said Person Insolvent the appraized value of his share of the said furnace and other Stock in Trade, at the time such Assignment shall be made. And also that within 1 month after determination of Partnership, a final Account, Partition, or Division, be made between the said Partners or their legal Representatives, of the said Joint Stock and Trade, and also of Debts, dues, etc., on account of same. And after payment as aforesaid of liabilities to receive his respective share, according to the proportions above recited; and in case the money and Stock at end of term not sufficient to clear liabilities, each Partner to bear his share and part, according to the foregoing proportions.

Arbitration Clause, in case of difference, doubt, Question, or meaning of these presents, or anything contained therein, two indifferent persons to be nominated and chosen from time to time by Co-partners so differing within 21 days after such doubt, etc., shall arise, each contending partner to choose one, to be by the same two Persons chosen, or else by an Umpire to be nominated by the said two persons, in case they cannot agree, and Parties to abide by such decision, and no suit or other proceedings were to be taken before such Arbitration had been determined.

And whereas the said Isaac Wilkinson hath obtained a Patent for his new invented machine for blowing furnaces, forges, and other Iron Works, by Valves, Cyphons, and other Engine or Engines for the term of 14 years, and hath agreed to and with the said other partners that they shall have the benefit of the said Patent in their said Furnace and other Iron works to be erected by them.

Now the said Isaac Wilkinson doth hereby for himself, his exors., and admors., and each of them covenant, promise, grant, and agree to and with the said Thomas Lewis, Thomas Price, Richard Jenkins, Thomas Harris, John Curtis, Nathaniel Webb, John Jones, and Edward Blakeway, that the said Partners shall, during the remainder of the said 14 years, have the full benefit of the said Patent at the Iron works belonging to the said Co-partnership.

In consideration whereof the said Thomas Lewis and above others, did covenant, promise, and agree with I. Wilkinson as follows: That if any one furnace erected by the said Co-partners should make on an average more than 20 tons of mettle per week during the first Blast, that then the said I. Wilkinson should receive the sum of £50 for every ton of Pig Iron so exceeding the Quantity of 20 Ton. And if said Co-partners should find it necessary and convenient to Blow more Furnaces than one, then in such case the said Wilkinson should receive the like Gratuaty for every additional Furnace.

Usual interchangeable Witnessing Clause.

---

A very important Lease was taken by the Dowlais Comyany in 1763 from Lady Windsor (who, we have seen, granted the 1760 lease to Messrs. Maybery and partners at Hirwain), and must be considered henceforth as the main lease, under which the Dowlais Works were held, superseding the lease granted by Lord Windsor in 1748-9, and specially providing that 22 acres of the Common land should be assigned to the Dowlais Company to build their Works upon.

### LEASE OF MINERALS AND THE 22 ACRES.

By Indenture dated 23rd June, 1763, between

THE RIGHT HONBLE. ALICE, LADY VISCOUNTESS DOWAGER OF WINDSOR, one part.

And

THOMAS LEWIS, of Newhouse, in the Parish of Llanishen, in the Coy. of Glamorgan, Squire.

THOMAS PRICE, of Watford, in the said County, Gent.; and

JOHN JONES, of Bristol, Ironmaster, other part.

RECITING the Rt. Hon. Herbert, Lord Viscount Windsor, decd., did by his Indre. of Lease of the 1st November, 1749,[1] demise and grant unto Thomas Morgan, of Ruperra, Esquire, amongst other things,

All the veins and mines of coal, iron, and stone upon all or any of the commons of the said Lord Windsor, in the several Parishes of Merthyr and Gelligare, in the said County of Glamorgan, above the Brook or River of Tayach, for the term of 99 years, at yearly rent of £26.

And reciting the said veins and mines of coal, iron, and stone, have been by due and proper Conveyances assigned, transferred, and set over unto the said Thomas Lewis for and on behalf the said Thomas Price and John Jones, and they are thereby become legally possessed of or entitled to the same.

It was witnessed that said Lady Windsor for and in consideration of the yearly rents, covenants, provisoes, conditions and agreements hereinafter specified and reserved, and by and on the part and behalf of the sd. Thos. Lewis, Thos. Price, and John Jones, their exors., admors., assns., to be paid, done, and performed, as also in conson. of the great expence they have been at and the large sums they have expended and laid out in the

[1] The date of this Lease is 10th March, 1748 (see *ante*, p. 21); and this is distinctly shown on various documents, and explained in Case submitted to Counsel.

building and erecting of an Iron Furnace, and of divers houses, outhouses, water engines, fire engines, kilns, pounds, wears, banks, and other devices needful and necessary for the carrying on of the said Iron Works in and upon the premes. therinafter granted.

And in consideration of the surrender and yielding up to the said Lady Windsor, her heirs and assigns,

All quarrs and quarrys of stone and slate, situate in or under any of the commons or waste lands of the said Lady Windsor, situate in the said several Parishes of Merthyr and Gellygare Supra Cayath, granted as aforesaid by the said original Lease, and all their right, title, and interest thereto, except the liberties and powers hereby after reserved to the said Thomas Lewis, Thomas Price, and John Jones, and their assigns, She the said Lady Windsor Hath granted, demised, set, and to farm lett, and by these presents doth grant, demise, sett, and to farm lett unto the said Thomas Lewis, Thomas Price, and John Jones and their assigns,

All that parcel of waste or uninclosed land, situate, lying, and being in the said Parish of Merthir, in the County of Glamorgan aforesaid, leaving the lands of Thomas Rees on the west part, the lands of David John and Mary Rice on the north part, and the waste or uninclosed land of the said Lady Windsor on the east and south parts, containing in the whole 22 Acres of land as sett forth, bounded, and described in the map hereunto annexed,

With free leave, licence, and liberty to and for the said Thomas Lewis, Thomas Price, and John Jones, and their exs., ads., and assigns, to enclose and fence in the same, leaving a proper space or breadth for a highway or road, and to sett up, erect, and build in and upon every part or parcel of the said hereby demised premises such and so many furnaces, blast furnaces, forges, mills, engines, store-houses, kilns, coal-houses, yards, courts, edifices, and buildings for the placing and keeping of oar, coal, coak, and charcoal, and the making and manufacturing of iron, as they, the said Thomas Lewis, Thomas Price, and John Jones, their exors., admors., and assns., shall think fitt and convenient.

And also full and free liberty of turning and conveying of the river and brook Dwylas, or such other water or watercourses as there are near adjoining to the said demised premises, to serve such works as they the said Thomas Lewis, Thomas Price, and John Jones, their exors., admors., or assigns, have built and erected, or from time to time shall build or erect as aforesaid, and for that purpose to have full and free liberty and power to make so much and so many channels, sluices, dams, ponds, pondheads, stanks, and Wears as they shall think fitt, With full and free liberty, licence, and authority to and for the said Thomas Lewis, Thomas Price, and John Jones, their executors, admors., and assigns, from time to time and at all or any time or times during the term hereby granted, to bore, try, dig, search, work for, raise, and land all such coal, culm, iron myne, and iron oar as shall or may be found in or under all or any the commons situate in the several Parishes of Merthyr and Gelligare aforesaid, above the Brook or River called Cayach aforesaid, and for the purpose aforesaid, to dig and sink all such pitts, groves, levells, aditts, drains, shafts, trenches, chanes, and other works whatsoever, on any part of the said waste or commons as they shall think fitt, and to convert any water and water-courses thereon found or to be found for the better raising, working, mineing, or landing of the said coals, culm, iron myne, or iron ore, and for drawing or carrying off waters that might be hurtful or prejudicial, or might be necessary for the scouring or cleaning thereof, and to take and carry away all such coal, culm, iron oar, or iron mines so found on the said Commons or part thereof. And with full and free liberty, license, and authority to and for the said Thos. Lewis, Thos. Price, and John Jones, to take, dig, leave from and out of any part or parcell of the sd. Commons, clay, sand, lime stone, or other stones, as can be there found or gotten, and which shall be necessary, needful, and used in the building or repairing the said furnaces, forges, mills, edifices, or other buildings erected on the said demised premises, with liberty of ingress, egress, and regress to and for the said Thos. Lewis, Thos. Price, and John Jones, their exors., ads., or assns., servants, etc., at all times during the term hereafter mentd., to pass and repass to and from and over the same, with horses, carts, and carriages, doing as little damage to the estate, tenants, etc., of sd. Lady Windsor as the nature of the works will permit of, and filling up all useless pitts and channells which be hurtful and an annoyance to the tenants of the said Lady Windsor.

Except and always reserved out of this demise and grant unto the said Lady Windsor, her heirs and assigns, All veins of tin, lead, and copper, and All quarrys of stone and slate, except so much as shall be necessary or wanted for the said works, and all other mines and minerals whatsoever, except iron oar and coal myne, and all springs of salt, brine, or copperas, and all veins of marl, sand, clay, peat, and turff.

To have and To hold all and singular the said premises, powers, and priviledges unto the said Thomas Lewis, Thomas Price, and John Jones, their exors., ads., and assns., from the 1st day of November last for and during the full term of 85 years from thence next ensuing.

Yielding and Paying yearly unto Lady Windsor, her hrs., etc., the rent of £5 over and above and exclusive of the yearly rent of £26 due as afsd. by the sd. original Lease for the coals and iron oar and other premises granted to the said Thomas Morgan, Esq., upon every feast day of St. Michael, without any deduction, etc.

Covenants by said Thos. Lewis, Thos. Price, and John Jones with Lady Windsor,

To pay sd. rent of £5, besides sd. rent of £26 reserved by sd. Lease granted to Morgan ; To pay all rates, taxes, etc. ; To fill up all useless pits and prevent any hurt as to depasturing, and all furnaces, forges, mills, houses, outhouses, etc., to be kept in good and sufficient repair, in default or neglect to repair, Lady Windsor to inspect and give notice to them.

Proviso for re-entry if rent in arrear for 15 days.

Covenant by said Lady Windsor with sd. Thos. Lewis, Thos. Price, and John Jones,

That they, observing and performing covts. and condons., and paying rent, might peaceably and quietly enjoy said premises.

(Signed) by Lady Windsor.

Sealed and duly attested.

---

In the course of time various changes of partnership took place, which we will now proceed to trace.

## CHANGES IN THE PARTNERSHIP FORMED 19th SEPTEMBER, 1759.

Under the Deed of Partnership of 19th September, 1759, called "The Myrthy Furnace," and previously Abstracted, the following are named as the original Partners :—

| | |
|---|---|
| Thomas Lewis. | John Curtis, |
| Thomas Price. | Nathaniel Webb. |
| Richard Jenkins. | Isaac Wilkinson. |
| Thomas Harris. | Edward Blakeway. |

By the recitals in the deed of this date (1st May, 1792) made between Thomas Guest, of Dowlais, Glamorgan, Ironmaster, who had become a partner in the firm, and Joseph Cowles, of Coed y Gric, co. Monmouth, Gent. (and which deed recites the deed of 1759),

It appears that Edward Blakeway, one of the Original Partners, had retired from the Partnership, and had sold his share to Thomas Harris for £60.

Also, that John Curtis, an Original Partner, had not advanced any money in joint Stock, and had sold his Share to the said Thomas Harris for *5s.*

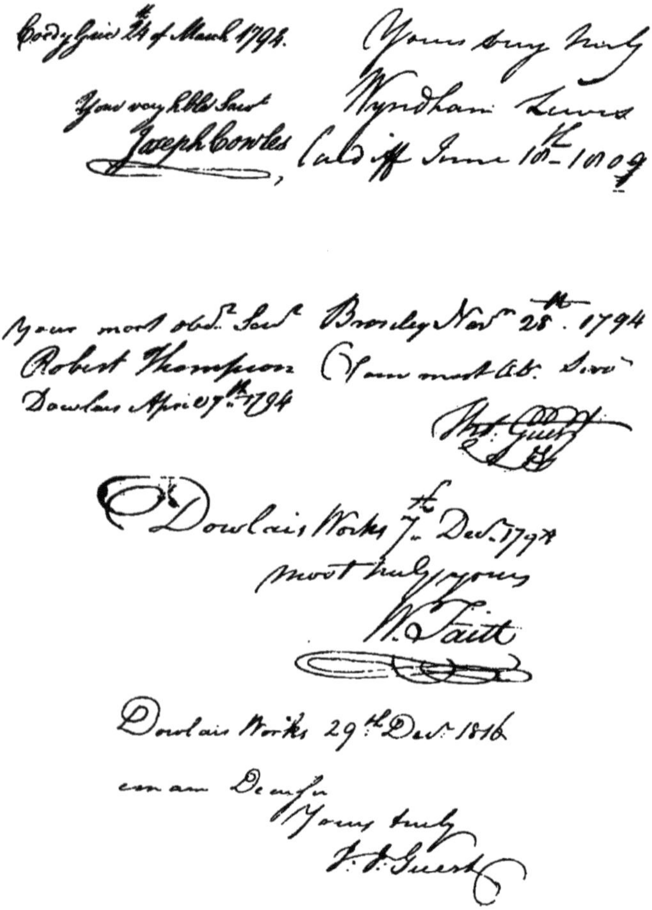

SIGNATURES OF PARTNERS IN THE DOWLAIS IRON WORKS.

Also, that by deed dated 10th October, 1782 (therein recited) made between John Guest, of Dowlais House, and Thomas Harris, The said Thomas Harris, who had become possessed of $\frac{6}{18}$ths of the Joint Stock, then greatly enhanced in value by the extension of the Works and Furnaces, and which had been lately greatly enlarged and augmented by the erection of an additional Furnace, sold and conveyed all his $\frac{6}{18}$ths interest to the said John Guest for £2,600, Thomas Guest, of Cardiff, his Son, and William Williams, of Brecon, banker, becoming surety.

Also, that by the death of John Guest, on 25th November, 1787, Thomas Guest, his son, became Administrator, and seized in possession of $\frac{3}{18}$ths in his own right, the remaining $\frac{3}{18}$ths being in trust for the rest of the family. And by this present deed (19th September, 1792),

It is declared That Thomas Guest had sold and conveyed $\frac{1}{18}$th of his interest to Joseph Cowles for the sum of £2,400.

By the recitals in the deed of this date (10th December, 1798), between Robert Thompson, of the Parish of Merthyr Tydfil, Co. Glamorgan, Ironmaster, and William Taitt, of the Town of Cardiff, Esquire, on May 1st, 1795, It appears that Joseph Cowles of Coed y Gric sold $\frac{1}{18}$th to Robert Thompson, and by this present deed It is declared that Robert Thompson had sold and conveyed $\frac{1}{18}$th to William Taitt for £3,817, and all his interest in the said Dowlais Furnaces and leases, etc.

---

1800.—By Mortgage deed of this date it appears that John Guest assigned $\frac{1}{18}$th interest to Robert Williams, of Brecon, in Mortgage for £1,500, and that John Guest having paid off the Mortgage, he, Robert Williams, as the Mortgagee, conveyed by request of John Guest the $\frac{1}{18}$th to Taitt.

---

1795.—By a recital in a deed of this date, made between William Taitt and other parties, It appears that by deed dated 1st August, 1787, between John Jones and William Taitt, and by other instruments, William Taitt became seized of $\frac{4}{18}$th Shares in the Works.

---

Descriptions of Partners in deeds of these dates.

1813.—William Lewis, late of Alderley, now of Cheltenham, Gloucester, Esq., William Taitt, of Cardiff, Esq. (being Proprietors of Dowlais Iron Works), do on behalf of themselves and Thomas Guest agree, etc.

---

1819.—Josiah John Guest, of Dowlais Works, Merthyr Tydfil, Glam., Esq.
Wyndham Lewis, of Greenmeadow, same Coy., Esq.
William Price Lewis, of the same place, Clerk.
Thomas Revel Guest, of Cork, Ireland, Esq.

---

1826.—Josiah John Guest.
Wyndham Lewis.
William Price Lewis.
Thomas Revel Guest.

---

It will be seen later, that the Penydarran Company, whose Iron Works closely adjoined those of the Dowlais Company, had a deficient supply of Coal, and, as early as 1786, they applied to their neighbours—who had an abundance—to lease to them certain veins of coal. The two Companies were then on good terms, and the lease was granted. It was arranged that a dead rent of £160 should be paid, and 6*d*. a ton additional rent for every ton over 5,616 tons that should be raised. We are inclined to think

F

that in the early days of Iron and Coal Mining the ground landlords charged fixed rents only, and that royalties were first introduced by the lessees in their sub-leases. It was a convenient form for them to obtain an increased rent.

The following is a copy of the sub-lease to the Penydarran Company.

## DOWLAIS COMPANY TO PENYDARRAN COMPANY.

### Lease of Veins of Coal.

By Indenture of 20 June, 1786, made between

William Lewis, of Pentyrch, in the Coy. of Glamorgan, Esquire;

Joseph Cowles, of Coed y Gric, in the Coy. of Monmouth, Gentm.;

John Guest, of Dowlais, Merthir Tydvil, Co. Glamorgan, Esquire, and Ironmaster;

John Jones, of the City of Bristol, Ironmaster; and

William Taitt, of Pwllywheaid, Parish of Merthir Tydvil, Gent. (Major part in number and value of the Company and Proprietors of Dowlais Iron Works, Merthir Tydvil), on behalf of themselves and Partners—one part.

And

Jeremiah Homfray, of Pendarren, in the Parish of Merthir Tydvil, aforesaid; and

Samuel Homfray, of the same place, Ironmasters—other part.

It was witnessed that in consideration of the Rents, Reservations, Covenants, and Agreements thereinafter expressed and contained, and on the part of Jeremiah Homfray and Saml. Homfray, their exs., etc., to be paid, observed, and performed.

They, the sd. Lewis, Cowles, Guest, Jones, and Taitt, by virtue of any powers enabling them,

Have and each and every of them, Hath demised, granted, and to fee, farm let, and by present Indenture doth demise unto said Jeremiah Homfray and Samuel Homfray, their exs., etc.

All veins, seams and Beds of Coal lying or being open and found, or which shall or may hereafter be discovered or found in or upon or under a certain part of the Common called Wain nant y bwch, situate in the Parish of Merthir Tydvil, and within the Lordship of Sengbenith; that is to say, All that piece or parcel of Land which lies in Breadth between a certain Rivulet, there called Nant y bwch on the South and the Point of Tor y fan Hill, in a straight line to the Gate leading from the Mountain to Pwll y wheaid House on the North, and in length bounded by the Lands of Pendarren, the lands of William David and Trebedda on the West, and by a line drawn from the Point of Toryfan Hill to the Road near Sarn Howell on the East, and measuring in breadth 1,232 yards, and in length 1,232 yards or about, and for better description and certainty a Plan thereof was annexed thereto.

Together with full and free power and license for the sd. Jeremiah Homfray and Saml. Homfray, their exors., etc., to bore, dig, delve, and trench in, upon, or under the said Piece or Parcel of land for the searching out, raising, having, and taking of the Coal there found and to be found; and to work, follow, and carry on the same to the most advantage, and for that purpose to dig, sink, and make all such pits, groves, Levels, Trenches, and Channels, and to erect all such Engines and other whatsoever works as shall be thought necessary for the working thereof.

And also to lay on the Land all such Coal as shall from time to time be so gotten or had, and all Rubbish forth in working, with full ingress, egress, and regress for the Homfrays, their exs., ads., servants, etc., during the term, with or without Horses, Carts, etc., to or from sd. Colliery, and such coal raised to carry away and use at their own pleasure.

And also with further liberty or power for the Homfrays, their exs., etc., to take, direct, and appropriate Water issuing from the said veins of Coal for the purpose of watering their Coaks and Coakyards at Pendarren ffurnace, but no other purpose.

To have and to Hold, use, and enjoy the said Coal and Colliery, with all the priviledges, liberties, etc., unto the said I. Homfray and Saml. Homfray, their exs., etc., from the 29th Septr., 1792, for and during the full end and term of 56 years.

Yielding and Paying unto Lewis, Cowles, Guest, Jones, and Taitt, their exs., etc., and the other proprietors of Dowlais Works afsd. for the time being, the yearly rent of £140 8*s*. 0*d*., upon 25th March and 29th September, the first payt. to be made on 25th March next, after commencement of term.

And also Yielding and Paying unto the said William Lewis, Jos. Cowles, Jno. Guest, John Jones, and William Taitt, their exs., etc., or other the Proprietor afsd., the additional Rent or sum of 6*d*., for every ton weight of Coal, which by virtue of these presents shall be had and taken by the sd. J. Homfray and S. Homfray, their exs., ads, etc., in any year of the Term over and above yearly allowance of 5,616 Tons, each Ton to consist of 2,500 weight, and each Hundred 112 Pounds, and the Compass of the year for taking the said Allowance of 5,616 Tons, to be computed from Michas. day to Michas. day next following, and not upon average taking of one year with another, on every 25th March and 29th Septr. which shall first next happen after the taking of such surplus Quantity of Coal over and above the said yearly allowance of 5616 Tons, free and clear of all Taxes, expenses, etc.

Covenants by sd. Jeremiah Homfray and Samuel Homfray, jointly and severally, and their heirs, with the sd. Lewis, Cowles, Guest, Jones, and Taitt, their exs., etc.

To pay sd. rent of £140 8*s*., and sd. additional rent of 6*d*. for every Ton of Coal over 5,616 Tons. To pay and discharge rates and Taxes. To at all times during term take from the hereby demised premises all the Coal to be used or consumed in the blast Furnace at Pendarren, and not from elsewhere.

And shod. not sell or dispose of the Coal from said Colliery to any person (Firing for the workmen only excepted);

And should at all times fence and fill up all pits and shafts from time to time made or sunk by virtue of now reciting Indenture when same useless.

And should fairly and justly weigh Coal and enter in Books kept for purpose, and which Books should be open to Dowlais Proprietors, with liberty to make copies.

And to make, manage, and work and carry on said Coal mines according to regular method of working, and at the expiration of term yield up with appurts. And lawful for sd. several Proprietors of Dowlais to view and to see want of Repair, and should any such be found to give notice to Counting House at Pendarren Furnace to rectify same, and would within one month after notice to Homfrays such were to be put into complete state of repair.

Covenant by Lewis and others with Homfrays That they, paying Rents and observing and performing covenants, should have peaceable possession.

Proviso that should any stipulation as to working of the Coal and disposal of same as above recited, be broken or violated, usual power of re-entry to Lewis and ors.

Further covenant by the Homfrays that they would not directly or indirectly until after expiration of term take on lease or treat for any property on said Lordship or said Mines or Quarries on same in possession, etc., of sd. Dowlais Coy.

In witness, etc.

NOTE.—There is a Memo. on the first page of this Lease:—"This Lease to be granted by Wm. Lewis, Joseph Cowles, Jno. Guest, Jno. Jones, of Bristol, and Wm. Taitt, for themselves and Partners, without making mention of any names. To Jere. and Saml. Homfray only."

---

The Dowlais Company were at this time (1796) able to turn out a large quantity of pig-iron from their furnaces, and their near neighbours, Messrs. Richard Crawshay and Watkin George, of Cyfarthfa Iron-works, being in want of an additional supply of pig-iron, the following contract was entered into between the Companies:—

## CONTRACT BY DOWLAIS CO. AS TO SUPPLYING PIG-IRON TO RICHARD CRAWSHAY AND WATKIN GEORGE, CYFARTHFA, IRONMASTERS AND CO-PARTNERS.

BY ARTICLES OF AGREEMENT of this date (November, 1796), between

WILLIAM LEWIS, of Alderley, in the Coy. of Gloucester;

WILLIAM TAITT, of Cardiff, in the Coy. of Glamorgan;

THOMAS GUEST, of the same place;

JOSEPH COWLES, of Coed y Gric, in the Coy. of Monmouth;

JOHN GUEST, of Brosley, in the Coy. of Salop; and

ROBERT THOMPSON, of Dowlais, Merthir Tydvil, Glamorgan, Ironmasters and Co-Partners—one part;

And

RICHARD CRAWSHAY, of Cyfarthfa, Merthir Tidvil afsd., and

WATKIN GEORGE, of same place, Ironmasters and Co-Partners—other part.

Whereby the sd. Lewis, Taitt, Guest, Cowles, Guest, and Thompson covenanted and agreed with sd. Crawshay and Watkin George That they, sd. Lewis, etc., their exors., etc., would sell and deliver to sd. Crawshay and Watkin George, their exs., etc., 2,000 Tons of Pig Iron yearly for the term of 5 years from 1st Jany. then next, at the price of £5 5s. for every Ton long Wt. of 20 Hds. to the Ton at 120 lbs. to the Hd., besides the usual allowance of 30 lb. on each Ton for breakage, the said Pig Iron to consist in Quality of two-thirds at least of Dark Grey fit for Forge and Foundry uses, and the Remr. of bright Grey mottle or white, and to be delivered at the Canal Lock No. One, in the Parish of Merthyr Tidvil, in regular Quarterly Quantities, of the Wt. and Quality before mentioned (casualties or accidents at Dowlais Works or otherwise inevitably preventing such regular supply only excepted).

Agreement by Crawshay and George with Lewis and their Exors. that they, Crawshay and George, would buy and take the sd. Pig Iron for the term at the price and in manner aforesaid and (on every 1st April, 1st July, 1st October, and 1st Jany.) to pay for the same by good or legal Bills of Exchange on London, within 3 months, Bills to bear date on Quarter days afsd., to order of Lewis and their heirs, so that they, Lewis, etc., should be paid for all Pig Iron they shod. deliver.

---

A little before this time, namely, in 1795, a serious interruption of the prosperous course of the Dowlais Works occurred, and it is hard to determine precisely what gave birth to it. Possibly the Commoners had found their sheep-walks injured, or even destroyed, by the extensive working of mine-patches on the open hill, the formation of tram-roads and large ponds, and the "scouring" practices resorted to in cleansing and washing the iron ore.

At any rate, the Commoners became uneasy, and questioned the right of the Dowlais Company to cut and carve about the common land to their detriment, without any

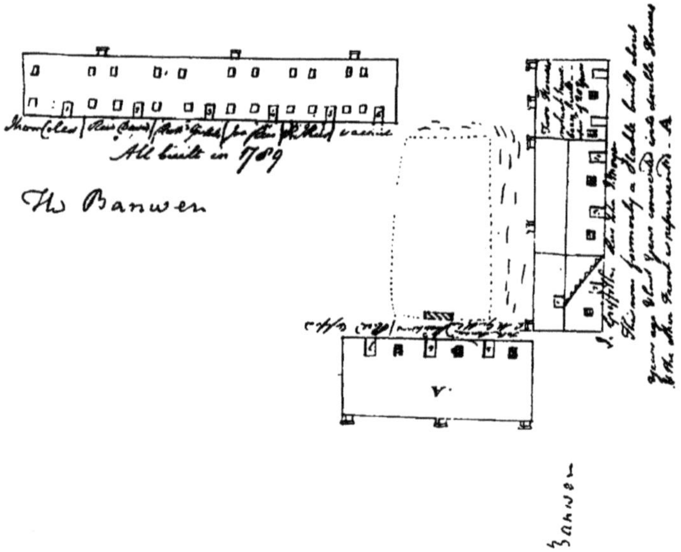


*Page* 37.

THE DOWLAIS WORKS. WATKIN HARRY'S CLAIM. 1795.

compensation being paid; and particularly they called in question the act of the Company in placing their works and workmen's houses on that part of the Common land known as the twenty-two acres, on which the Lady of the Manor had—perhaps unadvisedly—sanctioned the erection by the lease of 1763.

Mr. Samuel Homfray, of the Penydarran Works, no doubt from some strong reason or other, championed the cause of the Commoners.

In the result litigation ensued, and each individual member of the Dowlais firm was served with sixteen distinct writs of ejectment, and claiming damages at the instance of the Commoners.

We here set out the "Case" laid before Counsel by the Dowlais firm, and Counsel's opinion thereon.

## THE 22 ACRES—DOWLAIS COMPANY—WATKIN HARRY'S CLAIM.

### Case Submitted to Counsel in 1795.

Certain Commons in the Parishes of Merthir Tidvil and Gellygare, Co. Glamorgan, abound with Coal and Iron stone, which have been raised by the Lords of the Manor or their Lessees Time immemorial.

By Indenture dated 10th March, 1748 (here follows abstract of Lord Windsor's Lease to Morgan).

By Indenture dated 16th Augt, 1757 (here follows abstract of Lease by Morgan to Rees and John).

By Indenture dated 20th Septr., 1757 (here follows abstract of Lease, Rees and John to Lewis and Co.)

By Indenture dated 3rd June, 1763 (here follows abstract of Lease to Lewis Price and Jones by Lady Windsor).

Thomas Lewis and Co. had, previously to obtaining the last-mentioned Lease, erected an Iron Furnace called Dowlais Furnace on part of the 22 Acres thereby demised, which they began building in 1757. They not only built that Furnace, but made several other necessary Erections about it, such as a Smith's Shop, Storehouse, Lime Kilns, etc., and about 26 years ago they built a Dwelling House nearly at the Extremity of the 22 Acres, the whole of which (though not regularly inclosed) has been ever since more or less used in carrying on their Works.

The Company now consists of several Persons, who hold their Shares under different Assignments from the original Lessees, and have a Capital of over £20,000 engaged in their Works.

About 6 years ago they erected another Furnace, adjoining the old one, on a spot where some Buildings had stood since the Beginning.

About 10 years ago they built a stable for their working Horses contiguous to the before-mentioned Dwelling House, and about 5 years ago they erected six Workmen's Houses near the same spot, all on the 22 acres, and within the Line of the said Old House; and last year the Stable was converted into Dwelling houses. See the plan of these houses.

There never was any Notice not to erect any of these Buildings; on the contrary, several of the neighbouring Freeholders (Commoners) assisted in haling Timber for the first Furnace; and the Company have carried on the Works at this place without the least interruption for upwards of 30 years; and in so doing, among other things, have been all the time in the habit of digging clay and making bricks.

Scouring for Mine (by collecting Water and letting it down in large Quantities to carry off the earth and Rubbish) has been immemorially practiced on these Commons, and anciently the Ponds were much more numerous, but not so large as those used at present.

This Practice, from all appearance, has existed for Centuries.

At the Summer Assizes, in 1791, a Cause was brought on for Trial at Hereford in the name of Thomas Rees, a Commoner, against the Earl of Bute, then Lord Cardiff, and the Dowlais Company, and other persons, in respect to these erections, and for scouring, and also touching an Inclosure at a place called Brincaira, which the Dowlais Coy. had no concern with. On the Brincaira Business the Plaintiff (by a sort of consent) had a verdict, and that Inclosure has been since levelled, but we believe a verdict was entered for the Defendants on all the Counts which affected the Dowlais Company.

The Dowlais Company, in consequence of a dispute with a Mr. Homfray, are now harrassed with 16 separate Actions in respect of the several Dwelling-houses, and for the supposed Inclosure of that part of the Common leased to them, as before stated; and have been threatened with others for erecting the last Furnace, and for scouring and burning bricks on the Common; and the nominal Plt. Watkin Harry lives a great Way off, whose Cattle never graze within a Mile of the Furnaces unless they chance to stray from their usual walks, the Common being several miles in extent.

As the 22 Acres have been in great measure (tho' perhaps not completely) occupied by the Company for upwards of 30 years, and as such Buildings are absolutely necessary for getting and manufacturing the Mines, and they were made without any Complaint or Notice from any of the Commoners to the contrary. And the Piece of Ground in Question has been nearly, if not wholly, useless to the Commoners for that Length of time.

Scouring is, in a certain degree, prejudicial to the Commoners, but has been always uninterruptedly practiced. And the making of Bricks on the Commons for the use of the Works can be clearly proved for upwards of 30 years.

The Actions brought, and in which 16 Declarations have been delivered, Watkin Harry against the Company and their several Tenants are as follows, vizt.:

No. 1, against Wm. Lewis, Wm. Taitt, Thos. Guest, Joseph Cowles, Jno. Guest, and Robert Thompson (being the Company), and Jno. Griffith, one of their Tenants.

No. 2, agst. The Company and Richd. Lewis anor. Tenant.

No. 3, agst. The like and Richd. Lewis and Tenant.

No. 4, agst. The like and Jno. Morgan Do.

No. 5, agst. The like and Richd. Williams Do.

No. 6, agst. The like and Richd. Vippond Do.

No. 7, agst. The Company only.

These Declarations are substantially and almost Verbatim, the same varying only the Name of the last Deft.—complaining of a Deprivation of Plts. Right of Commoning on Blaen Romney, etc., and which he claims to be intitled to in Right of a Messuage and Lands held by him in the Parish of Kellygare (one of the Parishes in which the Common is situate), by Defts. having erected a Dwelling House and Stable, and a Fence inclosing and separating 10 acres of the Common. In which there are 6 counts, with very little variation; and some should have been spared, and probably might be expunged on a Complaint being made.

No. 8, agst. The Co. and John Coles, anor. Tenant.

No. 9, agst. The Co. and Rees David.

No. 10, agst. The Co. and Richd. Griffith.

No. 11, agst. The Co. and Joseph Thos. Rees.

No. 12, agst. The Co. and Rees John Rees.

The 5 last mentd. Declons. are the same as the first 7, leaving out the erecting of a stable.

The last four Declarations are:

No. 13, agst. The Coy. and Morgan Gwillim and S. Morgan, 2 Tenants.

No. 14, agst. Same and Jennett Thomas and Rosser Thomas, not Tenants or defended by Company.

No. 15, agst. Same and Margaret Harry, ditto ditto.

No. 16, agst. Same and Thomas Harry, ditto ditto.

The last 4 Declons. seem, as to the 2 first Counts, the same as the five preceding ones. The Remainder of the Counts are for erecting a House and fence on Part of the Common, Parish Gelligare, orwise. Kellygare, called Pant-y-waun.

*Vide* Copies of the three Declarations left herewith.

It is to be observed that the Plaintiff actually assisted Joseph Rees in carrying some of the Materials for Building the first House on Pant y Wain. That mentd. in Declon. 10, and for which Mr. Griffith received some Stabling Rent.

Your Opinion is desired whether any and which of the Actions can be maintained.

Whether some of the Counts could be expunged, and whether it would not be advisable to consolidate Actions.

Whether the Company have not, under the Title and circumstances above stated, a good ground of Right to the Furnaces and other erections that have been made above 30 yrs., tho' not 60 yrs., ago. Whether they have not a Right to dig for Mines, scour, etc., as hath been usual Time immemorial. And also to erect new Furnaces and other necessary Works for manufacturing Ore, etc.

And whether the Coy. can justify an actual Inclosure of the 22 acres granted by the Lord as before stated, marked out and in a great measure solely occupied by the Company and their Predecessors without any interruption or Complaint from any of the Freeholders, or those having a right of Common. And on the whole advise what to be done by Coy.

OPINION.

I do not understand from the Declons. whether the Buildgs., etc., the Pltf. complains of, applies to Buildgs. or Inclosure. With respect to Dowlais Furnace, Erections, and Dwghouse, erected and built upwards 20 yrs., and enjoyed by Coy. quietly ever since, I think Actions cannot be maintained, because a possessory Action by a Commoner, I apprehend, cannot be maintained, as he has not exercised his right within 20 yrs. in the place. After 20 years adverse possessn. against the Commoner, a release of his right *quâ* the past encroachments would be presumed. Supposing the Coy. are able to establish exclusive possession not only of Furnace and other erections, but also the whole 22 Acres comprised in the Lease against Commoners for last 20 years, then, I apprehend, Actions not maintainable even with respect to the modern Buildgs., etc., for the reason before mentd. But suppos'g the Plt. should be able to make out a *primâ facie* case, showing exercise of Common right on the 22 acres within 20 years, I think the Defts. may make out a good Defence on 2 Grods.: 1st, By custom to dig for mines, scouring, etc., erect Furnaces and other works for manufacturing Ore, and habitations for Workmen if they can shew the Works, etc., in question to be of that description; for I apprehend such a custom is a legal custom, and that the Commoner takes his Common right, subjt. to it. 2ndly, By shewg. that there is sufficiency of Common left for Plaintiff and all others who have a right, for the Lord or any by his Authority may inclose and hold in severalty by way of approvemt. on that Condition. The Coy. may justify the actual Inclosures upon that condition of the 22 acres. I think all the Declons. are too long, and that Court would expunge some Counts and Motion to do so advisable. I think afterwards it may be advisable to move to consolidate Actions, or all may abide event of a few, vizt., that all the 1st class, as above distinguished, may abide Event of one in that class, and so in the 2nd and 3rd Class of same; but before determined upon, Defts. shod. get information to what buildings, etc., each Declon. applys. The Comp'ny, I conceive, have under the Title and circumstances above stated, a good Title to the Furnaces and other Erections that have been made above 30 years.

(Sd.) Geo. Wood, Mid.-Temple,
2 Feb., 1795.

---

The Trial took place at Hereford in 1795, and there is little doubt that the result—though unfortunately on Counsels' briefs, which we have, there is no entry of the terms—was in favour of the Dowlais Company, and that the Works were allowed to remain on what had been once undoubtedly common land, and apparently on the ground that the Commoners had not been diligent suitors, and had through their non-interference for many years, acquiesced in the usurpation of the Common land sufficiently long to give a legal title to it to the Lord of the Manor and his Lessees.

On the day before the trial, Mr. John Powell, the Attorney of the Dowlais Company, when at the Green Dragon, received the following note from T. C.

T. C. was Thomas Caldecot, the eminent Counsel of that day. The 22 Acres we now know; and the Jury was a Herefordshire Special one. Whether Mr. Powell was able to interview any of those supposed to be favourably disposed, and with what effect, all my papers relating to the trial are discreetly silent!

---

## CALDECOT'S NOTE TO POWELL.

"Would it be amiss to look after the Special Jury, and to insure the attendance at 8 o'clock to-morrow morn of such as you think well disposed? And can any of your people speak of the point to which the 22 acres extended, and the grant extended: or if any reputation of the right, or any greater actual user, within that line than without?

"(Sd.) T. C."

---

This great trial having ended, we believe, wholly in favour of the Dowlais Company, a peaceful condition of things ensued for some few years, enabling that Company to develop their great concern.

However, the quarrel between the Dowlais firm and Mr. Samuel Homfray still continued, and Mr. Homfray was particularly angry with Mr. W. Taitt, one of the Dowlais partners, and threatened to indict him for perjury. Subsequently, Mr. Taitt brought an action against Mr. Homfray, at the Hereford Assizes, and obtained £500 damages.

The hostility extended to the members of both firms, and we find in 1811 the Penydarran Company bringing an action against the Dowlais Company for a variety of alleged injuries, the chief of which was the diversion of the Dowlais brook water at Dowlais top or bank into the Rhymney Valley. This statement as to the injuries done was supported on the part of the Penydarran Company by the affidavits in Chancery of Edward Martin, of Morriston; Wm. Llewellin, of Pontypool; Timothy Martin, of Merthyr Tydfil, Coal and Mine Agent, David Evan Harry, of the same place, coal and mine agent, John Homfray, Esqre., of the same place; and Richard Henry, master miner.

Their evidence seemed to show beyond a doubt that the little Dowlais brook, which formed the boundary between the two Works, had become choked up with cinders, slag, and refuse of all kinds; and that a condition of things had arisen, whoever might be most to blame, amounting to a regular *impasse*. Two kings were ruling in the little Dowlais Valley, where there was barely room for one!

The cause went to trial, and it appears from our papers that it was decided in favour of the Dowlais Company.

However, the difficulties of the case were so great that some remedy had to be found; and it was accordingly agreed between the parties to endeavour, by small concessions of land near the brook side, and in other ways, to establish a *modus vivendi* for the future. The terms, which are difficult to understand without the aid of a map, were then embodied in a lease dated November 30th, 1813, from the Dowlais Company to the Penydarran Company, the parties to the same being—

William Lewis, late of Alderley, but now of Cheltenham, Gloucester, Esq., and

William Taitt, of Cardiff, in Glamorgan, Esq. (the present Proprietors and Partners of certain Iron Works called Dowlais Iron Works), of the one part;

And

Thomas Homfray, of Hagley, near Stourbridge, Worcester, Esq.;

William Forman, of the Tower of London, Esq., and

Henry Forman, of Greenwich, Coy. Kent, Esq. (the present Partners and Proprietors, trading under style of Penydarran Iron Company), of the other part.

---

And again, in 1819, a further lease was granted by the Dowlais Company to the Penydarran Company, of a messuage and lands called Gwain y Varran, and the right to work Iron Ore and Iron Stone, at the rent of £120, with usual Lessor's and Lessee's covenants, the parties now being—

Josiah J. Guest, of Dowlais;

Wyndham Lewis, Green Meadow;

William Price Lewis, of same place; and

Thomas R. Guest, of Cork, Ireland, Partners (and Proprietors of Dowlais), of the one part.

And

William Forman, of Penydarran Place, Glam., and

William Thompson, of the City of London, Partners and Proprietors of Penydarran Furnace, of the other part.

---

A still greater difficulty at this time (1824) faced the Dowlais Company than they had ever met with. Their mineral landlord was now the Marquis of Bute, by descent from the Windsor family; and he realising the improvident character of the leases granted by his predecessors, in 1748 and 1763, and further being advised that there had been infractions of the Leases, both as to the working of Stone quarries and the improper working of the Collieries, proceeded to a review at Law of the whole position from the very first, as between himself in virtue of his inherited estate and his lessees. Every matter was reported upon, and expert engineers and managers, in the persons of Mr. David Stewart and Mr. Thomas Johnson, his assistant, were employed, and Counsel's opinion sought again and again, to test the validity of the leases. Messrs. Farrer, of Lincoln's Inn Fields, were the solicitors employed by the Marquis of Bute, and every possible step was taken to enforce what was claimed to be his strict and full rights.

Litigation between the parties continued for many years, with varying success, and the Briefs and papers in my possession connected with the proceedings are very voluminous.

Surveyors of eminence were employed to examine the underground workings, and also to report whether the land of the Marquis, claimed by him as his freehold, had not been indiscriminately worked for iron ore and coal by the Dowlais Company just as they had worked the open common lands; and we annex an extract from Mr. Johnson's affidavit as to the identity of the land, common, or private freehold, in question.

EXTRACT from an Affidavit of Thomas Johnson, of West Hatch, in the County of Essex, Esquire, in the Suit wherein The Most Honble. John Crichton Stuart, Marquis of Bute and Earl of Dumfries; The Right Honble. Frederick William, Earl of Bristol, and Henry Lewis Hobart were Plaintiffs; and Josiah John Guest, Wyndham Lewis, William Price Lewis, and Thomas Revel Guest were Defendants.—1825.

States—

He had for some years past been engaged on behalf of the Marquis in assisting Mr. David Stewart in investigating the state of the Glamorganshire property of the Marquis, and he found that the Estates of the Marquis had been very much neglected, and that a great number of encroachments on his rights and infringements on his property had been committed and suffered during the lifetime of his predecessors and during his minority; and that in course of such investigation he discovered that certain Tracts or pieces or parcels of Land called Bryn Glaes Gwayne, Menith Bryn Pyllog, and Pen y Vedw, or some of them, and the privilege of digging and getting coal in and under the three latter were held for 99 years, if Herbert Moses, Evan Moses, and Charles Herbert, or the survivors or survivor of them, should so long live, at the yearly rent of £15, and the privilege of digging and getting Iron Mine in and under the sd. tracts of land, if the sd. Herbert Moses, Evan Moses, and Evan Herbert, or the survivors of them, should so long live, at the yearly rent of £5, which said Land and privileges before mentioned had been in possession of said Defts. or the Dowlais Iron Company for the time being for many years past, and that he had been informed that Evan Moses, the surviving life of the sd. three lives, died in 1794, but the facts were not known by sd. Marquis until he discovered it through him, Johnson, and that the Dowlais Company continued to work the Coal under part of the Lands and occupied the surface, and have obtained a considerable annual profit from such coal, and from underletting the surface, and that he had been employed on the spot in investigating the identity of the said pieces of land, and that the same or such part thereof as had been held by the sd. defts. or Dowlais Coy. for the time being had for many years past gone by the name of the Carno tenement, from the circumstance that he supposed of the Brook Carno running thro' them, and that the sd. tracts of land called Bryn Pyllog and Pen y Vedw in his opinion formerly consisted of partly various Enclosures which were occupied by the defts. or the Coy., or their under-tenants, and which have been given up to the sd. Marquis, and partly of a tract of land now open to the Common, or only divided therefrom by several Brooks or streams, part of which is called Pen y vedw, or Twyn, or Ty Llysg, and other part Bryn Pyllog, and that he had been engaged in examining a lot of old people respecting the identity of sd. three pieces of land, and that there was no doubt or difficulty in ascertaining Boundary thereof from adjoining enclosed land (which all belonged to the Marquis) or from the Common, and that the sd. names of Bryn Pyllog, Pen y vedw, and Twyn, or Ty Llysg, are all descriptive names, having, as he believed, the following significations respectively, vizt. : Bryn Pyllog—Hill full of pits or Trenches or holes; Pen y vedw—The Birch Hill, or a Headland covered with Birches; and Twyn, or Ty Llysg—Whinberry Hill; and that the whole tract of land before stated to be unenclosed, except by Brooks or small streams, taken all together will correspond with the description of Bryn Pyllog—a Hill full of holes; and that on examining sd. witnesses he was informed of the name Twyn, or Ty Llysg, and that the same was the usual country name, and that it was generally so called until some Law proceedings took place, on which old leases were produced, and since that time it had sometimes been called Pen y Vedw, but more frequently Twyn, or Ty Llysg, and that old Witnesses speak of it as a distinct, well-known tract of land, and that there exists a Tradition of its once having been covered with Birch Trees, and that he had seen a parchment roll amongst the papers of one Lewis

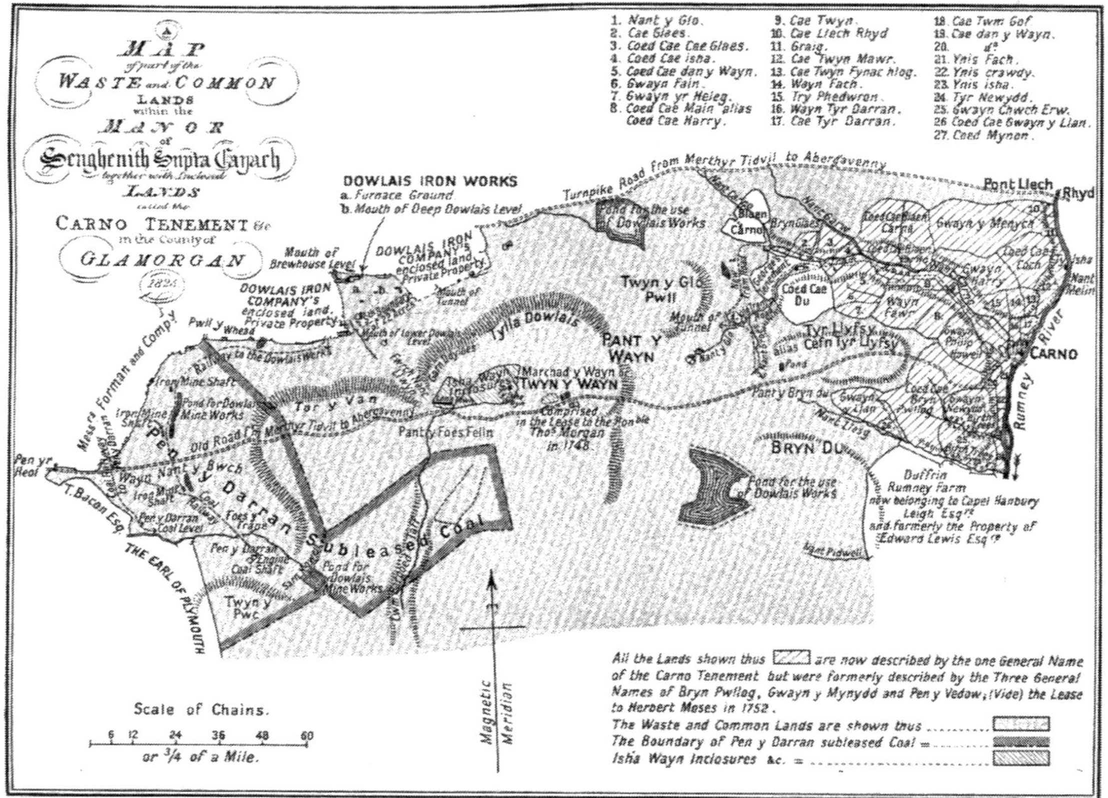


Plan by Thomas Morris, Land Surveyor, &c., Newport.

Edwards (who was, he had been informed, Vestry Clerk of the Parish of Gelly gare), deceased, of 8th Decr., 1803, purporting to be a valuation of every Tenement of Land in the Parish of Gelly gare, wherein is an entry, vizt., "Carno, £15; Ty Llysg, 10*s*; Blane Carno, £2," from which it appears to him that "Ty Llysg" was separately assessed at 10*s*. a year.

In the end an arbitration was agreed upon, and the following terms were settled as between the parties, more or less to their mutual satisfaction :—

## THE DISPUTE BETWEEN THE MARQUESS OF BUTE AND THE DOWLAIS IRON WORKS COMPANY.

(The Agreement made in 1828, for effecting a settlement of all matters in dispute, and the withdrawal of the suits in the Courts of Law, then pending, by the Marquess of Bute, is contained in twenty-nine brief sheets of paper.)

### The Articles of Agreement.

The Parties to these Articles were as under :—

The Most Honorable John Crichton Stuart, Marquess of Bute and Earl of Dumfries, of the one part (his solicitors were Farrer and Co., Lincoln's Inn Fields);

And

Josiah John Guest, Wyndham Lewis, The Revd. William Price Lewis, and Thomas Revell Guest (who formed a Company of Ironmasters in the Parish of Merthyr Tidvil, in Glamorgan, called the Dowlais Iron Company), of the other part (solicitors for the Dowlais Company, Gregory, Clement's Inn; Jones and Powell, Brecon).

After reciting the old Mineral Leases of

10th March, 1748—Lord Windsor to Thomas Morgan, of Ruperra.

19th September, 1752—Lord Windsor to Herbert Moses.

23rd June, 1763—Alice, Lady Windsor, to Lewis, Price and Jones.

22nd November, 1787—John Morgan, as devisee of Thomas Morgan above, to William Lewis, John Guest, and others.

And stating that the reversion of the Fee Simple in the premises in such Leases described was then vested in the said Marquis of Bute for his own use and benefit.

And specifying the questions at issue and now pending in the High Court of Chancery.

Declared, That in order to terminate the said Suits, and to adjust and settle amicably the same, and all other matters in dispute and litigation, the following Arrangement had been come to between them :—

(1) The Marquess of Bute, in consideration of the annual rents to be paid to him hereinafter specified, confirmed all the liberties and rights granted in the leases of 1748 and 1763, for the remainder of the terms; and also confirmed all the rights and privileges in the lease of 1752 to work the iron mines, and also granted the privilege of taking Limestone, Sand, and Clay therefrom, as they required for their own use. And further agreed that the Suits now pending should be withdrawn, without costs, and that all claims for damages and trespasses at law or in equity should be abandoned.

(2) And the said Dowlais Company agreed, by a legal instrument to be executed within 3 months, to surrender all estates, rights, etc., under the lease of 1752, in certain specified lands, in the mines of coal, and also to grant the said Marquess the right to take stones, sand, and clay, and all minerals except coal and iron ore, from certain common lands in the Manor of Senghenith above the brook Cayach; and they further agreed to pay an annual rent for the remainder of their terms, such annual rent, "as at the end of the same would amount to the same sum of money as £30,000, at 5 per cent. interest, payable half-yearly," such annuity to be calculated by an Actuary therein agreed upon, and to release the Marquess of Bute of all claims, etc., against him at law or in equity.

As to all other points, including the fixing the exact day that the old Leases terminate (presumably having reference to old and new style), and the construction of the Leases, It was agreed between the parties that all such questions should be referred to the decision of Arbitrators, then named, with an Umpire, also named, in case of difference.

---

## REVIEW NOTES.

Of the original "Myrthy" Firm formed in 1759, only the Lewis family, represented by Wyndham Lewis and William Price Lewis, are to be found as members in 1834. John Guest, of Broseley, the first in the Firm of that name, came in as a partner in 1782. He was succeeded by his Son, Thomas, in 1787; and Thomas, again about the year 1819, was succeeded by his sons, Josiah John Guest and Thomas Revel Guest. The firm, then consisting solely of the family of Guest and that of Lewis, remained unchanged in 1826 and 1834.

During that period of 75 years, from 1759 to 1834, the chief and leading men, who directed the operations of the firm were, first, Thomas Lewis, the Founder; then in succession, John Guest, who came from Broseley, William Lewis, of Alderley, Thomas Guest, William Taitt, Wyndham Lewis, and lastly Josiah John Guest. They were all men of mark and great ability, as they need to have been to conduct the affairs of a business which had grown to such immense proportions. Of the earlier members of the Firm, I have only a very few original autograph letters; but of William Taitt, Wyndham Lewis, and J. J. Guest, I have very many.

It will have been observed by the careful reader of the Leases previously fully abstracted, those to Thomas Morgan from Lord Windsor in 1748, and to Thomas Lewis and Partners from Lady Windsor in 1763, that while very extensive mineral rights were granted over the Common Lands of the Manor of Senghenith, no royalties whatever were reserved for working the iron ore and Coal Mines. The tin, lead, copper mines, stones, and slate, were excepted from the leases; but the only payment for the working of the iron ore and coal was a fixed rent of £26 per annum (with £5 additional by the 1763 lease).

Also that the term was to be 99 years from 1748.

With such a nominal rent, and granted an abundant supply of iron ore and coal over a large tract of common land, and capital and skill to utilise this most favourable position, the commercial success of any Iron Works established was assured. There were the drawbacks of want of communication to any Canal at the first start, and always of a small supply of water in the Dowlais brook, though supplemented by ponds; but there was the great advantage of the Works being placed in the very midst of the iron ore bed and coal veins, and with limestone conveniently near—every material was close at hand necessary for iron making.

Starting with a small capital of £4,000, Thomas Lewis and Co. were soon able to largely increase their Works out of the profits made, and to develope these into a large concern; and it is said, that in 1834, the Dowlais Company had from fourteen to seventeen furnaces in blast, besides large rolling mills for rails, and puddling furnaces.

---

## MEMBERS OF THE DOWLAIS FIRM IN PARLIAMENT.

| | | Seat. |
|---|---|---|
| 1826. June 1 | ... John Josiah Guest ... ... | Honiton. |
| 1830. July 30 | ... Do. ... ... ... | Do. |
| 1832. Dec. 11 | ... Do. ... ... ... | Merthyr Tydvil. |
| 1835. Jan 8 | ... Do. ... ... ... | Do. |
| 1837. July 27 | ... Do. ... ... ... | Do. |
| 1841. June 29 | ... Do. ... ... ... | Do. |
| 1847. July 28 | ... Do. ... ... ... | Do. |
| 1852. July 8 | ... Do. ... ... ... | Do. |

(Died between July and December. Henry Austin Bruce succeeded in December.)

---

| | | |
|---|---|---|
| 1820. March 15 | ... Wyndham Lewis, Barrister-at-Law, of Green Meadow, in the Parish of Whitchurch, Co. Glamorgan ... ... | Cardiff Borough. |
| 1827. May 22 | ... Wyndham Lewis, do. ... ... | Aldeburgh (Suffolk). |
| 1835. July 6 | ... Do. do. ... ... | Maidstone. |
| 1837. July 27 | ... Do. do. .. ... | Do. |

(Benjamin Disraeli, second Member. He married the widow of Wyndham Lewis.)

---

## MAKING OF THE CANAL TO THE SEA AT CARDIFF.

The difficulty of transport of their iron to market by the South Wales ironmasters must have been immense, down to the period of the making of the Glamorganshire canal from Merthyr to Cardiff, and of the Aberdare canal. Horse-loads of pig-iron, or even wagon-loads, were not suited to the carrying on of any great trade; and hence the much-needed formation of these canals gave a strong impulse to the iron industry of the Merthyr district; and it will be easy to understand that the ironmasters of Dowlais, Cyfarthfa, Plymouth, and Penydarran Works were their chief promoters; and the capitalists of Brecon — the Messrs. Wilkins, bankers — with considerable foresight, afforded their assistance.

This will be seen by a glance at the list of the original promoters named in the Preamble to the Act of 1790. The names are, for the most part, familiar to us, and especially the Breconshire ones of Thomas Maybury (*sic*), John Peirce, Walter Powell, John Powell, Walter and Jeffrey Wilkins, Walter Jeffreys, and Williams (the bankers), William Wilkins, Pennoyre Watkins (attorney), Robert Williams, William Williams, Thomas Wilkins, and, I think, the Rev. Thomas Davies was the old capitalist living at Glynde, Surrey, but owning large Breconshire estates. There was money and enterprise in those days in Breconshire, and the leading men were quick to see the future development of the new industry in the hill-district on the borders of their county. Our especial friends, Messrs. Powell, Jones, and Powell, of Brecon, were the solicitors for the Bill in Parliament, and Messrs. Wilkins and Co., of Brecon, the bankers.

The canal was twenty-five miles in length, and difficult to make, but Messrs. Radford—father and son—were experienced canal engineers, and all difficulties were soon overcome; and the canal when opened soon proved not only of the greatest advantage to the district, but a great commercial success.

The Dowlais Works sent the following weights of iron—chiefly manufactured—by this canal to be shipped at Cardiff.

| | Tons. | | Tons. |
|---|---|---|---|
| 1817 ... | 9,936 | 1829 ... | 23,352 |
| 1818 ... | 9,694 | 1830 ... | 27,647 |
| 1819 ... | 10,796 | 1831 ... | 22,075 |
| 1820 ... | 11,115 | 1832 ... | 29,395 |
| 1821 ... | 12,571 | 1833 ... | 35,072 |
| 1822 ... | 14,557 | 1834 ... | 33,447 |
| 1823 ... | 14,025 | 1835 ... | 39,145 |
| 1824 ... | 12,594 | 1836 ... | 39,286 |
| 1825 ... | 15,851 | 1837 ... | 38,914 |
| 1826 ... | 16,601 | 1838 ... | 39,361 |
| 1827 ... | 20,726 | 1839 ... | 40,495 |
| 1828 ... | 23,575 | 1840 ... | 45,218 |

## MINE PATCHES AND SCOURING.

The iron ore was worked mainly on the slopes and on the "Wain" or level land along and near the watershed divide line of the Dowlais brook and of the Rhymney river.

To each miner or ganger was marked off a "patch" of the hill to turn over, and these patches bore the name of the miner in charge of the patch, such as "Tom Jones's patch," "Rees Jenkins' patch," and this was the case all over the ground set out to be dug up and searched for iron ore. The gangers made contracts with the company to raise the ore at so much per dozen bushels, which weighed together 36 cwt.

The practice of "scouring" was extensively used by the ironmasters on these patches. The water having been panned up in the brook or in a pond to form a head of water, and the mixture of earth and iron ore being placed below, on the dam being opened the strong rush of water cleansed the heavier ore from the loose earth and clay, which latter were carried down the brook to the sea. It saved much labour, and the ore was at once clean and fit for being sent to and used in the furnaces. Sometimes, "scouring" continued night and day, if the water served; and no wonder the Commoners, who were sheep-farmers, complained when they saw their green pastures transformed into a waste of land, on which not even a blade of grass would thereafter grow. So completely was the natural soil washed away that nothing was left but mining shale; and these mining grounds, though long ago worked out and left severely alone by the ironmasters, are still to be seen perfectly barren and sterile, all along the line of mine patches between Dowlais and Brynmawr.

The recuperative powers of Nature have wholly failed to produce the semblance again of fertility, even after a rest of forty or fifty years.

## CONCLUDING REMARKS.

In September of this year (1905), we drove across what is known as the Hill district, from Hirwain to Brynmawr, and were pleased to find the three great last-century Iron Works, Dowlais and Cyfarthfa, now owned by the Firm of Guest, Keen and Co., and the Ebbw Vale Works of the Company of that name, in full vigorous operation; and, contrary to our original intention, we intend to give photographic views of these as they exist to-day.

On looking through our notes, we find we have omitted to notice at any length the position of the Dowlais brook. It would seem to me to come down on the very outcrop of the coal measures on the north from the high ground at Bryn pwllog, and to have a short, steep course to its junction with the Taff at Merthyr. On its right bank the Morlais brook, flowing from the bosom of the hills under Morlais Castle lime rocks, joins it in its mid-course. You have, however, to trust to information from others or to imagination, as the courses of both brooks are at the point of junction covered over, and unrecognisable. Dowlais is, it may be said, a corruption of Dulais, signifying "dark green water," a very common name for small streams in Wales.

The Waun Fair, or Twyn y Marchant, or Marchnad y Wayne, deserves a notice. It appears by the 1748 lease to have been in full force then; and probably its origin dates back to a very early period. The Fair ground is stated in the lease to be estimated "at 20 acres of Welsh measure in extent, be the same more or less." We saw the Twyn, or bank of table land on which the Fair is held, from the Abergavenny road, and were told that a large Fair had been held there recently, dealers, etc., attending from all parts of the three adjacent counties of Glamorgan, Monmouth, and Brecon.

We hope later to trace down the descent of the old Pembroke and Windsor family, the owners of the Senghenith Manor, and of the Manor at Hirwain, to the Scotch family of Stuart and Bute.

Here ends our Notice of the Dowlais Iron Works.

IV.

# The Cyfarthfa Iron Works.

---

[SCHEDULE OF DEEDS RELATING TO THE CYFARTHFA IRON WORKS,

INCLUDING

THE ORIGINAL 1765 LEASE FROM LORD TALBOT OF HENSOLL, CO. GLAMORGAN, AND MICHAEL RICHARDS OF CARDIFF, TO ANTHONY BACON AND WILLIAM BROWNRIGG.]

---

29th August, 1765.—Indenture of that Date between the Right Honble. William, Earl Talbot and Baron of Hensol, in the County of Glamorgan, and Michael Richards, of the Town of Cardiff, in the sd. County, Esqr., of the One Part, and Anthony Bacon, of Throgmorton Street, in the City of London, Esqr., and William Brownrigg, of the Town of Whitehaven, in the County of Cumberland, Esq., of the other Part. Purporting to be a Lease from said Earl Talbot and Micl. Richards to said A. Bacon and Wm. Brownrigg, of the Coal and Iron Stone in the Lands of said Earl Talbot and Micl. Richards, within the Parish of Merthyr Tydvil, with divers Priviledges, for the Term of Ninety Nine years, commencing 25th March, 1765, at the yearly Rent of One Hundred Pounds. Ex'ted by Earl Talbot and Micl. Richards.

24th June, 1766.—Indre. of that Date bet. said An. Bacon, of the One Part, and sd. Wm. Brownrigg, of the other Part, Purporting to be Articles of Copartnership in the Iron Business, and for carrying on the same in the Parish of Merthyr Tydvil. Ex'ted by both Parties.

22nd July, 1777.—Deed Poll of that Date indorsed on said Articles of Copartnership, purporting to be an Assignment from said Wm. Brownrigg to sd. A. Bacon, of his Share and Interest in the said Works and Premises, in consideration of Fifteen Hundred and four Pounds fifteen shillings and Five Pence. Executed by both.

2nd May, 1763.—Lease from John Williams, of the Parish of Chiriton, in the County of Glamorgan, Clerk to Edwd. Morgan, of the Parish of Merthyr Tydvil, Yeoman, of a Messuage and Lands in said Parish of Merthyr Tydvil, called Rhydycar, for the Term of Lives of the Lessor and his Sister Eliz'th Williams, at the yearly Rent of Twenty two Pounds. Executed by said John Williams.

30th June, 1766.—Lease and Counterpart of said Premises from sd. Edwd. Morgan to sd. A. Bacon and Wm. Brownrigg, during Edwd. Morgan's Term therein, at the yearly Rent of Thirty Six Pounds. Ex'ted by Edw. Morgan.

13th Sept., 1771.—Assignment of said Leasehold Premises called Rhydycar from said Edwd. Wm. Morgan to Wm. John and Morgan Williams for securing the payment of £40 and Interest.

4th July, 1765.—Lease from Lewis Wm., Daniel William, and Wm. Thomas, all of Merthyr Tydvil, to sd. A. Bacon and W. Brownrigg, of Two Fields near Cyfarthfa Rock, for the lives of sd. Lewis William and Margt., the wife of Edwd. Phillip, and the survr. of them, at ye yrly. rent of £7.

17th June, 1767.—Lease from Wm. Richard, of Merthyr Tydvil, yeoman, to said A. Bacon and Wm. Brownrigg, of Three Fields near Cyfarthfa Rock, for the Life of sd. William Richard, at the yearly rent of £6.

31st March, 1768.—Lease from Neast Morgan, Wm. and John Morgan, both of Merthyr Tydvil, to sd. A. Bacon and Wm. Brownrigg, of Three Fields near Cyfarthfa, with the Liberty of a Water-course through another Piece of Land, Coed Evan Maddock, for the Life of Jane, the wife of Lewis David, at the yearly Rent of £5 10*s*.

Y BACON'S FAVOURITE ROOM IN THE OLD HOUSE AT CYFARTHFA WORKS, 1784.
HIS CREST.

*(Photo R.W. 1905).*

7th October, 1765.—Lease from Said Earl Talbot and Michl. Richards, of Rhydycar Farm aforesaid, to said A. Bacon and Wm. Brownrigg, in Reversion expectant on the several Deceases of said John Williams and Eliz'th Williams, for the Remainder of a Term of 99 Years, to be then unexpired, at the yearly Rent of £36.

7th October, 1768.—A Reversionary Lease from sd. Earl Talbot and Michl. Richards to said A. Bacon and Wm. Brownrigg, of the Fields comprized in the Lease of the 17th June, 1767, at the yearly Rent of Six Pounds.

15th October, 1768.—A Like Reversionary Lease of the Premises comprized in that of the 31st of March, 1768, at the yearly Rent of £5 10*s.* 0*d.*

15th Oct., 1768.—A Reversionary Lease of the last-mentioned Premises from Earl Talbot and Michl. Richards to said A. Bacon and Wm. Brownrigg for the Remr. of a Term of 99 years, at the yearly Rent of £7.

23rd September, 1769.—Lease from Earl Talbot and Michl. Richards to said A. Bacon and Wm. Brownrigg, of Llwyn Celin Fawr, in the said Parish of Merthyr Tydvil, from the 13th Febry., 1769, for the Remainder of the Term of 99 years, in the first Lease granted, at the yearly Rent of £36.

29th April, 1771.—Lease from Henry Richards, of the Parish of Coyty, Gent., and Mary his wife, to Charles Wood, of Merthyr Tydvil, Gent., of Limestone, at Craigfawr y gurnos, in Merthyr Tidvil, for the Lives of Edward Harry, of Gurnos, David Edward his Son, and Anne John ap David, Wife of Rees David, of Merthyr Tidvil, at the yearly Rent of £2 2*s.* 0*d.*

16th June, 1772.—Assignment from said Wm. John and Morgan William, and said Edwd. Morgan to sd. A. Bacon and Wm. Brownrigg, of Rhydy Car, Leasehold Premises in Conson. of the several sums of £41 10*s.* and £68 and 10*s.*

28th June, 1775.—Lease from The Revd. Mr. Saml. Davies and wife to said A. Bacon and W. Brownrigg, of Bryn Tegall Faur, in Merthyr Tydvil, for the Life of Lewis David Llewellin, at the yearly rent of £6 17*s.* 6*d.*

1st July, 1738.—Lease from Lord Talbot and Michl. Richards, Esq., to Wm. Lewis, of Merthyr Tidvil, Yeoman, of a Moiety of a Tenement and Lands in the Parish of Merthyr Tidvil, called Aber-nant y gwenithdyr, for the Lives of John Lewis, Lessee's Brother, Lewis William, aged 9, and Margt. William, aged 10 years, his Son and Daughter, and the Survivor, at the yearly Rent of £5 and 6*s.*

10th April, 1772.—Assignment of sd. Lease from Lewis William and Dl. William to Timothy Thomas, Consr., for securing £180 and Interest.

10th March, 1777.—Assignment of the sd. Lease from sd. Timothy Thomas, Cordwainer, Lewis William and Danl. William, both of the same, yeomen, Ex'tors., etc., of said Wm. Lewis to said A. Bacon and W. Brownrigg, in Consion. of the several Sums of £120 and £180.

14th October, 1777.—Lease from Ann Richard, of Merthyr Tidvil, Wd., to sd. A. Bacon, of a Piece of Land used as a Coaking Bank, with a Piece of Wood Gro'd adjoining, at Cyfarthfa Furnace, also the Land under the Canal, and the Land taken for a Road on the Lower side thereof; also a Piece of Gro'd Part of Gwain arrw, in the Parish of Merthyr Tydvil, for the Lives of said Ann, Richard William, her Son, and Anne her Daughter, and the Survivor of them, at the yearly Rent of £2 10*s.* 6*d.*

2nd February, 1780.—Lease from sd. A. Bacon, Esq., to Lewis William and Dl. William, of Messuages and Lands, in the Parish of Merthyr Tidvil, from the 2d Febry. 1780, for the Term of 21 yrs., at the yearly Rent of £12.

1st May, 1782.—Lease from Evan Griffiths, of Gelly, in the Parish of Llanwonno, Gent., to said A. Bacon, of a Part of Ynis Vach, in the Parish of Merthyr Tidvil, for the Lives of said Evan Griffiths, Elizth. Griffiths, and Richd. Griffiths, his Brother and Sister, at the yearly Rent of £3 and 3*s.*

27th Sept., 1782.—Ind're of that Date between sd. A. Bacon, of the One Part, and Francis Homfray, of Stourton, in the Parish of Kinfair, in the County of Stafford, Ironmaster, of the other Part, Purporting to be a Lease of a Canon Boring Mill, Air Furnace, Forges, and other Erections, and some Land at Cyfarthfa, for the Term of 50 years, with Divers Covenants and Articles on both sides, for carrying on the Iron Business. Executed by Mr. Bacon and Mr. Homfray.

2d February, 1783.—Lease from Mary John, John Lewis, Wm. Lewis, Danl. Lewis, and David Lewis, all of Merthyr Tidvil, to sd. A. Bacon, of the Messuages and Lands called Tyr y Pandy, with Three ffields, Part of Tyr Gwailod y Garth, for the Lives of sd. Mary John and Mary, the wife of Lewis Edward and the Survr., at the yearly Rent of £30.

1st October, 1783.—Lease from Wm. Williams, Thos. Williams, and Jno. Williams, to sd. Anthy. Bacon, of several Fields, Part of Tyr Abernant y Gwenithdwr Farm, for the Lives of sd. Wm. Williams and Thos. Williams and the Survr., at the yearly Rent of £24.

26th April, 1784.—Lease from the Earl of Plymouth to said Anty. Bacon, of the Messuage and Lands called Gwyldy y Du Garth, and also House and Lands called the Pandy, situate in Merthyr Tydvil, for a Term in Reversion, expectant on the several Deceases of Mary John and Mary, the Daughter of David John, at the yearly Rent of Sixty Pounds.

1st November, 1785.—Contract between William Williams, of Merthyr Tydvil, Yeoman, for himself and on the Part of Thomas Williams and Jno. Williams, his Brothers, of the One Part, and Richd. Hill, Gent., on the Part of the sd. A. Bacon, of the other Part, for leasing certain Parcels of Lands, with Liberty of scouring, for the Lives of sd. William Williams and Thomas Williams and the Survivor, at the yearly Rent of £11 13*s*.

9th July, 1768.—Lease from Rees Thomas, of Aberdare, to Isaac Wilkinson, of Merthyr Cannaid, two Houses and Fields in the Parish of Merthyr Tidvil, for the Residue of a Term, at the Yearly Rent of £18.

25th March, 1772.—Contract for a Lease from Isaac Jones, Gent., to sd. A. Bacon, of Tir Cwm Cannaid, in Merthyr Tydvil, for the Lives of sd. Isaac Jones, Margt. his wife, and Margt. his niece, the wife of Wm. Watkins, at the yearly Rent of £20.

---

Anthony Bacon, of Throgmorton Street, in the City of London, is a good address to-day for a moneyed man, as it was in the times we are writing of; and we may safely conclude that by experience gained in the mineral district of Workington, in Cumberland, he was well competent to judge of the value of the Cyfarthfa mineral property near Merthyr Tydfil, in Glamorganshire, in conjunction with the water-power of the adjacent streams, when chance or design brought him that way. And if in doubt he could probably rely on the sound judgment of his companion, William Brownrigg, of Whitehaven, Esquire. Mr. Bacon was also Member of Parliament for Aylesbury at this time, having succeeded John Wilkes, expelled the House of Commons.

It appears that by their marriages with co-heiresses, Lord Talbot, of Hensoll, in the County of Glamorgan, and Michael Richards, of Cardiff, Esq., were possessed of a large mineral estate near Merthyr Tydfil, extending over, it is said, 4,000 acres of virgin mineral land; and on negotiations being entered into, they were induced to grant a lease of the coal and iron stone in their lands for ninety-nine years to the said Anthony Bacon and William Brownrigg, at the reserved fixed rent of £100 per annum.

It may be noted here that this is the third instance we have already met with of long mineral leases being granted at a low fixed rent, no royalties whatever being payable.

The partners having secured the main taking, prudently proceeded to acquire rights, sufficient for their purposes, over all of the freehold and leasehold lands that lay near to the proposed site of their intended Iron-works; and it will be seen by a reference to the above-given schedule that quite a number of small properties were so acquired by them.

A lease also was taken from Thynne Howe Gwynne, of Buckland, Lord of Pencelly Manor, of a feeder from the river Taf fechan, on the common land in the parish of Vaynor, for the supply of water-power, which was essential to the very existence of the Works.

For several years Messrs. Bacon and Brownrigg continued in partnership, until on July 22nd, 1777, it was dissolved, Mr. Brownrigg receiving in payment as his share the sum of £1,500 15*s*. 5*d*.

Mr. Anthony Bacon, being now alone interested in the Cyfarthfa Works, secured also, about this time, further mineral land at Plymouth, both by acquiring a lease granted by the Earl of Plymouth to Messrs. Wilkinson and Guest, and also by leasing some land direct from the Earl of Plymouth, where he erected a blast-furnace, in addition to the one he had already working at Cyfarthfa. He also, in 1780, as we have seen, by an assignment from Messrs. Wilkins and Maybery, became possessed of the Hirwain Furnace.

It will be remembered that in 1774, and just before and after, the great American troubles occurred, causing much disturbance and loss to the iron trade. In one respect it had a beneficial effect in causing a great demand for canon, or "ordnance," for the Government.

Mr. Bacon's Works were hitherto purely blast-furnaces for the production of raw pig iron; and whether it was that as a Member of Parliament, and therefore incapable of

OLD CYFARTHFA FURNACES. No. 5 IS FIFTH FROM RIGHT.
*(Photo 1870-75).*

taking Government contracts, or that he did not understand the special business of casting and boring canon, he does not appear to have entered into a class of probably very lucrative business.

However, in 1782, Mr. Francis Homfray, of Stourton, in the parish of Kinfair, county of Stafford, ironmaster, was granted by Anthony Bacon a mill for boring canon at Cyfarthfa, as also the Lower Works, called the Foundry, with the pool of water and other premises described in the lease, for a term of fifty years, at £20 per annum, subject to the following restrictions and reservations.

"That he, the said Francis Homfray, his heirs, etc., shall not nor will at any time during the continuance of this demise erect or cause to be erected any blast-furnace in the Co. of Glamorgan, for the purpose of casting or melting Pig metal, without the licence or consent first had in writing under the hand of the said Authony Bacon, his exors., etc.

And also that he, the sd. F. Homfray, his exors. and admors., shall and will from time to time and at all times during the continuance of this demise, when and as often as he shall be thereunto required by the said A. Bacon, his exors., admors., or assigns, find, provide, and "Supply the said A. B., his exors., admors, and assigns with all such Castings in Iron as shall be made in Flask, Loam, or Drye Sand for the use of the Works at Cyfarthfa aforesd. or elsewhere in the County of Glamorgan, on being from time to time paid by the sd. A. B., his exors., admors., or assigns, the Prime Cost only for such Castings respectively, and without any profit whatsoever therefrom." It is also covenanted "That whereas the said A. Bacon is possessed of two Furnaces and other Works at Cyfarthfa aforesaid, and Plymouth, in the County of Glamorgan, for making and Casting of Pig Iron, that he the sd. A. Bacon, his exors. admors., and assigns, shall and will yearly and every year During the present War, supply and deliver, or cause to be supplied and delivered unto the said F. Homfray, his exors. and admors., for his and their use at the said Works at Cy'fa aforesd. hereby demised, all the Dark Grey Metal which can, shall, or may be made at the sd. A. B. Furnace at Cy'fa and Plymouth aforesaid, and which the sd. F. Homfray, his exors. or admors., can, shall consume, or use at the said Works hereby demised to him, in founding or Casting of Guns, and as the said two Furnaces shall during the time aforesaid make, to be supplied and delivered at the sd. two Furnaces of Cyfarthfa and Plymouth, as herein above covenanted to be supplied, by the sd. A. Bacon, his exors., admors., and assigns, during that space of time." And also from and after the end of the present war, or the ceasing of demands from the Boards of Ordinance as aforesaid, during the then continuance of this demise, shall and will take all the metal made at the said Furnace of Cyfarthfa aforesaid by the said A. Bacon, his exors., admors., and assigns, and also all such further quantity as he, the said F. Homfray, his exors. or admors., shall have occasion from the other Furnaces of and belonging to him, the said A. Bacon, in the said County of Glam., in case the said Furnace at Cy'fa should not at any time during the time last aforesd. make metal sufficient to supply the demands of the said F. Homfray, his exors., or admors. And further, that he, the said Francis Homfray, his exors. or admors., shall not nor will at any time or times hereafter during this demise purchase any Iron whatsoever from any other Furnace or Furnaces, for the use of his or their Works hereby demised, or any other works which may be erected by him or them, other than from the Furnaces of and belonging to him, the said A. Bacon, his exors., admors., or assigns, in the said County of Glamorgan. And also that F. Homfray may be at liberty to erect Buildings on certain described pieces of land for the use of the sd. F. Homfray, "so as no act shall at any time during this demise be done by the said F. Homfray, his exors. or admors., as shall or may prejudice the said A. Bacon, his exors., admors., or assigns, in the carrying on and conducting the said Blast Furnace, or any Blast Furnace which he, the said A. Bacon, his exors., admors., or assigns, shall or may at any time hereafter erect, the same to be blown by the machinery now standing. And also that it shall and may be lawful for F. Homfray to make Cuts, Canals, etc., for diverting the Water for the use of his said F. Homfray's Works, so as nevertheless and upon condition that he, the said F. Homfray, his exors. or admors., do not divert the Stream to the Prejudice or hindrance of the said Blast Furnace now erected or to be erected at Cy'fa aforesd., or to the Prejudice to House and Gardens of the said A. Bacon."

In October, 1784, F. Homfray disposed of the Forge and Premises above mentioned at Cy'fa to Mr. David Tanner, and on or about March, 1786, Mr. Tanner disposed of the aforesd. Premises at Cy'fa to Mr. Crawshay.

The death of Anthony Bacon occurred in this latter year (1786), at the comparatively early age of sixty-seven, after a very successful and remarkable career as an ironmaster. At the time of his death, there were in hand the extensive Works of Cyfarthfa, Plymouth, and Hirwain, all in full operation, guided by his single will, and the difficulties of the situation were enhanced by his large family of children (natural) being at the time, and for many years to come, minors.

We now append a copy of Mr. Anthony Bacon's will :—

In the Name of God, Amen.

I, Anthony Bacon, of Cyfarthfa, in the County of Glamorgan, being of good Health and of Sound Mind and Memory, but considering the Uncertainty of Life, and how necessary it is for me at my Age, now past my Sixty-seventh year, to settle my Temporal Affairs, and particularly as I am circumstanced, Do make this my last Will and Testament, firmly hoping that (for Christ's Sake, on whose Merits and satisfaction I intirely depend) when I depart this Life my Soul will be received amongst the Blessed.

I give and bequeath to my exors., hereinafter named, all my Estate and Effects, real and personal, of what Nature or Kind soever I die possessed of, for the uses and purposes of this my will to be by them disposed of as followeth, that is to say :—

1st.—I give and Bequeath to my Wife, Elizabeth Bacon, a clear Annuity of Seven Hundred Pounds, to be paid to her Quarterly: that is to say, at the End of every Three Months, One Hundred and Seventy-five pounds, to commence from the Day of my Death, and to continue during her natural life. I also give to my said Wife all my Household Furniture and Plate that is in any House of mine at my Decease, except the Furniture in my House at Cyfarthfa, which I wish to remain there for the use of him to whom that Estate is left; and my Will is also that my said wife Elizabeth shall have the House, Offices, and Gardens during her life if she chuses to live there. I also give her my Coach and two of the best coach Horses, and one of the best Saddle Horses I may die possessed of.

2ndly.—I Give and Bequeath to my Niece, Eliz. Bacon, £5,000, to be paid to her out of the Produce of my Estates and Effects, as the same shall arise, after all my just Debts are paid and discharged; but in the Interim my Will is that she should receive interest for the said Sum at the Rate of 5 p. Cent. by the year, until it be convenient for my Exors. to discharge it, the Interest to commence from the Day of my Death.

3rdly.—I give and Bequeath unto my Relation, the Revd. Thomas Richardson, an Annuity to be paid him during his Natural life of Two Hundred Pounds, that is to say, £50 every three Months, to commence from the Day of my Death, and to be paid out of the Profits arising from Hirwen Furnace; and my Will is that he shall have a Room fitted up and furnished at Hirwen at the Dwelling-house there, and the same shall be kept in Repair for his Use, and he shall have a Horse found him and kept at the expence of the said Furnace during his life.

4thly.—I give and Bequeath to my Relation, Anthony Richardson, all the Debt which may be due to me at my Decease from Gilbert Francklyn, Esq., of the Island of Tobago, except £1,200 which he owes me for a Bond I entered into for him and paid to Mr. Appleton. It is my Will that that sum be paid into the Hands of my Executors.

5thly.—I leave to my Half Brother, William Bacon, the sum of Five Hundred Pounds, to be paid him the first Legacy after my Debts are paid, And I further leave to him and his Heirs Male all my Estate in the Province of Virginia, which I hold in Partnership with Sundry Gentlemen, called the dismal Swamp, containing about 30,000 Acres, with the Share of all the Buildings, Sluices, and Stock that may be thereon. I likewise leave him all the said Debts that shall remain due to me at my Decease in the several Provinces or States in North America, desiring him to pay one Fourth Part of such sums as he may recover to the two Daughters of my late Brother, the Revd. Thomas Bacon, now being in Maryland.

6thly.—I desire my Exors. will receive all the Income of my Estate and Works of what Nature soever, with all the Debts and Effects of every kind that may be due and owing or belonging to me; and after paying the Annuities left in this my Will, I desire they will in the first place pay all the just Debts that I may owe, with the Expenses of my Funeral; and that being done, I desire my Exors., and my Will is that they pay all the legacies left herein, beginning at the first and so on as they are named to the last, and when they are discharged my Will is that the surplus income of my Estate and Effects may be put into the Funds every half year with the Interest arising added, to accumulate for the purposes hereafter named, reserving always such sums as are necessary for keeping the works in repair, and also such sums as my Exors. may think proper to lay out or expend in the Education of the Children hereafter named which I acknowledge to be my Children; and I hereby nominate and appoint my Friends, the Revd. Dr. Saml. Glasse, Mr. William Stevens, of Broad Street London, Mr. Thomas Harrison, of Whitehaven, and my Agent, Mr. Richard Hill, at Cyfarthfa, my Exors. of this my Will.

7thly.—I give and Bequeath to my most affectionate Friend, the above-named Doctor Saml. Glasse, £1,000, in acknowledgment of the very singular Friendship I have received from him, and the great affection I bear him.

8thly.—I give and bequeath to my very worthy Friend, the above-named Mr. William Stevens, the sum of £500.

9thly.—I Give and Bequeath to my very worthy, kind Friend, Mr. Thos. Harrison, above named, £500.

10thly.—I give to my Godson, Anthony Bacon Richardson, £100; to my Godson, Anthony Speding, £50, and to my Goddaughter, Elizh. Hill, fifty pounds.

11thly.—I give to my Cousin, Ann Younger, £100.

12thly.—I give to my Cousin, Mary Browning, £100.

13thly.—I give to all my menial Servants that have lived with me at the time of my Decease Three years and upwards, One year's Wages more than is due to them, and £5 each for Mourning.

14thly.—I give and Bequeath to Mary Bushby £1,000, to be paid her after all the above Legacies is paid, and in the Interim my Will is that she shall be paid One Hundred Pounds Annually until the said Legacy of One Thousand Pounds be paid to her; and further my Will is that she the said Mary Bushby, do receive for the Maintenance of her four Younger Children, that is to say, Thomas, Elizabeth, Robert and William, Fifty pounds by the year for each of them, so long as they shall continue with her; but when my Exors. shall think it necessary to take away any of the Children from her for their Education, the sum of fifty Pounds for that Child shall cease to be paid.

15thly.—I give and Bequeath to Anthony, the Eldest Son of the said Mary Bushby, who is, at the Time I am writing this Will, at School at Gloucester, under the care of the Revd. Mr. Stock, by the name of William Addison, May 13th, 1785—I say I Give to him, the said Anthony, all the Lands and Royalties whatsoever which I hold under Lease from the late Right Honble. Earl Talbot, and the late Michael Richards, Esq., of Cardiff, in the Parish of Merthyr Tydvil, in the County of Glamorgan, together with all the Dwelling-house, Outhouse, Offices, and Gardens, that I have erected thereon, commonly known by the name of Cyfarthfa; and also all the Household Furniture, Plate, Linen, and Books that may be there at my Decease; and I also give to him the Blast Furnace called Cyfarthfa Furnace, that is now erected or may be erected, or any other that may hereafter be built upon the said premises, and also all the Materials that belong to the same, and also all the Coal and Mine that may be raised or upon the Banks of the said Furnace at the time which I have appointed for him to be put in possession of the same; and I also give him the Forge at Cyfarthfa, now let under Lease to Francis Homfray, and my Will is, that he the said Anthony shall not be put into ye possession of this Bequest until he arrives at the age of Twenty four Years, until which time the Produce of the Furnace and Works is to go into the Fund above named, for the Uses which will be hereafter named. I also give him the Lease of the Farm opposite Cyfarthfa House, which I hold from the Earl of Plymouth; it is further my will that Anthony, above named, when he shall come to the age of Twenty four years, and have the Possession of this Bequest given up to him, that he shall have lent to him Two thousand Pounds for one year out of the Fund above named to enable him to carry on his Works, after which he must return the same into the Funds aforesaid.

16thly.—I give and bequeath to Thomas, Son of the said Mary Bushby and Brother to the above-named Anthony, all the Leases of Lands and Tenements which I hold under the Earl of Plymouth, with all the Royalties of Mine and Coal contained therein, together with the Furnace erected thereon called Plymouth Furnace, and all other Buildings and erections whatsoever on the aforesaid Premises. And also all the Tools and Implements belonging to the said Furnace. And also all the Mine and Coal which may be raised for or brought upon the Bank of the said Furnace at the time he is put in possession of this Bequest, which is to be when he arrives at the age of Twenty-four years; and my Will is also that he shall have £2,000 lent him out of the Fund above named for twelve months, to enable him to carry on his Works, at the end of which time he must repay the same to the Fund from which it was taken. Note: The Farm I hold of Lord Plymouth, opposite my house at Cyfarthfa, is excepted out of this Bequest, as it is already given to his Brother Anthony. I also give the above-named Thomas all that Freehold Estate called Trebetha, which I bot. of Mr. Phillips, and lies near to Plymouth Furnace.

17thly.—I give and Bequeath unto Robert, Son of the above-named Mary Bushby, and Brother to Anthony and William, being the Third son, my Furnace called Hirwen Furnace, which I purchased of Maybery and Wilkins, of Brecon, together with all the Leases, Royalties of Iron, Mine and Coals therein, and all the Tools and Implements belonging to the same, and all the Houses and Erections that are or may be thereon, and also all the Mine and Coal that may be raised for or be upon the Banks of the said Furnace, to be put into his Possess'n when he shall attain the Age of Twenty-four years, and at that time my Will is that he shall have lent him £2,000 out of the Fund above named, to enable him to carry on his Furnace for Twelve months, after which time he shall repay the same into the Fund above named for the purposes hereafter named.

18thly.—I give and Bequeath to my worthy Friend, Mr. Thos. Harrison, of Whitehaven, my Estate in the Parish of Workington, in the County of Cumberland, called Banklands, with all the Houses, Offices, Collieries, Coals that may be raised, Gins, Engines, Tools, and Implements whatsoever, that are upon or belonging to the Estate for the Purposes hereinafter mentioned; that is to say, I desire him to take the entire Management of the said Estate under his Direction, and that he will every six months send the Profits that may arise from the Coal Works and other Matters that may accrue from the said Estate to be placed in the Fund before named, first paying all the debts due from the Estate, and retaining to himself for his Trouble Fifty pounds every six months, but when the said Estate is improved as much as reasonably can be expected, which I hope may be in three years from the date of this, my Desire is that he will sell the Estate as soon as he can get the value it ought to fetch; but at all events I would not have it kept more than five years after my Decease; if when it is disposed of by Sale my Debts and Legacies are not fully paid, I desire and my Will is that they may be immediately discharged, and the surplus I wo'd have as soon as may be put in the Fund above named for the following Purposes.

19thly.—I give and Bequeath to Elizabeth, Daughter of the said Mary Bushby, out of the Fund above named, which I have Reason to expect will be considerable in the Amount before anything will be demanded from it a clear Annuity of Three Hundred pounds, to be paid her Quarterly during her Natural Life: that is to say, Seventy-five pounds every 3 months, to commence from the Day that she comes to the age of 21 years. I think this the best way to provide for her, as it has pleased God to affect her with lameness.

20thly.—I give and Bequeath to William, the youngest son of the said Mary Bushby, who was born at Gloucester in the Month of March, 1785, the remaining Part of the above-named Fund, after leaving sufficient to secure the Annuity left to Elizabeth during her life, and at her decease my Will is that the whole sum may come to him, William. Provided the sum does not amount to more than £10,000, my Will is that he, William, sho'd have £10,000 first paid him, and the Rem'r to be paid or equally divided amongst them that are alive of the children above named of the said Mary Bushby. My Will is further That in case of the Death of any of the sons of the said Mary Bushby named in this my Will (which I acknowledge also to be my children), I leave the succession to be as followeth, that is to say, if the Eldest son, Anthony, should die before he is of age, as directed by this Will, then the 2nd son, Thomas, shall succeed to all the bequest left to his Brother Anthony, and he Thomas shall give up all that is bequeathed to him to the 3rd son Robert, and Robert shall give all that is bequeathed to him to his Brother, the fourth son William, and in that Case the fund above named must be equally divided amongst the remaining Brothers, and if more than one Bro'r of the above named sho'd die before they become of age, then the two surviving Brothers shall divide the Bequests left to those that shall so die equally betwixt them, and if only one of the children above named, my sons and the sons of the said Mary Bushby, my Will is that he shall succeed to the whole of my Estate, real and personal, left to the other three.

And I further Declare, and my Will is, that if any of the Sons above-named, vizt., Anthony, Thomas, Robert and William, sho'd desire to marry before they come to the age of Twenty-four years and not under the age of 21 years, and have the consent of the majority of my Executors as may then be living, so to do, he shall in that Case be deemed of age and put in Possession of his Fortune; and if any one of my Sons live until he is of the age of 24 years, my will is that he shall at that age be added to my Executors, and have Powers accordingly. And lastly, if all my Sons, the Children of Mary Bushby above named, should die before they come of age, as directed by this my Will, Then I leave the whole of my Estate and Effects to be equally divided between my Niece Eliz. Bacon, my Cousins Anthony and Thomas Richardson, they paying out of the whole £1,000, to my Cousin Ann Younger, or if she be dead, to be divided equally amongst her Children, and also £1,000 to Richd. Hill, if he be living, and continue in the care of my Works in Wales; or if he dies in the employment of the Works, the sum left to him shall be divided amongst his Children. And I do hereby declare this to be my last Will and Testament, revoking all other Will or Wills heretofore made by me. Dated this fourteenth day of June, 1785; having wrote the whole with my own Hand, and also signed the Bottom of every sheet, and in Testimony have here unto set my Hand and Seal now wrote to this on or about the 13th of last May, altho' I executed the day above written.

A. B.

Signed, sealed, and Delivered, the last Will and Testam't
of Anthony Bacon. In the Presence of us—
Richard Crawshay.
John Cockshutt.
James Sutton.

Will proved (A. Bacon).—This Will was proved in London, on the 25th February, 1786, Before Rt. Hon. George Harris, D.C.L., and Surrogate of the Rt. Worshipful Peter Talbot, D.C.L., Master Keeper of the Prerogative Court of Canterbury.

By the Oath of Thomas Harrison, one of the Executors, Power reserved to the other Executors to make the same Declaration, vizt., to Revd. Samuel William Glasse, D.D., William Stevens and Richard Hill, if they apply for the same.

On the 27th March, 1787, Richard Hill, as one of the Executors, came before the Court and proved the same.

The Executors were not very willing to take upon themselves such onerous duties and responsibilities, and eventually the aid of the Court of Chancery was sought, and the estates were placed in its charge, Mr. William Bacon, Brother of the deceased, being appointed Receiver.

The proceedings of the Court recorded in Orders, Decrees, Reports, Accounts, etc., are voluminous; and we have not attempted to examine all these documents. Suffice it to say, that the Court, acting on the advice of the Receiver, granted leases during the minority of the son, Anthony, of Cyfarthfa Works, to Messrs. Crawshay and Cockshutt (the old tenants of a portion in succession to Mr. Francis Homfray), of the Plymouth Works, to Mr. Richard Hill (Mr. Bacon's old agent, and one of his executors), and of the Hirwain Works to Mr. Glover, of Abercarne, all at reserved rents, and the leases terminable at the expiration of the minority.

During this minority period Mr. Hill, the lessee of the Plymouth Works, entered into an arrangement with Messrs. Crawshay and Co. to deliver 1,000 tons of pig iron to them at £4 per ton, and afterwards another 1,000 tons at the same price. Subsequently, Mr. Hill contracted with Mr. Crawshay to supply him with the whole make of the Plymouth Furnace at the same price, up to the date of the termination of the minority.

On that latter event happening, Mr. Crawshay, who had made large erections and additions in the Forge, and had erected a new Forge on the premises let to Mr. Homfray, and also a new Furnace let to Messrs. Crawshay and Co. by the Court of Chancery, capable of consuming a very large quantity of pig iron, could no longer claim the delivery of pig-iron under the recent agreement, but proceeded to call upon Mr. Hill to deliver the pig iron under the old Homfray agreement of 1782. To this Mr. Hill demurred, alleging that the 1782 agreement had ceased to be operative. How the dispute was settled our papers do not tell us, bnt it appears to have been amicably disposed of, one way or the other.

We now give a copy of what appears to be the first decree of the Court in the suit, dated July 24th, 1793, made to the Court of Chancery on the Petition of Anthony Bacon, when he had attained his majority.

## IN CHANCERY.

CHANCERY DECREES AND ORDERS, A 1792, FO. 552.

Wednesday, 24th July, 1793.

Between ANTHONY FRANKLAND, otherwise ADDISON, otherwise BACON; THOMAS SMITH, otherwise BACON; ELIZABETH SMITH, otherwise BACON; ROBERT SMITH, otherwise BACON; and WILLIAM SMITH, otherwise BACON, Infants, by WILLIAM BACON, their next friend, Plaintiffs;

And

ELIZABETH BACON, Spinster; SAMUEL GLASSE, WILLIAM STEVENS, THOMAS HARRISON, RICHARD HILL, ELIZABETH BACON, Widow, and others, Defendants.

## DECREE.

Whereas the Plaintiff, Anthony Frankland, otherwise Addison, otherwise Bacon, and now called Anthony Bacon, did on the 2nd day of July, 1793, prefer his Petition unto the Right Honourable The Master of the Rolls, setting forth—

That Anthony Bacon by his Will, dated the 14th day of June, 1785, gave to his Executors thereinafter named all his real and personal estate to be by them disposed of in manner following, vizt. :—

He gave to his Wife the Defendant, Elizabeth Bacon, Widow, a clear Annuity of £700, to be paid quarterly as therein mentioned; and he also gave to his said Wife all his leasehold Furniture that was in any house belonging to him at his Death (except the

Furniture at his house at Cyfarthfa, which he wished to remain there for the use of him to whom that Estate was left. And his Will was that his said Wife should have the House, Offices, and Gardens during her life if she should chuse to live there.

And he gave to his Niece, the Defendant, Elizabeth Bacon, Spinster, £5,000, to be paid to her out of the produce of his Estate and effects as the same should arise after all his Debts were paid, but in the interim she should receive interest for the same at £5 per cent. until it was convenient to his Executors to discharge the same, and the said Testator desired his Executors would receive all the Income of his Estates and Works of what Nature soever, with all the Debts and Effects of every kind that might be owing or belonging to him after paying the Annuities left in his said Will, he desired that they would in the first place pay all his debts, with the expenses of his Funeral, and that being done he desired his executors to pay all the Legacies left therein, beginning with the first, and so on as they were named to the last, and when they were discharged his Will was that the Surplus Income of his Estate and Effects should be put into the Funds every half-year, with the Interest arising added to accumulate for the purposes thereinafter mentioned, reserving always such sums as were necessary for keeping the Works in repair. And also such sums as his Executors might think proper to lay out in the education of the children thereinafter named, which he acknowledged to be his Children, and he nominated the Defendants, Samuel Glasse, William Stevens, Thomas Harrison, and Richard Hill, Executors of his said Will.

And he gave to the Petitioner by the description of Anthony, eldest son of Mary Bushby, then at School at Gloucester, under the Care of the Reverend Mr. Stock, by the name of William Addison, May the 13th, 1785,

All the Lands and Royalties which he held under Lease from the late Earl Talbot and the late Michael Richards, Esquire, with all the dwelling-house, Outhouses, Offices, and Gardens he had erected thereon, commonly known by the name of Cyfarthfa, and also All the Household Furniture, plate, Linen, and Books that might be there at his Death; and he also gave to the Petitioner—

The Blast Furnace called Cyfarthfa Furnace that was thereon erected, or any other that might thereafter be built on the said premises.

And also all the Materials that belonged to the same.

And also all the Coal and Mine that might be raised upon the Banks of the said Furnace at the time he had appointed for him to be put into possession of the same.

And also gave him the Forge at Cyfarthfa, then let under lease to Francis Homfray, and his Will was that the Petitioner should not be put into possession of the said Bequest until he should arrive at the age of 24 years, until which time the produce of the said Furnace and Works were to go into the Fund thereinbefore named, for the uses thereinafter mentioned.

And he also gave to the Petitioner the Lease of the Farm opposite Cyfarthfa House, which he held of Lord Plymouth.

And it was his Will that the Petitioner, when he should come to the age of 24 years, have the possession of the aforesaid Bequest given up to him, that he should have the sum of £2,000 lent to him for one year out of the Fund thereinbefore mentioned, to enable him to carry on his Works, after which he was to return the same into the Trust Fund.

And the said Testator gave to the Plaintiff, Thomas Smith, otherwise Bacon, Son of the said Mary Bushby, and Brother to the Petitioner,

All the Leases of Lands and Tenements which he held under the Earl of Plymouth with all the Royalties of Mine and Coals contained therein, called Plymouth Furnace, and all other Buildings and erections on the aforesaid premises.

And also all the Tools and Implements belonging to the said Furnace.

And also All the Mine and Coal which might be raised for or brought upon the Banks of the said Furnace at the Time he was put into possession of the said Bequest, which was to be when he arrived at the age of 24 years, and he was to have £2,000 lent to him out of the Fund thereinbefore mentioned for 12 Months, to enable him to carry on his Works, at the end of which time he was to repay the same to the Fund from which it was taken.

And he gave to the Plaintiff Thomas all that Freehold Estate called Trebetha, which he bought of Mr. Phillips, and which laid near to Plymouth Furnace.

And he gave to the Plaintiff Robert Smith, otherwise Bacon, Son of the said Mary Bushby, and brother to the Petitioner,

His Furnace, called Hirwin, which he purchased of Maybery and Wilkins, of Brecon, with all the Leases of Royalties of Iron Mine and Coals thereon, and all the Tools and Implements belonging to the same, and all the Houses and Erections which were or might be raised for or be upon the Banks of the said Furnace, to be put into his possession when he should attain the age of 24 years. At that time he was to have £2,000 lent to him out of the Fund thereinbefore named, to enable him to carry on the Furnace for 12 months, and then to repay the same into the Fund into thereinbefore (*sic*) named, for the purposes thereinafter mentioned.

And the said Testator also gave to the Plaintiff, Elizabeth Smith, otherwise Bacon, Daughter of the said Mary Bushby, out of the Fund thereinbefore named, an Annuity of £300, payable quarterly, during her life, and to the Plaintiff William Smith, otherwise Bacon, the Youngest son of the said Mary Bushby, the remaining part of the said Trust Fund, Provided it did not exceed £10,000.

And the said Testator directed that in case of the death of any of the said Sons of the said Mary Bushby, which he acknowledged also to be his children, he left the succession to be as follows, vizt. :—

If the eldest son, Anthony, should die before he was of the Age directed by his said Will, then the second son, Thomas, should succeed to all the Bequest left to his brother, And the said Thomas should give up all that was bequeathed to him to the 3rd Son Robert, and the said Robert should give all that was bequeathed to him to his Brother, the 4th Son, William.

And in that case the aforesaid Funds were to be equally divided among the remaining Brothers.

And if more than one Brother should die before they became of age, then those two surviving Brothers should divide the Bequests left to those that should so die equally between them.

And if only one of the said Children, his Sons, and Sons of the said Mary Bushby, should survive, such Son should succeed to the whole of his Estates, real and personal, left to the other three.

And the said Testator further declared that if any of the said Sons therein before named, vizt., the Petitioner Anthony and the Plaintiffs Thomas, Robert, and William, should desire to marry before they come to the age of 24 years, and not under the age of 21 years, and have the consent of the majority of his Executors then living so to do, he should in that case be deemed of age and put into possession of his Fortune.

And if any one of his Sons lived until he was of the age of 24 years, he should at that age be added to the Executors, and have power accordingly.

That the said Testator, Anthony Bacon, died on the 21st day of January, 1786, without revoking his said Will.

And the Defendant, Thomas Harrison, one of the Executors, alone proved the same, and the usual power being reserved to the Defendants, the other Executors who then declined acting.

That by Decree made on the hearing of this Cause, dated the 18th day of December, 1786,

It was among other Things referred to Mr. Ord, one of the Masters of this Court,

To take an Account of the said Testator's personal Estate, not specifically bequeathed, come to the Hands of the Defendant, Thomas Harrison, his only acting Executor.

And the said Master was also to take an Account of the Debts, funeral Expenses, and Legacies of the said Testator.

And also of the arrears of the Annuities given by his Will, and to compute Interest on the Debts and Legacies as therein mentioned.

And the said Master was to cause an Advertisement to be published in the *London Gazette* for the Creditors of the said Testator to come in before him and prove their Debts, and to fix a peremptory Day for that purpose, and such of them as should not come in by the Time to be therein limited were to be excluded the benefit of the said Decree.

And It was Ordered that the personal Estate of the said Testator (not specifically bequeathed) should be applied in payment of his Debts, and funeral expenses in a course of Administration.

And that the surplus of such personal Estate, after payment of his Debts and funeral Expenses, should be paid into the Bank with the privity of the Accountant General of this Court to the Credit of this Cause, subject to the further Order of the Court.

And the said Master was to consider in what manner the Iron Works and other Adventures of the said Testator therein mentioned might be best let and set for the Benefit of the said Testator's Estate and the persons interested therein, and to state the same with his opinion to the Court, and to make a separate Report as to the several Inquiries relating to the said Iron Works.

And it was Ordered that the Receiver then appointed of the rents and profits of the said Testator's Estate should be continued.

That William Bacon, the Receiver, having laid a proposal before the Master for letting Cyfarthfa Furnace till the Petitioner should be entitled to possession thereof under the said Testator's Will, the Master made his separate Report approving of such proposal, which was afterwards confirmed.

That on the 12th day of February, 1786, a Lease was executed, with the Approbation of the said Master, by the said Receiver, to Richard Crawshay, William Stevens, and Joseph Cockshutt, of Cyfarthfa Furnace, and other the Premises devised by the said Will to the Petitioner as aforesaid, from Christmas, 1786, for the Term of 9 years (the time the Petitioner would have attained 24 years), subject to the contingencies in the said Will, and to the several yearly rents reserved by the Lease and Agreements under which the said Testator held the same, and to the Covenants, Exceptions, Reservations, Conditions, powers, and Agreements therein mentioned, at the clear yearly rent of £1,000, payable as therein mentioned over and above the several yearly Rents reserved by the Leases and Agreements under which the said Testator held the said premises, and subject to the Covenants therein contained.

That the Petitioner attained his age of 21 years on the 14th day of February, 1793, and on the 21st day of the same February was married to Elizabeth Ramsbottom, Spinster, with the consent of the Defendants, Thomas Harrison, William Stevens, and Richard Hill, being the Majority of the Executors of the said Testator, according to his said Will.

That on the 30th day of May, 1793, the said Master made his general Report in this Cause, pursuant to the said Decrees, which has since been absolutely confirmed.

And Therefore it was prayed that the Petitioner might be let into possession of the said Furnace called Cyfarthfa Furnace, and other the premises so devised to him under and by virtue of the said Will, and might receive the rents and profits thereof from the 21st day of February, 1793, the time of the Petitioner's Marriage as aforesaid. And that the Lease so executed by the said Receiver to the said Richard Crawshay, William Stevens, and James Cockshutt, as aforesaid, might cease and be determined, and that the said Receiver might be discharged from receiving the rents and profits of the said premises, accrued and accruing, due for the same since the said Marriage of the Petitioner.

Whereupon all parties concerned were ordered to attend His Honour on the matter of the said Petitioner and Counsel for the Petitioner, and for all the other parties, and also for such of the Trustees as are not parties this day attending accordingly.

Upon hearing of the said Petition, the Probate of the will of the Testator, Anthony Bacon, the Decree dated the 18th day of December, 1796; the Master's Report, dated the 30th day of May, 1793; an Extract from the Parish Register, and an Affidavit veryifying the same; an Affidavit of Mary Bushby, whereby it appears that the Plaintiff, Anthony Frankland, otherwise Bacon, hath attained his age of 21 years; an Extract from the Parish Register of the Marriage of the Plaintiff; an Affidavit verifying the same; an Instrument dated the 15th day of February, 1793, being the Consent of the Majority of the Executors of the Testator to the said Marriage, read and what was alleged by the Counsel for the said Parties,

His Honour doth by Consent of the Defendants by their Counsel, and also by the Consent of Gilbert Franklyn and such of the Legatees named in the said Testator's Will as are adults by their Counsel, And the Counsel for such of the Legatees as are infants by their Counsel not opposing the same,

Order that it be referred to the said Master, Mr. Ord, to approve of a proper Security to be entered into by the Petitioner, Anthony Bacon, for payment of the Rent and performance of the Covenants in the Lease stated in the said Petition of the premises called Cyfarthfa Furnace, part of the said Testator's Estate, and upon the Execution of such Security,

It is Ordered that the said Petitioner be let into possession of the said premises from Michaelmas next until the further Order of the Court.

And it is Ordered that the said Petitioner do pay the rent reserved in the said Lease to the Receiver of the Rents and profits of the said Testator's Estate by quarterly payments, but this is to be without prejudice to the Claims of the said Gilbert Franklyn and the Legatees of the said Testator, with liberty for them to apply to the Court from time to time as they shall be advised.

S. K. L.

---

It would seem that Mr. Anthony Bacon, the eldest son, was desirous—acting under this order—to obtain so much of the Cyfarthfa Works as were not included in the Homfray lease.

Mr. Richard Crawshay demurred to this, and the following is the account of the formal conference held between Anthony Bacon and Richard Crawshay on the subject of this dispute, in the presence of their mutual friend, as a recording witness, Mr. Richard Hill:—

" Plymouth Furnace,
"Septr. 29th, 1793.

" Dear Sir,—The following is the conversation that passed between Mr. Crawshay and myself this morning as nearly *verbatim* as we can recollect. The sense and effect is perfect. As soon as you can conveniently draw out the rough draft of an affidavit I'll thank you, that Mr. Richard Hill and myself may swear to it, and forward it to London :—

"Minutes of a conversation between Richd. Crawshay and A. Bacon, in the presence of Rd. Hill, Junr., at Cyfarthfa, on the 29th Septr., 1793: 'A. B. informed Mr. C. that he came in consequence of the Order obtained from the Court of Chancery for his being put into possession of Cyfarthfa Furnaces on that day. That he was ready prepared to fulfil everything contained in the Order on his part, and was ready to name a person to value the Ore, Stock, etc. Mr. C. then said he was sorry he could not give possession, as they so materially differed in the construction of the Contract between Bacon and Homfray. A. B. said he considered that quite a distinct thing from the possession being given, and had nothing to do with it. A. B. then asked Mr. C. if he had a copy of the Order of the Court of Chancery. R. C. said he had. A. B. asked him if he had been served with it. R. C. said, No, not served. A. B. said he had ordered Mr. Pearson to send him (R. C.) a copy of the Order. R. C. said that he supposed, in consequence of that Order, he (A.B.) came to ask possession, to which A. B. answered, Yes. R. C. then said he was sorry he could not then give it to him, as he intended to ask the Court of Chancery what he was to do.'

"ANTHO. BACON.
"RICHARD HILL, Junr.

"Mr and Mrs. Hill and family unite with Mrs. Bacon and myself in best compts. to Mrs. Powell and all friends.

"To John Powell, Esq., Brecon."

---

Eventually it would seem that an arrangement was come to for Mr. Richard Crawshay to take to the whole of the Cyfarthfa Works, including Cyfarthfa, and the benefit of all the original leases granted by Earl Talbot and Mr. Richards, of Cardiff, in respect of the properties. The sum paid to Mr. Anthony Bacon—no doubt a large one—is not stated in our papers.

[The disposal of the Plymouth and Hirwain Works is dealt with elsewhere.]

The following are the last letters of Mr. Anthony Bacon we have relating to the Cyfarthfa property, and are interesting as fixing May 20th, 1794, as the date when the purchase was to be completed by Mr. Crawshay; and also in showing that Lord Dynevor and John Richards, Esq., had become lessors in succession to the Earl of Talbot and Michael Richards, Esq.

COPY.

Plymouth, May 2nd, 1794. Copy from John Richards, Esq.

Dear Sir,—Yesterday I received your letter relative to some Land, which you mention that the Proprietors of the canal have taken, and to which you have an objection as having a Lease so long a time of which is unexpired. As Lord Dynevor has an equal right with myself (if you have no objection), I will enclose a copy of your letter to Mr. Bold; as I think, from knowing more of the business than myself, he will be better able to judge how to prevent their taking more Land than will be absolutely necessary for the use of the canal. And I conceive they cannot have the least right either to lett or sell any Land for any other purpose but that of building store-houses for their use,

And am, Dear Sir, Yours, etc.,
J. R.

---

London, May 7th, 1794. Copy from Lord Dynevor.

Dear Sir,—I received your letter transmitted me by Mr. Bold, and am sorry to hear that there is any difference of opinion on the subject of the Lands sold to the canal Company. I own I am so totally unacquainted with the subject, the transaction having taken place before I had any concern with the Estate,[1] that I can only refer you to Mr. Bold,

[1] Baroness Dynevor succeeded to the property in 1791, as only daughter and heir-at-law, and also devisee under the will of Earl Talbot.

to give you an Account of the proceedings; he will probably be at Merthyr in a short time, and I will desire him to wait upon you and give you every information on the subject. I can only add that I very well remember Mr. Bold having declared his resolution that no more Land than was absolutely necessary for the Canal Proprietors to have in order to carry their work into execution should be spared to them.

I am, Dear Sir, Yours, etc.,
(Sgd.) DYNEVOR.

---

COPY.

Llandaff, May 12th, 1794.

Dear Sir,—Enclosed you have copy of Letters recd. from Lord Dynevor and Mr. Richards in reply to those I sent you. As both the Gent'n refer to Mr. Bold, I think you may with propriety call upon him and inform him of our decided intention to proceed immediately for the recovery of the Land. I think we should state the whole of the proceedings to him, that if he can adopt any mode to prevent the unpleasantness of a Litigation, we shall be happy to follow it. Every piece of Land now becomes an object to the Works; but if Mr. Bold can hit upon any mediating system, I shall be happy to meet him for that purpose. On Tuesday, the 20th, I meet Mr. Crawshay to sign and settle the Deeds. If Williams's business can be settled by that time, I shall be happy. Also, if you can send John Lewis's Lease for execution. Excuse haste. United by Mrs. B. and Mr. Ramsbottom in Compl'ts to Mrs. Powell, Family, and all friends at Brecon,

I remain, Your mo: obt., hble. Servt.,
(Sgd.) ANTHO. BACON.

---

The following refers to the valuable Feeder from the Taff fechan river, for which £300 rent was paid to Mr. Thynne Howe Gwynne, of Buckland;

COPY.

Near Newbury, Jaury. 24th, 1801.

Dear Sir,—I have by this day's Post sent you Copy of Extracts from Correspondence bet. Mr. Gwynne, Mr. Jones, Mr. Crawshay, and myself, relative to Mr. Gwynne's confirming Lease of Land and Water at Coedcwmma—the particulars of which, I have no doubt, will be fresh in your memory. In my engagement with Mr. Crawshay, I have assigned to him Mr. Gwynne's Lease, and I pay the Rent to Mr. Gwynne; consequently, you will see I am bound to enforce the performance of Mr. Gwynne's confirmation of the further term. You will see by the correspondence the steps already taken, and how I have been baffled and prevented. I have now to request you will, in the most expeditious way, at the same time giving the parties all due notice, take every legal measure to enforce the fulfilment of Mr. Gwynne's engagement. You will observe I want no further power than the present Lease grants. I only want the term lengthened. As to the trespass, I don't believe any is committed; and if there is, I have nothing to do with it. I apprehend, by waiting upon Mr. Gwynne, he will refer you to Mr. Jones, with whom I beg to have no acct., as he and Mr. Gwynne have already made me pay the piper pretty handsomely. If you wish for the Lease, shall I write to Mr. Crawshay?

Yours most obt.,
(Sgd.) ANTHO. BACON.

[It may be stated that the widow of Anthony Bacon lived at Cyfarthfa during the whole period of the minority of her husband's natural children.]

OLD BLAST FURNACES AT YNYSFACH, CYFARTHFA.

*(Photo R.W. 1905).*

PAGE 63

ONE OF THE YNYSFACH FURNACES.
C & G (CRAWSHAY AND GEORGE) 1801, INSCRIBED ON ARCH.
*(Photo R.W. 1905).*

PAGE 63

ONE OF THE YNYSFACH FURNACES.
C & G (CRAWSHAY AND GEORGE) 1801, INSCRIBED ON ARCH.
*(Photo R.W. 1905).*

PAGE 63

CYFARTHFA IRON WORKS IN 1813.

*(Wood's Rivers of Wales).*

## ANTHONY BACON AS MEMBER OF PARLIAMENT.

(The first of that name.)

| | | | Seat. |
|---|---|---|---|
| 1764. Jany. 25 | ... Anthony Bacon | ... ... | Aylesbury, Co. Bucks. |
| | *Vice* John Wilkes, Esq. Expelled the House. | | |
| 1768. March 16 | ... Anthony Bacon | ... ... | Do. |
| 1774. Oct. 6 | ... Do. | ... ... | Do. |
| 1780. Sept. 7 | ... Do. | ... ... | Do. |
| | [He died Jany. 21, 1786.] | | |

We now pass from the Bacon tenure of the Cyfarthfa Works to that of Richard Crawshay and the Crawshay family.

---

## THE CRAWSHAY DYNASTY.

Whether Anthony Bacon, who, though short-lived, securely laid the foundation of the great Cyfarthfa Works, or Richard Crawshay, or his grandson William, who both successively developed them to a state of marvellous greatness and success, is to rank the highest among the ironmasters of their times, it is difficult to decide. The one laid the stone, the other built upon it.

We are not now concerned with the examination of ancient leases and documents of title, but with a going concern, which passed by purchase from the heir of the founder to Mr. Richard Crawshay in 1794, and which, under his management, assisted for a time by his partner, Mr. Watkin George, assumed vast dimensions.

[The site selected by Messrs. Bacon and Brownrigg for the erection of these Works was immediately below the junction (or Cymmer—Welsh) of the Taff Fawr and Taff Fechan rivers, and on the right bank of the united streams now bearing the name of the Taff. It was also on the very outcrop of the South Wales mineral basin, and at the northern end of their immense mineral takings from Lord Talbot and Mr. Richards, and which extended several miles down the Taff Valley to the south, and westwards to the centre line of the Aberdare mountain—an area, it is said, of 4,000 acres. The Dowlais, Plymouth, and Penydarran Works are all on the left bank of the Taff, and somewhat intermixed; but the Cyfarthfa had the sole undivided possession of the right bank, and sovereignty there incapable of being interfered with. There is little doubt that this site was so chosen at the first start of the Works, when unfailing water was a first necessity, on account of the abundant supply of water there provided in the twin streams of the Taff.

This, at least, has been the impression formed on our mind by a recent visit, when, by permission of Mr. Wm. Evans, the manager of the firm of Guest, Keen, and Co., we were taken through the old part of the great Cyfarthfa Iron-works.

The guide placed at our disposal was Mr. Henry Jones, the mill manager, one of the oldest of the Cyfarthfa officers, and possessed of great experience and a well-stored memory. Unfortunately, the day was a little inclement, and we were unable to visit the old Furnace—No. 5—or rather the remains of it—which dates from Anthony Bacon's time, and is some little distance higher up the river than the present main Works. This No. 5 has a plate on it dated 1765, W C, 1827, and is one of the sights of Merthyr. We were rather disappointed at this, but the fates were adverse.

However, it was dry and pleasant within Anthony Bacon's old house, still standing in good order, and which is immediately facing the puddling mills, etc., and water-wheels of olden time, and which I recognised as those depicted in the sketch given in Wood's *Rivers of Wales*, as they stood in 1817. The master's house was close to his main

Works, as it should be, in the early days of any experiment, and the glaring light of the furnaces, and the thud of the hammers were, to the master who had brought them into existence, a welcome sight and sound.

Of course, we were shown the fireplace with the fat hog cast upon it in Anthony Bacon's favourite room, now the drawing-office; and one of the draughtsmen kindly offered to send me a photo. of it, which shall duly appear hereafter.

Then followed a visit to the range of four old Blast Furnaces, known as Ynysfach, placed at some little distance down the river, the Works having extended in a south direction. These were built by C. and G. (Richard Crawshay and Watkin George) in 1801, according to the inscription chiselled out on a stone in the arch of No. 4. These were also no longer in use, being superseded by other furnaces of modern times.]

But we must now return from this short digression to the marked pathway of our historical sketch.

The opening of the canal to Cardiff about this period gave facilities, hitherto unknown, for the delivery of the iron produced at the Works; and the war, when the casting and boring of cannon was a leading article in the trade, and the times generally favoured the iron industry.

There is little doubt but that Mr. Richard Crawshay was no ordinary man, and that he possessed great skill in and knowledge of the mystery of iron-making, with the capacity to organise and arrange the conduct of a large business employing certainly hundreds, if not thousands, of workmen. And he had a large, almost virgin field of iron ore and coal to work upon. He soon amassed great wealth, as quickly as a pool of water fills after heavy rain. To me, one trait in his character stands out for admiration, which his letters amply prove: that of his true and firm friendship to those who were true and faithful to him. A thousand pounds or so was nothing to him, if he could help a good neighbour, and it was a common expression of his: "We must not let that poor fellow go to the wall." The Freres, of Clydach, he assisted in a time of difficulty with a loan of £10,000; and it is said that on one occasion the wealthy bankers of Brecon, so Mr. Charles Wilkins tells us, were glad to have his moneyed support.

And one fine morning he made a present of the Abercarne Estate—of what value I do not know—to his son-in-law, Benjamin Hall.

"London, December 10th, 1808.

"My dear Sir,—You already know the kindness and munificence with which Mr. Crawshay has presented me with the Abercarne Estate. The completion of the purchase has been retarded by various events, the Death of Glover, the Broils in his family, and the number of parties necessary to join, there being two Mortgagees, one of whom Mr. Anstey has given most unconceivable trouble, tho' nowonly an Incumbrancer of £600, besides several judgment Creditors. Mr. Glover agreed to convey to Mr. Crawshay, or any person that he should appoint. When Mr. Crawshay put me into possession, 6th August last, he wrote to Mr. Kaye to make out the Deeds to me. I have, therefore, desired Mr. Kaye, who has managed this Business, to prepare an Appointment from Mr. Crawshay to me, and Mr. Crawshay desires me to bring it down with me, tho' wished me to put it in your Hands to prepare. You will do me the justice to believe that it would have been pleasing to me to have been able, but Mr. Kaye having been throughout engaged, I thought it impossible. However, having stated the transaction shortly, I shall send you all the Documents by Monday's post, and the Deed when prepared, that you may peruse it, and give your opinion fully, and shall be much obliged if you can meet me at Cyfarthfa when I go down, that it may be executed. I leave Town for Abercarne on Wednesday, 14th, or Thursday. Write me a few lines on this statement by return of post on Tuesday, and I shall get them *here;* if not, direct to *Abercarne.*

"Mr. Crawshay writes me of your better health, in which I shall always feel interested, being D'r Sir,

"Very truly yours,

"John Powell, Esq. "BENJN. HALL."

There were two matters, however, that caused him great trouble: the one in relation to the Union Works in the Rhymney Valley, which he sought to establish for the benefit of his son-in-law, Benjamin Hall. Richard Crawshay was himself a partner in conjunction with Benjamin Hall, Watkin George, his great mineral expert, and Mr. Richard Cunningham, the latter as manager. Apparently Mr. Cunningham, to say the least of it, made mistakes, and was dismissed; and hence an angry correspondence, and a very painful interview, with a sharp lawsuit at the end, was the result.

The other trouble was that with his eldest son, William, of whom he complains bitterly in his letters that "he would never do anything he wished." Happily we find, according to the pleasing note in a codicil to his will, that the father and son were fully reconciled, and instead of cutting him off with £100,000, he left him a three-eighth share of the Cyfarthfa Works.

Mr. Richard Crawshay was, however, especially fortunate in having such able nephews—the brothers Joseph and Crawshay Bailey—to assist him in the management of the Works; and how much of his great success was due to their careful attention to every detail, and possibly sagacity in suggesting savings in cost, or original improvements in the Works themselves, will never be known. His nephews were themselves bred and born great ironmasters.

Richard Crawshay died in 1810, having appointed his son-in-law, Benjamin Hall, sole Executor, and we herewith append a full copy of his Will:—

This is the Last Will and Testament of me, Richd. Crawshay, Esqr., of Cyfarthfa, in the County of Glamorgan, in my own handwriting, Septr. 26th, 1809. First, I give and bequeath to my wife Mary, one Annuity of two thousand pounds a year during her life, in lieu of all other Claims soever on my Estate and Effects; also the use of the House and Furniture she now lives in at Sunbury, she paying Rents and Taxes, and keeping the same in proper repair, on condition that she gives up all Title to 20 Canal Shares standing on the Company's Books in her name. I give and bequeath to my daughter Ann Franklen three Brecon Canal Company's Notes for Six thousand pounds each, and Two thousand pounds in money. I give to my Daughter Elizabeth Williams, two Brecon Canal Cos. Notes for Six thousand pounds each, and the Twenty Canal Shares standing in her name. I give to my Sisters Susan Bailey, Elizabeth Thompson, and Sarah Moses, each two hundred pounds a year for their lives; to Mrs. Pulling, Mrs. Maber, and Miss Sarah Mosser one thousand pounds each; to the Children of Su. Bailey, one Thousand Pounds, except Joseph, who I have otherway provided for, the share of his Brother Thomas, an Idiot, shall be vested in Joseph to support the Idiot, as he shall Judge best; to the Children of Sarah Moses I give One Thousand pounds each, except Richard, Robert, and Mrs. Heazle, who have had £500 each before, they shall have only £500 each now. To my only son, who never would follow my advise, and has treated me rudely in very many instances, instead of making my Executor and Residuary Legatee, as till this day he was, I give him one hundred Thousand pounds on Condition that he delivers my Leasehold Premises at Paul's Wharf, the Iron Chest Containing my writings as they now are, when demanded by my Executor. If he is desirous of purchasing the Premises at Geo. Yard, which are partly Freehold and part Leasehold, he shall have the refusal of them for three thousand pounds; if not, they shall be sold by Auction, as my Great Aim is to create peace and Civility to Mr. Hall in this. I order, in conformity with past experience on this subject the amount of the Legacy, 100,000, will most likely be in the hands of Wm. C. and his Partners, if Less be due to me, the balance shall be paid, and so, if contrary, received by my Executors.

| | | | | |
|---|---|---|---|---|
| To James Cockshutt, Esq., of Yorkshire, I give | | ... | ... | £500 |
| Jos. Kaye, Esqre., London | ,, | ... | ... | 500 |
| Thos. Charles, Gent., Cardiff | ,, | ... | ... | 1000 |
| Thos. Pierce, Gent., Cyfarthfa | ,, | ... | ... | 1000 |
| C. Waters, do. do. | ,, | ... | ... | 800 |
| Mat. Wayne, do. do. | ,, | ... | ... | 800 |

K

| | | | |
|---|---|---|---|
| To Jos. Probyn, Gent., Cyfarthfa, I give | ... | ... | ... £150 |
| For my Goddaughter (dau: of) Dr. Turton, M.D., Swansea, I give | | | 300 |
| Thos. Bee, Son of Thos. and Ann Bee, I give | | ... | 300 |
| James Sutton, "Crawshay's Arms" | ,, | ... | .. 100 |
| Jane Newman, "Bridgewater Arms" | ,, | ... | ... 100 |

Three Women Servants and Morgan, Fifty pounds each; Jack Jones and Ruce Perrot, one hundred each, and my wearing apparel to Perrot. To Peggy Thomas, my kind Nurse ever since Patty's Death, I give one hundred a year for her life; Hoar, the Gardiner, 100, To Joseph Bailey, Twenty-five Thousand pounds, to be Transferred from my Account on the Ledger to his, intended as a Capital to him to become Partner with my Executor of one-fourth share in the Trade of all those Works, so long as the Lease endures with the Principal and profits a-growing therefrom, to be his own for Ever; and Lastly, I give and bequeath to Benjn. Hall, Esq., and his Wife, now of Abercarne, and to their Heirs for ever, all the rest and residue of my Estates and Effects whatsoever, as Freeholds, Leaseholds, Bonds, Bills, Notes, Mortgages, and whatever else is found to be my property any where; and I do hereby appoint the sd. Ben. Hall, Esq., my only Executor, for carrying this my Will into execution, he paying all Debts due from me, my Funeral Expenses on a decent but not Extravagant Scale, and resting remains at Landaff Cathedral. In witness whereof I have hereunto set my hand and Seal the Date above written.

RICHD. CRAWSHAY (L. S.).

Witness to the signing and sealing hereof, and declared to be my last Will and Testament, of me, Richd. Crawshay, without Informing the Witnesses of the Contents of it, on the Twenty-sixth day of Septr., 1809, in the presence of each other, and at my request.

Crawshay Bailey, Joseph Probyn, Rees Parrott (all of Cyfarthfa).

First.

I give Rings as under, of the like left me by the late John Wilkinson, Esq.;

Thomson Bonar, Esq., London;
William Porter, Esquire, London;
Sr. John Sinkclair, Baronet, London or Scotland;
Edwd. Morgan, Esq., Landaff;
Dr. Hall, Landaff;
John Williams, Esquire, Landaff;

and

Thos. Charles, Gent.; Thos. Browne, Esq., Cardiff; William Williams, Esq.; Mrs. Williams, his Wife, Brecon; Honble. Judge Moisey; and to Joe. Bailey, Cyfarthfa. And to any others my Executors may think fit. To Jno. Franklen, Esq., my Jonas Hanway Ring.—RICHD. CRAWSHAY, Jany. 27th, 1810.

Second

By my Will, dated the 26th Septr., 1809, I have made a mistake by supposing I had Six Brecon and Abergavenny Canal Notes for Six thousand pounds each, whereas they are Six for £5,000 each. To Correct that error I make this Codicil, vizt.: To my Daughter Anne I give three of those Notes for £5,000 each, and Five Thousand Pounds in money; and to my Daughter Elizabeth, the other three Canal Notes, and five thousand pounds in Money, in lieu of 20 Canal Shares. I give and bequeath to my Grandson Richard Franklen my Dehrivid Farm, now Let to Robert Brooks and Robert Brooks for two hundred and fifty pounds a year, to him and his heirs for ever. It shall be held in trust for him by his parents till he attains the age of 21 years. I give David Davis, Esq., Surgeon, £200; his Partner has a Note from me for £300. I give to the Revd. Thos. Jones, Curate of this Parish, one hundred pounds.

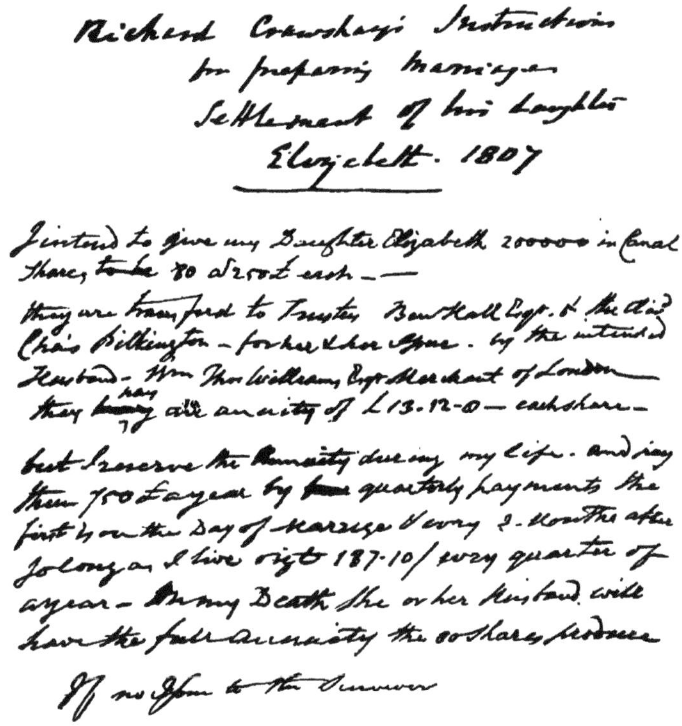

Richard Crawshay's Instructions
for preparing Marriage
Settlement of his Daughter
Elizabeth. 1807

I intend to give my Daughter Elizabeth 20000 in Canal
Shares, ~~to be~~ 80 at 250£ each —
they are transferred to Trustees Benj Hall Esqr. & the Revd
Chas Pilkington – for her & her Issue. by the intended
Husband – Wm Thos Williams Esqr Merchant of London
they ~~bring~~ pay an annuity of £13-12-0 — each share —
but I reserve the Annuity during my life. and pay
them 750 £ a year by ~~two~~ quarterly payments the
first 4 on the Day of Marriage & every 3 Months after
So long as I live viz 187-10/ every quarter of
a year – On my Death She or her Husband will
have the full annuity the 80 Shares produce
If no Issue to the Survivor

RICHARD CRAWSHAY'S SETTLEMENT ON HIS DAUGHTER ELIZABETH, 1807.

PAGE 66

Given under my hand and Seal this 2nd February, 1810, In presence of three Witnesses: Richd. Crawshay (L.S.). Witness: Edwd. Waters, Joseph Probyn, Crawshay Bailey, all at Cyfarthfa.

Third.

My Bodily health is out of repair, 4th May, 1810, that I will not now take the Trouble of making a Fresh Will, but do now make this Codicil, that is to say, being reconciled to my Son Wm. Crawshay, I hereby give him three-eight Shares of my Concerns at this Iron Works, and of the Premises at Cardiff, so the Partnership will stand at my demise.

| | |
|---|---|
| William Crawshay, | three-eighths. |
| Benj. Hall, | three-eighths. |
| Jos. Bailey, | two-eighths. |

Witness my hand and Seal, the Date above written.—Richd. Crawshay.

Proved at London, with three Codicils, 26th July, 1810, before the Worshipful Maurice Swabey, Doctor of Laws and Surrogate by the Oath of Benjamin Hall, Esquire, the sole Executor, to whom admon. was granted, having been first sworn duly to administer.

Geo. Gostling.
Nathl. Gostling. } Deputy Registrars.
R. C. Cresswell.

Ex. July, 1810 (15), J. E.

The above is an office copy extracted from the registry of the Prerogative Court of Canterbury.

---

We shall now trace briefly the history of the Cyfarthfa Works, from the time of Richard Crawshay's death to about the year 1840.

The arrangements entered into for carrying out the terms of his Will were mainly as follows:

While William Crawshay, the only son, and Benjamin Hall, his son-in-law, and sole executor, and who were each entitled to a three-eighth share of the Works, carried on the concern jointly for a time, Joseph Bailey, the Nephew, who had been given a two-eighth share, elected to sell his interest to the holders of the other shares.

Mr. Hall, the sole executor, had much to do the next few years in settling the affairs of the estate, and was also responsible, as partner, for the conduct of the Works; inasmuch as it is understood Mr. William Crawshay took no personal interest or part in the management, and seldom, if ever, visited the Works.

The following invoice (copy) shows that on March 25th, 1815, the Cyfarthfa firm was styled Crawshay and Hall.

"Cyfarthfa,
"George Overton, Esq., "25th March, 1815.

| | £ | s. | d. |
|---|---|---|---|
| "To Crawshay and Hall. | | | |
| "Rent of Gwaelodygarth house and land, etc., from 2nd August, 1814, to 25th March, 1815—½ year and 51 days—at £130 per annum . | 83 | 0 | 0 |
| "Deduct property tax . . . . . . | 8 | 6 | 0 |
| | £74 | 17 | 0" |

The exact date when Benjamin Hall left the firm our papers do not show, but it would seem that it was very shortly after the year 1815.

Though William Crawshay had taken no part in the management of the Works, his eldest son William, hence known as William Crawshay, junr., when he came of age, took a great interest in them, and on Mr. Hall seceding from the firm, assumed the sole management on behalf of his father.

The first letter we have of his bears the date of November 29th, 1820:

"Cyfarthfa, Novr. 29th, 1820.

"My dear Sir,—I have made a purchase in this County which makes me inclined to part with the Lwyn Rios farm, adjoining your upper farm in the Parish of Vaynor. The 2 farms are situated thus, and it certainly is desirable to you to possess the one I wish to sell, and consequently I make you the first offer.

"I am willing to take £2,000 for it; and to prove to you that I think it worth the money, I will take a 21 years' lease at £60 p. annum, and keep everything in repair, you receiving the exact clear income of £60, free of all tenants' claims whatsoever.

"Have the goodness to consider this matter, and give me your reply, as I am desirous of taking advantage of the present high price of land.

"I have another farm to sell in Breconshire, near Hirwain, which I will sell to pay 3 p. cent. clear, if you are buyer in that part of the world.

"I am, Dear Sir,
"Yours very truly,
"W. Crawshay, Jr.

"John Powell, Esq.

"You see, I am not so good a Manager as Mr. Bailey. I have bo't only £30,000 worth of land, and cannot pay for it without selling other land, and cutting and contriving."

We have inserted this letter because there is a trace of a joke in it. It was well known that the Crawshay family invested their yearly accruing and immense wealth in Consols and liquid securities of the gilt-edge class, as bankers call them (there was one exception in case of "Turks"), while Joe Bailey, their relation, of Nantyglo, put every spare pound he had in the purchase of land. In after-years, when there came a panic in the money market, or either firm were short of cash, the Crawshay family sold out their Consols, and had the laugh at Bailey posting up with his title-deeds to pledge at the Bank of England. Land, however, we know gives special social privileges, but the Crawshays never sought political power and seats in Parliament, with a baronetcy or peerage perhaps in view! They cared for none of these things.

At the same time, they were fond of a good house to live in, and on a site finely placed on an open, sloping bank on the left of the Taff, but within easy sight and reach of the Works, Cyfarthfa Castle was built by William Crawshay in the year 1825, at a cost of £30,000. And there, and at Caversham more particularly, the vineries and hothouses supplied the famous firm of Solomons, at Covent Garden, with the finest grapes and fruit that England can produce. The Crawshay family never did things by halves!

In 1837, the valuable water right from the Taff Vechan river was purchased by Mr. William Crawshay for £7,000 from the trustees of the estate of Roderick Gwynne, of Buckland, who died as far back as 1808. During Mr. Thynne Howe Gwynne's life (he died in 1826) it could not be sold, and £300 a year was paid him as rent. Strictly speaking, the Lord of the Manor never had the power to lease the water from off the common land. It is a right unknown to the law.

This William Crawshay, junr., was certainly a wonderful man, and is said to have equalled his grandfather in skilled knowledge, industry, and ability to manage a great iron-works, and in that he was backed by the great realised wealth of his father. The latter enabled the Works to be carried on in full productiveness in bad times and in good, the pig-iron being stored and stacked when prices were low; and the Cyfarthfa Works then enjoyed a great era of development and prosperity, every improvement in the manufacture of iron being taken advantage of, and rolling mills erected to meet the new and great demand for railway rails.

The original letters of his, which I have, are written in a bold, round hand, and denote the vigorous character of the writer, and up to the year 1835 are signed "Wm. Crawshay, Jr." In that year, and subsequently, the letters are signed "Wm. Crawshay," and I presume his father died about that date, but the exact year shall be given when ascertained.

At one time, an event not uncommon in the history of a vigorous family, there were three William Crawshays in existence—father, son, and grandson—William, William, junr., and William 3rd. Of this William 3rd I have two original letters, the one dated August 2nd, 1831, in which he asks Mr. John Powell, the solicitor, of Brecon, to get him some grouse shooting on the Penkelly manors of Miss Gwynne, of Buckland; and the other of August 19th, 1835, also dated from Cyfarthfa, referring to his father's absence from home:

"Cyfarthfa, Augt. 2nd, 1831.

"My Dear Sir,—Your kindness hitherto in getting us permission to sport on Miss Gwynne's (now Mrs. Holford's) hills has once more induced me to ask the favour of again being permitted to shoot this year, and to allow the keeper to take our dogs up once or twice in Company with Edwards, Nant gwine, before the 12th, to just see and accustom them to the birds. They are old dogs, and will not want breaking in. My father (who has just left for London, or would have written himself) joins me in kind regards to you.

"Believe me to be, Dear Sir,

"Your Most Obliged Friend,

"J. Powell, Esq., Brecon. "W. CRAWSHAY 3rd."

---

"Cyfarthfa, August, 1835.

"Dear Sir,—My father is from home; his return is Tuesday next, and on Wednesday he will remit you Amount of your Claim for Rent,

"And I am, Dear Sir,

"Yours very truly,

"John Powell, Esq. "W. CRAWSHAY, Jr."

We have given these letters in full, on account of the painful interest attaching to this young man's death. In crossing at the Old Passage at Beachly-on-Severn, on a very stormy day (Sunday, September 1st, 1839), the boat was swamped, and every one on board was drowned.

The following is the account in *The Times* of September 4th, 1839:—

"MELANCHOLY AND FATAL ACCIDENT ON THE RIVER SEVERN: ELEVEN LIVES LOST.

"On Sunday last (September 1st) a most melancholy accident, attended with the loss of eleven fellow-creatures, occurred at the Aust Passage across the Severn.

"It appears, from what we can learn on the subject, that the steamboat which crosses the Passage, does not usually ply on Sundays. Consequently, those parties who wished to cross on Sunday last, were obliged to avail themselves of a small boat, called the 'Mail Boat,' and of a passage-boat for carriages, called the 'Little Western.'

"The day having been throughout exceedingly boisterous, the wind blowing a complete gale produced a very heavy sea in the Severn, which, together with the tide which there runs with extreme rapidity, made it very dangerous for boats to pass across.

"At about five minutes after three o'clock in the afternoon, the Mail Boat proceeded from the Monmouthshire side, and was followed in about ten minutes by the 'Little Western,' having on board six passengers, five horses, and two carriages, besides the crew, consisting of her Captain and four men. The sea was at that time running high, and the wind almost a complete hurricane. The vessel, though labouring much, continued to progress to the destined shore, when about half-way across a sudden gust of wind, called a land squall, carried her on her side; and the horses, as it is supposed shifting, she was capsized, and in a few moments she was filled with water, and went down, every soul on board perishing with her.

"The Mail Boat had at this moment reached the beach on the English side; and, as her passengers were ascending the beach, they happened to turn round, when they saw the unfortunate vessel dismasted, and in a sinking condition. They uttered an exclamation, and in the space of a minute, while they were gazing, the unfortunate boat went down.

"The Mail Boat immediately put off again to endeavour to save the lives of some of the passengers, but were unable to reach them, and being herself swamped, so heavy was the sea.

"One or two of the passengers were seen for a moment struggling with the waves, but they soon sank to rise no more. The Mail Boat succeeded in reaching two of the horses, but for their plunging were unable to tow them to shore.

"The following are the names of those who were drowned: Mr. Crawshay, junr. (it is not known which), one of the large ironmasters of Merthyr; Mr. Andrew Bland, brother of Mr. Bland, coach proprietor, of Bristol; Mr. Jones, of Welsh Newton, Monmouthshire; a Mr. Jenkins, and Robert Harmer, a servant of Capt. Jenkins, the one who was proceeding with his master's carriage to meet him at Bristol; Capt. Whitchurch, the master of the boat; William Whitchurch, his son, about seventeen years of age; and three men of the crew, some of whom have left wives and families.

"We have heard that it was the intention of Mr. R. H. Blewett, M.P., to have crossed by the boat but he was too late."

And in the *Times* of September 10th, the following further particulars are given:—

"We are informed that the Mr. Crawshay, who was lost on Sunday last in crossing the Passage, was William, the eldest son of Mr. William Crawshay, the proprietor of the Cyfarthfa, Hirwain, and Forest Iron and Tin Works, in the Counties of Glamorgan and Brecon, and of Cinderford and Abbots Wood Iron and Coal Works, in the Forest of Dean; and of the House of Crawshay, etc., London. The son who was unfortunately drowned, was the resident and active manager of the above Works, and was on his way to visit his father at Caversham Park, near Reading. He had just entered his thirtieth year, and was a young man of high honour and talent. And, on September 11th, it is stated that Mr. Crawshay's body was found by a Gloucester pilot, William Morgan, at Lydney, about five miles from the place where the boat was lost. Morgan will receive the reward of £20, offered by the Messrs. Crawshay, brothers of deceased, for the recovery of the body. Mr. Crawshay had £25 in gold, and some loose silver, and also a gold watch and guard chain, the property being found quite safe."

This remarkable and unparalleled accident created a deep sensation at the time, and is fresh in people's memories even to-day, though the precise details of the catastrophe have been forgotten.

Mr. William Crawshay continued to occupy, and occasionally visit Cyfarthfa Castle, which he had built, down to 1847, I think, when he bade farewell to the Merthyr district and to the Works, the management of which he handed over to his son, Robert Thompson Crawshay; the other Sons, Henry and Francis, having been placed in possession of the Iron Works in the Forest of Dean and at Treforest.

One of the characteristics of the Crawshay rule and management was, I believe, that they would never have "Shops" or "Truck Shops" connected with their Works, and always set their faces against the practice, which we have already seen, and shall see still further, prevailed among the Welsh Iron Works. And in other ways the interests of the work-people were studied, which had the effect of giving the Firm in all ordinary times the devoted attachment and affection of their workmen. The exception was, perhaps, the time of the Chartist riots in 1831, when the passions of men became wholly ungovernable.

In his farewell speech, at a public dinner held at Merthyr in 1847, Mr. William Crawshay told the story at length of his family's connection with the Iron Trade. I have read that interesting speech in a copy of a Merthyr paper, filed at the British Museum, and went there a few days ago for the purpose of taking a copy for insertion. But, unfortunately, the authorities are rearranging and carting away to new buildings a great store of these old newspapers; and all access to them for the present is neccessarily refused. I shall hope, however, to obtain a copy in time to add it in an Appendix.

In the year 1856, I remember going to see Mr. R. T. Crawshay at the Castle, taking him three fine Salmon caught in our fishery in the Usk, at Caerleon, in which he and I

VIEW OF CYFARTHFA IRON WORKS IN 1905.

(Photo R.W.)

PAGE 71

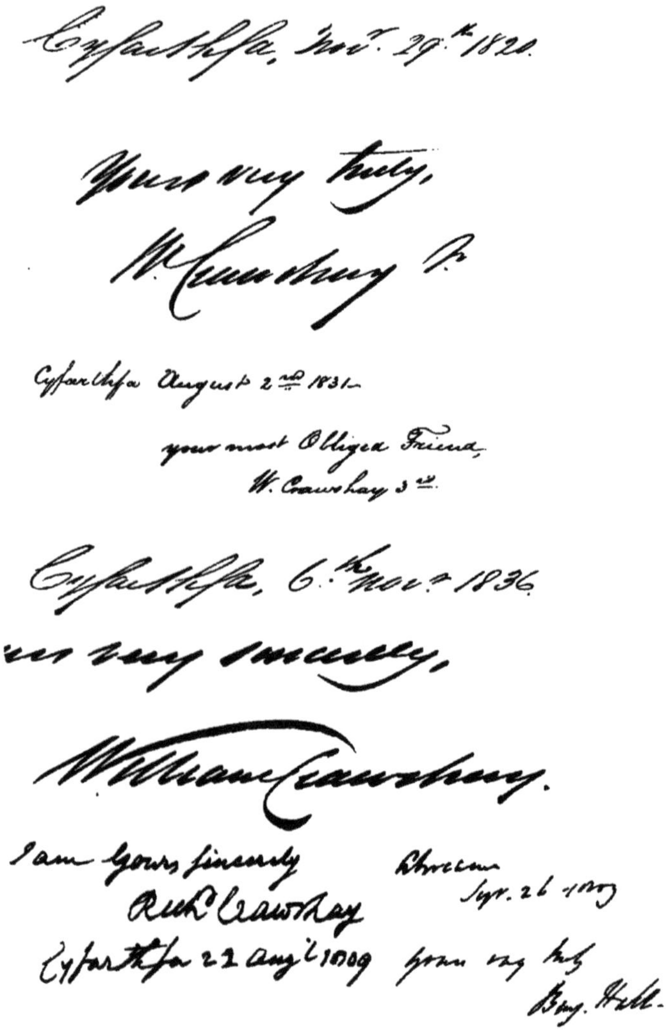


SIGNATURES OF PARTNERS IN THE CYFARTHFA IRON WORKS.

Page 71

were partners in conjunction with the late Major Stretton and Mr. Cobb, of Brecon (our Capital was £80, of which £40 was paid up). The fish were beauties, and one especially, a very thick fish—we called them "Uskers"—he was so struck with the shape, that he then and there laid it on a flat board, and outlined the form with a pencil.

Mr. William Crawshay, the father, lived to a grand old age, at Caversham Park, on the breezy and healthy chalk ridge north of the Thames, at Reading, and died there, I think, in 1867; but the later fortunes of the family and of the Works being of comparatively modern date, are not included in the scope of these papers.

Mr. George Forrest was a much-trusted Agent—at the Works from 1820 to 1830; and, at a later period, the well-remembered Mr. William Jones filled a similar capacity.

A Book to itself might be written of this great Firm, and we can only give but this brief notice.

---

## GLAMORGANSHIRE CANAL: RETURN OF IRON SENT FROM CYFARTHFA (AND HIRWAIN) TO CARDIFF, 1817 TO 1840.

| | | Tons. | | | Tons. |
|---|---|---|---|---|---|
| 1817 | ... | 14,191 | 1829 | ... | 24,768 |
| 1818 | ... | 15,706 | 1830 | ... | 19,892 |
| 1819 | ... | 16,646 | 1831 | ... | 15,465 |
| 1820 | ... | 19,010 | 1832 | ... | 24,668 |
| 1821 | ... | 18,070 | 1833 | ... | 37,380 |
| 1822 | ... | 17,137 | 1834 | ... | 34,952 |
| 1823 | ... | 19,452 | 1835 | ... | 35,090 |
| 1824 | ... | 20,399 | 1836 | ... | 34,654 |
| 1825 | ... | 23,063 | 1837 | ... | 33,580 |
| 1826 | ... | 20,206 | 1838 | ... | 36,986 |
| 1827 | ... | 29,312 | 1839 | ... | 37,009 |
| 1828 | ... | 30,011 | 1840 | ... | 35,507 |

V.

# Plymouth Iron Works.

---

THE early history of these Works is attended with some little uncertainty. It would seem that Anthony Bacon was not the original lessee, but was possessed of them, when he died, by virtue of an assignment from the original lessees from the Earl of Plymouth, namely, Isaac Wilkinson and John Guest.

It is stated in a Case before us that, in exercise of a power contained in a deed dated December 14th, 1763, between the Right Hon. Lewis Windsor Hickman, Earl of Plymouth, of the one part, and Isaac Wilkinson and John Guest of the other part, it was intended to erect and build on some part of the lands and estates of the said Earl, situate in the parishes of Merthyr Tydfil and Aberdare, in the County of Glamorgan, or one of them, certain furnaces, forges, mills, pothouses and works, for making and manufacturing of iron.

And the Case also states that most of the lands of the said Earl were held by lease for one, two, or three lives, the veins of iron ore and coal being excepted and reserved to the Earl.

Under these circumstances, Messrs. Wilkinson and Guest had promised to agree with some one of the Earl's tenants for the interest, or for liberty and licence to erect and build on the said lands such furnaces, forges, iron-works, as they should think necessary; and in consideration thereof the said Earl agreed to grant a lease of the same for ninety-nine years; and also for the better accommodation of the Works the said Earl had procured a lease of the river Taff from New Bridge up the said river, as far as the lordship of Senghenith extended, with liberty to erect weirs to divert the said river for the use of any furnace or forge to be erected.

And also that the said Earl, for the better carrying on of the iron-works, had agreed to grant them liberty of digging and raising and carrying away coal or iron ore under such land, except any coal or iron ore granted by his ancestors, said coals and ore raised to be consumed in such furnaces, forges, and iron-works, the term to be ninety-nine years, from May 1st, 1765, at the annual rent of £60.

We had written thus far, when a copy of the original counterpart lease was sent us by the courtesy of Mr. R. Forrest, with the permission of Lord Windsor, and we subjoin so much of it as is material to our history of these Works:—

This Indenture, made December 14th, 1763, Between The Right Honourable Other Lewis Windsor Hickman, Earl of Plimouth, of the one part, and Isaac Wilkinson, of Plasgruns, in the parish of Wrexham, in the County of Denbigh, Ironmaster, and John Guest, of the parish of Broseley, in the County of Salop, Ironmaster, of the other part. Whereas the said Isaac Wilkinson and John Guest intend shortly to erect and Build on some part of the lands and Estate of the said Earl of Plimouth, situate in the several parishes of Merthir Tidvil and Aberdare, in the County of Glamorgan, or in one of them, certain ffurnaces, fforges, Mills, pothouses, or other Works for the making and Manufacturing of Iron.

And whereas all or most part of the lands and Tenements and Estate of the said Earl of Plimouth in the said parishes are now held by Lease for one, two, or three lives, determinable on certain terms of years not yet expired, out of which leases, or the greatest part thereof, the veins of Iron Oar, and Coal are excepted and reserved to the said Earl of Plimouth and his heirs.

And whereas the said Isaac Wilkinson and John Guest have taken upon themselves and promised to Contract and agree with some or one of the Tenants of the said Earl of Plimouth for their interest or term, or for liberty or license to erect and Build on some or one of their lands or Tenements such ffurnaces or fforges or other Ironworks as the said Isaac Wilkinson and John Guest shall think proper or necessary; and the said Earl of Plimouth hath in consideration thereof agreed to confirm and corroborate such agreement, and to grant a term of 99 years on such lands on which such ffurnaces, fforges, or Ironworks shall be so erected, on the rents, payments, and conditions hereinafter specifyed.

And whereas the said Earl of Plimouth, for the better accommodation of the said Ironworks, hath lately taken a Lease from the Right Honourable Alice, Lady Viscountess Dowager Windsor, of the ffishery of the river Taff, in the County of Glamorgan aforesaid, from the bridge there called New Bridge up the said river as far as the Lordship of Senghenith Extends, with liberty to erect any wears in the said rivers to divert the river Taff to the use of any Ffurnaces or fforges to be erected on the lands or Estate of the said Earl of Plimouth, and to convert the stones there found to the use of the said wears or works.

And whereas the said Earl of Plimouth hath also agreed for the better carrying on of the said Ironworks to Grant unto the said Isaac Wilkinson and John Guest the liberty of Digging, raising, and carrying away any Coal or Iron Oar which can or may be found in or under any of the lands, Tenements, or Estate of the said Earl of Plimouth, situate in the said several parishes of Merthir Tidvil and Aberdare, in the said County of Glamorgan, except such Coal or Iron Oar as may be held by any former Grant or Lease granted heretofore by ancestor or predecessor of the said Earl of Plimouth, and in such case only from and after the expiration of such Lease, and so as such Coal and Oar so to be raised and carryed away, be made use of, applyed, and consumed in such ffurnaces, fforges, and Iron Works so to be erected on the lands and Estate of the said Earl of Plimouth, and not elsewhere or otherwise whatsoever.

Now this Indenture witnesseth that the said Earl of Plimouth, in pursuance of the said agreement and in consideration of the costs, charges, and expenses which the said Isaac Wilkinson and John Guest must necessarily expend and be at in the erecting, finishing, and compleating such Iron Works, and in consideration of the rents, covenants, payments, conditions, provisoes, and agreements herein-after mentioned, and which on the part and behalf of the said Isaac Wilkinson and John Guest, their Exo'rs, Adm'ors, and assigns, are to be paid, done, and performed, Hath demised, granted, and to ffarm let and set, and by these presents,

Doth demise, grant, and to ffarm let and set unto the said Isaac Wilkinson and John Guest, their Ex'ors, Adm'ors, and assigns, The power, liberty, priviledge, and license to set up, erect, and build in and upon any part or parts of the Lands, Tenements, or Estate of the said Earl of Plimouth, situate in the said several parishes of Merthir Tidvil and Aberdare, in the said County of Glamorgan (having first procured for that purpose the assent of the Tenants of such lands and made proper satisfaction to them for their term and interest in the same), such and so many ffurnaces, fforges, Mills, Engines, Storehouses Coal-houses, Yards, Courts, edifices, and buildings for the placing and keeping of Oar, Coal, Coak, and Charcoal, and the making and manufacturing of Iron as the said Isaac Wilkinson and John Guest, their Ex'ors, Adm'ors, or assigns, shall think it proper and convenient.

And also full and free liberty of erecting any wear in the said River Taff, and conveying and diverting the water of the said River Taff, or any other water or waters, Brook or Brooks, as are belonging to any lands or Estate of the said Earl of Plimouth, to the use of such Ironworks so to be erected by the said Isaac Wilkinson and John Guest, their Ex'ors, Adm'ors, and Assigns, as aforesaid, and for that purpose to make such and so many channels, Sluices, Dams, ponds, pondheads, stanks, and wears as they shall think fit, with full and free liberty, license, and authority to and by the said Isaac Wilkinson and John Guest, their Ex'ors, Adm'ors, or assigns, to bore, try, search, work for, raise, and land all such coals and culm, Iron oar, and Iron mine as shall or may be found, or are now open in, upon, or under all or any of the lands, Tenements, or Estate of the said Earl of Plimouth, situate in the several parishes of Aberdare and Merthir Tidvil, and whereof no lease is now subsisting; and if such Lease is subsisting, then only from the expiration thereof and for the purpose aforesaid, to dig and sink all such pitts, groves, levells, aditts, drains, shafts, trenches, channels, and other works whatsoever, as shall be thought necessary or convenient to the working thereof.

Yielding and paying each and every year the clear yearly rent of £60, free from all rates, taxes impositions, and deductions whatsoever, etc.

Except and always reserved out of this demise and grant unto the said Earl of Plimouth, his heirs and assigns, all Coal, Culm, Iron Oar and Iron Mine, Clay, and sand, and all quarries of stone and slate which shall be over and above supplying the said Iron Works, and all veins of mines of Tin, Lead, Copper, and all other mines and minerals whatsoever, and all springs of salt, brine, and copperas, and all veins of marl, peat, and turf. To have and to hold all and singular the powers, priviledges, and authoritys aforesaid unto the said Isaac Wilkinson and John Guest, and their Ex'ors, from May 1st, 1765, For and during and unto the full end and term of 99 years from thence next ensuing, and fully to be compleat and ended.

(Signed and witnessed.)

Endorsement on deed. Dated 14th December, 1763.

EARL OF PLIMOUTH
to
Messrs. WILKINSON and GUEST,
Plimouth Company.

Counterpart of Lease
of the
Ironworks in Glamorganshire.

For 99 years, from 1st May, 1765, at £60, and to commence from 1st May, 1765, payable on 1st Nov. and 1st May in each year. Expires in 1864.

There was, however, great difficulty in obtaining possession of the lands of the long-leasehold tenants, and it is not clear from our papers whether Wilkinson and Guest ever succeeded in doing so, and whether the Plymouth Furnace was built by them. It would seem that, on finding such difficulties in their path, they assigned all their interests to Mr. Anthony Bacon, and that the first Plymouth Furnace was erected by him.

We have as yet been unable to find the date and particulars of this assignment, but that such was made is beyond question; and also the fact that Anthony Bacon died possessed of the Plymouth Furnace, and of the interests in the Plymouth lease.

[It may be noted that the Plymouth lease extended to the parish of Aberdare, and a question arose at a later period between Mr. Thomas Bacon and the Earl of Plymouth's guardians as to what his powers were as devisee of Anthony Bacon.]

The Plymouth Works were, prior to Anthony Bacon's time, even if they existed, quite small in extent, but having an abundant and powerful water supply in the river Taff, the situation possessed special advantages.

It will be seen by a reference to Mr. Bacon's will that these Works were left to his second (natural) son, Thomas; and we have also stated that the complexities of the case were such, that it was the wish of all parties to place the estate in the Court of Chancery until the children attained their majorities, as fixed by the will.

An application being made to the Court, and granted, it followed that guardians were appointed for the children, and a receiver, Mr. William Bacon (brother of Anthony, deceased, and natural uncle to his children), was selected, with instructions to let on lease the various iron-works during the minority of the children to whom these Works respectively were left by will.

Mr. Richard Hill had been the trusted agent of the late Anthony Bacon, and was further the one of the executors who had proved the will, and on his applying to the Receiver for a lease of the Plymouth Works, it was, no doubt, readily granted.

The lease was as follows:—

## LEASE OF PLYMOUTH FURNACE.

### William Bacon, Receiver in Chancery, to Richard Hill, 1788.

This Indenture, made May 9th, 1788, between William Bacon, of Thavies Inn, London, Gentleman, Receiver of the Rents and of the Estates in Question in a Cause now depending in the High Court of Chancery, between Anthony Frankland, otherwise Addison, otherwise Bacon, Thomas Smith and others, Infants, by the sd. Wm. Bacon, their next Friend, Plts., and Elizabeth Bacon, Spinr., and others, Defts., of the one part; and Richd. Hill, of Cyfarthfa, in the County of Glamorgan, Gentleman, of the other Part.

Whereas Anthony Bacon, late of Cyfarthfa, in the County of Glamorgan, Esqr., deced., was at the Time of his Death, which happened on or about January 21st, 1786, possessed of sevl. Leasehold Farms and Estates, situate at Cyfarthfa and other Places in the said Countys of Glamorgan and Brecon, where he had erected several Iron Furnaces, and carried on very considerable Iron Works, and one of the sd. Furnaces, called Plymouth Furnace, was erected and worked upon several pieces or Parcels of Land held by the sd. Testator, Anthony Bacon, or his Agents, under different Leases and Agreements, for certain unexpired Terms of years, and subject to sevl. reserved Yearly Rents therein mentioned. And whereas the sd. Anthy. Bacon, by his last Will and Testament in writing, bearing Date on or about June 14th, 1785, gave amongst other things to the sd. Thomas Smith, otherwise Bacon, who is now in the 9th year of his Age, the sd. Furnace called Plymouth Furnace, and the Leases of Lands and Tenements which the sd. Anthy. Bacon held under Lord Plymouth, with all the Royalties of Mine and Coal contained therein, whereon the said Furnace was erected, and all other Buildings and Erections whatsoever on the said premises, and also all the Tools and Implements belonging to the sd. Furnace, and all the Mine and Coals which might be raised for or brought on the Banks of the sd. ffurnace at the Time the sd. Thos. Smith, otherwise Bacon, was to be put in possession of the afsd. bequest, which was to be when he Arrived at the Age of 24 years, and appointed Samuel Glasse, William Stevens, Thos. Harrison, and the sd. Richd. Hill, Exors. of his sd. Will.

And whereas the sd. Anthony Bacon, soon after making and executing his said last Will departed this life without altering or revoking the same, and the said Thomas Harrison and Richd. Hill, two of the Exors. named in the sd. Will, have since duly proved the same in the Prerogative Court of Canterbury, as, in, and by the sd. Will and Probates, reference being thereto had, will more fully appear. And whereas by the sd. Bill brought in the sd. Cause, now depending in the sd. Court of Chancery, it was prayed amongst other things that the will of the sd. Anthy. Bacon might be established, and the Trusts thereof performed and carried into Execution. And whereas, by an Order made in the sd. Cause, bearing Date July 5th, 1786, stating to the effect hereinbefore recited, it was ordered to be referred to Mr. Graves, one of the Masters of the sd. Court, to appoint a proper Person to be Recr. of the Rents and Profits of the Freehold and Leasehold Ests. in question in the sd. Cause, and to allow him a reasonable Salary for his care and Pains therein, such Person so to be appointed Recr. first giving security to be allod. of by the sd. Master duly and annually to account for and pay what he shod. so receive as the Court shod. Direct. And the Tenants of the sd. Ests. were to attorn and pay their Rents in arrear and growing Rents to such Recr., who was to be at Liberty to let and set the sd. Estates with the Approbatn. of the sd. Master as there shod. be Occasion. And whereas, in pursuance of the sd. Order, the sd. Master by his Report of July 27th, 1786, appointed the sd. Wm. Bacon to be Receiver of the Rents and profits of the Estates in Question in the sd. Cause.

And whereas by Anor. Report made in the sd. Cause, bearing Date Decr. 13th, 1786, in pursuance of the sd. Order of July 5th, 1786, the sd. Master after taking Notice of a proposal brought in before him by the sd. Wm. Bacon, the Recr. whereby the sd. Wm. Bacon conceived it would be for the benefit of the Plts., the Infts. entitled to the said ffurnaces under the sd. recited Will as afsd., and those interested in the sd. Testator's Ests. and Effts. to let the same to a Tenant or Tenants for a term of years. at a net annual Rent, and for such Tenants to take the Ore, Coals, Materials, and Stock of each Furnace at a fair valuation; therefore the sd. Recr. proposed that a Lease shod. be granted to the sd. Richd. Hill of the sd. Furnace, called Plymouth ffurnace, from Xmas, 1786, for a Term of 15 years and one half, Subject to the contingencies in the sd. Testator's Will, at and under a net yearly Rent of £650. And also to pay the several yearly Rents amog. to the sum of £268 7*s.*, reserved by the several Leases and Agreements, under which the sd. Anthy. Bacon held the same, and to take the Ore, Materials, and Stock then on and belonging to the sd. ffurnace at a fair Valuation, to be ascertained by Two Persons, one to be named by the sd. Richd. Hill and the other by the sd. Wm. Bacon, the Recr., and to enter into Covenants in the said Lease to carry on and preserve the Works of the sd. Furnace, and to leave the Stock thereon at the Time of the Expiration of the sd. Lease, not exceeding the Value of the Stock then upon and belonging to the same, to be taken at a like Appraisement as afsd. by the Person or Persons who shod. then be entitled to the same, and that the sd. Richd. Hill had offered to take a Lease of the sd. ffurnace, called Plymouth Furnace, on the before-mentd. Terms, upon consideration thereof the sd. Master did by his sd. Report approve of the sd. proposal, and was of opinion that it wod. be proper and for the benefit of Plaintiffs, the Infts., and those interested in the Testors. Este. and effects to grant a Lease to the sd. Richd. Hill of the sd. Furnace, called Plymouth Furnace, from Xmas, 1786, for a Term of 15 years and one half of a year, at the Rents and on the Terms mentd. in the sd. Recers'. proposal respectg. the sd. Furnace, called Plymouth Furnaee, and which sd. last-mentd. Report, by an Order made in the sd. Cause, stands absolutely confirmed as in and by the sd. Bill, Orders, and Reports, reference being thereto respectively had, will more fully Appear.

And whereas, in pursuance of the sd. last-mentd. Report, a fair Valuation hath been made of the Ore, Materials, and Stock, on and belonging to the sd. Furnace, called Plymouth ffurnace, by two Persons, one named by the sd. Richd. Hill and the other by the sd. Wm. Bacon, the Recr., who have valued and appraised the same at the sum of £490 12*s.* 7*d.*, which has been accordingly paid by the sd. Richd. to the sd. Wm. Bacon, the Recr.

This Indenture witnesseth, that in pursuance and Obedience of the sd. sevl. Reports and Orders, and in conson. of the yearly Rent, Covenants, and Agreements hereinafter reserved and contd. on the Part and behalf of the sd. Richd. Hill, his Exors., etc., to be paid, Done, kept, and performed, He the sd. Wm. Bacon, under and by virtue of the Power and Authority in him as Receiver as afsd., by these Presents Doth demise, Lease, etc., to farm lett unto the sd. Richd. Hill, his Exors., etc., All that the sd. Furnace, called Plymouth Furnace, and all those several Pieces of Land whereon the sd. Furnace is erected and worked, situate in the Parish of Merthir Tidvil and Aberdare, in the County of Glamorgan, late in the Tenure or Occupation of the sd. Anthy. Bacon, and now of the sd. Richd. Hill, and also all the Messes or Erections, Buildings, Farm Lands, Tenements, Royalties, Mines, Veins of Coals, Quarries of Stone, and Priviledges held and enjoyed by the sd. Anthy. Bacon with and in working the sd. ffurnace, with their and every of their Appurts., togr. with all Ways, Ponds, Waters, Watercourses, Woods, Priviledges, etc., to the sd. furnace and premes. hereby demised, belonging and enjoyed by the sd. Anthy. Bacon, or which he was entitled to under and by Virtue of the Leases and Agreemts. whereby he held the same, and which said Furnace and premes. hereby demised were given by the Will of the sd. Anthy. Bacon to the sd. Thos. Smith, otherwise Bacon, as aforesaid.

To have and to hold the sd. Furnace, pieces of Land, Messes, Farm Lands, Buildings, and all and singular other the premises hereby demised, etc., with their Appurts., unto the sd. Richd. Hill, his Exors., etc., from Xmas. day, 1786, for and during and unto the full end and Term of 15 years and one half of a year from thence next ensuing, and fully to be compleat and ended, subject nevertheless to the Contingencies in the sd. Will of the sd. Anthy. Bacon, and also to the paymt. of the sevl. yearly Rents reserved in and by the sevl. Leases and Agreements under which the sd. Anthy. Bacon held the same, and to the sevl. Covenants, Reservations, Conditions, etc., therein contained,

Yielding and paying therefore yearly, and every year During the sd. Term hereby granted unto the sd. Wm. Bacon, the Recr., as afsd., and his Assns., or to such other Person or Persons who for the time being shall be entitled to receive the Rents, Issues, and Profits of the sd. premes. hereby demised the clear Yearly Rent or sum of £650 of l'full money of Great Britain, free and clear of and from all Rates, Charges, or deductions whatsoever, on the four sevl. Days of Payment of Rent in the Year herein after mentd., that is to say, March 25th, June 24th, September 29th, and Decer. 25th in each and every Year, by even and equal Portions, the first paymt. thof. to begin and be made on March 25th now next ensuing over and above the sevl. yearly Rents reserved by the sevl. Leases and Agreements under which the sd. Anthy. Bacon held the sd. premes. hereby demised,

And the sd. Richd. Hill doth hereby for himself, his Heirs, etc., covenant and agree with the sd. Wm. Bacon, the Recr. as afsd., and with such other Person or Persons who for the time being shall be entitled to receive the Rents, etc., of the sd. premes. hereby demised, that he the sd. Richd. Hill, his Exors., etc., shall every year during the Term hereby granted well and truly pay unto the sd. Wm. Bacon, the Recr. as afsd., and his Assns., or to such other Person or Persons who for the Time being shall be entitled to receive the Rents and Profits of the demised premes., the sd. clear yearly Rent or sum of £650, free and clear of and from all Charges, Deductions, etc., whatsoever on the sevl. Days and Times, and in manner herein before appointed for payment thereof, And also that he, the sd. Richd. Hill, his Exors., etc., shall during the sd. Term hereby granted, pay and Discharge all Rates, etc., which shall at any time be charged or assessed on the said demised premises, either by the authority of Parliament or otherwise.

Further covenant on part of the said Richard Hill, his exors., etc., to save harmless the said William Bacon, and the Exors. of the said Anthony Bacon, in respect of all agreements and leases entered into by the said Anthony Bacon.

Further covenant on the part of the said Richard Hill, his exors., etc., to uphold and repair the premises, and to deliver up the same in good repair.

Provision for entry to view state of repair.

And the sd. Richd. Hill doth hereby for himself, his Heirs, Exors., etc., further Covenant and agree with the sd. Wm. Bacon, the Recr. as afsd., and such other Person or Persons who for the Time being shall be entitled to the sd. premes. hereby demised, that he, the sd. Richd. Hill, his Exors., etc., shall from Time to Time and at all Times hereafter during the Continuance of the sd. Term hereby granted, to the Uttmost of his and their power, well and sufficiently carry on, work, preserve, and support the Works of the sd. Furnace, and every part thereof. And also shall, at the expiration of the sd. Term hereby granted, leave Ore, Coals, Materials and Stock of the sd. Furnace on the sd. demised premes., not exceeding the Value of the sum of £490 12s., to be taken and paid for by the Person or Persons who shall then be entitled to the sd. demised premes. at a fair valuation and appraisment, to be ascertained by two persons, one to be named by the sd. Richd. Hill, his Exors., etc., and the other by the Person or Persons who shall then be entitled to the sd. demised premes.

Usual covenant for re-entry by Receiver on rent being in arrear.

Lastly, covenant by Richd. Hill not to sublet without leave given in writing, or if subletting should take place, then power of re-entry by Receiver.

In witness, etc.,

---

About the year 1794, Mr. Richard Hill had very serious trouble with the Glamorganshire Canal Navigation, then recently opened, for improperly, as he said, taking the water he required for his Plymouth Works, and had a right to. Mr. Hill, junr, aged twenty, took an active part in this, closing or shutting the sluices communicating between the Canal and the mill-race, according to his father's directions, when required. This the lock-keeper, named William Williams, resisted, and hence, on the 1st August, 1794, a desperate encounter took place between them on the canal bank. Mr. Hill was victorious, but his opponent being seriously hurt, brought an action against him at the Glamorgan Great Sessions, and obtained substantial damages.

However, at the ensuing Great Sessions—a Bill having been previously filed in the Chancery Court—Mr. Hill, senior, brought an action against the same Canal Company. claiming £2,000 damages, for injury to the Plymouth Works, by the cutting off their usual supply of water from the river Taff.

The Attorney-General of the Great Sessions, Mr. Nichol, and Mr. Hughes, were counsel for Mr. Hill, the plaintiff, and the brief of his counsel is now before me, with an elaborate plan of the Plymouth Weir on the Taff river, the canal locks, the overflow weir, and tail-races, cuts, etc.; and the plan was supplemented at the trial by a model, which the Attorney-General explained to the jury and Court. The case resulted in Mr. Hill obtaining a verdict in his favour, with £300 damages.

On a recent visit to the Merthyr district, I made a special point of seeing the head of the famous Glamorganshire Canal. I found, to my surprise, it had fallen into complete disuse: not a vestige of a canal boat was to be seen, and the water supply turned off into the river! Very little more than one hundred years have been long enough to bring about this marvellous change from high dividends and great prosperity to absolute ruin. A hundred years, I thought, can do much!

Then I had a good look at No. 3 Lock—Parliament Lock, as it is called—a copy of the Canal Act having been kept there for public reference. Here it was the battle-royal raged on that August day between Mr. Hill, junr., and the lock-keeper, and round this famous lock suit after suit at law was maintained; and it is obvious that the difficulties were immense to find sufficient water in summer time both for the mills at Plymouth and for a large trade through the canal lock. Several special contrivances were used, such as a sluice leading back to the river from Half-Chamber Lock. All the troubles are now, however, at an end; and on the day of my visit the water in the lock was green and stagnant, and the massive lock gates had not apparently turned upon their hinges for months past!

Mr. Hill appears to have thought it desirable to increase the extent of the mineral property attached to the Works, and during his tenure of the property, added what appears to be considerable properties—at least in number—to the original taking, such being in his own name, and held on long leases, extending in duration far beyond that of the lease granted to him by the Court of Chancery.

Similarly, with the view of permanently providing for a supply of limestone to his furnaces for fluxing purpose, Mr. Richard Hill entered into an agreement, or contract, dated February, 1795, with Mr. Richard Crawshay, of Cyfarthfa, for the long term of sixty-six years.

The stone was to be quarried in the limestone rocks in Graig y Gwinos, and being "good and proper furnace limestone," was to be delivered by Mr. Crawshay on the side of the railroad at the canal warehouse at the price of 1*s.* 9*d.* per ton long weight, as accustomed at furnaces, from time to time, on reasonable notice.

The agreement was entered into subject to Mr. Crawshay retaining his right and interest in the limestone rocks named, or in any other limestone rocks.

And he also entered into a contract to deliver a larger quantity of pig-iron annually to Mr. Crawshay (p. 56).

In 1799, when Mr. Thomas Bacon became twenty-one years of age, he granted a lease, which he subsequently confirmed, when his minority fully terminated, and he became twenty-four years of age in 1803, for sixty-four years of all his interest in the leases from the Earl of Plymouth and in the Plymouth Works on payment of £815 per annum rent to the Earl of Plymouth, and to Mr. Bacon of £1,262 for 2,000 tons of pig-iron, and 5*s.* per ton for every additional ton of pig-iron made in the year.

And about the same time, being now fully possessed of the property, Mr. Richard Hill and his son entered into an agreement with the Dowlais and Penydarran Companies for the construction of a tram-road for the joint use of the three Works in conveying their iron to the Glamorganshire Canal. The agreement is dated 1799, but the particulars of it are not given in our papers. But it was the subject of an arbitration at a later date by Mr. Richard Blakemore, of Melingriffith in 1809, the terms of which we now give.

---

## THE TRAM ROAD AGREEMENT.

### The Arbitration.

Questions having arisen between the Dowlais, the Penydarran, and the Plymouth Companies as to the interpretation to be placed on the terms of the Agreement, I. I. Guest, Samuel Homfray, and Richard Hill, on behalf of their respective Companies, entered into bonds to submit the dispute to the Arbitration of Mr. Richard Blakemore (M.P. for Wells), the Ironmaster, of Melin Griffith Works and Monmouth Forge.

The following is his Award:—

The following Question having been refer'd to me by Messrs. Hills and the Penydarran and Dowlais Companies, vizt. —

"Whereas a difference has arisen between Messrs. Hills and the Penydarran and Dowlais Companies respecting the Distance they ought to pay for their Iron, it is agreed that the Question be left to R. Blakemore, Esq., who is to take into consideration the spirit of the Agreement of the 18th January, 1799, and the subsequent conduct of all parties as explanatory thereof; and if Mr. Blakemore should not accept it, or should not make an Award before the 1st of February, then to be left to two persons, one to be chosen by each Party.

"And having accepted of the Reference and heard and fully considered all that the Parties have chosen to offer in support of their several Pretensions,

"I do now declare :—

"That it appears to me that, however ambiguous the words of the Agreement of the 18th January, 1799, are as touching the Question at issue, and under whatever difficulties I might have found myself in bringing the consideration of it within the Provisions of that Agreement, yet I think the subsequent Conduct of the Parties, which I am specially directed to have regard to, has put a practical construction upon it, which in a great degree divests it of ambiguity or difficulty; and enables me, therefore, in a satisfactory manner to make up my Mind upon the subject refer'd to me, and I accordingly award as follows :—

"That Messrs. Hills do pay to the Tram Road Company Tonnage upon all the Iron made at the Plymouth Furnaces in the state or process of manufacture in which it is sent away from those Works, viz., as Finers' Metal, for what is made into and delivered as Finers' Metal, Pig Iron, or Castings, etc., for what is delivered in those states.

"And that the Distance for which such Tonnage be paid be for the Tram Road Distance (as formerly acted upon) between the Furnaces and Forge. And that Tonnage be paid by Messrs. Hills to the Tram Road Company upon all Iron made at or delivered from the Forges in the state or process of manufacture in which it is sent away from thence, whether as Puddlers' Bar or Bar Iron, etc.

"And that the Distance for which such Tonnage be paid be for the Tram Road distance (as formerly acted upon) from the Forges to the Basin.

"Dated at Melin Griffith, January 16th, 1809.

("Signed) Richd. Blakemore."

(Original document in our possession.)

---

In 1807, Mr. Richard Hill, who was a good practical engineer, and accustomed to tram-road making, arranged with the Dowlais Company and the Penydarran Company to lay down a tram-road of 4 ft. 2 in. gauge, from a point, where it was already laid of that width, to the lime rocks at Castle Morlais, for their joint use on the terms stated in the following Memorandum of Agreement.

Memorandum, 22nd June, 1803.

It is agreed and determined to lay a Tram Road of the Width of the Road already laid (4ft. 2 in.) from where it is already laid of that width to the Lime Rock at Castle Morlais, the present Road to remain on the inside of the Wide Road, and kept in repair. R. Hill is to be allow'd £150 for making and laying the Wide Road on having what Materials are already prepared, and the Rails delivered on the Road. The whole Road to be completed by the 25th Decr., 1803, and what plates each party may have furnished more than their proportion to be paid for the same by the Treasurer at six pounds sixteen shillings and 6*d*. p. ton Long Wt. On the 25th Decr., 1803, the Accots. to be settled and the Capital of each party adjusted, after which the Repairs of the Road and all Expences to be paid from the Tonnage arising upon the Road, Provided the Tonnage is sufficient; if not, to be paid in the proportions as hitherto by each party. The Rails that are laying on the narrow Road to Calon-ucha to be considered as part of Messrs. Homfray's proportion. The Narrow Road to be considered as part of the General Road, and kept in repair as such. Proper Articles of partnership to be drawn and executed at Xmas next.

SAML. HOMFRAY,
For Jere. Homfray and Co.

WM. TAITT,
For Dowlais Co.

RICHD. HILL and SON.

Exd., ANTHONY HILL.

(Original document in our possession.)

The Plymouth Company were, it will be seen, good friends with all their neighbouring Works, unless we make one slight exception. This was the dispute as to a tip of cinders with which the Penydarran Company had covered the Rector of Merthyr's (Mr. Maber) glebe field. Under a supposed lease from the Rector, Mr. Hill began to cart away the cinders to be re-melted at their Plymouth Works, but Messrs. Homfray soon stopped that by tipping a quantity of rubbish over the cinders! The aid of the law was invoked, but the whole of this very small affair soon ended. What has become of the Rector's glebe land, and whether it is recognisable and capable of identification to-day, is another matter.

---

Having, probably, a very small capital to start with, and many additions and improvements of and to the Works becoming necessary, Mr. Richard Hill sought the assistance of partners in obtaining financial support, and he found them in Mr. Struttle and Mr. Miers, his own son-in-law; and it was also resolved to add his son, Mr. Richard Hill, junior, who had taken an active part in the management of the Works, as a fourth partner.

The following heads of Agreement for Partnership were then drawn up (to be followed by a formal deed executed by them) :—

1803, May 5th.—Heads of Partnership Agreement of this date between Mr. Richard Hill, Mr. Amos Struttle, Mr. John Natl. Miers, and Mr. Richd. Hill, Junr., whereby they agreed to enter into Partnership for 21 years, from 24th June then next, under the Title of the Plymouth Forge Company, and to be conducted under the Firm of Hill, Struttle, Miers, and Hill.

The Capital was to be £20,000, three-fourths, or £15,000, to be advanced by Mr. Struttle, and one-fourth, or £5,000, by Mr. J. N. Miers; any further advance, if found necessary, to be made by parties in proportion to shares in concern.

Messrs. Richd. Hill and Son to be paid by the Company the annual Rent of £500, in consideration whereof they agree to grant a Lease for 21 years of all such quantity of land as shall be necessary for erecting all such Buildings, Shops, Warehouses, Workmen's and other houses, as shall be found requisite, together with the liberty to cut and make all necessary Watercourses, Roads, or other Conveniences as shall be found necessary for the Works to be 1st erected, as well as for any further extension of them as may afterwards be mutually agreed upon; with full liberty to raise Coal, Stone, Clay, or Sand for the use of the Works, either upon the Lands first set out, or in case a sufficient supply cannot then be found, then upon any other lands they (Rd. Hill and Son) may have the power of doing so where they shall point out, without any further payment for the same beyond the £500 mentioned. The Rent not to commence until the Forge and Mill begin to Work.

In case the Works shall become unprofitable, and not capable of being carried on to advantage, the Term and Rent to cease, and the whole Stock to be Valued and the moveable part thereof sold, and the fixed part thereof to be taken by Richd. Hill and Son at such Valuation, payable in 5 years by equal annual instalments, with Interest, each partner bearing loss according to his Share.

The Capital to be advanced as fast as may be thought eligible to complete the Erection, and on completion of the Works the whole Capital to be deposited as forthcoming.

Richd. Hill and Son engage to find a sufficient supply of Coal for the Works, Workmen, and all other purposes of the Works, from Lands Richd. Hill and Son may have a power to do so, the Coal to be raised and carried at the expense of the Company, but R. Hill and Son to be paid 9*d.* p. ton (the ton to consist of 21 hundred, and each cwt. of 120 lbs. for every ton so raised and carried).

The Works and Buildings to be erected necessary and sufficient to work up the Metal produced from the present three blast-furnaces at Plymouth, the whole of which it is agreed shall be delivered to the Company, either in Castings necessary in the future consumption of the Works, such as Rolls, Hammers, etc. (except such castings as said Rd. Hill and Son may want for their own use), the remainder to be delivered in run-out Metal at the Forge, the Price to be regulated by the Price Bar Iron has sold for, deducting therefrom all the expences from the Works, which of course leaves the net price at the Works; One moiety of that remainder to be the price of Run-out Metal.

| | | £ s. d. |
|---|---|---|
| Thus the present price in London or elsewhere being £16 p. ton | | 16 0 0 |
| *Deduct* Carriage from the Works to Cardiff | 0 10 0 | |
| Loading and Charges at Do. | 0 5 0 | |
| Insurance | 0 5 0 | |
| Freight to London or elsewhere | 1 5 0 | |
| Lighterage, Landing, etc. | 0 10 0 | |
| Commission | 0 10 0 | |
| | | 3 5 0 |
| Present net price at the Works per Ton | | £12 15 0 |

a moiety of which will be £6 7*s.* 6*d.* for the present price of Run-out Metal per ton.

The amount of the Run-out Metal to be paid by the Company to Rd. Hill and Son at the end of every 3 months, by Bills at 3 months, payable in London. For the first year, the price to be paid shall be £7 per ton till the price of that year shall be ascertained as above, and in all future years the amount to be paid every 3 months shall be the price of the preceding year till the price from the Accounts of the year can be adjusted, when the difference upon the whole year shall be determined and paid or received as the price of that year shall turn out to be greater or less than the amount paid. And in like manner before explained, the Price of Run-out Metal shall continue to be determined. If Bar Iron is sold Long Wt., Rd. Hill and Son shall be paid Long Wt. for the Run-out Metal, or if sold Short Weight, then they shall be paid short weight.

Rd. Hill and Son shall supply all necessary Castings to be used in the Erection of the Works at the price of £8 per Ton long wt., other castings that shall be afterwards wanted for the use of the works, or any further extension of them, shall be charged at the same price with Run-out Metal, determined as above. Hammers and Rolls if needful to be cast from an Air furnace. Rd. Hill and Son engage to be the purchasers of all old and broken Castings at a price which shall be £2 p. ton less than the price of new Castings.

Rd. Hill and Son agree to secure and allow to the Company the use of the Rail Road now made, and which passes within 100 yards of the proposed situation of the intended Work, the Company paying Rd. Hill and Son $1\frac{1}{2}$*d.* p. Ton per Mile on Manufactured Iron, and 1*d.* per ton per Mile on all rough Articles, as Wood, Stone, Clay, Coal, Sand, the above not to apply in case Rd. Hill and Son shall enter into any Compromise with the Canal Company, they, Rd. Hill and Son, engaging not to give up the said rail-way without securing to the Forge Co. a right of way along it, and guaranteeing to the Forge Co., and that the amount of rates upon the rail-way and Canal Collectively shall not exceed the amount of rates upon the Canal and rail-way now paid Collectively, and as the Tonnage shall be from time to time regulated by the rail-way and Canal Compy. The Management of all the Erections and Works, as well as the future conduct of them, to be under the Direction of Rd. Hill, Junr., at a Salary of £400 per annum, to be continued for the first 5 years, but after that period he shall be at liberty to resign the conduct of them on giving 1 Month's notice.

The profit and loss of the concern to be divided or borne in the following manner (vizt.) :—

Rd. Hill, three-eighths
Mr. Struttle, three-eighths
Mr. Miers, one-eighth
Rd. Hill, Junr, one-eighth
} eight-eighths.

The interest of the Capital shall be paid before any Division of Profits, which division for the first 5 years shall not exceed £125 a share of one-eighth, and after the first five years not to exceed £250 a Share one-eighth without the general consent of the parties.

No extension or increase of the Works to be made during the last 6 years of term without all parties' consent.

In case of death of Struttle before end of term, his or his Executor's interest should only continue to the end of the Year in which he should happen to die, but if that event happened within 1st 6 years of Term, then the Stock and all kinds of Implements, Buildgs., and Machinery should be valued by two indifferent persons, whose determination should be final, and his part of the then valued Capital should be paid in the following manner by five yearly and equal payments, with interest at £5 per cent. on amount unpaid till the whole shall be discharged.

But in case of Struttle's death after expiration of 6 years, or on determination of Partnership at end of 21 years, beyond such valuation it was agreed that further sum of £1,000 should be paid by Rd. Hill and Son to Struttle in respect of his interests in Workmen, Customers, etc., commonly termed the Goodwill of the Works and business; but this last sum of £1,000 not to be paid unless Struttle, surviving the Partnership, enters into an engagement that he will not enter into any manufacture of Bar Iron for the space of 2 years after the expiration of the said Term of 21 years.

Mr. Miers to be paid £250 on the same Terms.

All Drafts or Bills to be drawn by Rd. Hill, Junr., who was to be Cashier, and all Books to be open for the inspection of Partners. All Accounts to be made up to Midsummer of each year, or within 2 months afterwards.

In case of dispute—Arbitration. The Rent Salary and Royalty of 9*d.* per Ton on the Coal to be paid half-yearly.

Lastly, it was agreed by all Parties that during Partnership they would not engage in similar concerns; those already engaged in not to be considered.

Rd. Hill and Son to be paid an amount to be agreed upon as an equivalent for the damages that may be done to their lands before the Rent commences. The interest on the Capital to be paid half-yearly.

In case of death of Rd. Hill, Senr., J. N. Miers, or Richd. Hill, Junr., this Agreement to extend to their exors. and admors.; and if Struttle and Miers should continue in the concern till the expiration of the term, the Capital of each was then to be paid by R. Hill and Son.

In 1806, Mr. Richard Hill the elder having died, it became necessary to make an arrangement under his will in family matters, and the parties to it are Richd. John Hill, his eldest son; John Hill, of London, another son; Anthony Hill, of Plymouth, youngest son, Mary Hill, the widow of Richd. Hill; Elizabeth Hill, his daughter; and John Nathaniel Miers, of Cadoxton Lodge, Glamorgan, and Mary his wife (the other and youngest daughter of said Richd. Hill).

But it is not necessary to refer to this deed at any length.

By the year 1813, the firm had undergone several changes: Mr. Richard Hill, senior, was, as we have seen, dead; Mr. Struttle and Mr. Miers had seceded, and the partners were now the three brothers, Richard John Hill, John Hill, and Anthony Hill; and from various causes the Works had become indebted to Messrs. Wilkins and Co., of Brecon, in the large sum of £54,000; and hence, Bankers naturally requiring security for advances, a formal mortgage deed was executed.

About 1820, Mr. Anthony Hill (one of the sons above) became the Managing Partner, and the Works were carried on with great vigour and ability; and it is said that the brand of bar-iron made at these Works had a special value, and was known for its excellence throughout the world.

On 26th August, 1826, Mr. John Hill sold all his interest in the Works to his brothers, Richard and Anthony, and the Agreement of that date was entered into, of which the following, so far as material facts are concerned, is a summary:—

1826, August 26th.—By Agreement of this date, made between Richard Hill and Anthony Hill, one part; and John Hill, other part. John agreed to sell to his Brothers, Richard and Anthony, All the property and interest he possessed in Firm of R. J. and A. Hill.

In consideration of which the two Brothers agreed to pay him an Annuity of £3,000 per annum and a sum of £10,000 to his Heirs, etc., after his death, the annuity to be by quarterly instalments of £750 by Bills of not more than 3 months, the first payment on 1st January, the £10,000 to be payable 5 years after death of John Hill, with interest from death to payment at 5 per cent. per ann. The two Brothers also agreed to make arrangements for payment to him immediately of £2,000 or £2,500, which sums to be deducted from annuity, amounting to sufficient to liquidate same in two years from date.

Dissolution to be gazetted. Jones and Powell to draw documents.

Signed by all Parties.

---

Probably, however, the large standing debt due to Messrs. Wilkins, the bankers, was hard to wipe off; and from that and other reasons it was resolved to put up the Works for sale in July, 1834, then called the Plymouth and Dyffryn Works.

The particulars of sale shortly given are as follows:—

The Property offered for sale by
Winstanley and Sons, at the Auction Mart, London,
On Friday, 4th July, 1834, at 12.

The lawyers were Mr. Scadding, of 1, Gordon Street, Gordon Square, and Messrs. Jones and Powell, of Brecon.

Seven well-constructed Blast Furnaces, capable of making 500 Tons per week of Pig Iron, with Bridge Houses, Cast Houses, Mine Kilns, Coke Yards, etc., attached.

Thirteen Running-out Fineries, Foundry, with Air Furnaces, Cupola, Stoves, Crane, Carpenter's Shops, Smith's Shops, etc. All in excellent Repair.

Of these Blast Furnaces, Four are situate at Plymouth, and Three at Duffrin; to the former the Blast is supplied by means of two Water Wheels about 8 feet wide, each with a head and fall of 28 feet, supplied by the River Taff; and to the latter by a Water Wheel of 14 feet wide, with a head and fall of 24 feet, supplied by the same water, and also by a Double power Steam Engine, the Steam Cylinder of which is 52½ inches, and the Blowing Cylinder 122 inches in diameter, with a stroke of 8 feet.

## THE VALUABLE MINES

Of Coal and Iron Stone lie under upwards of Eleven Hundred Acres of Land, the greater part of which are worked by Level and amply sufficient for the supply of the Works. There are also abundant Supplies of Lime Stone, Hearth Stone, Sand Stone, Fire Clay, and other Materials necessary for an Iron Work, together with Counting Houses, Agent's Houses, Warehouses, Stabling for 150 Horses, and about 200 Workmen's Houses. The whole being in good Repair.

## THE PLYMOUTH PREMISES,

Containing 500 Acres of Mineral Ground, are held of Thomas Bacon, Esq., as Lessee of the Earl of Plymouth, for a term of years, of which 32 Years are unexpired, on payment to Lord Plymouth of about £815 per annum, and to Mr. Bacon of £1,262 for 2,000 Tons of Pig Iron, and *5s.* per Ton for every additional Ton of Pig Iron made in the course of the year.

## THE DUFFRIN PREMISES,

With Pentrebach and Abercannaid Farms and Lands, containing 450 Acres of Mineral Ground, are held of Thomas Thomas, Esq., for a term of years, of which 80 Years are unexpired, at an annual rent of £1,360. Part of the Minerals, containing about 160 Acres, are held under Lease from Mr. William David, for an unexpired Term of 27 Years, at the annual rent of £250. There are also reserved Rents payable for the same term as the Plymouth premises are held, amounting to about £174 per annum, for the use of Water-courses, Land, Grist Mill, and various other privileges, Rolling Mills and Puddling Forges worked by two Water Wheels, with head and fall of 24 feet, also supplied by the River Taff; one of the Wheels being 10 feet, and the other 6 feet wide, capable of making 300 Tons of finished Bars per week, with the requisite Puddling and Balling Furnaces, Carpenter's Shops, Smith's Shops, Warehouses, etc.

Also Lathe for turning Rolls, worked by one of the Water Wheels.

## A BRICK YARD,

With Clay-wheel, Rolls, Stones, Kiln, etc., amply sufficient for the manufacture of Bricks for the supply of the Works. Also Dwelling-house for the Brickmaker attached.

## A COMMODIOUS MANSION HOUSE

For the residence of the Manager of the Works, with Grounds, Garden, Stabling, Coach-houses, and suitable Offices. The Rolling Mill, Brick Yard, and Mansion House, are included in the Lease of the Duffrin and Pentrebach Premises, being erected on part of the latter property.

The Farm, with suitable Buildings, comprises about 320 Acres of Land in good Cultivation, and is included in the before-mentioned Leases.

There are various Ground Rents belonging to these Works for Land let on Building Leases, which produce about £140 per annum.

The whole of the Premises are compact, and the Buildings and Machinery erected in a substantial manner, on the most improved principle. A Tram Road, four-fourteenths of which belong to these Works, connects them with the Glamorganshire Canal at the Navigation House, about Seven Miles from the Works, from whence the Produce is conveyed for the distance of 17 Miles by Canal to the Port of Cardiff, at a very moderate rate.

---

Whether the property was sold or not my papers do not show, but it certainly did not pass from the possession of the Hill family, for we find up to 1841 the brothers, Richard and Anthony Hill acting as managers of the Works.

Numerous letters of theirs are extant, and it is evident from these that they carried on the Works with great industry and ability, and were able gradually at last to turn the corner financially, and realise large profits.

In 1840 it was resolved to turn the private firm into a company, and a prospectus was issued of the Plymouth, Pentrebach, and Dyffryn Iron Company, with £400,000 capital.

The Plymouth leases had 24 years unexpired; Pentrebach, 74 years; Dyffryn, seventy-four years. The valuation of the Works by Mr. William Needham amounted to £384,000.

The property also included the hematite ore in the neighbourhood of Whitehaven, in Cumberland, held under the Earl of Egremont. The ore was stated to have contained 62 per cent. of iron.

The managing directors of this company were to be Messrs. Richard and Anthony Hill.

Mr. Anthony Hill lived to an old age; and, being possessed of great wealth, is said to have been most kind and liberal to his agents, workmen, and to all in any way connected with him.

---

## RETURN OF IRON FROM THE PLYMOUTH WORKS, CONVEYED BY THE GLAMORGANSHIRE CANAL.

| | Tons. | | Tons. |
|---|---|---|---|
| 1817 | 7,095 | 1829 | 13,534 |
| 1818 | 7,337 | 1830 | 12,177 |
| 1819 | 7,633 | 1831 | 10,498 |
| 1820 | 7,941 | 1832 | 9,200 |
| 1821 | 9,943 | 1833 | 12,093 |
| 1822 | 8,833 | 1834 | 12,073 |
| 1823 | 10,920 | 1835 | 12,631 |
| 1824 | 9,499 | 1836 | 13,573 |
| 1825 | 11,269 | 1837 | 15,353 |
| 1826 | 7,836 | 1838 | 16,143 |
| 1827 | 12,907 | 1839 | 15,762 |
| 1828 | 12,976 | 1840 | 12,922 |

VI.

# The Penydarran Iron Works.

---

THIS is the last of the group of four great Iron-works near to Merthyr Tydfil that we have to notice.

Called Penydarran, the head of the steep bank or rocks, it was situate on the left bank of the brook Dowlais, a little lower than the great Dowlais Works, which it adjoined. The same brook supplied water for the use of both, but the Dowlais being higher up on the stream, and the older-established concern, had the first call and command of its use. The Plymouth Works were, on the other hand, quite away on the low ground on the left of the Taff, where the old corn-mills of early days stood.

With the latter, except in the cinder-tip case, good terms seem always to have existed; while from one cause or another fierce lawsuits, with intervals of peace, raged between Penydarran and their immediate neighbours, the Dowlais Company. After reading the briefs and evidence in three or four great lawsuits, directly or indirectly promoted by the Penydarran Company, they seem to me to have been the aggressors, and in the wrong throughout, and to have deserved to fail, as they appear to have done in nearly every instance.

The circumstances of this position led doubtless to this irritation, and their chief managing partner, Mr. Samuel Homfray, was of a somewhat haughty, masterful character. Their great neighbour had an immense tract of mineral ground—of iron ore and coal—held at a nominal fixed rent, while these smaller Works were very short of coal, and both for that and the iron ore raised, had to pay more than nominal royalties to their ground and mineral landlords. In some cases they were themselves lessees of coal-mining ground from the Dowlais Company, by leases granted when they happened to be good friends. In the Black Ball vein there was a joint user, and the same was the case in the Pwllywhead premises, the Dowlais Company winning the coal and the Penydarran Company winning the iron ore; and besides all other matters, causing petty or serious annoyance, there was the brook Dowlais flowing from the upper ground of the Dowlais Works down to and through their own, with the ever-standing grievances of alleged diversion of its waters, and the fouling and choking of its bed by the tipping of rubbish. We are reminded of the saying of Dr. Marigold, in one of Dickens's tales, that if you share a cart as your abode with your wife, you need to have a wonderfully good temper to get along, anyhow. And in truth these Iron-works were placed too close to each other for practical and convenient working without interference.

Still, though quarrelsome, some admiration must be felt for the plucky fight they made to hold a high position in the iron-mining and iron-making world, with limited means and under adverse circumstances; and in enterprise and skill in conducting their business they had no superiors. They turned out from their Works, for a long series of years, manufactured iron in large quantities, and of the best quality; and Mr. Homfray was quick to avail himself of the inventions of Trevethick, the Cornishman, who made the first steam-engine to travel on the old tramroad, nine miles in length, leading from the Penydarran

Works to the Cardiff Canal. He also engaged the services of another eminent Cornishman—John Petherick, of Camborne.

The first origin of the Penydarran Works was undoubtedly in 1784.

Mr. Francis Homfray, of Wollaston Hall, Worcester, and of Hyde Kinver, in the County of Stafford, himself an ironmaster in one of those counties, and of good family and of ample means, became acquainted with Mr. Anthony Bacon, of Cyfarthfa, in or about 1782, and leased from him a mill for boring cannon, and a foundry at Cyfarthfa, for the term of fifty years. The conditions of the lease have been given previously in our notice of Cyfarthfa Works.

In 1784, however, Mr. Francis Homfray assigned his lease over to Mr. David Tanner, of Monmouth; and presumably he did this for the reason that he intended to establish his three sons in a new Iron-works at Penydarran, on some freehold land then available for the purpose.

Accordingly, two of his sons, Jeremiah the eldest and Samuel the youngest, both describing themselves as then of Cyfarthfa, took a lease of all, and all manner of iron mine and iron ore in, upon, and under the lands of Pwllywhead, in the parish of Merthyr Tydfil, with powers to work the same, from Mr. John Rees, of Merthyr, gentleman; to hold the same for ninety-nine years, at a royalty of 1*s.* for every ton of iron ore raised, such ton to consist of 21 cwt., and every cwt. of 120 lbs.; or if 300 tons were not raised in any one year, the annual rent of £15 was then to be paid. The coal on the taking was expressly excepted, that being already leased to Mr. John Guest, of Dowlais.

About the same time, the Coed Cae Daren, and other small properties, were secured on long leases, and though there was no great landowner or lord of the manor in this instance to lease a great tract of land from, sufficient mineral ground was rented to justify the establishment of an Iron-works.

We may assume that the father, Mr. Francis Homfray, with his experience, really chose the site and laid out the Works, finding the capital, but preferred not to be a partner, but to give his sons a free independent start on their own account, himself being always in the background in reserve to assist and advise when needed.

The first partners, therefore, were his three sons—Jeremiah, Thomas, and Samuel, and the business was commenced in their names, the elder brother Jeremiah and Samuel the younger being the joint managers. Thomas never seems to have taken an active part, but to have returned to his father in Worcestershire, and stayed there. He, however, remained a partner in the Firm, probably representing his father.

This was in 1786 or thereabouts, and in the course of the next six or eight years a pretty little Iron-works, complete in every respect, had been established close to the left bank of the Dowlais brook. We shall give a view of these, from Wood's *Rivers of Wales*, as they appeared in 1813. A commodious mansion-house, called Penydarran House, had also been built on the opposite side of and a little above the Dowlais brook, for the use of the partners.

We shall see later that the brother Jeremiah was on the look-out for fresh fields to conquer, and in 1789 had, with Walter Watkins and Cracroft, started the Ebbw Vale Iron-works. With these in hand it soon became necessary for him to give up his share of the management of the Penydarran Works to his brother Samuel. This he did, but had reason to be sorry for it afterwards, if we may judge from the following letter to his solicitors, our friends, Walter and John Powell, of Brecon:—

"Cardiff, 4th August, 1796.

"Gentlemen,—Having an opportunity by Mr. Wynter, have sent on Articles of Pendarran for your perusal against the time of Mr. J. Powells coming here, when I shall have much to say upon them. The particular advice I want most is respecting the Manager's power over the concern and the control of the Partners over him.

"I must here observe Samuel Homfray is now sole Manager from the circumstance of my resignation.

"Some curious discriminations are made by him upon the Arbitration clause, etc., etc., and we are all sett at defiance, and as he says without any possible remedy. He insists he has a right without our knowledge or consent to lay out our money in whatever he pleases to think is for the benefit of the concern—say in Peach Houses, Fish ponds, Mortgages, Turnpikes, or even cleansing the Thames to sail our Iron to London. Some of the circumstances having happened, I make an objection to signing the Yearly Accounts, upon which he promises me no money till I do, which is not very convenient to a poor man with no other resource. Some remedy to check his unbounded ambition, misapplication of that Power and money he is entrusted with, and procuring a certain income without being obliged to beg it from him, is what I aim at. The mode of doing this in the most delicate manner I shall be glad you'll think of against Mr. J. Powell comes here, that I may be determined when we meet what steps to pursue to make my mind (which is now tormented by his unkind and arbitrary proceedings) more at rest, and procure some necessary provision for myself and family, which I shall very shortly be in want of.

"Meantime, I remain,

"Your most obedt. Servt.,

"JERE. HOMFRAY.

"Messrs. W. & Jno. Powell, Brecknock.

"Whilst writing this letter my friend Wynter has given me the slip. I'm not quite sure whether you have not got a copy of our Articles; if so I'm right in sending this by post. Bring Richd. Thomas's Agreement with you."

There is little doubt that money was quickly got at Penydarran under Samuel Homfray's skilful management, and was spent as freely, and Jeremiah's description of his brother's character is not far from the truth. The celebrated "Lazarus" case is an instance in proof of this: where, after a dinner at Cardiff in 1790, Mr. Samuel Homfray lost £250 at that game of cards to Richard Griffith, Surgeon, of Cardiff, and then refused to pay, alleging that he had been cheated. In this he was confirmed by Mr. John Richards, Jun., of the Corner House, one of the party, who was prepared to swear that the cards were improperly marked by Mr. Griffith, and so used when dealing. To receive the black deuce, the lowest card in the game, was a certain lose on that deal, and Mr. Homfray complained loudly that he was for ever being dealt "that——black deuce!"

And then Mr. Homfray took the strong step of indicting Mr. Griffith at the Hereford Assizes, for an offence against the Statute of 1711, which made it unlawful to play at a game of cards and win any sum above £10 at one sitting. The case, entitled "The King, on the Prosecution of Samuel Homfray against Richard Griffith," came on for trial at the summer assizes at Hereford, 1790, by a special jury. The following counsel were retained on behalf of the prosecution: Messrs. Caldecot, Nichol, Bowen, and Leycester; but their skill was of no avail, and the Jury gave a verdict for the Defendant; no doubt being of opinion that a curious run of bad luck (as we have seen recently in the Australian Cricket Matches) accounted for Mr. Homfray's loss, rather than unfair play.

A few years later—in 1795—the case of Harry *v.* Dowlais Co. was tried at Hereford Assizes, and it was a matter of common knowledge that Mr. Samuel Homfray was the instigator of that unsuccessful action.

All this was *trop de zéle*, and the outcome of superabundant energy; and it was fortunate that in 1800 Mr. Homfray was able to devote some of his spirit to the Tredegar Iron-works, which he then leased in partnership with Richard Fothergill and Matthew Monkhouse from Sir Charles Morgan, Bart. Here was a new field for his energy to be displayed in; and added to this he took to himself a wife, one of the Tredegar family, and also in 1806 issued an address as a candidate for a seat in Parliament for Breconshire against Colonel Wood, of Littleton, and the following is the address which he then issued:—

PENYDARRAN IRON WORKS IN 1813.

*(Wood's Rivers of Wales).*

PAGE 89

GENERAL ELECTION.

To the Gentlemen, Clergy, and Freeholders of the County of Brecon.

Gentlemen,—A dissolution of Parliament having taken place, I beg leave to announce to you the intention which my friends have emboldened me to adopt, of offering myself as a Candidate to represent you in the ensuing Parliament, in the Room of Sir Charles Morgan, Bart. The repeated proofs of your kindness which the Tredegar family (with whom I am so nearly connected) have experienced upon so many occasions, joined to the cordial support so flatteringly tendered to me by my Friends on the approaching Election, give me the greatest hopes of success.

I intended to have honoured myself with a personal attendance upon each of you, had it not been judged equally respectful by the other Candidate as well as by myself, to abstain from a Canvass until the County Meeting should have been held.

I have the honour to be, Gentlemen,
Your obedient and devoted Servant,
Samuel Homfray.

Tredegar, October 26th, 1806.

Mr. Homfray does not, however, appear to have gone further than issuing this address.

The Penydarran Company especially devoted themselves to the manufacture of merchant iron, and bought largely of pig iron from their neighbours, beyond what their own furnaces produced.

On the 23rd January, 1802, we find the following agreement entered into between Joseph Harrison, the then managing partner of the Nantyglo Iron-works, and Mr. Samuel Homfray, the head of the Penydarran Company:—

"Its agreed, that the present price of Merchant Bar Iron at Cardiff, £19. Pig Iron £6. When Bar Iron rises and falls, Pig Iron to rise and fall one-third of the amount. Quality of Pigs to be 1/3 Dark Grey and 1/3 Mottle. When it happens that the Penydarran do not find it their Interest to have the Iron over here, they are to have the Privilege of taking it upon the Bank, deducting the Carriage out, and ordering it to Newport or elsewhere; and if it costs more money carrying it there than to Penydarran, they are to pay the extra charge, but if it costs less, Mr. Harrison to allow it. The quantity to be 15 Tons per week between this and Midsummer next, and 30 Tons per week after for the Term of 21 years, subject to be given up by either party on giving one year's notice previous to the expiration of every seven years.

"Payment at the end of every Quarter by Bills, half at three months and half at five months.

"23rd January, 1802.

"Subject to any exchange that may be made between the Sirhowi and Nantyglo Company for any part of the above quantity for the supply of Langroiney Works.

"(Sd.) Saml. Homfray.
Joseph Harrison."

The luxurious mansion of Mr. Samuel Homfray at Penydarran, of which his brother Jeremiah wrote in terms of despair, is thus described in Wood's *Rivers of Wales*, p. 57.

"The splendid Mansion of Mr. S. Homfray at Penydarren—situated upon a gentle declivity—is sufficiently removed from the town by the extent of the pleasure-grounds, and contains all the conveniences and luxuries requisite for a family of wealth and importance. The gardens, which at first wore the appearance of sterility and barrenness, are now abundantly productive. The hot-houses, grape-houses, etc., furnish their respective fruits in profusion; and walks laid out with taste and judgment present several points, from whence the silver Taff may be seen to great advantage.

"And the singular effect from the numerous fires viewed by night, when the immense columns of flame, the incessant noise of the hammers, and the continued buzz of voices, impresses the mind with a sensation perfectly new. This effect is heightened by a near approach to the Works, where, through a long range of buildings, innumerable human beings are seen busily employed in their various occupations: some stirring the liquid metal in a kind of oven, others drawing heated masses along the ground, and others again carrying bars of red-hot iron, which—as they pass through the rollers—may be compared to the windings of so many serpents. Add to all this the strong reflection of the fire upon the figures covered with the black dirt of the Works, and it will not be surprising that such a scene should recall to the recollection the fabulous description of the infernal regions, and their inhabitants."

And we may be quite certain that Mr. Homfray kept there a most hospitable house: no lack of the best of viands and wines of the best vintages, for his many friends.

Mr. Homfray, though taking a leading part in the management of the Tredegar Iron-works, still continued to manage the Penydarran Works; and not forgetting his old prejudice against the Dowlais Co., accused Mr. Wm. Taitt, one of the partners, of perjury; and Mr. Taitt brought an action against him at the Hereford Assizes, in 1807, with the result of £300 damages being awarded to Mr. Taitt.

And in 1811, when Thomas and Samuel Homfray were both still partners in the Penydarran Works, jointly with William and Henry Forman, the action for fouling the Dowlais brook was brought by them against the Dowlais Co., to which we have referred previously. The language used in the Case prepared in the Brief we have, shows that a terribly bitter feeling then prevailed between the two Companies.

A few years pass, and the Homfray family and also Henry Forman retire from the firm, and Alderman William Thompson, with—I think—Mr. William Forman in partnership, carried on the Works.

We pass on now for a good many years, to 1824-5, when it will be remembered an important action was brought against the Dowlais Company by their Mineral Landlord, the Marquis of Bute.

And it was somewhat remarkable—a singular coincidence, it may be said—that just at that moment the Penydarran again commenced a suit against their neighbours, for interfering with and damaging their mineral workings in an important Level called The Black Ball Level. It thus happened that the Dowlais Company were at the same time confronted with two lawsuits, prosecuted by nominally independent parties, but both contending that the Dowlais Company had been at fault in their mode of conducting their mineral workings.

An Injunction was moved for but not granted. and other proceedings were being instituted, when probably—as in the case of the Marquess of Bute's claims—a settlement was arrived at. As to this, our papers give us, however, no precise information.

It will be seen by the Returns of Iron sent to Cardiff by Canal that the produce of these Works increased year by year, until it amounted in 1840 to 16,130 tons. This was under the proprietorship of Alderman William Thompson & Co.

---

## MEMBERS OF THE PENYDARRAN FIRM IN PARLIAMENT.

[Samuel Homfray issued his Address to the Electors of the County of Brecon on October 26, 1806, in opposition to Col. Thomas Wood, of Littleton, but did not, we believe, go to the Poll.]

On June 19, 1818, Samuel Homfray was elected as Member (with Mr. Richard Benyon) for the Borough of Stafford.

[Alderman William Thompson was also in Parliament, representing the City of London.]

---

RETURN OF IRON, CHIEFLY MANUFACTURED IRON, SENT DOWN THE GLAMORGANSHIRE CANAL TO CARDIFF BY THE PENYDARRAN COMPANY, 1817 TO 1840, INCLUSIVE.

| | | Tons. | | | Tons. |
|---|---|---|---|---|---|
| 1817 | ... | 8,275 | 1829 | ... | 10,085 |
| 1818 | ... | 8,634 | 1830 | ... | 11,744 |
| 1819 | ... | 7,549 | 1831 | ... | 11 819 |
| 1820 | ... | 8,690 | 1832 | ... | 10,582 |
| 1821 | ... | 10,018 | 1833 | ... | 12,150 |
| 1822 | ... | 9,924 | 1834 | ... | 12,752 |
| 1823 | ... | 10,920 | 1835 | ... | 12,634 |
| 1824 | ... | 10,358 | 1836 | ... | 12,537 |
| 1825 | ... | 10,611 | 1837 | ... | 12,834 |
| 1826 | ... | 8,691 | 1838 | ... | 12,707 |
| 1827 | ... | 10,369 | 1839 | ... | 15,540 |
| 1828 | ... | 10,223 | 1840 | ... | 16,130 |

Here end our Notes of the Penydarran Iron-Works.

# General Notes

RELATING TO THE

# Four Great Merthyr Tydfil Iron Works.

DOWLAIS. PLYMOUTH.
CYFARTHFA. PENYDARRAN.

## EXTRACT FROM MALKIN'S "SCENERY OF SOUTH WALES,"

Vol. I, Page 264, 1807.

"Merthyr Tydvil continued a very inconsiderable village till about the year 1755, when the late Mr. Bacon took more notice of the iron and coal mines, with which this tract of country abounds, than they had before excited. For the very low rent of two hundred pounds per annum he obtained a lease of a district, at least eight miles long and four wide, for ninety-nine years. It is to be understood, however, that his right extended only to the iron and coal mines found on the estate, and that he had comparatively a very small portion of the soil on the surface, on which he erected his Works for smelting and forging the iron. He possessed, in addition, some fields for the keep of his horses, and other necessary conveniences. He at first constructed one furnace; and little besides this was done, probably for at least ten years. The next advance was the erection of a forge for working pig into bar-iron. About the beginning of the American War, Mr. Bacon contracted with Government for casting cannon. Proper foundries were erected for this purpose; and a good turnpike road was made down to the port of Cardiff, along an extent of twenty-six miles. At Cardiff, likewise, a proper wharf was formed, still called the Cannon Wharf, whence the cannon were shipped off to Plymouth, Portsmouth, and wherever the service required. These were carried in wagons down to Cardiff, at a prodigious expense of carriages, horses, and roads. There are those who do not hesitate to assert, but I know not with what truth, that sixteen horses were sometimes employed to draw the wagon that contained only one cannon. It is likewise said that the roads were so torn by these heavy wagons and the weight of their loads, that it was a month's work for one man to repair the turnpike after every deportation of cannon. I had no opportunity of inquiring properly and minutely into the truth of these relations, but I cannot help suspecting them to be matter of fact in the main, hyperbolically aggravated, though I derive the account from very respectable sources of information.

"This contract is supposed to have been immensely lucrative to Mr. Bacon; but he was obliged to relinquish it about the close of the American War, or rather to transfer it to the Caron Company, in Scotland, as I have been informed, where most, perhaps all, of the cannons are now cast. He made this disposal that he might be enabled to hold a seat in Parliament, to which he had been elected. Soon afterwards, about the year 1783, he granted leases of his remaining term, in the following parcels: Cyfarthfa Works, the largest portion, to Mr. Crawshay, and the remainder to Mr. Hill. Mr. Bacon never had any interest in Penydarren or Dowlais Works; but his heirs have from the other two a clear annual income of ten thousand pounds. Mr. Crawshay's Iron-works of Cyfarthfa are now by far the largest in this kingdom; probably, indeed, the largest in Europe, and in that case, as far as we know, the largest in the world. He employs constantly fifteen hundred men, at an average of thirty shillings a week per man, which will make the weekly wages paid by him two thousand two hundred and fifty pounds; and the monthly expenditure, including other items, about ten thousand pounds. From the Canal accounts, it appears that Cyfarthfa Works sent nine thousand nine hundred and six tons of iron to Cardiff between the first of October, 1805, and the first of October, 1806, so that the average may be reckoned from one hundred and eighty to two hundred tons every week. Mr. Crawshay now works six furnaces and two rolling mills. For procuring blast for the furnaces and working the mills, he has four steam-engines—one of fifty, one of forty, one of twelve, and one of seven horse-power.

"The quantity of iron sent from Penydarren Works by the Canal, from October, 1805, to October, 1806, was six thousand nine hundred and sixty-three tons; so that the men employed by Mr. Homfray must amount to about one thousand, and his monthly outgoings must be about seven thousand pounds, and the weekly average of iron from one hundred and thirty to one hundred and forty tons. Dowlais Iron-works, belonging to Messrs. Lewis and Tate, are next in the scale to those of Penydarren. Their produce last year amounted to five thousand four hundred and thirty-two tons. Plymouth Works, belonging to Mr. Hill, sent out within the same period three thousand nine hundred and fifty-two tons, or twenty-six tons per week. They employ about five hundred men, at a monthly expense of four thousand pounds. The total of the iron sent to Cardiff down the Canal, from the first of October, 1805, to the first of October, 1806, was twenty-six thousand two hundred and fifty-three tons, or about five hundred tons weekly; whence it is shipped off to Bristol, London, Plymouth, Portsmouth, and other places, and a considerable quantity to America.

"The number of smelting furnaces at Merthyr Tydvil is about sixteen."

## EXTRACT FROM WOOD'S "RIVERS OF WALES,"

Part I, Page 5, 1813.

"In Leland's time, Merthyr Tydvil was undoubtedly an insignificant village, and continued so to the middle of the last century, when its iron and coal mines attracted the attention of Mr. Anthony Bacon and others, who obtained leases for ninety-nine years of a great extent of mine and coal ground at very trifling annual rents. A furnace was built at Cyfarthfa for smelting iron; and some years after, a forge was erected for working the pig-iron into bar-iron, by means of pit coal, but without success. At the same time a Company was formed, who took the mines and coals near Dowlais, where they built a furnace for making pig-iron. Another Company, also, about the same period, rented the mines from Lord Plymouth, and built a furnace, called Plymouth; but these different Works made very little progress, nor did their projectors derive any advantage from them for many years.

"About the beginning of the American War, Mr. Bacon contracted with Government for the casting of cannon, and in consequence erected proper foundries for casting, and mills for boring them out of the solid. These Works were let to Mr. S. Homfray, who contracted for all the pig-iron produced from the Cyfarthfa Furnace at £4 10*s*. per ton, long weight, and as many coals as he should have occasion for, at 4*s*. per ton, for the term of fifty years. This gentleman, who came to Merthyr in 1782, began by improving the boring of cannon, and erecting forges for the milling of bar-iron. He also brought a number of most approved workmen from England, in order to establish the manufactory, in which he fully succeeded.

"Some difficulties having arisen between Mr. Bacon and Mr. Homfray, the latter parted with those parts of the Cyfarthfa Works which belonged to him to Mr David Tanner, of Monmouth, who sold them soon after to Mr. Richard Crawshay, an iron merchant of London.

"In 1784, Mr. Homfray, in company with others, began the Penydarran Iron-works, and about the year 1793 discovered the method of making the Finer's metal, which is considered as the leading feature in the manufacture of bar-iron, both by improving the quality and increasing the quantity made; and from which has arisen the great and extensive manufacture of that useful article throughout the Principality.

"In 1791, the Canal to Cardiff, navigable for barges of from twenty to twenty-four tons, was begun. This Canal has upwards of forty locks upon it in the space of twenty-six miles, its head at Merthyr being near 570 feet above the level of the sea.

"Upon the death of Mr. Bacon, his different Works were let till his children came of age: Cyfarthfa to Mr. Crawshay, Plymouth Works to Mr. Hill, and Hirwain to Mr. Glover.

"Upon Mr. Crawshay's arrival in the country with a great command of money, he availed himself of the new discovery of the Finer's metal; and, with the advice of Mr. Homfray, immediately proceeded to enlarge the Works at Cyfarthfa, and increase the make of bar-iron, and at length brought these Works to a state of perfection, universally allowed to exceed that of any of a similar nature in Great Britain. In the year 1800, an overshot wheel, 50 ft. in diameter, formed entirely of cast iron, and said to have cost £4,000, was constructed at Cyfarthfa. The water by which it is turned is brought from a distance, and crosses the river Taff upon an aqueduct, elevated more than 80 ft. above its bed.

"The number of Furnaces now at Merthyr Tydfil (1813) are as follows: At Cyfarthfa, four; at Penydarran, three; at Plymouth, four; at Dowlais, four; and at Ynis Fach, two.

"The quantity of pig-iron produced weekly is, on an average, not less than fifty tons per furnace, which amounts to 850 tons per week, or 42,200 tons per annum.

"The different Works produce, likewise, of bar-iron: Cyfarthfa, about 11,000 per annum; Penydarran, 7,000 tons; Dowlais, 5,000 tons; and Plymouth, 4,000 tons; making a total of 27,000 tons, which is expected to increase this year to 30,000 tons, all of which is sent down the Canal, and shipped at the port of Cardiff."

Mr. Wood adds: "Not far from Merthyr Tydfil, lower down the river Taff, there are at Gethin the remains of a small, very old furnace, between the Canal and the Taff; and about two miles lower down the river still, at Pont yr Gwaith, are the remains of another furnace; and near it in the river are the oak stakes which formed a wear, called Wattle Wear, but not the slightest tradition has reached the present period relating to these Works."

---

## THE DOWLAIS COMPANY AND SHOPKEEPING.

It may be confidently stated that, at an early period, at least, a shop was kept by the Dowlais Company for the supply of their workmen: because we read that it was the bringing of forty bushels of barley meal by Evan Evans, a servant of the Dowlais Company, to supply their workpeople from the Moor Park Mills, near Abergavenny, that led to the riot among the workmen at Mr. Kendall's Works at Beaufort, on the 22nd March, 1800.

There was a troop of five horses and three mules laden with meal and bran; and as these were passing by Beaufort, they were stopped and detained by a mob of one hundred persons.

And the annexed case, prepared to be submitted to Counsel, is sufficient to prove that the Dowlais Company kept a shop in 1816:

## CASE FOR THE OPINION OF COUNSEL.

### Ex-Parte Ironmasters (Dowlais Co.) as to Shopkeeping.

"The Iron Masters in South Wales being obliged to reduce the Wages of all the persons employed in their different Manufactories, have adopted every mode for supplying them with the necessaries of life at as moderate a rate as possible.

"To effect this object they have established Shops at their Manufactories, where the Men employed have an opportunity of purchasing their different articles at a much lower rate than they can possibly get them from the Shop of any general Tradesman. The Benefit of this reduction in price is, however, entirely confined to the Workmen employed in the Manufactory to which the particular shop belongs. The shop is conducted by a confidential person, who does not sell any Article without having a written authority to do so from one of the Partners in the Works, or one of the Pay Clerks. This written authority is, in some instances, to the following effect:—

"'Mr. A. B. (the Manager of the Shop). Let the Bearer have goods worth Five shillings.'

"'E. G.' (The Pay Clerk.)

"In another Works the following cheque is adopted:—

"'No. 153, Dowlais Iron Works, 6 Augt., 1816. Wm. Jones, Dowlais Shop.

"'Deliver Morgan Collier, goods to the amount of Ten shillings, which place to the account of Dowlais Compy.

"'Wm. Thompson' (Pay Clerk).

"The Masters settle their Account of Wages with the Workmen at the end of every four weeks. The amount of the Cheques that each man has received during the current four weeks is deducted from the total of his Wages, and the Balce. either paid him in Money or a Cheque, according to his option.

"This system thus adopted by the Iron Masters has naturally occasioned every opposition from the regular Tradesmen in the neighbourhood, and they now threaten to lay information against the former to recover the penalties inflicted by the different Statutes which have been made for protecting the relative situations of Master and Servant.

"Sometimes the following cheque is adopted:—

"'No. 20, Value in Goods at Dowlais Shop, Sixpence.'

"The first Statute that occurs as applicable to the Iron Trade is the 1st of Anne (St. 2), Ch. 18, which is made perpetual by the 9th of Anne, Chap. 30. Then comes the 12th of Geo. the 1st, Chap. 34, the provisions of which are made applicable to the Iron Trade by the 12th Sectn. of the 22 Geo. 2nd, Chap. 27.

"In one Iron Works the Workman, at the time he presents his Cheque, has his option either to receive the Amount in *Money* or in Goods. But this is not the case in other Works, tho' he is not in any Works *compell'd* to take goods in part of payment; but if he takes a Cheque, he must receive Goods in discharge of it. In short, it is entirely an Act of choice.

"It was evidently the object of the Legislature to prevent an undue influence on the part of the Master, to protect the Workman from the oppression of his Master if he compell'd him to take his Goods (by which he might make an unfair profit by) in lieu of his Wages.

"But as the Masters in the present instance are affording a very great advantage to their Workmen, it is unfortunate that the Legislature has not allowed the Workman, in this description of Manufacture, to exercise their option as by the 6th Sectn. of the 13 Geo. 2nd, Chap. 8, they have given to the Workmen in the Manufactories of Gloves, etc.

"The Iron Masters being desirous of ascertaining whether the course they are thus following does or does not subject them to both or either of the penalties imposed by the respective Acts before referred to,

"You are requested to advise—

"Whether they have made themselves liable to the penalties imposed both by the 1st of Anne, Chap. 18, and the 22nd of Geo. 2nd, Chap. 29, or to which of these; and whether the Cheques before described, and which are never given for a Sum amounting to £1, are liable to any and what Stamp Duty because they are reissued; and also whether the payment in one instance of the penalty mentioned will compensate for all the Breaches committed.

"If you should be of opinion that the Ironmasters have incurred the penalty, you will be pleased to point out the mode that can be followed to effect their object of rendering the advantage to the Workmen before described without infringing the law.

"As the Ironmasters are not expressly restricted from trading in the commodities applicable to the support of their Workmen, it is presumed that if the Workman is first paid his Wages in Money, there is nothing to prevent his purchasing of his Master the articles that he may require.

"Your advice and opinion is, however, requested upon the whole circumstances of the case, for the future guidance of the Ironmasters."

[The opinion of Counsel given is not among our papers.]

And I have been informed by one who has known the Merthyr district for nearly sixty years that the shop was not given up until 1845.

---

## PENYDARRAN SHOP.

The shop was in existence in 1800, when it was sacked by rioters; but how much later I am not able to state.

---

## A FEW NOTES ON RICHARD CRAWSHAY'S WILL.

Two names are mentioned in his will which may possibly serve as an Index to Character.

The first name is that of Sir John Sinclair, of Scotland, well known as one of the most intelligent, far-seeing statesmen of his age. To him Richard Crawshay leaves a ring, as to a friend.

The other is that of Jonas Hanway, who had either given or left by will a ring to Mr. Crawshay, as a memento or a memorial of his friendship. Well, Jonas Hanway—he is said to have invented the umbrella—was one of the chief of the band of philanthropic men and women that were to be found in Bristol from 1780 to 1800.

*Noscitur a sociis*, and to have known such men and to be their friend is, shall I say, a proof to me that Richard Crawshay shared their noble views and feelings.

---

WINGFIELD.

# LLANCAIACH ESTATE, CO. GLAMORGAN.

(ONE UNDIVIDED MOIETY.)

## THE CYFARTHFA PROPERTY.

### Statement of Title.

1. Edward Prichard, of Cardiff, High Sheriff of Glamorgan, 1599, owned the Llancaiach Estate.

2. He was succeeded by his eldest son, David Prichard, then of Llancaiach, and the latter by his eldest son, Edward Prichard.

3. Edward Prichard had two daughters, Jane and Mary. Jane married John Wightwick, of Marleston, Berks., and Mary married David Jenkins, of Hensol. By a Settlement, 2 Car. II, 1662, one moiety of the Llancaiach Estate was settled on Mr. and Mrs. Wightwick, and the other on Mr. and Mrs. Jenkins.

4. The moiety owned by Mr. and Mrs. Wightwick was sold to Mr. Michael Richards between the years 1685 and 1729.

5. David and Mary Jenkins, of Hensol, left an only daughter, Cecil, who married Charles Mathew, second son of Thomas Mathew, of Castell-y-Mynach.

6. Charles and Cecil Mathew left an only daughter, Cecil, who married, November, 1713, Charles Talbot, first Baron Talbot of Hensol, Lord Chancellor of England.

7. Cecil, Baroness Talbot, died in 1720. Lord Chancellor Talbot died in 1737, and his wife's share of the Llancaiach Estate then descended to their son William, second Baron Talbot, afterwards first Earl Talbot and first Baron Dynevor, Lord Steward of the Household, who joined in granting the Cyfarthfa Lease to Anthony Bacon in 1765, and died 27th April, 1782.

8. William, Earl Talbot, married Mary de Cardonnel, and left an only daughter and heiress, Cecil, who became by special remainder Baroness Dynevor on her father's death.

Cecil de Cardonnel, Baroness Dynevor, married George Rice, Esqre., son of Edward Rice, Esq., M.P. for County Carmarthen, and had, with other issue, George Talbot, third Baron Dynevor, who married the daughter of Viscount Sydney, and had issue George Rice, fourth Baron Dynevor, who married the daughter of Lord Charles Fitzroy, who had no male issue, and devised the Llancaiach and Cyfarthfa Estate (Moiety) to his grandson Edward Rhys Wingfield, the eldest son of his eldest daughter. He died March 14th, 1901, when the Estate descended to his eldest son, Mervyn Edward George Rhys Wingfield, the present owner.

BUTE.

## THE DESCENT OF THE BUTE ESTATES (GLAMORGAN).

Sir Richard Herbert, of Ewyas (natural son to William, first Earl of Pembroke, K.G.), buried in Abergavenny Church; *ob.* 12th September, 1510.

Succeeded by his second son, William, who married Anne, the sister of Catherine Parr, wife of Henry VIII.

The King (10th July, 1 Edw. VI, 1547) granted to Sir William Herbert, Lord-President of the Marches of Wales, afterwards Earl of Pembroke, Miscin, Glynrhondda, and other Manors and property in Glamorgan.

The King (7th May, 4 Edw. VI, 1550) granted to the same, Senghenydd and other manors, castles, towns, etc.

(Sir William, created Earl of Pembroke, 1551.)

The Earl died 15th March, 1570. Succeeded by his son.

Henry, Second Earl, died 19th January, 1601.

Succeeded by his son.

William, Third Earl, died 10th April, 1630.

Succeeded by his brother, Philip, who had been created Earl of Montgomery, 1605.

Philip, Earl of Pembroke and Montgomery, died 23rd January, 1650.

Succeeded by his son.

Philip, Earl of Pembroke and Montgomery, died 1669.

Succeeded by his son.

William, Earl of Pembroke and Montgomery, died 8th July, 1674.

Succeeded by his brother.

Philip, Earl of Pembroke and Montgomery, married Henrietta de Queronaille, sister of the Duchess of Portsmouth (who married, secondly, Timoleon Gouffier, Marquis de Thois).

The Earl died 29th August (some say 8th September), 1683, when he was succeeded in the Earldom by his brother Thomas, but his Welsh Estates went to his only daughter, Charlotte Herbert, who married, first, John, Lord Jeffreys,[1] Baron of Wem, who died 1703; and, second, Thomas, Viscount Windsor, who died 1738. Charlotte (Lady Windsor) died 1733, and was succeeded by her son,

Herbert Hickman, Second Viscount Windsor. [He granted the Senghenydd Manor lease of 1748, and the Hirwain lease of 1757.]

Married Alice Clavering.

On the death of Herbert, Viscount Windsor, in 1758, Alice, Viscountess Windsor, granted the Hirwain lease of 1760, and the Senghenydd lease of 1763.

Viscountess Windsor died 24th November, 1776, leaving two daughters, Charlotte Jane, who married John, Lord Mountstuart, who afterwards became first Marquis of Bute; and Alice Elizabeth, who married Viscount Beauchamp, son of the Earl of Hertford, and died leaving no issue.

[See Præcipe Book, Great Sessions, Co. Glamorgan, 1770 to 1790.]

John, First Marquis of Bute, died 1814.

Succeeded by his grandson.

John, Second Marquis of Bute, died 18th March, 1848.

Succeeded by his son.

John Patrick, Third Marquis of Bute, died 8th October, 1900.

Succeeded by his son.

John, Fourth Marquis of Bute.

[1] Son of "Judge Jeffreys." Their Trustees, with the approval of Lord and Lady Jeffreys, sold the Llwyd Coed Forest, in the Manor of Miskin, Aberdare, in 1698, June 14th and 15th, to Richard Hughes, of Brecon. See also lease to Edwards, *ante*, p. 19.

WINDSOR.

# PLYMOUTH ESTATES (GLAMORGANSHIRE).

## DESCENT OF THE PLYMOUTH ESTATES TO LORD WINDSOR, 1905.

How did the Estates of the Rt. Hon. Lewis Windsor Hickman, Earl of Plymouth, grantor of the Lease of December 14th, 1763; and

How did the Estates of the Earl of Plymouth, a Minor, 13 years of age, in charge of Guardians (according to the "Case" quoted), in 1800,

Become and are vested in Robert George, Lord Windsor, in 1905?

---

### Ancient Title.

## OTHER OR OTHO.

(*Lived* temp. *Edward the Confessor.*)

WALTER, OR WILLIAM, CASTELLANE, OF WINDSOR, AND OF ALL THE BERKSHIRE FORESTS.

(Temp. 1066, *William the Conqueror.*)

WILLIAM DE WINDSOR, BARON, 1135.

(*Creation of Baron.*)

INTERVENING BARONS IN DESCENT.

* * *

---

Henry, Baron Windsor, of Bradenham, 1605.

Thomas, who died 1640, *s. p.*

Elizabeth, elder sister and coheir, who married Dixey Hickman, of Kew.

Elizab., second sister and coheir, who married Andrew Windsor, nephew of Henry, Lord Windsor.

(Barony fell into abeyance between these two sisters.)

*a*

| *a*

Thomas Hickman, son and heir of the marriage of elder daughter, had the title of Baron Windsor restored in 1660 (1 Chas. II); created Earl of Plymouth, 1682.

By his first marriage—
Had a son and heir, Other Windsor (died *vita patris*).

By his second marriage—
Had a son, Herbert, Viscount Windsor and Mountjoy. *See* Bute.

Succeeded by his son, second Earl of Plymouth; *ob.* 1727.

Succeeded by his son, third Earl of Plymouth; *ob.* 1732. = Elizabeth, only daughter and heir of Thomas Lewis, of The Van and of St. Fagans, bringing with her large Glamorganshire estates.

Succeeded by his son, Other Lewis, fourth Earl of Plymouth.

Granted Lease of Plymouth Works, December 14th, 1763.

Succeeded by his son, Other Hickman, fifth Earl of Plymouth; *ob.* 1790.

Succeeded by his son, a Minor, then 11 or 13 years (?) of age; born in 1789 (*see* "Case" in 1800). Other Archer, sixth Earl of Plymouth, who, dying without issue (1833), the Barony fell into abeyance. His two sisters—

Maria = Marquess of Downshire.

Harriett. = Hon. Robert Henry Clive, second son of the first Earl Powys; *ob.* 1854, of the Clive branch.
(In 1855, Lady Harriet had then the abeyance of the Barony terminated in her favour, and became Baroness Windsor.

Their eldest son, Robert Clive; *ob.* 1859. = Lady Mary Bridgeman (died July, 1889).

His only son is the present Robert George, Lord Windsor, succeeding to the Barony of Windsor on his grandmother's death, November 9th, 1869; and has issue.

(Created Earl of Plymouth, November 9th, 1905.)

(Lord Windsor is said to own nearly 17,000 acres of land in Glamorganshire—St. Fagans, Penarth, Plymouth, etc.; besides his Worcestershire property—Hewell Grange—and Shropshire Estate—Oakly Park.)

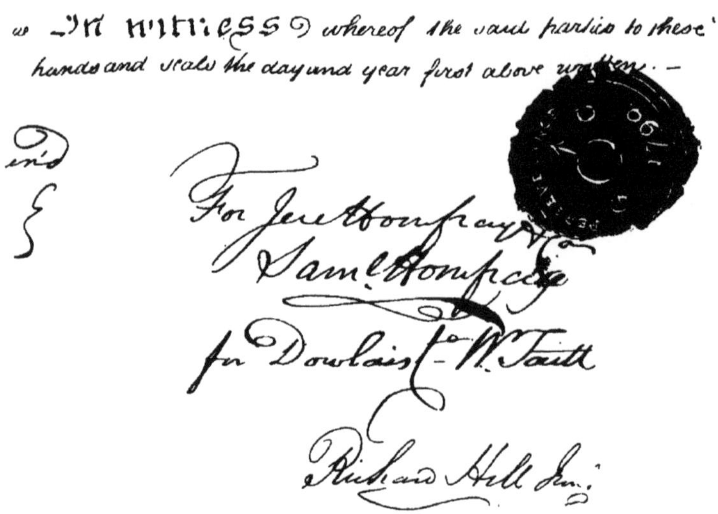

In witness whereof the said parties to these
hands and seals the day and year first above written. —

For Jere Homfray & Co
Saml Homfray

for Dowlais Co — W. Taitt

Richard Hill Junr

*Page* 101.

SEAL OF CANAL COMPANY, AND SIGNATURES OF IRONMASTERS.

## PROPOSED RAILWAY FROM DOWLAIS TO THE VALLEY OF THE USK.

Sir J. J. Guest, of Dowlais, was a profuse letter-writer, and we have probably a hundred of his original letters in our possession. But, as far as we have read the pretty, small, but far from clear, handwriting in which they are written, we have found little interesting information. One, however, of his letters contains a memorandum of importance, showing that he seriously proposed the making of a railway from Dowlais to the Valley of the Usk, if not to Brecon, pretty nearly along the same route as that adopted by the Brecon and Merthyr Railway Company in 1860.

His plan, as proposed in 1836, was to carry the line up the Taff Fechan Valley, along the mountain side, at such a level as to avoid making any tunnel at the Torpantau summit of the Beacon range of mountains; and when the railway reached that point, it was to be taken on an inclined plane of several hundred feet fall down to the level, or nearly so, of the Glyncollwm Valley.

The proposal, however, proceeded no further, and we may assume that the necessity of an expensive inclined plane killed it. It is quite possible to make a railway with a decent gradient from Merthyr to the Usk Valley, given a long tunnel on the same line; but from Dowlais to the Usk Valley it is impossible, as the making of the Brecon and Merthyr since has amply proved.

The true course the line should have taken was up the Taff Fawr Valley, and by the Storey Arms to Brecon; but it must be remembered that Dowlais and Merthyr were distinct places then, and the Iron-works at Dowlais and Cyfarthfa in different hands; and so Breconshire and Glamorganshire will apparently ever remain subject to the infliction of the badly-engineered, hill-climbing, steep-gradient railway known as the Brecon and Merthyr Railway—a line to be avoided by travellers, if at least in a hurry.

## THE IRONMASTERS AND THE CANAL COMPANY.

In 1804 a dispute arose between the Dowlais, Penydarran, and Plymouth Companies—all making common cause—and the Glamorganshire Canal Company. In forming a new tramroad to bring their iron to the Canal, these firms had built a bridge across the Canal, taken some land, and made a basin on or interfering with the Company's property, without any leave or licence. This the Company resented, and legal proceedings ensued, settled only by the payment of an annual wayleave, and the costs of the Company, as "between solicitor and client."

The original agreement of settlement is now before us, and in the space of three or four inches at the foot are the signatures of Samuel Homfray, Wm. Taitt, and Richard Hill, Junior, and the seal of the Company.

The seal bears the motto: "Perseverance," the north point, and G. C., with the date of the formation of the Canal Company, 1790.

The seal and the signatures together form an interesting little group.

The following is the aggregate total of the weights sent down the Glamorganshire Canal to Cardiff, by these Four Works respectively—1817 to 1840 (or twenty-four complete years).

| | Tons of Iron. |
|---|---|
| Dowlais ... ... ... ... | 585,448 |
| Cyfarthfa ... ... ... ... | 613,154 |
| Plymouth ... ... ... | 261,348 |
| Penydarran ... ... ... | 265,796 |
| Total in Tons ... ... | 1,725,741 |

VII.

# The Neath Abbey Works.

OUR readers are probably tired of the description of the great Iron-works at Merthyr, and will be glad to hear about the smaller Forges that were established in South Wales at a very early period; and so we will take them to the Neath Abbey Works, to shake hands with the Quaker families of Fox and Price.

These Works are of old date, and were placed, for the sake of the water power, on the little brook Clydach, which, rising on the upland ground at Cilybebwl, falls into the Neath river at Neath Abbey. We have no papers showing when this Forge was first formed, and, as far as we know, these Works have always been in the hands of Quaker families.. It is quaintly said that "they never tried to grow large," but were contented to jog on at a moderate rate, but ever mindful to turn out work of the best make. Unlike other iron-masters in South Wales, they did not get together a fortune by casting or boring cannon for scenes of warfare.

I have no other papers than these four subjoined letters of 1818, which are given *in extenso*, from the quaintness of the Quaker phrases, and some interesting particulars as to prices. The Harfords of Nantyglo were also Quakers, as we shall see presently.

---

Neath Abbey,
24/4 mo./1818.

Est'd frd.,—We will ship the pipes at 15*s*. p. Cwt. The tram plates will be governed by their length and wt. p. foot. Please state this for our governmt.

It may take 3 wks. or a Month to complete the order; less if there is distress.

Thy ass'd fr'd;
JOSEPH T. PRICE.

Wm. Ives, Coleford, Gloucestershire.

---

Neath Abbey,
2/5 mo./1818.

Estd. frd.,—On examining our Stock of pipes, wh. we have now under hand, we find we have a 13½ in. Working barrel, 10 ft. long; and we have 27 yards of 13 in. pipes, with brackets, as you Order. If you choose to have the working barl. 12½ Dis., these pipes are exactly.

Your reply by return,
Your frds.,
FOXES AND PA. CO.

Wm. Ives, Coleford.

Neath Abbey,

Messrs. Ives and Speedwell Mine Co. 7/11 mo./1818.

Bot. of Price Bros.

| | | Tons. | | | | |
|---|---|---|---|---|---|---|
| 287 Plates, 4 ft. long | . . . | 3 | 18 | 1 | 6 | |
| 168 ,, 2 ,, | . . . | 1 | 2 | 3 | 3 | |
| 30 Wing and Box | . . . | 0 | 12 | 3 | 0 | |
| 485 Plates . . . | Long Wt. | 5 | 18 | 3 | 9 | |
| | Short Wt. | 6 | 1 | 3 | 23 | at £8, £48 15 7 |

p. John Thomas Hiscox, Mr.

Esteemed frd.—We have pleasure to transmit Invoice of the remainder of yr. Order, etc., etc.

We are, Yours faithfully,

Wm. Ives, Monmouth. PRICE BROTHERS.

---

Neath Abbey,

7/5 mo./1818.

Estd. frd.,—As you have been used to such very much longer Cr. than it is our practice to give, we will go as far as to take an Acceptce., payable in London at 6 months, but cannot exceed that.

Seeing that you declined the tram plates at £9 per ton frm. the Air furnace, we refer it to Price Brothers. See their letter annexed.

For Foxes and Neath Abbey Co.,

Thy assd. frd.,

Wm. Ives, Coleford. JOS. T. PRICE.

---

Neath Abbey,

9/6 mo./1818.

Esteemed frd.,—Thy favr. of 2nd Inst. speaks of our delivering the pipes and tram plates at Lidney Basin.

Our delivery is at our own Port. We have no objection to deliver at Lidney (Lydney, Glos.), charging the freight and Insurance.

Thou art, we hope, fully aware it was not our proposition to deliver at Lidney. Thy reply p. return will oblige

Thine truly,

Neath Abbey Co.,

p. JOS. T. PRICE.

Wm. Ives, Speedwell Mine Co., Coleford, Gloucestershire.

---

Neath Abbey,
8/9 mo./1818.

Speedwell Mine Co.

Bot. of Price Brothers.

| | T. | c. | qrs. | lbs | £ | s. | d. |
|---|---|---|---|---|---|---|---|
| 1,109 Tram plates, Wt. Long. . . | 15 | 2 | 2 | 1 | | | |
| Short Wt. . . | 16 | 3 | 2 | 9/8 = | 129 | 8 | 8 |

Esteemed frd.,—We enclose bill lading and Dft. for amt. of above acct. of Tram plates shipd. p. "Lovelilass."—Wm. Hiscox, Master, for Lidney. We request the favour of thy returning the Dft. accepted p. return. And also the Dft. for the Pump work, sent Jno. Jones. Waiting which, we are

Thy friends,

Wm. Ives, Coleford or Monmouth. PRICE BROTHERS.

The Works were on Lord Dynevor's property, and have been abandoned as such, I am informed, for thirty years, and are now in ruins, covered with moss and ivy.

VIII.

# The Afon, Ynis y Penslwch, Ynis y Gerwn, and Dylais Iron Forges.

THESE Forges were of early date, the Afon being on the ——— river, Ynisypenslwch on the Tawe river, the Dylais on the Dylais brook, near Neath, and Ynisygerwn on the Neath river, and in the year 1782 were in the hands of Mr. John Miers, Ironmaster, of Neath.

These Sites had doubtless been chosen for the Forges on account of the available water-power: as we have previously seen in the case of the Brecon Furnace and Pipton Forge.

The following Invoice of Bar Iron, etc., supplied to Mr. Lewis Williams' Estate (Mr. Williams was a Ship Chandler and Ironmonger in a large way of business at Neath) by Mr. John Miers, is given as mentioning the names of these 4 Forges, and also the prices existing at that day.

## THE ESTATE OF THE LATE LEWIS WILLIAMS

IN ACCOUNT WITH

## THE EXORS. OF THE LATE JOHN MIERS, ESQ,

*Dr.* *Cr.*

| Date | Description | Tons. | Cwt. | Qrs. | Rate | £ | s. | d. | £ | s. | d. |
|---|---|---|---|---|---|---|---|---|---|---|---|
| | Balance Brought Forward | | | | | | | | £188 | 4 | 10 |
| 1793. | | | | | | | | | | | |
| April 27. | To Bar Iron at Neath | 1 | 0 | 12 | At 20s. | 1 | 2 | 2 | | | |
| | Rod Iron at do. | 9 | 2 | 26 | „ 22s. | 10 | 14 | 1 | | | |
| | | | | | | | | | 11 | 6 | 8 |
| | Rod Iron at Ynisph. | 8 | 0 | 0 | „ 20s. | 8 | 0 | 0 | | | |
| | Do. at do. | 11 | 0 | 10 | „ 21s. | 12 | 4 | 0 | | | |
| | | | | | | | | | 20 | 4 | 0 |
| May 25. | Bar Iron at Dylais | 1 | 3 | 21 | „ 22s. | | ... | | 2 | 0 | 8 |
| | Rod Iron at Neath | 3 | 0 | 7 | „ 22s. | | ... | | 3 | 7 | 4½ |
| June 22. | Do. at do. | 2 | 2 | 6 | „ 22s. | | ... | | 2 | 16 | 2 |
| | Bar Iron at Dylais | 3 | 2 | 9 | „ 21s. | | ... | | 3 | 15 | 2 |
| | Rod Iron at Ynisph. | 5 | 0 | 24 | „ 22s. | | ... | | 5 | 14 | 9 |
| | Bar Iron at Avon Forge | 11 | 2 | 3 | „ 21s. | | ... | | 12 | 2 | 1 |
| eb. 20. | Bar Iron at Dylais | 3 | 3 | 3 | „ 21s. | | ... | | 3 | 19 | 4 |
| | Rod Iron at Neath | 3 | 1 | 10 | „ 22s. | | ... | | 3 | 13 | 6 |
| | Rod Iron at Ynisph. | 10 | 1 | 5 | „ 22s. | | ... | | 11 | 6 | 6 |
| | Bar Iron at Avon Forge | 5 | 0 | 14 | „ 21s. | | ... | | 5 | 7 | 7 |
| Aug. 17. | Rod Iron at Neath | 10 | 1 | 11 | „ 22s. | | ... | | 11 | 7 | 8 |
| | Bar Iron at Dylais | 0 | 0 | 21 | „ 21s. | | ... | | 0 | 3 | 11 |
| | Rod Iron at Ynisph. | 6 | 1 | 19 | „ 22s. | 6 | 19 | 3 | 7 | 1 | 3 |
| Sept. 14. | Do. at do. | 2 | 0 | 11 | „ 22s. | | ... | | 2 | 6 | 1 |
| | Rod Iron at Neath | 5 | 3 | 19 | „ 22s. | | ... | | 6 | 10 | 2 |
| Oct. 12. | Do. at lo. | 6 | 3 | 6 | „ 22s. | | ... | | 7 | 9 | 8 |
| | Rod Iron at Ynisph. | 8 | 3 | 10 | „ 22s. | | ... | | 9 | 14 | 5½ |
| Nov. 9. | Rod Iron at Neath | 2 | 0 | 11 | „ 22s. | | ... | | 2 | 6 | 2 |
| 1794. | | | | | | | | | | | |
| Jany. 4. | Bar Iron at Avon Forge | 2 | 0 | 23 | „ 21s. | | ... | | 2 | 6 | 4 |
| | Rod Iron at Neath | 2 | 2 | 0 | „ 22s. | | ... | | 2 | 15 | 0 |
| Feb. 1. | Rod Iron at Ynisph. | 12 | 3 | 15 | „ 22s. | | ... | | 14 | 3 | 5 |
| | Bar Iron at Avon Forge | 0 | 3 | 23 | „ 21s. | | ... | | 1 | 0 | 0 |
| | Rod Iron at Neath | 7 | 1 | 16 | „ 22s. | | ... | | 8 | 2 | 7½ |
| Mar. 1. | Rod Iron at Ynisgn. | 0 | 2 | 0 | „ 22s. | | ... | | 0 | 11 | 0 |
| „ 31. | Rod Iron at Neath | 5 | 0 | 16 | „ 22s. | | ... | | 5 | 13 | 1 |
| | | | | | | | | | £355 | 19 | 1 |

It will be seen that a Mr. Cuthbertson—a name not unknown in Neath to-day—was Mr. Miers' Cashier, and as will appear, on reference to the original receipt, had a very elaborate style of signature:—

"Reced. 3d. January, 1786, of Mr. Lewis Williams, Forty-Six Pounds Eighteen Shillings, and Four Pence, being the Balance of the within Account, and the above Sum for the use of Mr. Jno. Miers.

"£46 18s. 4d. "R. CUTHBERTSON."

Mr. John Miers, being possessed of these Four Forges, must have been in a large way of business. He died in 1786.

Apparently a Son of his, John Nathaniel, married the daughter of Richard Hill, of Plymouth; and if the son-in-law continued the working of the Forges, no doubt he proved a good customer for the Plymouth pig-iron, being himself also for a time a partner.

This John Nathaniel's daughter was the celebrated beauty and accomplished Molly Miers, who first became Lady Mackworth, and subsequently the wife, when quite young, of Capel Hanbury Leigh, of Pontypool Park, the Lord Lieutenant of Monmouthshire.

I have seen her driven on to the Abergavenny race-course in great state, with an open barouche, and four horses with postillions, with powdered hair or white wigs, and, I think, outriders in scarlet. Several letters of hers I have, and in them she shows great affection for her nephews, Richard and Capel Miers, of Ynisypenslwch. The Miers family have to this day retained the Ynisypenslwch estate and Works in their hands, the Works, like many other old forges, being changed into a tin-plate works.

---

# IX.

# Ynis y Cedwyn Furnace, 1729.

---

## IN A DEED OF RELEASE, DATED 30TH AUGUST, 1729.

Between

ROBERT POPKINS, of Forrest, in the parish of Llansamlet, in the County of Glamorgan, Esquire;

RICHARD SEYS, of the Town of Swanzey, in the same Coy., Gentleman, 1st part.

CHRISTOPHER PORTREY, of Yniskedwyn, in the Parish of Ystradgunlais, in the County of Brecon, Esq., 2nd part;

HENRY WILLIAMS, of Brecon, in the County of Brecon, and

GABRIEL POWELL, of Pennant, within the Town of Brecon, afsd., Gent., 3rd part;

And

JOHN LEWELLIN, of Ynisgeryn, in the Parish of Cadoxton-juxta-Neath, in the County of Glamorgan, and

ROBERT MORRIS, of the same Parish and County, Gent., 4th part;

Certain messuages and premises are conveyed to uses, including all that messuage or dwelling-house, *Furnace*, lands, etc., situate at Yniskedwyn, in the parish of Ystradgynlais, in the County of Brecon, in the occupation of Ambrose Crowley, Gent, and partners.

---

We have taken some trouble to get later information as to the Yniskedwin Furnace, or the Ironworks that succeeded it, but wholly without success, as regards the long period from 1729 to 1800. Mr. E. Roberts, of Swansea, writes me word that when digging a foundation for a new Furnace about 1870, a cast-iron plate was unearthed, with the date "1711" on it, so there must, he thinks, have been a Furnace there prior to 1729.

Ynisedwyn has, however, Mr. Roberts writes, played an important part in the history of the iron trade in the nineteenth century, as it was there the first hot-blast furnace was erected.

Mr. Crane, the owner of the Yniskedwin Works, which were situate on the anthracite coal formation, in a Paper to the British Association (1838), says:—

"One evening, after I had placed a piece of the anthracite upon my parlour fire (which had before been made up with bituminous coal), and had allowed it to arrive at a red heat, upon my applying as fierce a blast to this piece of coal as I could raise from a pair of bellows, I noticed the appearance of a black mark, or spot, upon that part of it where the air impinged upon it. On my continuing the like rapid current in the same direction, I shortly blew the fire out of it.

"I at once perceived that the strength of a current of air, when cold, which we are of necessity obliged to blow into our furnaces to secure the passage of the blast through the high and dense columns of materials contained in an erection like a blast-furnace, instead of encouraging ignition, was actually unfavourable to it.

"On giving the thing but a moment's reflection, the question promptly occurred to me, what would be the effect of turning a blast into a furnace upon this coal, which would itself burn, which would itself melt lead! I at once determined that it was a thought which was really worthy of mature reflection."

And then he adds :—

"The further consideration which I gave to the matter, and the further experiments which I shortly afterwards instituted, have at length been crowned with full success."—Scrivenor, *Iron Trade*, p. 303.

Mr. Strick, of Swansea, in articles in the *Iron and Coal Trades Review* of August 28th and September 25th, 1896, gives the credit of the invention of the hot blast to Mr. Thomas. There is little doubt that it was a most important discovery, and that certainly Mr. Thomas took over the invention to America, and was the founder of the anthracite iron industry in that country.

Mr. David Mushet, I find, in his *Iron and Steel* work, 1840, page 424, gives the credit of the invention wholly to Mr. George Crane, of the Yniskedwin Works. Mr. Charles Wilkins, in his *History of the Iron Trade*, at page 269, has a very full note, and gives the credit to Mr. Thomas rather than to Mr. Crane, his employer. It seems to me that Mr. Crane's own version of the discovery is the one that we can most safely rely upon, having been publicly given before the British Association at the time.

## X.

# The Melin Griffith Iron Works.

THESE important Works were situate on the river Taff, in the parish of Whitchurch, in Glamorganshire. First it was a Forge only, and the manufacture of tin plates and of other specialities in the make of iron plates to meet foreign requirements and orders was added.

There was a notable firm of ironmasters in South Wales, of whom we have heard little as yet, but shall soon hear a good deal, named Harford, Partridge and Co.

They held at one time or another, in Monmouthshire, the Nantyglo Works, the Ebbw Vale Works, and the Monmouth Forge, the Harfords being several brothers of that name of a wealthy Quaker family of Bristol, and Mr. Partridge, of Bishopswood, Ross, being an ironmaster of New Weir Forge (in succession to Mr. George White, my ancestor) and of the Monmouth Forge.

Possessed of great enterprise, and seeing the advantages of having a mill low down on the Taff river, with great water-power, they extended their operations to the Taff Valley; and, as far as I know, were the first to found the Melin Griffith Works.

Probably, for each of the undertakings, the partnership differed a little, though always one partner was a Harford; and we find that in the Melin Griffith Works Mr Richard Blakemore was the added partner: the friend of the Partridge family, and himself a partner in the Monmouth Forge; and it was he that assumed the management, and proved the life of these Works, and developed them largely.

In 1803 we find Mr. Richard Blakemore writing from Monmouth Forges, and signing his letters "For Harford, Partridge, and Co., and Self," and in which he brings charges against the Glamorganshire Canal Company of taking away water from the Taff, to the injury of the Melin Griffith Works, and in breach of the provision of their statutory powers:—

"Monmouth Forges,
"Jany. 19, 1803.

"Messrs. W. and J. Powell,

"D'r Sirs,—Mr. John Harford being from Home, the Declaration was sent from M. G.[1] to Bristol, and from thence to me, yesterday. I have this morning perused it. Each Count contained therein seems to me founded solely upon the Breach of that Clause in the Act of Parliament, made with a particular reference to M. G. Works, for securing to them the Surplus Water; but it has always appeared to me that we have a much broader and clearer ground of Action than any that can be founded upon a breach of this particular clause, which every body condemns as insufficient and loose, vizt., upon the ground that the Canal is not executed, 'doing as little damage as may be,' which the Canal Company are bound to do by the Words in the latter part of the 1st Clause, and which we can prove is not done, inasmuch as they may and ought to supply themselves with Water without interfering with our Works, by taking the Water below the Works instead of above them. I do not by any means disapprove of the Declaration; on the contrary, the Gentleman who has drawn it seems to have made himself a perfect master of the Case, and to have drawn it with great clearness and propriety: but I wish to have a Count introduced into it, founded upon this Ground. Would it not also be well to introduce a Count into it respecting the two Weirs erected near the Quakers' Yard, across the River Taff (the Canal Company have a power to divert Brooks and Streams of Water, but not the *main River*), whereby all the Water of that River is at some seasons of the year diverted into the Canal. The Parish in which the Works are situated, and the other Blanks, are filled up—the former accurately, the latter near enough.

"It was my intention to have written you about this time respecting the intended prosecution of Hopkin David for Perjury in the Court of Chancery. It is our serious wish and intention that that Prosecution should be carried into effect at the next Assizes, for which we therefore doubt not you will do the needful. Pray, have you made any progress in the Conveyance of the Premises lately bought of Mr. Glover? I shall be glad to hear from you upon anything important transpiring upon this and the other affairs now pending in your hands.

"Wishing you the compts. of the season,

"Yours, with much respect,
"Richd. Blakemore,
"For Harford, Partridge, and Co. and Self."

[1] Melin Griffith.

The following is a memorandum written on this letter from Powell to Jno. Allen, of Clem ent's Inn, no doubt his London agent :—

"Melin Griffith Works, in the Parish of Whitechurch.—Mr. Blakemore observes at ye end of the 1st. Col. that Plts. have sustained great damage by paying play wages to their Workmen, 1st January, 1796, erecting . . . 13 feet wide, 4 inches lower, 1 Jany., '98. Lock out of repair. 1st Jany., 1796, Canal Leaky. Do. Left open, Paddles and Gates of Lock."

It was, no doubt, a very serious matter to the Firm, this lessening of the water supply. It was for the abundance of water power the Firm had taken the Mill, and laid out large sums of money.

Not without great difficulty, some terms were arranged between the Firm and the Canal Company, which are embodied in an Agreement, in 1806, between the Canal Company of the one part, and the proprietors of Melin Griffith Works of the other part, which was to the effect that Harford and Co. were to receive from the Canal Company the sum of £700, to set up a fire-engine to throw into the upper level of the Canal the water of the Taff after passing Meliu Griffith Works; and were also to pay to Harford, Partridge, and Co., during the continuance of their interest in Melin Griffiths Works, the yearly sum of £90, the first payment being made on 1st Jany., 1807; and that the old water engine to be given up to them which was in the ditch; and the arrangements as to the carrying out of the practical portion of the works were placed under the direction and control of Mr. Rennie and Mr. Jessop by the parties.

Notwithstanding this Agreement, differences constantly occurred as to the respective water rights between the proprietors of the Works and the Canal, and the question was one long continuous dispute.

In dry seasons, no doubt the situation became acute, the Works claiming to have the first right and pull of the river Taff, and the Canal Co. advancing the claim to be supplied under their statutory powers. It is easy to be wise after the event, but what should have been done is obvious. The Canal Company, then earning a very large dividend, could easily have made—and should have been compelled to make—large compensating reservoirs to hold the winter rains, benefiting themselves and the Works by ensuring a regular and constant supply of water in dry seasons.

It may be said that the Canal Company did think of doing so, but when they were told by Counsel in 1807 (in a Case submitted for the opinion of John Williams, Serjeant-at-Law), "That they had no Parliamentary power to expend money in making this reservoir out of their Capital, but only power to do so out of Revenue," they did not proceed further. Serjeant Williams recommended their applying for Parliamentary powers to raise fresh capital for the purpose; but this was never done.

And it will be seen from the following letter that there was perpetual trouble caused by the defaults of the Company in their engagements to the Works :—

"Cardiff, March 2nd, 1810.

"Dear Sir,—Our old Friends, the Glamorganshire Canal, are again repeating their njuries to us at Melin Griffith, which has compelled us to commence proceedings at law against them. On reference to the Papers in Mr. Wood's possession, we find many are wanting of our former proceedings, which, of course, I presume, are with you. Will you, therefore, permit me to request that you will collect the whole of them and transmit them to Mr. Wood by his Clerk, who will, I understand, be the bearer of this.

"I am, Dear Sir,
"Your Obedt. Servt.,
"RICHARD BLAKEMORE."

"Walter Powell, Esq., Brecon.

And this state of things continued, for as late as August 11th, 1835, we find Mr. Blakemore writing to Mr. Ives, his solicitor, that: "he was extremely impatient to have the costs from the Glamorganshire Canal Company paid, and must urge you to compel the same being done without further delay;" and when received to pay to his bankers, Masterman, Peters, and Co., and advise him of the same.

At what time Mr. Richard Blakemore became sole owner of the Melin Griffith Works our papers and his letters do not reveal to us, but we have reason to believe that he soon acquired the sole interest in the Works, and directed the management down to as late a period as 1838.

Many years before that time he had amassed a fortune, and was able to purchase the Leys property near Monmouth, where he lived.

In 1830, by the following letter, it will be seen that he was a candidate for Wells, in Parliament, and for which he was returned :—

"Wells, July 31, 1830.

"Dear Sir,—The hurly-burly in which I am engaged have altogether withdrawn me from attention to matters of business, and will continue to do so until the excitement is over. On this account it is that your letters respecting Morgan's Annuity have not been replied to. It would, I think, be very improper that I should make a Profit, or obtain any personal advantage, in that matter; and I feel extremely obliged to you for your kindness in drawing my attention to it; but a question arises who is entitled to the difference between the computed and real value. It strikes me, in the hurry in which I wrote, that I ought to account for it to the Estate, and not to Morgan. Will you, therefore, let the matter be postponed till I can talk it over with you.

"On Monday, I expect the State of the Poll will indicate something decisive as to the strength of the Votes here. The Poll of to-day—the 1st Poll—has been merely nominal on my part.

"I am, Dear Sir,
"Yours very truly,
"RICHD. BLAKEMORE."

There is little doubt that Richard Blakemore, the contemporary of Richard Crawshay, Richard Hill, and of some of the chief partners of the Dowlais Firm, was one of the most respected and successful men of his time in South Wales.

He died leaving no children, the Works passing to his nephew, Thomas Booker, who took the name of Blakemore, and who afterwards became Member of Parliament for Herefordshire.

We must close this account by saying that we fear, from various causes, the same great success that attended the uncle did not wait upon the nephew.

---

## EXTRACTS FROM MALKIN'S *SOUTH WALES.*

### 1807, Vol. I, Page 152.

"The Tin Works at Melin Gruffyth are perhaps the largest in the Kingdom. Not less than 13,000 boxes of the very best tin plates—containing 225 plates in each box—have been known to be sent within the year from the manufactory. The scraps of iron plates, from which the tin is made, are converted into bolt-iron, for ship-building. This place is four miles north of Cardiff."

## XI.

# Treforest Works.

In connection with the Hirwain Iron-works, Mr. Crawshay purchased from Mr. Christopher James the "Forest" property, situate in the Taff Valley at Treforest, on the western side of the river Taff, about a mile below Pontypridd; and also acquired a small Works situate on an adjoining property, supplied with water power from the river Taff. Soon afterwards Mr. Crawshay transferred to his then eldest son, Mr. Francis Crawshay, the Hirwain Iron-works and the properties at Treforest. The greater portion of the pig-iron made at Hirwain, as well as some of the bar-iron, was conveyed by the Aberdare Canal tramway to Canal Head, Aberdare, and thence by the Aberdare and Glamorganshire Canals to Treforest, where it was manufactured into bars and plates.

About the date of the expiration of the lease of the Hirwain Iron-works, Mr. Francis Crawshay, with the view of being independent of Hirwain for the supply of pig-iron, commenced erecting blast-furnaces at Treforest, and completed three modern blast-furnaces, with the necessary equipments; but, owing to some dispute with his father, Mr. William Crawshay, he never set them in blast.

In the year 1873 Sir William T. Lewis, of Aberdare, entered into negotiation with Mr. Francis Crawshay, and purchased the Forest Blast-Furnaces, together with sixty acres of freehold land in connection with them, abutting upon the Taff Vale Railway; and with the view of providing fuel, he also purchased a bituminous colliery in the Rhondda Valley, for supplying the furnaces with first class-coke.

Sir William, soon after the acquisition of the properties, took into partnership Mr. Menelaus, the General Manager of the Dowlais Works; Mr. Edward Williams, the General Manager of Bolckow, Vaughan and Company's extensive Works at Middlesborough; Sir Isaac Lowthian Bell, Mr. G. T. Clark, the Trustee of the Dowlais Works, and some London bankers, who formed themselves into a limited liability Company, called the "Forest Iron and Steel Company."

This Company immediately proceeded to alter the furnaces in accordance with the more recent experience in the modern Works in the North of England; and after expending a considerable capital at the furnaces and collieries, they were set going for the manufactnre of Bessemer pig-iron, and kept at work successfully up to the year 1900, when, owing to the exhaustion of the coal at the Company's collieries, and the necessity of acquiring additional Works for manufacturing pig-iron into plates, rails, and other uses, the Works were dismantled, and the Company was ultimately wound up and the property sold.

## XII.

# The Aberaman Iron Works.

When, or soon after, Anthony Bacon (the eldest son of the Anthony Bacon who died in 1786), sold his interest in the Cyfarthfa Iron-works to Mr. Richard Crawshay, he bought what is described as the fine domain of Aberaman, in the Vale of Aberdare. It consisted of (1,528 acres being in a ring-fence) a total acreage of nearly 1,700, of which the Aberaman mansion, with 963 acres, and hanging woods of 100 acres on the hill-side, formed a part.

Mr. Bacon, having retired from the iron industry, made this his residence for a great many years, until he died about the year 1836. It would seem that, though every acre of the land had valuable seams of coal, and iron-ore veins were to be found there, no workings of these took place in Mr. Bacon's time, nor ever previously, except to a slight extent in olden time, as hereafter alluded to.

And on Mr. Bacon's death, and the entire property being sold by the devisees of his will in trust, in 1836, the auctioneers, in their florid description of the natural beauties of the estate in the particulars of sale, never alluded to the rich veins of coal that lay under the estate, nor to the veins of iron ore, except in respect of the Tir y Llaithty farm, in the following brief paragraph:—

"There are the remains of an Old Furnace on the Farm, and a branch of the stream bounding one side of it, and is distinguished as 'the Furnace Brook,' from which it may be presumed that Iron may be found among the minerals which belong to and pass with the Estate."

Here was an opportunity, where geological knowledge, either acquired by education or through practical experience, was invaluable to an intending purchaser: a lesson those of our present generation may well take to heart; and Mr. Crawshay Bailey came over from Nantyglo, and saw and bought the estate solely for its mineral wealth and capability.

The Aberaman Iron-works were then founded by him, and he himself went to live at Aberaman House, leaving his nephew, Henry Bailey, in charge for himself and his brother Joseph, of the Nantyglo Works.

The history of these Works is quite modern, but I believe, from some causes, they did not prove as profitable as were expected, and Mr. Crawshay Bailey is said to have lost money by them. But that loss was amply made up in the working of the coal measures, which contained the finest seams of the Aberdare steam coal, and the estate has ever since proved one of great mineral value to its owners.

---

Aberaman, 26th Oct./44.

Dear Sir,—If you want to look at my Aberaman deeds, you must send up Tom Gabb at your expense, as I don't understand what is wanted.

Yrs. truly,
C. Bailey.

Henry Maybury, Esq.,
Solr., Brecon.

---

During my recent visit to the Valley of the Cynon (Aberdare), I was taken to see the site of these Works, which is on the little Aman brook, a short distance from the main stream, the Cynon.

On the engine-house the date and initials—1845, C.B.—were inscribed, but the form of the blast-furnaces and rolling-mills, as they once stood, was hardly recognisable. Just in the centre was one of the Powell-Dyffryn great pits, from which trams of the very best of steam coal, two at a time in quick succession, were being brought up at each winding journey made by the stationary engine. Of course, day and night shifts, and every modern contrivance to produce the greatest possible output! All was changed now, and King Coal reigned where the Iron King once held unchallenged sway. A scene of the utmost activity, and the earth was yielding her bounteous treasures in another form to promote the employment and the wealth of man.

Mr. Nixon, of the Tower Colliery, needed not a passport, and the manager and he were soon the best of friends, and I was shown everything in my particular enquiry line that they could think of.

Casually, I mentioned the old Furnace that was stated to exist, giving its name to a little brook. No sooner was that alluded to than the manager said: "Why, it is in the field below my house;" and away we went up a very steep hill, and there, sure enough, were the remains plainly visible, and capable of identification as a furnace; *and it was square inside.* Evidently, this was of older date than the Brecon Forge of 1720, but how much older deponent sayeth not—will not even guess! We know that the Romans formed rectangular camps; not circular, like the British did.

And there we must leave this interesting ruin, covered with grass and plants, and picturesquely placed at the junction of the two little streams, the lesser and the greater Aman: though there is very little to choose from in their amount of flow.

And how changed these valleys! One at least has a great colliery upon it, besides that we had seen, and the teeming population of small towns high up along the mountain sides.

Might I suggest that those who own the splendid rich coal veins there should not be too hard upon the coal, not too anxious to get wealth in a day; and, easing the strain on the colliery, give it a longer life, to the advantage of their children and to the future welfare of our country.

XIII.

# Aberdare Iron Works.

It is necessary, in our survey, to follow still the Cynon Valley, two of the old iron-works being situate there, and yet to be described: the Aberdare, famous for the family of Scale, and Abernant for that of Tappenden.

But first, as to the little river Cynon, for which I have a fondness. It rises on the south of the Cefn Cadlan ridge of mountain limestone, on which there are numerous swallow-holes, or pit-holes, familiar to geologists, and some little distance down its course are marked on the map Gelli Ffynnonau, or "the Wood abounding in Springs." Then it forces its way through the limestone gorge by Penderin church, and entering the broad plain and common of Hirwain Wrgan, sweeps round, like a comma, to the east on its way to join the Taff river. Many a brave warrior who fell in the famous battles fought hereabouts lies buried in the Cynon Valley; and high up in the rocky churchyard of Penderin rests one of our great modern ironworks managers, William Menelaus, of Dowlais, as well as his talented brother-in-law, Rees H. Rhys, who had great influence in all the public Boards of the district for fifty years after losing his sight.

If you inquire of the local residents, you will learn that the little Cynon, in its upper part, seldom floods, like those of our Breconshire red-sandstone formation streams; but, on the other hand, has an unusually equable flow in summer and winter. That we may attribute to the passage of the falling rain through the sandy millstone grit, and the porous limestone rock beneath, thence issuing in perennial springs at the base of that formation. Though of small size, the Cynon would, therefore, prove a surprisingly good brook to supply water, and even water-power, for mills, or even iron-works, on its course. Once there stood on its banks the Melin Rhydian, but that was long ago absorbed by the Hirwain Works, even in Maybery's day.

And when passing by, we may note that the Penderin limestone quarries have a history. They are the property of private freeholders; but it was from these the large supplies of stone required for fluxing their iron ore were brought to the Hirwain, Aberdare, Abernant, Aberaman, and Gadlys Iron-works, or to some of them. Either a fixed annual rent, or a royalty of 1½*d.* per ton was charged; and it is on record that £500 was once received in a single year by one of the quarry-owners.

But we must follow our stream onward in its course to meet the Taff; and passing by the Hirwain Iron-works, already noticed, we soon come in sight of the old Iron-works of Aberdare, and which now claim our attention.

In describing or speaking of rivers, it is the proper and good rule to call the banks right or left, as you are following them down from their source: the right bank is always the right, and the left the left, whether you are descending or ascending a river course. It is said that the battle of Inkerman was lost through the Russians misunderstanding this order, and marching up the wrong bank of a little stream!

The Hirwain Works were, as we have seen, built in Breconshire, just on the brook side on its left bank, while their leased mineral property lay on the right bank, mainly on the Windsor property under the Hirwain common. There were no minerals at this point on the left bank of the Cynon river; but now comes a change, and at Aberdare or Llwyd Coed Iron-works, which we are about to describe, the beds of iron ore and coal have crossed the stream, and are now to be found on the left, as well as on the right, of its course. And both the Aberdare Iron-works and the Abernant, a little lower down, were placed on the left side of the valley, and the whole of their mineral takings were on the same side also.

It will be remembered that Mr. Samuel Glover, of Abercarne, was the lessee of the Hirwain Works under the Court of Chancery during the minority of the brothers Anthony and Thomas Bacon—1786 to 1794—and doubtless saw the capabilities of the Llwyd Coed Forest Estate for establishing an iron-works there.

From a very early period the Earls of Pembroke had stood possessed of what was known as the Forest, or Chase, or Common of Y Llwydcoed; and it appears, by an Indenture of Lease and Release of June 14th and 15th, 1698, that the Trustees, Jeffery Jeffreys and John Jeffreys, of the marriage settlement of John, Lord Jeffereys, Baron of Wem, and his wife, Lady Charlotte, daughter and heir of Philip, late Earl of Pembroke, made a sale, under the general powers of settlement, of a part of the Llwydcoed Forest to Richard Hughes, of Brecon, for £200.

The property is thus described: " All that Forest, with the appurtenances, called Forest y Llwyd coed, being divided into several tenements, in the Occupation of the following persons:

" 15 acres held by Nicholas Herbert.
" 7 „ by Llewellyn Rees.
" 18 „ by Maud Owen.
" 13 „ by Elizabeth Thomas.
" 20 „ by Neast Morgan, widow.

[" And various other tenements of 10 to 16 acres each.]

" All which said Premises are in the Manor of Myskin, in the County of Glamorgan and were, by Indenture of May 22nd, 1690, granted by Jeffrey Jeffereys and John Jeffereys, Esqrs., Trustees of the Rt. Hon. Henrietta, Countess Dowager of Pembroke (see *ante*, p. 19), to the said Richard Hughes for 99 years, determinable on the deaths of the said Richard Hughes, Lamarock Hughes, and Charles Henry, all living, at the yearly rent of Four and Fifty shillings and Two Capons."

The property having thus become vested in the Hughes family in 1698, it appears by an abstract of title, now in our possession, prepared by Mr. Glover's solicitors, that there had been various marriage settlements, mortgages, etc., dealing with the estate during the next ninety or one hundred years, into which it does not concern us to enter.

*Page* 115. *Photo.*, 1906.

OLD ABERDARE IRON WORKS FURNACE. 1827.

And on March 26th and 27th, 1787, by formal lease and release, Samuel Hughes, of Tregunter, in the County of Brecon, conveyed to Samuel Glover, of Birmingham, County of Warwick, and Wm. Maud, of Abercarne Works, County of Monmouth, in consideration of the sum of £6,800 paid,

"All that Royalty or Lordship, or reputed Lordship, of Llwyd Coed, theretofore called the Forest of Llwydcoed, and also several tenements in various occupations, and described as being in the parish of Aberdare, in the Co. of Glamorgan, and as abutting on the lands of Edward Matthew, of Aberamman, to the lands of Thomas William Watkin, and to the river or rivulet of water called Cunon river, and a brook called Nant heere, on all or most parts and sides thereof, and by other mears and bounds there well known and distinguished.

"Also several premises the said Samuel Hughes had recently purchased from Edward Matthew, Esqre., such lands being intermixed with those previously described.

"And also all that tract of Freehold land, being part of the said Forest, called Carn y Brwdyr, and adjoining to unenclosed land of Lord Plymouth, called Carne Bearth Maen, to enclosed land formerly belonging to Lord Talbot, and now to Lord Dynevor and John Richards, Esqre., and to the unenclosed lands of Thos. Will. Watkin."

Executed by the parties, and a receipt for the £6,800 conson. endorsed.

There was a farm called Tir Ergid immediately above a portion of the Llwydcoed estate, and of which it was essential to lease the minerals if the iron-works were placed on the spot, which no doubt was thought best by Mr. Glover, and where they were subsequently built by his lessees.

Accordingly, in 1799, Mr. Samuel Glover, described as of Birmingham, engineer, obtained a lease from Rees David, of Pyle and Kenfigg, in the County of Glamorgan, and Mary Thomas, widow, of Abernant, in the parish of Cadoxton, in the same county, of Tir yr Ergid Farm, in the parish of Aberdare, with all mines, minerals, coal, and iron ore under the same (timber excepted), for seventy years, from 25th March, 1800, at the rent of £40 per annum. [There are no royalties named.]

Mr. Glover, being now possessed of these properties, mainly his freehold, but partly leasehold, and deeming their extent and the minerals therein sufficient to warrant the establishment of a new iron-works, proceeded to induce the following four gentlemen to lease from him the said lands for the purpose stated.

And on the 8th February, 1800, with the consent of Peter Rigby, Esq., of Usk, in the County of Monmouth, then mortgagee of the forest land, an indenture was made

Between

Samuel Glover, of Birmingham, in Co. of Warwick, of the one part;

And

John Thompson, of Lye Hall, in the parish of Quatt, in Co. of Salop, Ironmaster;

John Hodgett, of Cothersley, in the parish of Kinver, in the Co. of Stafford, Ironmaster;

George Scale, of Hansworth, in the said Co. of Stafford, gentleman, and

John Scale, of the same place, gentleman, of the other part.

And the following were the principal terms of the lease then granted:—

The lands of the Forest of Llwydcoed having been described and the names of the occupants of eleven different farms therein given, the extent of land being estimated at 702 acres, the lessees were to hold the same for the purpose of erecting an Iron Works thereon, with all necessary conveniences, and with full powers as to turning watercourses, opening levels, etc., for the term of 70 years from the 24th June, 1799, at a fixed rent of £1,000 per annum, payable for two years half-yearly, and thereafter quarterly each year.

And, of course, there were the usual covenants on both parts, as to payment of such rent and for quiet enjoyment, and a proviso for arbitration, in case of disputes arising.

---

Apparently this was a strong, capable firm, knowing their business, and possessed of capital; and we may assume that in the course of the next few years, one or more Blast Furnaces were built on the property leased, with all necessary works, cottages for workmen, and stabling, etc., and the waters brought by an ample leat from the Cynon brook to supply the many wants of the Works.

---

And now we must turn to their immediate neighbours—

## XIV.

# The Abernant Iron Works,

AND which came almost at once on the scene, and in this way:—

Our old friend, Mr. Jeremiah Homfray, first of Penydarran, next of Ebbw Vale (as we shall see later), and of Hirwain, was evidently a great prospector in the South Wales mineral field, and now Abernant engaged his attention. He arranged leases of mineral properties, and then sought Partners; and, after helping to establish the respective Iron Works, and set them going, he retired, and like the bee roving from flower to flower, then sought out fresh and likely mineral estates for development.

In this case of Abernant, Mr. Homfray first took Mr. James Birch, of Aberdare, engineer, as partner; and the original lease of the mineral land on which the Works were placed was taken from Mr. Walter Wilkins, of Maesllwch, in the County of Radnor, in their joint names only.

We now give this lease somewhat fully, because it was granted by the Walter Wilkins who then held himself a beneficiary interest in the Hirwain Works, and was conversant in that way with the Iron trade; and it was drafted by the Solicitor, Thomas Maybery, of Brecon, who, through his father, John Maybery, the Ironmaster, knew better the conditions to put in a lease than even our old friends, W. and J. Powell.

And the lease wholly differs from any we have seen previously, and one shilling per ton is charged on iron ore raised, and sixpence on coal. True, Mr. Glover has just led the way with a big ground rent of £1,000, but there were no royalties; and it will be readily seen that these two young Works were much handicapped in comparison with the old Works, where a £23 or £25, or even £100, fixed rent was the total sum to be paid to Lord or Lady Windsor, or Lord Talbot, for far greater mineral takings than these were.

---

WALTER WILKINS, ESQ., TO MESSRS. JERE. HOMFRAY AND BIRCH.

ABERNANT WORKS, 1801.

(COPY.)

Draft Lease of Tyr y Werva and Gorangon vach Farms, sit. in Ystradyvodock; and of Abernant y Wenallt, in Aberdare, Glamorgansh.; and also of Iron Mines and Coal under same, with power of erecting Works, etc.

Term, 99 yrs., from Michas., 1801.

---

MAYBERY, BRECON.

This Indre. made August 24, 1801, between WALTER WILKINS, of Maeslough, in the County of Radnor, Esqre., of the one part; and JEREMIAH HOMFRAY, of Llandaff, in the County of Glamorgan, Esqre., and JAMES BIRCH, of Aberdare, in the same County, Engineer, of the other part, witnesseth that in Conson. of the Rents, Royalties, etc., hereinafter reserved,

*Page* 117. *Photo.*, 1906.

OLD ABERNANT IRON WORKS.

He, the said Walter Wilkins, Hath Demised and Granted unto the said Jereh. Homfray and Jas. Birch, their Exrs., All those sevl. Messes., Farms and lands comly. called and known by the Name of Abernant-y-Wenallt, sit. in the sd. Par. of Aberdare, and now in the Occupon. of the said Jere. Homfray and Jas. Birch, their Underts; And also all those sevl. Messes. or Farms and Lands comly. called and known by the Names of Tyr y Werva and Gorangon Vach, sit., lyg, and being in the par. of Ystradyvodock, in the said County of Glamorgan, and now in the Occupon. of Willm. Morgan Jenkin and Thos. Morgan, and their Underten'ts, together with all Commons, Common of Pasture, Sheepwalks, Turbaries, Priviledges, and Appurts. whatsr. to the sd. sevl. Messes. and Lands belong'g. Except and always reserved out of this present Demise unto the sd. Walter Wilkins, his Heirs and Ass's, all Timber Trees and Underwood growing upon the said Premss. herein before mentd., with free and uninterrupted Liberty of Ingress, to and for the sd. Wr. Wilkins, his Heirs, etc., to fell, cut down, and carry away the same, doing no willful damage to the Grain or Grass on the sd. demised premes.

To have and to hold all the several messes. and Lands hereinbefore mentd., with the Appurts., unto the sd. Jere. Homfray and Jas. Birch, their Exors., etc., from Sept. 29 next ensuing the Day of the Date hereof for the full end and term of 99 years.

Yielding and paying unto the sd. Wr. Wilkins, his Exors., etc., yearly during so many years of the sd. Term hereby granted, as Nicholas John, the present Tenant of Abernant-y-Wenallt Farm shall live, the rent or sum of £31 and 10*s*. by two half-yearly payments. And also yielding and paying unto the sd. Wr. Wilkins, his Exors., etc., yearly after the decease of the said Nicholas John for all the residue of the said Term hereby granted, the rent of £91 and 10*s*. of l'full money as aforesaid by two half-yearly paymts., which sd. yearly rents of £31 and 10*s*. during the Life of the said Nicholas John, and of £91 and 10*s*. after his decease, are to be paid clear of all Rates, Taxes, etc.

And this Indenture further witnesseth that in conson. of the rents, Reservons., Royalties, Covts., etc., hereinafter reserved on the part of the sd. Jerh. Homfray and Jas. Birch, their Exors. to be paid and observed, He, the sd. Wr. Wilkins, Hath Demised unto the said Jerh. Homfray and Jas. Birch, their Exors., etc., All the Veins, Mines, and Seams of Coal, Culm, Iron Ore, Iron Mines, and Iron Stone, sit., lying, and being in, upon, or under all those the afsd. sevl. Messes. and Lands comly. called and known by the Names of Abernant y Wenallt, in the said Par. of Aberdare and Tyr Y Werfa and Gorangon Vach, and also in, upon, or under all other the lands of the sd. Wr. Wilkins, sit. in the sd. Par. of Ystradyvodock, in the same County; Together with full Lbty to and for the sd. Jere. Homfray and Jas. Birch, their Exors., etc., at all times during the Term hereby granted, to try, search for, and dig for the said Coals, Culm, Iron Ore, Mine or Iron Stone hereby demised. And for that purpose to drive and sink all such Pits, Grooves, Levels, etc., as shall be thought necessary to the finding and working of the same; Together also with full Lbty. to the sd. Jerh. Homfray and Jas. Birch, their Exors., etc., to Erect and Build upon any part of the sd. premes. herein before demised, such Furnaces, Forges, Houses, Cottages, etc., as the sd. Jere. Homfray and James Birch, their Exors., etc., shall think fit. And also with full and free Lbty. to dig and raise such Earth, Clay, Sand, Quarry Stones, and other Stones, as shall be necessary in the building of such Furnaces, Forges, Houses, etc. And also with full Lbty. to the sd. Jerh. Homfray and Jas. Birch, their Exors., etc., to use and Convert all Brooks, Waters, Streams of Water found or to be found on the sd. premes. hereby demised, as well for the benefit, use, and service of the said intended Furnaces, Forges, Mills, and or. Works to be erected on the sd. demised premes. for the making and manufacturing of Iron, as for the better raising, working, mining, and landing the said Coal, Culm, Iron Ore, and Iron Stone, and Draining or carrg. off any Water or Waters that may be hurtfull or prejudicial thereto, and for any other use that ye sd. Jerh. Homfray and Jas. Birch, their Exors., etc., shall at any time during the term hereby granted, think proper.

To have and to hold the said Coal, Culm, Iron Ore, Iron Mines, and Iron Stones herein before mentd., with the Liberties aforesaid, unto the sd. Jerh. Homfray and Jas. Birch, their Exors, etc., from the 29th September next ensuing the day of the date hereof, during the full term of 99 years from thence next ensuing.

Yielding and Paying therefore unto the said Wr. Wilkins, his Exors., etc., the sum of one shilling for every Ton of Iron Ore, Iron Mine, and Iron Stone, and also the sum of six pence for every ton of Coal or Culm which at any time during the sd. Term hereby granted shall be raised upon the sd. sevl. tenemts. and lands of the sd. Wr. Wilkins hereby demised by the sd. Jerh. Homfray and Jas. Birch, their Exors., etc., such Tons of Iron Ore, Iron Mine, and Iron Stone, and also of Coal and Culm, to consist of twenty-one hundred weight of One Hundred and twenty pounds, comly. called long weight, and in default of raising, getting and working such number of Tons of Iron Ore, Iron Mine, or Iron Stone, or Coal or Culm, in each of the sd. Terms hereby granted as will produce by the reservon. and rate of Tonnage afd., the sum of £300 yearly, then yielding unto the sd. Wr. Wilkins, his exors., etc., yearly, and every year, for and during so many years of the said Term hereby granted as the sd. Jerh. Homfray and Jas. Birch, their Exors., etc., shall make such default as afsd. the clear yearly rent of £300, the sd. Reservon., Royalty, and Rent, or such of them as shall arise and be payable, to be paid half-yearly (that is to say), on every the 25th day of March and 29th day of Sept. during the said term hereby granted, without any manner of deduction, the first paymt. whof. to be made on March 25th next ensuing the date hereof.

Covenant on the part of lessees to pay rents, royalties, etc., on the appointed day.

Covenant to keep account books and allow the same to be examined.

And that it shall and may be lfull. to and for the sd. Wr. Wilkins, his Heirs and Ass's, and his and their Agents, Servants, and Workmen, from time to time, and at all times, during the sd. Term hereby granted to enter and pass into all Pits, Mines, Shafts, Levels, and Works hereby demised for the purpose of Inspecting, surveying, or Dialling the same.

And Also that they, the said Jerh. Homfray and James Birch, their Exors., etc., shall build on some part of the Farm and Lands herein before demised, called Abernant y Wenallt, at their own Expence, one substantial Blast Furnace, for smelting and manufacturing of Iron, and shall finish such Furnace ready to blow within two years from the date hereof. And shall erect and build upon such o'r part of the said Premes., called Abernant y Wenallt, as they shall think most convenient, at their like expence, one other substantial Blast Furnace for the smelting and manufactoring of the said Iron Ore, Iron Mine, and Iron Stone of the said Wr. Wilkins hereby demised, and shall finish such last-mentd. Furnace ready to blow within five years from the Day of the Date of these Presents, both which Furnaces to be of such dimensions and of such plan and plans, and to be worked after such manner and Process as they the said Jerh. Homfray and Jas. Birch, their Exors., etc., may think proper. Covenants as to fencing-in mines, paying all rates and Tallages, and upholding premises in good repair.

Proviso on breach of covenants as to payment of rent, or of other matters, for re-entry by lessor.

Covenant on the part of the lessor for quiet enjoyment.

In witness whereof, etc.

And a lease had also been taken by Jeremiah Homfray and James Birch from William Llewellyn, of Cowbridge, and Wyndham Lewis, of Lanishen House, both in the County of Glamorgan, of all the seams of coal and veins of iron ore under the lands of

Tyr William Cant pwynt,
Blaenant y Wennallt,
Tyr Ralph,
Cynnon Farm, and
Ty Llwyd,

to hold the same for ninety-nine years, at a yearly rent; all which farms were on the same side of the valley, and adjacent to their main taking.

Upon these leases having been obtained, Messrs. Homfray and Birch sought the assistance of partners to form an iron-works and develop the property, and these were found in the Kentish family of Tappenden.

The Works were designed to be made and placed on the Nant brook, near its junction with the Cynon, and little less than a mile up the valley from the head of the Aberdare and Cardiff Canal; and on February 26th, 1802, Articles of Partnership were entered into

Between

JEREMIAH HOMFRAY, of Landaff House, Co. Glamorgan, Esq., of the first part;

JAMES BIRCH, of Abernant, Co. Glamorgan, Ironmaster, of the second part;

JAMES TAPPENDEN, of Faversham, Co. Kent, Gentleman, of the third part;

JAMES TAPPENDEN, of Stourmouth, Co. Kent, Gentleman, of the fourth part;

And

FRANCIS TAPPENDEN, of Foster Lane, London, Gentleman, of the fifth part;

and after reciting that the above leases had been entered into, and after reciting that proposals had been made by Messrs. Homfray and Birch to the Messrs. Tappenden to form a partnership for the purpose of erecting iron-works, etc., on the lands,

It was witnessed that the persons named in the preceding Articles formed a partnership for the purposes stated, the capital to be £40,000, Messrs. Homfray and Birch to give a bond of £20,000 for their share, such partnership to continue during the terms of the leases before referred to.

Under these leases, the Abernant Company had already expended a large sum of money in erecting iron-works; and on the signing of the Articles, the bond was produced by Messrs. Homfray and Birch for £20,000 to secure the advances by the Messrs. Tappenden up to that date, being one-half or a moiety of the total capital of £40,000.

The following is a summary of the Bond:—

Know all Men by these Presents That We, Jeremiah Homfray, of Landaff House, in the County of Glamorgan, Esquire, and James Birch, of Abernant, in the said County, Ironmaster, are held and firmly bound to James Tappenden, of Faversham, in the County of Kent, Gentleman; James Tappenden, of Stourmouth, in the Coy. of Kent, Gentleman; and Francis Tappenden, of Foster Lane, London, Gentleman, in the sum of Forty thousand pounds of good and lawful money of Great Britain to be paid to the said James Tappenden, James Tappenden, and Francis Tappenden, or any or either of them, or their certain Attornies, exors., etc.. for the true payment whereof they did bind themselves jointly and severally, and their Heirs, etc.

Dated the 26th day Feby., 1802.

The condition of the above Bond was that J. Homfray and Birch, or either of them, their heirs, etc., sho'd truly pay unto the Tappendens (three) their exors., etc., sum of £20,000 moiety of sum of £40,000 by the Tappendens (three), lent or agreed to be advanced under the above Articles, of even date of Bond, being the proper debt of Homfray and Birch. And also if the sd. Homfray and Birch permit and suffer the said Tappendens (three), without any interruption, to receive and take by and from the said Co-partnership in the said Articles mentioned, and the Goods, Wares, and Merchandize should fully liquidate, pay, and discharge to them, the said James Tappenden and or's, their exors., the residue of the sd. sum of £40,000, and other such sum advanced by them under the sd. Articles of Co-partnership and the Interest thereof resply., in full discharge of the same, and according to the true intent and meaning of the same Articles, then the several Covenants, stipulations, conditions, and the above-written Obligation to be void and of no effect, or else to remain in force.

Signed, sealed, and delivered, after being duly stamped, in presence of John Tappenden.

JERE. HOMFRAY (Seal).
JAMES BIRCH (Seal).

It appears that a great want had been felt by this Firm, as by their neighbours, the Aberdare Company, of easier or cheaper access to the sea than that enjoyed; because, as late even as August 1st, 1800, the making of the Aberdare Canal and the tram-road to join their Works was only proposed, and not even then undertaken, or it may have been the wish to have two communications to the sea: the one at Cardiff by the Taff Valley, and the other to Neath and Swansea by the Neath Canal.

Be that as it may, the Abernant Company resolved upon undertaking the making of a tram-road from the Works, passing by and accommodating the Aberdare Works as well, to the Neath Valley, some eight or nine miles in length, the tram-road having an artificial inclined plane to reach the low level of the Canal. As the matter was one of mutual advantage to both Works, an agreement was entered into between them: the Messrs. Tappenden to be the owners finding the money. (This was a private undertaking by the Messrs. Tappenden, and outside their partnership with Messrs. Homfray and Birch), and the Aberdare Co. agreeing to pay certain tolls for using the road, and to other conditions.

The Messrs. Tappenden also, under the well-known power of the Eight-Mile Clause Act in the Aberdare Canal, entered into an agreement with Mr. John Scale, of the Aberdare Company, for the construction of a short length of tram-road from the Aberdare Canal at Tydraw, a mile and a-half in length to their respective Works. The connection was then made complete by tram-road between the Neath Canal and Aberdare Canal, and a trader could use either route for sending his iron for shipment. This length of tram-road appears to have been made at the joint expense of the two Companies.

However, no sooner were the tramways constructed than serious differences arose between the neighbouring Works as to the construction to be placed upon the Agreements entered into, and almost civil war raged in the district with, of course, costly lawsuits.

These serious difficulties, and the heavy outlay made in various directions by the Messrs. Tappenden, tended much to injure the position of the firm. One result was the retirement of Messrs. Homfray and Birch from the partnership, and the following terms of dissolution were agreed to on 26th January, 1807 :—

"MEM., 26TH JANY., 1807.

"Messrs. Jere. Homfray and Jas. Birch to relinquish their Shares at Abernant to Messrs. Tappenden at Lady Day next.

"Mr. Homfray to be paid £1,000, optional with Messrs. Tappenden as to time, they paying one Hundred per annum in the interim.

"Mr. Birch exactly the same.

"Mr. Jno. Powell to do the conveyance at Messrs. Tappenden's expense.

"Mr. Homfray to have in addition a Pipe of Port given him.

"Mr. Birch, in addition, to have One hundred and fifty pounds per annum, payable half-yearly, for his own life. He is to quit his house at Lady Day next, or as soon after as he can, not exceeding Mich's.

"We agree to the within arrangement, and authorise Mr. Fothergill to give Mr. Powell Instructions to get the Writings done accordingly.

"JERE. HOMFRAY.
"JAMES BIRCH.
"JAS. TAPPENDEN.
"JAMES TAPPENDEN.
"FRANCIS TAPPENDEN.

"Witness: RICHD. FOTHERGILL.

"No. 4.

"11th February, 1807.—Received the sum of Sixteen Shillings, the duty due to his Majesty on the above Agreement.

"£0 . 16 . 0. "THOMAS BOLD."

The above document, the original of which is in my possession, is remarkable for the boldness of the signatures.

It will be observed that Mr. Richard Fothergill witnessed the deed, and appears to have acted as mediator between the parties.

The annexed letter of Mr. James Tappenden, written the day but one after (28th January, 1807), alludes to the dissolution of partnership, and gives us some further particulars of interest:—

"S'r,—I have the pleasure to inform you that, under the mediation of Mr. Fothergill, an amicable and liberal adjustment has taken place between Messrs. Homfray and Birch, and myself and Relations. The former for the Considerations after mentioned have signed an Agreement as sketched out by Mr. Fothergill (and which he will send you to get stamped), to assign to us absolutely their Shares and Interest in all our Works and all Claims and demands respecting the same.

"For your Information in drawing the necessary Instruments on this Occasion, I now send you Copies of the Articles of Co-Partnership, which contain Recitals of the Lease from Mr. Wyndham Lewis of the Mines and Minerals, and the Lease from Mr. Wilkins of Farms, Mines, and Minerals.

"I also send Copies of Lease subsequently granted by Mr. Wilkins of Coppice, and of Lease also afterwards granted by Mr. Lewis of two Farms in Aberdare, being part of the Lands of which the Mines and Minerals were before granted, and which last Lease contains extensive powers, as well respecting the Farms as the other Estates of Mr. Lewis. There has been also another Lease granted by Mr. Wilkins of some Land in Ystradyvodock, on

"In a Word, the Assignment to Messrs. T. is to include every Thing relative to the Abernant Concern and its appendages.

"I have only to add that as Mr. Birch's health is precarious, the immediate Dispatch of this Business is most particularly and earnestly requested, and that the Transmittal of the Draft of the Deed of Assignment, etc., to me by the Mail, addressed Faversham, Kent, will be esteemed a favour. It shall be perused and sent to Mr. Homfray for his Inspection without delay.

"I am, Sir,

"Abernant, "Your very humble Servt.,

"28th Jan. 1807. "JAMES TAPPENDEN,

"And addressed, John Powell, Esq., Brecon."

Thus far our papers carry us with certainty as to the early history of both the Aberdare and Abernant Works, and we find them at this point close neighbours, each possessing three blast-furnaces, holding considerable takings, and with convenient roads and canals formed to convey their produce cheaply to market.

But at this stage our original documents—so far as our search has extended—fail us, and we have not been able to give in detail the changes that took place in after-years, and to fix with certainty the dates.

There is a good deal in Mr. Charles Wilkins' *History of the Iron and Coal Trades*, p. 165, on the subject of both these Works, much of it resting on the high authority of Sir W. T. Lewis, to which we must refer our readers. But we venture to trace down the history of both these Works, as far as we are able, but must not be held responsible for perfect accuracy.

It will have been noticed that Mr. Richard Fothergill was the witness to the dissolution of partnership of the Abernant Company, when Messrs. Jere. Homfray and Jas. Birch left it. He had also, in 1804, agreed on the part of the Aberdare Company on the terms under which the tram-road to the Neath Canal was made by the Messrs. Tappenden; but whether he was acting as their manager or managing partner, he appears to have been, in 1804, the chief ruling power in the Aberdare Company. It will be seen that he was not one of the original partners.

Our information, such as we have, goes to show that the Messrs. Tappenden did not long continue the concern. I believe they retired from the Works about 1812; and in 1819, or thereabouts, the property was purchased by the Aberdare Company, and thence the two Ironworks were managed as one concern.

---

Our papers tell us very little about these Works until 1831, when Edward Morgan Williams, of Gadlys, who had become the freehold owner of the farm of Tyr yr Ergid, comprised in the lease of 1799, granted a release to the partners in the Aberdare Iron Company, their names being given as—

William Thompson, George Scale, Thomas Forman,
Thomas Fothergill, Rebecca Scale, and

from all claims he had made against them for damages and waste to the said property; and further covenanted to allow them to work the mines and veins of coal on the said farm in such a manner that they might think to be to their most advantage, on payment, for the remainder, from 25th March, 1826, of £50 a year rent, beyond the sum of £40 agreed to be paid under the original lease of 1799.

which Ranges of Houses have been built. The Copy of this is for the Moment mislaid. I have a copy of it at Faversham, and as soon as I get Home I will transmit a sufficient Extract from it.

"Presuming you to have read the Articles, I would only add that Messrs. Tappenden have erected 3 Blast Furnaces, with a large number of Houses, Offices, and Buildings, opened many Ranges of Levels for Mine and Coal, and from unforeseen events were under the necessity of making a Rail Road 8 Miles in Extent from the Abernant Furnaces to the Neath Canal, terminating with an inclined Plane worked by a Steam Engine; and in consequence of executing these Great Works have expended a sum of money to a great amount; and from the peculiar circumstances in which they have been placed, have not received any Interest on the Monies by them so expended, and which Interest has, therefore, been unavoidably added to their Capital, the whole making an aggregate of £ (*sic*), or thereabouts.

"It being deemed expedient that Messrs. Homfray and Birch should advance a Loan to Messrs. Tappenden, in Ease of their Account, application was made for that purpose. On their declining to do it, Proposals were offered to release them from Responsibility, if they would resign their respective Interests in the Works. A Meeting was holden, and the Terms were settled that Messrs. Homfray and Birch, in consideration of quitting, are to receive from Messrs. Tappenden, at the expiration of years (or sooner, if Messrs. Tappenden think proper) £1,000 each, and in the meantime each of them is to be paid an annuity of £100. In addition to this, Mr. Birch is to receive during his Life £150 p. annum

"These Payments may remain as a Charge on the Works until liquidated.

"The Rail Road made by Messrs. Tappenden passes through the Lands of the Earl of Plymouth, Sir Wm. Douglas, the Marquis of Bute, Samuel Rees, Miss Williams (deceased), and Walter Wilkins, Esq. They have all been paid for the same. Miss Williams conveyed her Part to Messrs. Homfray, Tappenden, and Birch, and their heirs and assigns. The Conveyances from the other parties were entrusted to Mr. George, of Neath. What progress has been made in them I do not know. I rather apprehend that nothing has been done in them. If so, they will now be made with the omission of the names of Messrs. Homfray and Birch. The Road is a Freehold.

"Messrs. H. and B. must release all their Claims, Estate, and interest in the Rail Road and the Tonnage thereof to Messrs. Tappenden and their heirs and assigns for ever. Note that H. and B. have never been supposed to have any legal claim to this Road. The Receipts and Disbursements respecting the same have been always kept separate, and Messrs. J., J., and F. Tappenden are always called the 'Tram Road Company.'

"Mr. Birch is to resign to Messrs. Tappenden the occupation and possession of his Dwelling house, with the Garden and appurts., at Lady day next, or as soon after as may be, and not later than at Michaelmas.

"The present partnership is to be dissolved on the 25th March, 1807. Mr. Birch's Office of Manager is at an end, and all interference in the concern of Abernant has ceased, both with respect to him and Mr. Homfray, but Mr. Birch is to receive his present salary of £200 up to the said 25th March.

"There must be mutual Releases between the parties: that is, from Homfray and Birch to Messrs. Tappendens and è contrá,' and H. and B. are to be indemnified by Mess. T. from all Claims to be made respecting the Abernant Works or Concerns, and from all Guarantees, etc.

"In Mr. Birch's Dwelling House are divers Articles of Furniture, which were purchased at the Cost of Messrs. Tappenden upon the commencement of the Concern. These are to be assigned to Messrs. T.

*Page* 121. *Photo.*, 1906.

OLD ABERNANT IRON WORKS FURNACE.

The following few letters, amongst many we have, may throw some further light on the history of these works:—

"Aberdare, 11th Octr., 1829.

"My dear Sir,—I send over the Bearer to say that the Birmingham Iron Masters' day will be held on Thursday next, and I shall have great pleasure in accompanying you there. I propose being at Brecon on Tuesday afternoon, as I think you named to me that a coach left your place on Wednesday mornings at five o'clock, reaching Birmingham that evening. I could very much wish it arrived early enough to avail ourselves of an invitation to dine at Mr. Thompson that day: where he had wished us, by his letter to me this evening, to meet the Messrs. Botfields, of Shropshire. I hope we may be in time to join them after dinner, as you are no doubt aware of their being very influential Iron Masters. We shall, at all events, see them on Thursday; and if you can so manage your time, perhaps we might contrive to see one or two of the Staffordshire Works on Friday. We can arrange this when I see you. I have an opportunity of going to Brecon on Tuesday with Mr. Dudley and the Revd. Mr. Berkeu, who have to attend your Bible Society that evening. May I ask you to name your dinner-hour at four o'clock, as I feel an anxiety to witness the proceedings, which, I understand, commence at six o'clock?

"Be kind enough to reply to this, and the Bearer will bring it to me at Merthyr, and oblige,

"John Powell, Esq. "Yours, etc., Geo. Scale."

. . . . . . . . .

"Aberdare Iron Works, 18th March, 1831.

"Dear Sir,—Mr. Williams has been with us lately, surveying the disputed boundaries, and Maps are preparing to be attached to the Leases. We feel anxious that this business should be brought to a close as soon as possible, and I should be glad to receive the Drafts as early as convenient for you to send them, Mr. Williams proposing to accompany us to Brecon in the course of next month to sign the Deeds. We shall, therefore, feel exceedingly obliged by your informing us how soon we may expect they will be ready for our perusal, as we shall have to send them to London for the approval of Mr. Thompson.

"John Jones, Esq. "Yours, etc.,

"For Aberdare Iron Co. and Self,

"Geo. Scale."

---

"Dear Sir,—Mr. Scale omitted yesterday in his note to you, asking whether it is necessary upon Mr. Williams signing the two leases and the release, to cancel or give up the old ones.

"Please to say what is usual upon such occasions; and, as I expect Mr. Williams up every day, may I beg the favour of an answer in a post or two?

"I cannot resist the opportunity of begging you to do all in your power to protect us from Williams' and Morgan's attempts—if we do not beat them we shall have one lawsuit after another—ten times more vexatious than even Bar Iron at its present price.

"I am, my dear sir, yours very truly,

"Rowd. Fothergill.

"Please to direct your answer to the Merthyr Post Office, as I will send for it on Monday."

There were difficulties arising from divided control in 1837, and we find the following letter written by Mr. George Scale, complaining of the conduct of Mr. Rowland Fothergill at the Works, who was, he said, neither manager nor a partner:—

"Penydarran Iron Works, March 5th, 1837.

"My Dear Sir,—Mr. A. Hill has seen Rowland Fothergill, and bids me not think of anything from that quarter. The Fothergills seem to have forgotten the balance of power in a partnership. I must now depend upon your doing what you can for me, as arranged at Plymouth. I shall have to leave Penydarran if the Debt is to be resisted, and my best course will then be to go to Aberdare at once and take the management. I am sure of Thompson's support, and I believe he is waiting for some such step being taken; he will not put me there without having the reins in his hands, to which you and Mr. Hill very properly object, but when he finds me there I believe he will use me. Rowland Fothergill is not a partner, nor has he been appointed manager; and, if I am not much mistaken, I should have as great a right to take matters into my own hands at the Aberdare Works out of Fothergill's, as Mr. Thos. Forman has to come to these works and take them out of mine, which he does when he comes into the country.

"If Rowland Fothergill had a grain of sense, he would ask me to come to Aberdare, and, taking the sale of iron into his own hands, leave the management of the works to me.

"You will please let me hear from you soon.

"To John Jones, Esq.

"Very sincerely yours,

"HENRY SCALE."

"Aberdare Iron Works, 9th Novr., 1832.

---

## STATEMENT OF ABERDARE LEASEHOLDS IN 1837.

| Names of Properties. | Years Unexpired. | No. of Acres. | Fixed Rent. £ | s. | d. | Royalty per Ton. Coal. | Mine. | — |
|---|---|---|---|---|---|---|---|---|
| | 1837. | | £ | s. | d. | Coal. | Mine. | |
| Llywd coed ... ... | 32 | 900 | 1200 | 0 | 0 | No Royalty | | Surface and Minerals. |
| Tyr yr Ergid ... | 62 | 70 | 90 | 0 | 0 | Ditto | | Ditto ditto. |
| Bryn David ... ... | 32 | 70 | 15[1] | 0 | 0 | 6d. | 1s. | Minerals only. |
| Abernant, No. 1 ... | 86 | 92 | 50[1] | 0 | 0 | 6d. | 6d. | Ditto and Surface buildings, etc. |
| | | | 267 | 0 | 0 | ... | ... | |
| Abernant, No. 2 .. | 63 | 1366 | 600[1] | 0 | 0 | 6d. | 1s. | Minerals and Surface. |
| | | | 343 | 0 | 0 | ... | — | Ditto ditto. |
| | Acres ... | 2498 | 2565 | 0 | 0 | | | |

[1] The Royalties are *not* in addition to the fixed Mineral Rents. On the Llwydcoed Property are three Blast-Furnaces; on the Abernant No. 1 are two ditto; on the Abernant No. 2 are one ditto; on the Abernant No. 2, is a Forge. There are seven Steam Engines, vizt., two at Llwydcoed, and five at Abernant. Total, seven.

Some few years after this, the difficulties which had arisen between the Fothergills and the Scales seemed to have reached a crisis. And after a costly lawsuit between the parties—Scale *v.* Fothergill—the Court of Chancery decided that the whole of the Aberdare and Abernant properties should be put up for auction and sold.

The printed particulars are now before me, setting forth all the properties, accompanied with a large lithograph drawing of all the mineral takings, and stating that the same would be sold at Gray's Inn Coffee House, on Thursday, June 11th, 1846.

It is impossible to deal with this document at any length, and I have resolved to send a copy of the same to the Cardiff Free Library, to be filed there for future reference.

---

We append a copy of Mr. Fothergill's letter of 1804, respecting the Tramroad agreement:—

"W. FOTHERGILL, WITH AGREEMENT BETWEEN ABERDARE AND ABERNANT CO.'S, 26TH NOV., 1804.

"Dear Sirs,—Herewith I send you back the draft of Agreement between the Aberdare and Abernant Cos.

"I have read it over, and believe all fair enough except as to the Incline Planes, viz., that of the Neath Canal Co.'s and also that of the Abernant Co's., both which, it seems, are to be worked by the Abernant engine. The parties have now agreed on what I have put on your additional sheet, which please to reduce into proper language, &c.

"I have kept this far too long; its but a bad reason for hurrying you, but its a true one.

"I am, Dr. Sir,<br>"Yr. most Hbl. Servant,<br>"Signed, RICHD. FOTHERGILL."

"26th Nov., 1804.

"To Messrs. Powells.

"P.S.—Messrs. Tappenden and Co. have agreed that the Hirwain Co. shall travel on similar terms to the Aberdare folks, and Mr. Overton requests me to get an Agreet. made accordingly, Do you like to do it? If so, I will get the needful instructions."

And also some interesting letters relating to the making of the Aberdare Canal Navigation.

"The Aberdare Iron Company propose, that if the Aberdare Canal Company will open a communication from the Glamorganshire Canal to their Furnaces, by a Canal as far as the same can be conveniently made, and then the remainder by a Tram-Road, and will engage to reduce the Tonnage upon the Iron from their Works to three-pence per Ton per Mile, the said Aberdare Iron Company will engage, that if the Tonnage does not amount to the sum of Seven Hundred and Fifty Pounds per Annum, to Guarantee the deficiency from the time the said Canal and Road are completed, 'till the expiration of the said Aberdare Iron Company's Lease.

"JOHN SCALE,

"August 1st, 1800. "For Aberdare Iron Company

"To the Proprietors of the Aberdare Canal.

"Gentlemen,—In Pursuance of your orders of the 11th July, I have surveyed and examined the Country between Aberdare Furnaces and the Glamorganshire Canal, and am clearly of opinion that the best communication will be partly by a Canal, and partly by a Rail Road, a plan and estimate of which I have prepared for your inspection. I recommend cutting a Canal from the Glamorganshire Canal, at the head of the 7th Lock above the Aqueduct over the River Taff, to a place called Ty Draw, nearly opposite Aberdare Village, which will be 7 Miles in length, with a rise of only 25 Feet, and wanting about 12 Bridges, and I estimate the same, all expences included, at ten Thousand Five Hundred Pounds.

"From this Canal to the Furnaces, I propose a Tram Road one Mile and a half in length, which I estimate at One Thousand Five Hundred Pounds, including every expense.

"August 1st, 1800. "T. Dadford.

"Sir,—In obedience to an Order made at the last General Assembly of the Company of Proprietors, I send you the above Proposals and Report, which are to be taken into consideration at a Special Assembly to be held for that purpose, at the Star Inn, Merthyr Tidvil, on Friday the 29th instant, at 11 o'Clock in the Forenoon.

"I am, Sir, Your obedient Servant,

"P. Griffiths,

"August 8th, 1800. "Clerk to the Company of Proprietors."

XV.

# The Gadlys Iron Works.

MATTHEW WAYNE had been one of the trusted servants of Richard Crawshay, and as we shall see later, left the Cyfarthfa Works soon after the death of his old master in 1810. He then linked his fortunes with the nephew, Joseph Bailey, and they together in partnership bought the Nantyglo Iron Works from Harford, Partridge and Co. This was in 1811. A few years later, namely 1820, Mr. Wayne retired from the partnership, and apparently settled down at Aberdare, where he was already possessed of some landed property.

We have no precise information when the Gadlys Iron Works were built, except that certainly they were of modern date, and formed since 1820, and by Matthew Wayne and Co. They were placed on the right bank of the Cynon River, almost in the centre of Aberdare, then a mere village, near the point where the Cwmdare brook joins the larger stream. Only one blast-furnace was built, and the whole works were evidently designed on a small but complete scale. The mineral takings are said to have been 350 acres, and were, like the Works, on the right bank of the Cynon, and held from the Marquess of Bute.

In 1835, the entire property was put up for sale by auction, and we give the particulars nearly in full, the flowery descriptive hand of the well-known auctioneer, Mr. George Robins, being marked in every line.

THE GADLYS IRON-WORKS,

Particulars of Sale of Valuable Property, consisting of the Gadlys Iron-works, at Aberdare, in the County of Glamorgan, in full operation, and employing about 150 people.

The Ore is principally procured One Mile and a Half from the Works, and the Property consists of 350 Acres of Mineral Property, with a good Residence, etc.

Mr. Geo. Robins will Sell at the Auction Mart, opposite the Bank of England, on Thursday, the 30th Day of July, 1835, at Twelve o'clock, a very Valuable Property, for the Employment of Capital, consisting of Gadlys Iron-works, at Aberdare, in the County of Glamorgan. The extent and value of these Works need no comment or remarks in the neighbourhood of Merthyr Tydfil, or indeed for upwards of 100 Miles around the Country. Their fame is stamped, and a certainty attendant on their proceedings fully established. It is for the purpose of illumining those at a distance that the following concise and inadequate remarks are respectfully submitted :—

The Iron Trade being unusually brisk, the latter observation will, no doubt, be fully understood and conceded, now that it is in full operation. The old Proverb of "Make Hay while the Sun Shines" applies just now to the Iron Trade. It has received an invigorating impetus, and fast making up lee-way for unprofitable and bygone days. Gadlys would form a valuable appendage to a very large Iron Foundry, being capable of making, in its present state, from 1,700 to 2,000 Tons of Iron Annually, and extensive Iron Founders will find this work "A most valuable appendage for making their large Castings at once from the Furnace."

It possesses besides unusual facilities for sending them to a Shipping Port, by Water. The power of these Works, although in extent not to be put in comparison with the Great Leviathan hard by, is quite sufficient to ensure large Annual Profits, and the *materielle* to secure it is perfect, and in every respect complete. All the Buildings essential, and every Article in Trade necessary for keeping the Works in the fullest operation is included in the purchase, a short List of which is here subjoined, viz :—

A Powerful Steam Engine (calculated to blow a Furnace and a Refinery), from the Neath Abbey Company, executed in their best manner; a large Blast Furnace, Cast House, Stove Room, Turning Room, Refinery, Cupola, Smith's Shop, Weighing Machine, Three Calcining Kilns, Bridge House, Carpenter's Shop, and an Office; all kinds of Workmen's Tools, Coal Mine and Limestone Trams, Coke Barrows, Punching Machine, Turning Lathe, etc. There are about 5,600 Yards, or 200 Tons, of Plates, laid in and About the Works.

The Iron made is much esteemed, and particularly adapted for strong Castings and Engine purposes. The Coal is worked by a Pit close to the Works, which has, besides, the convenience of a Drift or Road for taking down Horses, a Balance Jet for raising Coal, two Eight-inch Pumps, One Worked by a Water Wheel, 24 feet in diameter, the other by a High-Pressure Steam Engine. The Works are well ventilated, and most advantageously situate for Working the extensive and hitherto untouched Mineral District of Cwm Dare.

The Ore is principally procured about a Mile and a Half from the Works, and within 500 Yards of the public tram road.

Some good veins of Ore are likewise being opened upon in the Coal Works. Limestone is about Five Miles distance. There are good Quarries of Stone, and, indeed, every thing required, close at hand. The whole of the Works adjoin the Public Tram Road, which communicates with the Cardiff and Aberdare Canal, from which Port they are distant only about 24 Miles; therefore the facility of dispatching the Manufactured Iron is obvious, and consequently renders a quick and lucrative sale more certain. Indeed, Liverpool and Bristol have hitherto alone taken off all that can be spared.

The property altogether consists of nearly 350 Acres of Mineral Property, held on advantageous Leases, of which abstracts of the Covenants and Conditions will be produced on the day of Sale. Also, a good Dwelling House, with Stable, Beast House, and productive Gardens, etc., surrounded by a Paddock, and all kinds of Appendages in the shape of comfort, renders the Property indeed complete.

Mr. Robins is earnest in his appeal to all those who, having Capital, and no distaste for employing it successfully, to give their immediate attention to this most excellent opportunity to amass wealth, with a little industry, and without more than ordinary exertion to obtain it.

Any further information can be obtained on application to Mr. Morgan, Gadlys, Aberdare, near Cardiff. Stocks of Pig Iron, Coke, and Ore are to be taken at a fair valuation.

---

David Mushet, at page 414 of his *Iron and Steel*, states that in 1839 Thompson and Co. had six Furnaces in blast at Aberdare (including Abernant). Also, that there was one Blast-Furnace at Gadlys, owned by Wayne and Co. He estimated the output of each Furnace at only 55 tons of pig-iron per week, or 2,680 tons per annum, on account of the Works being situate in the Anthracite and Stone Coal district west of the river Taff.

---

Mr. Jeremiah Homfray, after retiring from the Abernant firm, appears to have settled down at Cyfeillon, in the Rhondda Valley; but whether he opened and worked a Colliery on the property of Walter Wilkins there, our papers do not tell us. We next find him knighted, and his name appears as "Sir Jeremiah Homfray." His son Jeston was articled to Mr. Thomas Maybery, Solicitor, of Brecon, in 1815; and we are informed that his grandson, Jeston Homfray, is in business as a Solicitor at Stourbridge (not far from the family's original home) at the present time.

---

We must yet add another Note. *Place aux dames!* Mary Maybery, of Powick Forge, and mother of John Maybery, was not afraid to stand behind her son in the Hirwain Works, sharing the responsibilities.

And, again, we see Rebecca Scale, the widowed mother of John, Henry, and George Scale, sharing the risks of the Aberdare and Abernant—*Fortes creantur fortibus.* I have a great admiration and reverence for brave women!

---

HERE ENDS THE WESTERN DIVISION OF THE OLD SOUTH WALES IRON WORKS.

XVI.

# The Bute Iron Works.

WE have now described the old Iron Works in the Western Group, and are turning our heads eastward, taking the different Works in succession from the Rhymney Valley to Blaenavon.

The first we come to are the Bute Works in the Rhymney Valley, in Glamorganshire, and of the history of these our papers tell us very little. Apparently they were of the quite late date of 1825—and had a very short life.

As in the rush to the gold diggings of Australia and California, in the rush to Klondike, and, more recently, to Johannesberg and Kimberley, so in this new-found mineral district of South Wales (to-day it is the case with coal, not iron) capitalists tried to be the first to seize the best takings, and when they had succeeded, they found, as the Dowlais Company found, that they were the objects of the jealousy of their neighbours.

It would almost seem that the establishment of the Bute Works was a stroke in the game of the jealous landlord, the Marquess of Bute, and their jealous neighbours, the Penydarran Works, whose old feud we have described previously at length, acting more or less in concert.

And we find on October 24th, 1825, Messrs. Josiah John Guest, Wyndham Lewis, Rev. William Price Lewis, and Thomas Revel Guest (the Dowlais Company), granting a lease to William Forman, Thomas Seton Forman, and Thomas Johnson (the Bute Iron Works Company), of the lands of Bryn-pyllog and Gwayn y Mynydd (Newydd?) for the purpose of getting ore thereon, on certain rents and conditions, in the Parish of Gelligaer.

It may have been that the Dowlais Company were forced by pressure of circumstances to grant this lease: because this was the very land around which the great controversy between the Dowlais Company and their landlord, the Marquess of Bute, had raged, and as to which Mr. David Stewart, the eminent North-Country expert, and his assistant, Mr. Thomas Johnson, had reported adversely to the Dowlais Company (*ante*, page 42); or, possibly, it may have been a voluntary act on the part of the Dowlais Company, and intended in their own interest and advantage.

To me, I confess, the establishment of the Bute Works seems, as I have stated, to have been a move in the desperate game played by their opponents in the anxious years preceding the settlement of 1825.

Be this as it may, in 1825 the Bute Works were built on the land of the Marquess of Bute, on the right bank of the Rhymney River, immediately opposite the main Works of the Union Company. Their first partners were Messrs. William Forman, Thomas Seton Forman, and Thomas Johnson, and the blast-furnaces erected were of a somewhat pretentious style of architecture, having a front of Egyptian design; and we are informed that a picture of them was exhibited in the Royal Academy about that period.

Between the Brynpullog property and the Furnaces there intervened the farm of Mr. Capel Hanbury Leigh, called Duffrin Rumney (formerly the property of Mr. Edward Lewis); and of this the new Company were able to obtain a lease of the minerals.

The lease of the land on which the Works themselves stood commenced on the 2nd of February, 1824, and was to run for 92 years.

On July 4th, 1837, we find a second lease granted by the Marquess of Bute, and from which it appears that all the original partners had then retired from the concern, the names of their successors, the new lessees, being Messrs. Henry Rowles, William Thompson, and John Pirie.

An amalgamation shortly after followed of these works with their neighbours, the Union Works, on the other side of the River Rhymney, in Monmouthshire, the joint firms hence to be called and bear the name of the Rhymney Iron Company.

## XVII.

# The Union Iron Works.

On a certain plot of land in the Rhymney Valley, part of it being in the County of Brecon, and the property of the Duke of Beaufort, another part being in the County of Monmouth, and the property of Mr. Glover, and the third part being in the County of Glamorgan, and the property of the Dowlais Company, and at the meeting-point of the three Counties of Brecon, Glamorgan, and Monmouth,

Messrs. David Evans, John Ambrose, and
Thomas Williams. Richard Cunningham.

entered into an Agreement in 1800, to build a Furnace, and to carry on an Iron Works, and the Cast Iron trade.

The Capital to be advanced by each Partner was £1,000, and it was further agreed to advance in equal portions, by each of the Partners, the additional sum of £6,000 as Capital, when required.

The first-named Capital (£4,000) was advanced, and the Works commenced, Richard Cunningham and Thomas Williams being the Active Managing Partners, to superintend the Building of the Works, with an allowance of £100 a year each for their trouble, up to such time as the Furnace should be actually in blast.

It was agreed that the said concern should be carried on and continued under the firm of "The Union Iron Company," Richard Cunningham and Thomas Williams having the management of the concern during their lives, and the existence of the term.

Unless we include Thomas Lewis, of Newhouse, Co. Glamorgan, who may be said to have founded the Myrthy Furnace or Dowlais Works, this Thomas Williams is the first South Wales man (judging by his pure Welsh name) who has taken part or share in any of the Iron Works we have yet noticed. We shall find one later in Walter Watkins, of Dany Graig, at Ebbw Vale and Llangrwyney. Unfortunately, though they had enterprise and skill, neither had probably the staying power of sufficient capital behind them; and both, we shall see, looked back from the plough, and left the field for English promoters and English capitalists to exploit and to capture.

But all credit to these men for having at least started on the road to fame and fortune.

The position of this little Works—the old Furnace of which still stands—was well chosen, close to very rich fields of iron ore and coal; and either the little brook, Nantmelin, or the large stream, the Rhymney—I do not know which, as I was unable to trace the mill-leet through the effacement of the natural features of the ground—served as water-power for the blast. The Furnace itself was built just within the boundary of the County of Brecon.

The taking from the Dowlais Company on the right bank of the Rhymney was full of iron ore in patches on the surface, and of coal easily obtained by levels, and, similarly, that from Messrs. Glover in Bedwellty parish in Monmouthshire: but I do not think there were any minerals of importance in the Duke of Beaufort's Breconshire portion (Manor of Tretower, in the parish of Llangynidir) of their taking. And it appears that by the year 1802 a considerable iron furnace had been erected, and Iron Works of considerable extent established upon the premises, and a Dwelling-House built on the leasehold land adjoining to the furnace as a residence for the Manager, Mr. Richard Cunningham.

This little Works no doubt attracted the attention of their larger and longer-established neighbours; and Mr. Richard Crawshay, of Cyfarthfa, being desirous of starting his son William, and his son-in-law, Mr. Benjamin Hall, in an Iron Works of their own, or partly of their own, independent of Cyfarthfa, with the assistance of Mr. Watkin George, as an experienced and well-known man in the business, thought the acquisition of the Union Works desirable, and negociations were entered into for purchase with that company. Meanwhile, Mr. William Crawshay, the son, declined to join in the proposal, and Mr. Richard Crawshay took himself the position in the arrangement, as a proposed partner, which he had intended for his son.

The negociations were chiefly conducted by Mr. Benjamin Hall, and as the result, a fresh partnership was formed on the 27th September, 1803, on certain terms, the partners then being—Richard Crawshay, Watkin George, Benjamin Hall, Richard Cunningham, and Thomas Williams, to be and to form "The Union Iron Works Co." And it was agreed that Richard Cunningham and Thomas Williams should devote their whole time to the management of the concern; in consideration of which they were not to be called upon to advance any money beyond the £1,000 each which had been already advanced, and they were to be allowed the keep of a Horse and Cow each.

And then appears the following remarkable provision:—

> "It is also agreed that Coal may be used for manufacturing iron on the premises."

[Possibly it refers to a Small Forge or Smith's Shop being established.]

The purchase of the shares of David Evans and John Ambrose, and subsequently that of Thomas Williams, was then completed by Richard Crawshay, Watkin George, Benjn. Hall and Richard Cunningham, each having one-fourth share in the concern, and a deed of partnership was entered into. The amount paid to Mr. Thomas Williams was, however, £3,000, and the total capital of the concern is stated to have been £29,000. This probably included the cost of the new Blast Furnaces built at a point lower down the river, where the large Works were finally placed.

And so matters went on for a year or so, Mr. Cunningham, as by agreement, superintending the concern, until the 31st August, 1804, when he was suddenly ordered by Mr. Richard Crawshay to attend him at his Dwelling-house at Cyfarthfa, some five miles distant.

The following is the sworn account given of the interview by Mr. Cunningham :—

"He found Mr. Benjamin Hall in Mr. Crawshay's room, and on being admitted, he was at once charged by Mr. Crawshay, in terms of great violence, with having improperly drawn bills on account of the co-partnership, and with being a swindler, or words to that effect. Mr. Crawshay, who is a Magistrate and a person of great property and influence in these parts, threatened to send him to the County Gaol at Cardiff, and desired Watkin George or Thomas Peirce, his Clerk, to fetch a Constable, so that he might be taken immediately to Gaol.

"Mr. Crawshay insisted that he should not continue a Partner, and that he should immediately sign an instrument dissolving the same. Accordingly, Mr. Cunningham, being in an ill state of health, and being afraid of being sent to prison, consented to sign any papers presented to him.

"Benjamin Hall then drew up on a stamped paper an Indenture, whereby Mr. Cunningham relinquished all his interest in the concern to Mr. Richard Crawshay, Watkin George, and Benjamin Hall, in consideration of receiving the sum of £1,654 9s. 3d., the sum computed to be the amount of his Capital in the concern, after adjustment and investigation by Mr. Thomas Peirce. The document is dated 31st August, 1804, and signed by

"Richard Cunningham,
"Richard Crawshay,
"Watkin George, and
"Benj. Hall,

and as to the balance agrees Richd. Cunningham and Thomas Peirce."

Subsequently to this, Mr. Richard Cunningham commenced a suit against Mr. Richard Crawshay and others, alleging that his signature to the deed of Dissolution of Partnership had been improperly obtained and under threats and duress, and was altogether void ; and he also complained that the statement of accounts prepared by Mr. Peirce, and which he had signed for the same reason, was wholly wrong.

The pleadings of Mr. Richard Crawshay and his partners give a different version of the interview, maintaining that Mr. Cunningham had committed irregularities in the accounts, and that the deed of Dissolution of Partnership had been agreed to and signed without any threats and undue pressure on their part being employed.

What was the result of the action our papers do not show, but it may be assumed that Mr. Cunningham could not, and did not, continue a member of the firm any longer. But it was not a very happy beginning for a young Works!

Among the documents we have are a number of draft building leases granted by Messrs. Richard Crawshay and Benjamin Hall, of lands in the vicinity of the Works.

So far our old papers carry us with certainty, but now comes a period, say after 1806, when, the works being a going established concern, there was little need of intervention of lawyers; and if there had been, Mr. Benjamin Hall, being a barrister himself, probably easily arranged the little legal business necessary.

A whole troupe of English Ironmasters had invaded the Welsh Hills, the indigenous Welsh inhabitants being either lookers-on, or hewers and drawers for those who, with capital and skill, soon changed the solitudes of the high plateau land and the valleys and slopes of the mountains, from a solitude into a teeming hive of human industry.

The Welsh looked on and wondered at the changes effected before their eyes: great furnaces being erected in every direction, and money lavishly expended by strangers, of whom they scarcely knew the names, and nothing as to where they came from, except from Staffordshire, London, or Bristol.

It is not surprising to find that mythical stories in the minds of the country people wreathed the hills like a mist; and tradition, mixing up the true with the fabulous, invested everything almost with romantic surroundings.

This I found to be the case in the Rhymney Valley, when I sought to add information derived from local witnesses to my paper information. For instance, we know for certain, that, including £3,000 paid to Mr. Thomas Williams, Messrs. Richard Crawshay and partners bought out all interests in the Union Works for under £10,000, and that the total sum invested, including their own shares, was only £29,000.

And what does tradition tell us, and that in the best-informed quarters? The story has been handed down, and is still current as truth in the district, that Thomas Williams and Co. were first offered £75,000 for their Works by Crawshay Bailey; but that Richard Crawshay, of Cyfarthfa, being anxious to obtain the Works for his son-in-law, Ben. Hall, stepped in and bought them for £100,000!

There is a foundation or admixture of truth in the story—the Works were purchased by Richard Crawshay, and with the object stated, but the sum given was £10,000, not £100,000; and as for Crawshay Bailey being a competitor, probably at that time he was under twenty years of age: a young lad without any capital whatever, in his uncle's office at Cyfarthfa.

From the circumstances stated, tradition on the Welsh hills, if anywhere, cannot safely be trusted; and I felt that, as I had set out on the task with the avowed intention to supply facts only capable of proof, I must close my ears to the tales handed down by tradition, though implicitly given credence to by even the oldest and best-informed of the local people. I should be much pleased, and my task would be greatly simplified, were it otherwise.

In the absence of full and certain documentary evidence, I will endeavour, however, to carry on the narrative of the history of these Works, and do the best I can to place it before my readers for what it may be worth.

The Works were fully acquired, as we have seen, by Richard Crawshay and Co. in 1804, and we may assume were extended and vigorously conducted until his death in 1810. Ben. Hall, his son-in-law, became by the terms of Mr. Crawshay's will sole owner of the Works, and carried them on to, shall we say 1820, or thereabouts. We cannot well say later, as Mr. Benjamin Hall died at the early age of 39.

Then, or soon after, Mr. Johnson came on the scene as manager of the Works, but whether as part owner or not I do not know; but from all accounts he was a man of great ability and skill in the Iron industry, and added largely to the Works.

There are two dates I cannot fix—that when Ben. Hall ceased to be the principal partner in the concern, and the other when the Rhymney tramway to Bassalleg was made by Crawshay Bailey. Nor do I know the circumstances under which Crawshay Bailey came to make that tramway at all. In fact, of the early history of Crawshay Bailey after he left Cyfarthfa, until we find him in partnership with his brother Joseph at Nantyglo, in 1820, I have no certain knowledge.

However, in 1825, or thereabouts, as we have seen, the Bute Works were formed on the opposite side of the river, and in a few years after it was proposed by the owners of the two Works that they should be amalgamated and form one Company, to be called the Rhymney Iron Company. The amalgamation was carried out, and from that day to this, the Rhymney Company, in one form or another, have held and worked the large mineral fields leased on either side of the Rhymney as one great concern : as an Iron Company, as long as it was profitable to make iron, and since as a great Coal-producing Company.

In 1839, according to David Mushet, *Iron and Steel*, p. 415, the Rhymney Iron Company (Rhymney and Bute) had six blast furnaces.

Of the more modern history of these Works, Sir Henry W. Tyler, the Chairman, has been good enough to supply me with an account; though of the period intervening after the date when my documentary evidence ends, he is unfortunately able to give no certain information.

Sir H. W. Tyler writes me as follows:—

"Rhymney Iron Company, Limited (Established 1836),

"26, Martin's Lane, London, E.C.,

"John Lloyd, Esq. "Oct. 25th, 1905.

"Dear Sir,—I have had the pleasure of receiving your letter of the 17th inst., which has been handed to me to-day. I have been making enquiry to see whether I could find any information which would be useful to you in your valuable work, but I am afraid the records at this office are very scanty indeed. I was only born in 1827, and therefore cannot remember what happened between 1810 and that date; and even after 1827 I did not become Chairman of the Rhymney Iron Company until, I think, 1877, previous to which I had very little acquaintance with it except as a Shareholder. We formerly used to make excellent Steel Rails, and got a very good reputation for Iron and Steel Work generally; but when the price of Steel Rails fell, in consequence of foreign competition, we could not continue the Steel Works without serious loss, and they were discontinued in 1891, and the Furnaces and the Bessemer Plant were demolished, fortunately for the Company at that time, inasmuch as it has been doing better as a Coal Company than it was possible to do as a Steel and Iron Company. We now turn out about 850,000 tons of coal a year, and we are sinking four new Pits, one of which has already reached Coal, and the others are expected to do so at the end of this year or early next year, which will, we hope, commence a new era of prosperity to the Company. I have asked the Secretary to search diligently in this office to see if he can find anything that might be interesting to you, and to send you any records that he can find.

"Yours, &c.,

"H. W. Tyler."

And here must end our account of these Iron Works, but it would be incomplete without some notice of —

## BUCHAN'S SHOP.

When recently at Rhymney, I was taken to see Andrew Buchan's Shop, of which I had often heard, and the fame of which was great throughout the Hill district, and far away in the Counties of Monmouth, Brecon, Carmarthen and Cardigan. While a great seller of goods and food to the large labouring population there and around, he was a large purchaser from the farmers and millers in the Counties I have named. Williams, of Maenest, Bendall, of Abercynrig, and others, supplied his shop weekly with fat cattle, sheep, poultry, eggs, cheese, and butter, salted and fresh; while troops of "Cardie Carts" from Cardiganshire brought hundreds of half-cured fat pigs, and tons of salt butter there through the early autumn and winter. The Moor Park Mills, at Llangrwyney, and the Velindre Mills, at Brecon, with John Handley as the skilful miller, sent there four-horse millers' vans with a weekly or bi-weekly supply of flour through the year.

And the shop is even now a sight, though shorn, from various causes, of much of its original business. It consists of a long, low, rectangular building, divided into compartments, with counters round, and ample space for its throng of customers that came on busy nights towards the week-end. There was a division for one class of articles like drapery, and another for grocery, and there were butcher's shops attached; and, in fact, every provision made for carrying on a general if not universal trade for a large industrial population.

And who was Andrew Buchan? He was a Scotchman, as the name denotes, and he first became a somebody in the district by contracting to divert the course of the Rhymney River for the Company. This led to his opening a shop for the convenience of his own work-people, and he soon extended the premises to meet the requirements of the workpeople at the Works generally. Whether there had been any arrangement financially between the Rhymney Company and the shop, I have never heard, and do not care to enquire too closely. All I know is that Andrew Buchan was a name to conjure by, in that and a wide district around for forty years, and he lived to a good old age, and respected by every one.

His house at the back of the range of shops had a pleasant parlour, where a farmer from Breconshire, or other, doing business with him, had a hearty welcome, and no one ever had to call there twice for his money.

All this is a bit of hearsay, but derived from living witnesses, and partly as well from my own knowledge.

XVIII.

# Tredegar Iron Works.

We now leave the valley of the Rhymney River, and crossing the narrow intervening ridge of mountain to the eastward, find ourselves in the valley of the Sirhowy River.

It would seem that here, at Tredegar, some Iron Forges had been earlier established in a small way, but of the particulars of such we have no record.

Our history commences in 1764, when Thomas Morgan, of Rhiwperra, Co., Glamorgan, Esqre., granted a lease for 40 years of Tredegar Forge to John Maybery, gentleman, the Ironmaster of Brecon Furnace and Hirwain Iron Works, of whom a full account as regards those two Works has been already given in this Volume at pp. 3 and 11.

But we have now to write of his connection with Tredegar, to which, though far distant, the attraction of a profitable venture in the mineral world had led him.

It is a somewhat strange introduction, but in order to make clear what follows afterwards, we have thought it desirable to give here at the outset the pedigree of the family of Morgan of Tredegar and Rhiwperra, which includes, of course, that of his lessor, the above-named Thomas Morgan, Esqre., of Rhiwperra:—

Wm. Morgan, of Tredegar, Esq., M.P., Mon., 1659-79. = Blanch, dau. and heir to Wm. Morgan, of Derw, Co. Brecon, Esq.

- Thos. Morgan, of Tredegar, Esq., M.P., co. Brecon, 1689-90, co. Mon., 1690-99; *ob.* 1699. = Martha, dau. to Sir Edward Mansel, of Margam, Knt.
- John Morgan, of Machen, Esq., Lord-Lieut. of cos. Brecon and Mon., M.P., co. Mon., 1701-20; *ob.* 1720. = Mary, dau. to Gwyn Vaughan, of Tre-barried, co. Brecon, Esq.
- Other issue.

Issue of Thos. Morgan:

- Son and dau., *ob. infants.*
- A. Sir Wm. Morgan, of Tredegar, K.B., Lord-Lieut. cos. Brecon and Mon., M.P., co. Mon., 1722; *ob.* 1731. = The Lady Rachel, dau. to Wm., 2nd Duke of Devonshire.

Issue of John Morgan:

- C. Thos. Morgan, of Rhiwperra, Esq., M.P., Breck., 1723-34, co. Mon., 1734-47, co. Brecon, 1747-69. = Jane, dau. to Maynard Colchester, of the Wilderness, co. Glou., Esq.

Issue of Sir Wm. Morgan (A):

- B. Wm. Morgan, of Tredegar, Esq., M.P., co. Mon. 1747-63; *ob. coel.*, 1763.
- Wm. Jones, of Clytha, Esq. = Eliz'th, *ob. s. p.*, 1787.

Issue of Thos. Morgan (C):

- D. Thos. M., of Tredegar, Esq., M.P., Brecon, 1754-63, co. Mon., 1763-71; *ob. coel.* 1771.
- E. Charles M., of Rhiwperra, Esq., M.P., Breck., 1763-69; *s. p.* = Mary, dau. and heir to Thos. Parry, of Arkston, Esq., and widow of Robt. Mynors, of Treago.
- F. John M., of Derw, Esq., M.P. Will dated June 23, 1785.
- G. Jane, eventual heir. = H. Sir Charles Gould, Knt. (son of King Gould), LL.D., Judge-Advocate-General. Created a Baronet, 1792; assumed the name of Morgan, 1792; *ob.* 1806, æt. 82.

Issue of Jane and Sir Charles Gould:

- I. Sir Charles M., 2nd Baronet.
- Jane, m. Samuel Homfray, of Penydarran.

Issue of Sir Charles M., 2nd Baronet (I):

- J. Sir Charles Morgan Robinson Morgan. Created Baron Tredegar.
  - Godfrey, 2nd Lord Tredegar.
- K. Charles Gould Morgan, M.P.
- L. Rev. Charles Augustus Morgan.

It will be seen that by the death of Sir Wm. Morgan (A), of Tredegar, and subsequently of his son, William (B), the latter without issue, the estates, being in tail male, went to his Uncle, Thomas Morgan, Esqre., of Ruperra (C), and thence to his eldest son Thomas, of Tredegar (D); then to the next son, Charles, of Ruperra (E); then to the next son, John Morgan (F), of Dderw; who, all dying without issue, Jane (G), their sister, became the eventual heir of the Morgan Settled Estates. Jane married Sir Charles Gould (H), Judge-Advocate-General, and had issue. The question of right of his father (C) to grant so long a lease as 40 years, was raised by his son Charles (E) on succeeding to the estates.

We now give the Case thereon, submitted to Counsel by Messrs. Maybery and Wilkins, the occupying tenants.

---

## TREDEGAR FURNACE, JANUARY 12, 1764.

### CASE FOR MESSRS. MAYBERY AND WILKINS, SUBMITTED TO MR. BEARCROFT IN JUNE, 1778, AND HIS OPINION THEREON.

By an Instrument of that date intituled "Articles of Grants, Covenants and Agreements," made between the Honble. Thomas Morgan of Ruperra (C) in the County of Glamorgan, Esq., of the one part, and John Maybery, Gent., of the other part. The said Thomas Morgan, for the rent thereinafter reserved, Did Demise, grant, and to Farm let unto the said John Maybery,

All that Forge called Tredegar Forge with the Store-house, Quay, Furnaces, and other Forges and Coal works therein particularly mentioned. To hold unto the said John Maybery, his exs., ads. and assigns, from the 2nd day of February next for and during and unto the full end and term of 42 years from thence next ensuing, and fully to be completed and ended at and under the Yearly Rent of £260, payable as therein mentioned. Also the said Thomas Morgan did bargain and sell unto the said John Maybery, his exs., ads. and assigns, All the woods (except Timber Trees of Ash, Oak, Elm and Beech), standing and growing on any Lands of the said Thomas Morgan in the several Counties of Monmouth and Glamorgan, fit for making Charcoal, at 10*s.* 6*d.* p. Cord, to be Cut and paid for at the times and in the manner therein mentioned. Among several other Covenants and Clauses in the said Articles contained, the said Thomas Morgan Did for himself, his heirs and assigns, also covenant that he, the said John Maybery, his exors., admrs. and assigns paying the said Yearly Rent and performing the covenants on his and their parts to be done and performed, should quietly enjoy the said Forges, Furnace and Store-house, Woods and premises and liberties aforesaid, during the term thereby granted, without the Interruption, Claim, and demand of any Person or Persons whatsoever.—*Vide* Copy Articles. In pursuance of this Agreement, Mr. Maybery entered upon the premises, and soon after took Mr. Thomas Wilkins into Partnership, but no Articles of Partnership have been executed between them.

In the lifetime of Mr. Morgan, the Lessor, and of Mr. Thomas Morgan, his Eldest Son, who succeeded him in the Estate, Messrs. Maybery and Wilkins, in confidence of the Lease and not doubting, or having any kind of Notice, but that he had power to grant it for 42 years, laid out several large sums of money in Digging for Coal, Additions to the Buildings, and making Levels and water Engines, amounting to £1,400 and upwards, and in many other respects much improved the Works, and paid all monies due for Rent, Cordwood, etc., to the time of the death of Mr. Thomas Morgan, the Son, which happened about the year 1771.

The Disturbances in America greatly affecting the Iron business, and finding themselves great losers in carrying on the Trade, they on the 8th March, 1775, Assigned over part of the Demised Premises to Messrs. Morgan and Price, at the clear Yearly Rent of £260 (being the same Rent they Paid Mr. Morgan for the whole) for the term of 30 years.

On the death of Mr. Thomas Morgan, the Son (D), the Estate came to Mr. Charles Morgan (E), who entered thereon as Tenant in Tail Male, under the Will of Sir William Morgan, late of Tredegar; and he now insists that Mr. Thomas Morgan, his late Father, being only Tenant for life, with Remainder to his first and other Sons in Tail Male, had no right to make any Lease that could be binding on the Remainderman, but such as he was empowered to do by the Clause in the Will. This Clause empowers his (the Testator's) Brother, Thomas Morgan and his Sons, etc., when they or either of them should be in possession of his Messuages, Manors, Lands, Tenements and Hereditaments, or any part thereof, to Grant any Leases or Grants under their or either of their hands and seals respectively, of the said premises, or any part thereof, for any Term or Terms of years not exceeding One and twenty years, or for the term of Lives not exceeding three Lives, so as upon such Leases or Grants to be made or Granted there be reserved the accustomed and ancient Rents.

Mr. Morgan insists that this Lease for forty-two years is not binding upon him as the Remainderman in possession, it exceeding the power given by the Will; and that at the expiration of twenty-one years he will demand the Possession, and, if not given up, make a Re-entry to ground ejectments, etc.

There is an Arrear of Rent due to Mr. Morgan for the Works, and a considerable sum for Cordwood, amounting, in the whole, to upwards of £2,000, as now computed; and as Messrs. Maybery and Wilkins are at present unable to carry the Iron Business on, that part of the Works remaining unlet, they, for want of being worked, are in some degree decayed; but a computation has been made by the Partners that they may be put in compleat Working Order for One hundred and fifty pounds, or thereabouts, tho' Mr. Morgan says that by an Estimate made by his direction, it will amount to £430 or, thereabouts.

Mr. Morgan also insists that ye Lessee, or the person concerned for him, knows or might have known the title of Mr. Morgan, the Lessor, who was not heir to his Nephew or Brother, the preceding owners, and therefore must have taken under the Will of one of them which is on record.

It is contended on the part of Messrs. Maybery and Wilkins that if Mr. Charles Morgan will not permit them to have the benefit of the whole Term of Forty-two years granted by Mr. Thomas Morgan, the Father, that his Executor is bound by his Covenant for quiet enjoyment, and that as he left Assets sufficient, such Executor, if they are Evicted, must Recompense them all the Damage they may sustain, as well for what they have already laid out in improvements, which were then done at a great risque and uncertainty, as for the profits they could make of the residue of the Works, for the Remainder of the Term, which they value, if let to Undertenants, at clear £200 p. ann. at the least—they also contend that Mr. Morgan cannot be injured in the meantime, as the Rent reserved by their Lease to Messrs. Morgan and Price amounts to as much as is reserved by the Original Lease, and which is agreed to be for the future paid by the Underlessees (whose responsibility is not doubted) to Mr. Charles Morgan.

Messrs. Maybery and Wilkins, being under Terms of Assigning all their property for the benefit of their Creditors, are very desirous to do every justice in their power as well to Mr. Morgan as to all others to whom they are Indebted; and as the remainder of this Term and the Advantages which they compute will arise from the monies by them laid out in the Works, will amount to a considerable sum, they, in justice to their Creditors, and to acquit themselves of any suspicion of partiality, would wish to be advised in what manner their Interest is to be estimated; and if the Lease, so far as respects the Number of years exceeding Twenty-one, is void, how the damages they may sustain for want of having the compleat Term of 42 years are to be averaged or computed, the Executor of the Lessor having Assets sufficient.

Your Opinion is therefore desired whether the Lease granted by Mr. Thomas Morgan to Mr. Maybery for 42 years is at this time or at the expiration of 21 years (for which last-mentioned term he had power to Grant), void or voidable—if made void by Mr. Morgan by Re-Entry and proceedings in Ejectment, have not Messrs. Maybery and Wilkins, or Mr. Maybery alone, any and what remedy against the heir or Executor of Mr. Thomas Morgan, the Lessor, for any damages they may sustain by being evicted before the expiration of the 42 years.

### Opinion on Above.

"Supposing the Power of Leasing to be such as it is here stated to be, I am of Opinion that the Lease in question is good for 21 years, but no longer. If, at the expiration of that Term, the Lessee shall be evicted by the person who shall at that time be entitled to the Freehold or Inheritance, certainly Mr. Maybery will have a remedy by Action of Covenant, founded on the Covenant in the Lease for quiet Enjoyment for 42 years, against either the Heir or personal Representative of the Lessor, as far as their respective assets will extend, in which he will be entitled to recover a satisfaction for the Damages occasioned by his being evicted before the end of the Term granted by the Lease."

Supposing your Opinion to be that the Assets of Mr. Morgan, the Lessor, are liable to the Damages Messrs. Maybery and Wilkins may sustain by not having their full Term of 42 years, how will those damages be averaged, should the matter go before a Jury? Is it probable that a Jury would find in damages what the Works may be estimated to be worth or rented for yearly, for the residue of the 42 years over and above the reserved Rent, deducting for Repairs and other casual Expenses, or only the money which can be proved to be laid out by the Partners in improving the Buildings, making Fire Engines, and Digging and Opening new Coal Works at a great risque, etc., or how otherwise? If some medium could be pointed out by which those Damages could be estimated, it would prevent any dispute between the parties, who on each side seem to wish to avoid it, and to settle matters consistent with what a Court of Justice might probably do, if litigated. If such a medium should occur to you, be pleased to point it out.

OPINION ON ABOVE.

"I think a Jury would probably estimate the Damages in such a Case, not merely from the money laid out by the Lessee in improving the Buildings, etc., but by giving a reasonable satisfaction to the Plt. for the probable clear profits which might have arisen to him by reason of the occupation of these premises, if he had been permitted to keep them to the end of his term. And I have known that Line followed by Juries on the Trial of questions of this kind, when proper Calculations have been laid before them in Evidence.

"EDWD. BEARCROFT,
"Linc. Inn, 15th June, 1778."

We may assume that with this complication of troubles overtaking the Firm, Messrs. John Maybery and Thomas Wilkins, his brother-in-law, withdrew from any connection with the Tredegar Works; but as to how their affairs were settled, our papers do not tell us.

Neither have we any Documents relating to the period down to March 20th, 1800, when Sir Charles Gould, now Sir Charles Gould Morgan, had become, in right of his wife, Jane, the owner of the Tredegar and Ruperra Estates.

It appears that his daughter, Jane, had married Samuel Homfray, the well-known Ironmaster of Penydarran (and of whom we have written earlier), as her second husband; and, in view of this family connection, it was arranged that Mr. Samuel Homfray, in conjunction with other partners, should become lessee of the Tredegar Iron Works.

And we now find that the following Memorandum of Agreement entered into on 20th March, 1800, for a Lease of the Coals and Mines under Bedwelty Common, between Sir Charles Morgan, Bart., and Samuel Homfray, Richard Fothergill, and Matthew Monkhouse.

. . . . . . .

## THE LEASE FROM SIR CHARLES MORGAN, BART., TO SAMUEL HOMFRAY RICHARD FOTHERGILL, AND MATTHEW MONKHOUSE.

To consist of all the coals and mines, etc., of all descriptions, of Clay, Sand, Stone, Slate, Firestone, etc., etc., under Bedwelty Common and Cwm Tyssog Inclosure, and under the whole of the Inclosed Lands, abutting North on Nantybwch and Breconshire, East on Sirhowy River and Abercarne Manor in the Hamlet of Mamhole, South on the Freehold of Morgan Watkin, near Pont Gwaith yr Harn, and West on Bedwelty Common aforesaid, together with the surface of the said Inclosed Lands and of two pieces opposite, adjoining Sirhowy River—subject to the existing Leases—the Tenants of all which paying their Rents to the Takers of this Lease, who are to pay a nett Rent of £300 p. annum for the first 5 years, and £500 p. annum afterwards for the term of 99 years, which rent is to include the Tythes and Land Tax.

The rent to commence from the 25th Inst., payable half-yearly. If no good sand can be found on the aforesaid premises, the Takers to have liberty of getting it from other premises belonging to Sir Charles, as near as it can be found, on paying reasonable damages for the Land injured thereby. Timber to be had from the Tredegar Estates, as required, provided its ready for Falling, on paying a fr. price for the same.

The Like in Pitt Timber when the Lease to Harford Partridge and Co. permit it.

The Takers are to have liberty of using all the Water they can collect on the premises, as well as Sirhowy river, together with Liberty to erect any Forges, or other Works on the said River, between the aforesaid Premises, and where it empties itself into the Ebbw, or within one Mile below, on paying a times price, or fair valuation, of the necessary Lands wanted for such Purposes, and a sufficient Colliery, if any one near it can be found then unlet, at a fair annual Rent.

The Takers to be at liberty to improve the Lands, clear old Fences, Grubb Wood, etc., Make Water Courses, Ponds and Ditches, with other usual Clauses; and to have Liberty to make a Tram or other road down Sirhowy Valley, to join the Canal, and of erecting Warehouses there, paying reasonable damages for the Land.

The Takers to engage to expend on the Premises £10,000, at Least, in erecting Works. The Takers to engage to make use of Mr. Morgan's Wharf at Newport for all Articles and things they may have occasion to bring down there for shipping, and to send all the Iron, etc., by his Vessels to Bristol, which they may have occasion to send there, Mr. Morgan engaging to charge no more than the customary and then times price for the Wharfage and Freight.

We do engage to grant the Lease of the Mines, etc., and Lands, as mentioned on this paper, introducing in such Lease the usual and Customary Clauses between Landlords and Tenants; and though we have it not in our power to confirm the same for the Term mentioned, yet we will execute such Instruments on some plan hereinafter to be determined as shall secure the same to the Lessees, or indemnify them from any Loss they may sustain by Erection of Works, etc. And they have this Authority under our hands, to commence immediately on the erection of Works, etc., making satisfaction and agreeing with the Tenants for any damage they may do to the Lands before the Leases fall into their hands. Samuel Homfray, on behalf of himself, and Richard Fothergill and Matthew Monkhouse, agrees to take this Lease.

London, Grafton Street,
20 March, 1800.

CHAS. MORGAN.
CHAS. MORGAN.
SAML. HOMFRAY.

This document, it will be seen, was signed by Sir Charles Morgan, the father (H), and Charles Morgan, the son (I); and for the purpose of further assuring the Lessees against loss by the remainderman claiming the right to set aside the Lease, on succeeding to possession, the following further Deed was executed by all the parties:—

1800.—By an Indenture made between Rt. Hon. Sir CHARLES MORGAN, Bart, of Tredegar, in the County of Monmouth, a Member of the Privy Council, Advocate-General and Judge Martial of his Majesty's Forces, and Lord of the Manor of Machen, in the said County, and

CHARLES MORGAN, of Ruperra, County of Glamorgan, Esquire, Son of the said Sir Charles Morgan, Baronet, of the one part;

And

SAMUEL HOMFRAY, of Penydarran Place, in the Coy. Glamorgan, Esq.,

RICHARD FOTHERGILL, of Sirhowy Furnace, in the Parish of Bedwelty, Co. Monmouth, Ironmaster,

MATTHEW MONKHOUSE, of the same place, Clerk;

WILLIAM THOMPSON, of the City of London, Merchant; and

WILLIAM FORMAN, of the same place, Merchant, of the other part.

After reciting the Agreement of 30th March, 1800, And stating that by the Will of John Morgan, Esq., late of Tredegar, deceased, dated 23 June, 1785, the said Sir Chas. Morgan was only entitled to the premises so agreed to be demised for his life, with remainder to the said Charles Morgan, his son, for his life, with remainder to the first and other Sons of Charles Morgan, successively, in tail male, with divers remainders over.

And stating that the said Charles Morgan (I) had 3 Sons, Charles Morgan Robinson Morgan (J), of the age of 10 years, Charles Gould Morgan (K), of the age of 8 years, and Charles Augustus Morgan (L), of the age of 3 years.

And stating that soon after entering into the said Agreement of 20th March, 1800, Samuel Homfray and others entered into an Agreement with Sir Charles Morgan and

Charles Morgan to lay out the sum of £3,000, in addition to the £10,000 agreed to be expended; and that on the faith of such agreement the said partners had laid out the sum of money, being a large one, in erecting a Dwelling-house, Furnaces and Forge upon the said premises; and that with the consent of the said Sir Chas. Morgan and Charles Morgan, the said Samuel Homfray and his Co-partners proposed to make a Tram road down part of the Sirhowy Valley to join the Monmouthshire Canal, and to erect warehouses.

It was witnessed that, in pursuance of the said recited Agreement, and of the moneys agreed to be expended, and of the rents, covenants and agreements thereinafter contained on behalf of the said Samuel Homfray and co-partners, to be paid, observed and performed,

The said Sir Charles Morgan, Bart., and his son, Charles Morgan, have and each of them hath demised not only in respect of their and each of their estate and interest, but by virtue and in exercise of all powers and authorities whatsoever, do by these presents demise to the said Saml. Homfray and his co-partners.

All that dwelling-house wherein Matthew Monkhouse now dwells, with all the several farms, tenements, etc., now in possession of the said Samuel Homfray and his Co-partners in the Manor of Machen in the Parish of Bedwelty, in the County of Monmouth, particularly set down in the Map thereto attached, the same being bordered by the brook called Nant y Bwch and the confines of the County of Brecon on the North, and by Sirhowy river and Abercarne Manor in the Hamlet of Mamhole on the East, and by the freehold land of Morgan Watkins near Pont Gwaith yr Harn on the South, and by Bedwelty Common on the West parts and sides thereof, except 2 Closes that are on the east side of the river Sirhowy.

Also All Mines, veins, seams and beds of coal, culm and iron ore, stone, clay, etc., in, upon, and under the said premises, and in, upon, and under the said Bedwelty Common, or any part thereof, and in, upon, and under any and every part of the Cwm Tyssog Inclosures, severally delineated on the said Map.

With full power to the said Samuel Homfray and his Co-partners to dig and trench in and upon the said lands for the purpose of and getting iron ore and coal, and working the same, and to make tramways on any part of the said lands and over the same down to the Sirhowy Valley to join the Monmouthshire Canal, and to take all Waters and Streams for the purpose of working and scouring the said Coal and iron ore; and with full power to erect Engines, Furnaces, Forges, Mills, etc., and also with full power to have pit timber, etc., on paying prices to be agreed upon.

Reserving to Sir Charles Morgan All timber-like trees and also the right of hunting, hawking, fishing and fowling, and all Mines of lead ore, tin and copper.

To have and to hold, subject to existing leases, for 99 years thence next ensuing.

Yielding and Paying for the first 5 years £300, and for the remaining 94 years £500 per ann., free of rates and taxes now imposed or hereafter to be imposed by Parliament.

Covenants by Saml. Homfray for himself and his co-Partners. To pay rent on days named,

And to lay out the sum at least of £40,000, in building Furnaces, etc., on or before September 29, 1808.

And to deliver to the Wharf at Newport and Pillgwenlly, belonging to Sir Charles Morgan, Bart., and Charles Morgan, his son, for shipping and unshipping the iron, coal, and other goods, belonging to them, for export or import on the river Usk; and should also freight all goods to Bristol by the Vessels of the said Charles Morgan at the customary freight times prices or rate for such freight, and at the rate of wharfage regulated by the Monmouthshire Canal Acts of Parliament. And the said Sir Charles Morgan Covenanted with Saml. Homfray and Partners, For quiet enjoyment for the term of 99 years, and against any molestation by any person claiming by or under them or under the Will of the said John Morgan, or otherwise howsoever.

Special Covenant that the Sons, on attaining the age of 21 years, should join in the execution of further securities, such as may be advised by Counsel learned in the law, by means of a Recovery or otherwise by the remainderman, and make the title of the leases good for the whole period of 99 years. Executed and attested.

The Covenant in the Deed requiring all coal to be shipped at the Wharf at Newport and Pillgwenlly, belonging to Sir Charles Morgan and his son Charles, and that all goods to Bristol should be conveyed in the vessels of the said Charles Morgan, would seem to show that the son, Charles Morgan, was then engaged in a shipping business at Newport; and it may be that the well-known Tredegar Wharf Company had its origin in this circumstance.

1803.—By Special Deed of Defeasance,

It is by that Indenture witnessed (*inter alia*), That if Sir Charles Morgan, Bart., and Charles Morgan shall use their best endeavours to prevail upon the said Charles Morgan Robinson, on his becoming 21 years of age, or, in case of his decease, the said Charles Gould Morgan, on his attaining the age of 21 years, and in the case of the decease of him, of the said Charles Augustus Samuel Morgan, on his attaining the age of 21 years, and in case of his decease, of such other person to whom the inheritance by virtue of the Will of the said John Morgan shall devolve, and who shall be of 21 years, to suffer a good and lawful Recovery in and upon the premises, to secure the same effectually to Sam. Homfray and his co-partners.

But if the remainderman would not execute the same, then Sir Charles Morgan and Charles Morgan not to be liable to Homfray and Co. partners for more than £40,000, Homfray to have one-third of such sum; but Homfray was willing to waive by a separate deed, as by a note on this present reciting deed appears; and as such waiver could not be embodied in this deed, a separate deed was prepared and executed by him to that effect.

---

Of course it was essential to the success of the New Works, that there should be a convenient means of access to the Seaport Town of Newport, and Samuel Homfray and his Co-partners had actually commenced to make a line of tram road down the Sirhowy Valley from such new Works, the whole way to a place called Pill, on the river Usk.

This line of tramroad was to be wholly independent of the Monmouthshire Canal Company, who, under the powers of their 1792 Act, had constructed a Canal to Crumlin, in the Ebbw Valley, by way of Crinda Pill.

Under these circumstances, Mr. Homfray and his Co-partners were approached by the Canal Company, and induced to abandon their independent tramroad the whole way to Newport, and to adopt the Canal as part of the communication from Risca down to Newport. The Canal Company further undertook to make the whole length of tramroad from the Tredegar Works to the junction with the Canal at Risca.

The following Agreement, dated 18th December, 1800, was then entered into

Between

The Company of Proprietors of the Monmouthshire Canal Navigation (at a Special General Assembly for this purpose held at Newport), of the one part;

and

Samuel Homfray and his Co-partners in the Tredegar Iron Works, of the other part.

After reciting that Homfray and Co. were then erecting the Tredegar Iron Works, in consequence of a Lease granted to them for 99 years by Sir Charles Morgan, Baronet, in the Parish of Bedwelty,

And reciting that Homfray and Co. had begun to make a tramroad to convey their iron, etc., from their works to a place called Pill, at Newport, and that such tramroad would take a different line to any of the roads or branches of the Canal Navigation;

And reciting that the Canal Company were apprehensive that such tramroad might prove injurious to their interests, and being desirous also to secure the tonnage on their Canal of all iron and coal to be exported from the said New Works;

And reciting that, in consideration of Homfray and Co. abandoning their proposed line of tramroad, the Canal Company would undertake, at their own expense, to make a good and sufficient tramroad from the said Works to communicate with the Monmouthshire Canal Navigation at or near Risca Church, on the following terms:

"It was witnessed that the Monmouthshire Canal Company shall, on or before the 25th December, 1801, make a good and sufficient tramroad, according to the plans of Benjamin Outram, of Butterly, in the County of Derby, Engineer, from the Tredegar Iron Works, to join their Canal near Risca Church, with all convenient turnouts, and, if required, to construct a double rail;

Such tramroad should be made of a sufficient width for Carts to pass by the side, and the road to be open to the public on payment of the same tolls as are taken in the Newport District of Turnpike Roads;

Provision as to reimbursing Homfray and Co. the money already expended by them;

And that the through Tonnage rate per ton from the Works to the Wharf at Newport should be 3*s*. per ton for all iron, and 2*s*. per ton for all coal, and for timber and other goods 3*s*. per ton, the whole distance being reckoned at 24 miles. For shorter distances, proportionate tonnage to be charged. Tonnage for coal to be at the long weight, each Ton consisting of 21 Hundred of 120 lbs., and of iron and other goods at 20 cwt., of 120 lbs., with the usual allowance of 30 lbs. for Breakage.

Samuel Homfray and Partners bound themselves to send all Iron, Coal, etc., from their Works to Newport by that line.

And the Company agreed to keep the Tramroad in good repair and the Canal well supplied with Water, and in times of frost to keep the navigation open by means of ice-boats.

Both parties agree to do their utmost to secure the passing of an Act of Parliament carrying the terms of such Agreement into effect."

---

[The large Aqueduct at Risca, built to convey the Sirhowy Tramway across the Ebbw Valley to the level of the Canal, being long since disused, has recently been partly pulled down.]

---

The tenure of the Estates held by Sir Charles Morgan under the Will of John Morgan, dated 1785, has, as we have seen, proved so difficult to deal with in any satisfactory and legal manner as regards granting long leases, that it was resolved to apply for a Private Act of Parliament.

This was obtained in 1802 (42 Geo. III.), and thereby power was given under the direction of the Court of Chancery in the County of Monmouth, for leasing said Estates for 99 years; and in the Schedules to the Act (Parts I., II. and III.), the Building Estate at Newport, and the Mines and Mineral properties at Sirhowy and Tredegar, were specified as such and set out, and that they might be so dealt with.

The Minerals under Bedwelty Common are stated to 1,000 acres, under the Valley of Cwm Tyssog 500, and under lands in the Parish of Machen and Risca, 1,500 acres.

On the 26th June, 1802, the Monmouthshire Railway Act (42 Geo. III.) was passed, carrying out the Agreement for the Sirhowy Tramroad, and also for empowering Sir Charles Morgan and Owners of Tredegar Park to make a railway through the Park, and then was formed what was known as the Park Mile.

Under the same Act, Samuel Homfray and his co-Partners were authorised for the purpose of getting Limestone for their works to make a Tramroad, with the consent of the Duke of Beaufort, to the Limestone works at Trefil, in the Parish of Llangynider, in the County of Brecon.

---

These Works were now carried on uninterruptedly by Samuel Homfray and Co. for a long series of years, and we give the tonnage of iron sent down for shipment at Newport by the Monmouthshire Canal.

---

## TREDEGAR IRON WORKS. SAMUEL HOMFRAY AND CO.

(From Scrivenor's *Iron Trade*, p. 126—1802-1830.)

| | | Tons. | | | Tons. |
|---|---|---|---|---|---|
| 1805 | ... | 956 | 1818 | ... | 8,258 |
| 1806 | ... | 3,124 | 1819 | ... | 7,140 |
| 1807 | ... | 4,138 | 1820 | ... | 8,211 |
| 1808 | ... | 5,529 | 1821 | ... | 9,923 |
| 1809 | ... | 9,105 | 1822 | ... | 8,102 |
| 1810 | ... | 7,696 | 1823 | ... | 9,903 |
| 1811 | ... | 6,643 | 1824 | ... | 11,444 |
| 1812 | ... | 7,862 | 1825 | ... | 11,012 |
| 1813 | ... | 7,597 | 1826 | ... | 10,962 |
| 1814 | ... | 9,131 | 1827 | ... | 13,837 |
| 1815 | ... | 9,225 | 1828 | ... | 14,341 |
| 1816 | ... | 7,499 | 1829 | ... | 13,349 |
| 1817 | ... | 10,350 | 1830 | ... | 12,303 |

(From Scrivenor's *Iron Trade*, p. 294—1831-1840.)

| | | Tons. | | | Tons. |
|---|---|---|---|---|---|
| 1831 | ... | 13,340 | 1836 | ... | 12,133 |
| 1832 | ... | 13,304 | 1837 | ... | 12,640 |
| 1833 | ... | 12,323 | 1838 | ... | 15,526 |
| 1834 | ... | 12,858 | 1839 | ... | 14,861 |
| 1835 | ... | 13,909 | 1840 | ... | 15,288 |

---

In 1839 (Mushet, *Iron and Steel*, p. 415), there were five Blast-Furnaces, and the title of the Firm is there given as "Thompson and Co."

---

(End of Tredegar Iron Works.)

XIX.

# The Sirhowy Iron Works.

We are still keeping on sound historical ground, and have the draft leases drawn by the famous firm of solicitors of Brecon, Walter and John Powell, to refer to. If any ironmaster was contemplating taking a lease of minerals from a great Manorial lord or humble freeholder, the advice given him and acted upon was to seek the counsel and assistance of this firm, who knew exactly what were the requirements of a mineral lessee, and the enabling and protecting clauses necessary to be inserted in the Leases; and I entertain a strong opinion that they were trusted by lessor and lessee alike to draw up the formal binding document, of which the terms had been previously in brief arranged between the parties.

Few, perhaps, dream that the late Sir William Vernon Harcourt, the West Monmouthshire Member of Parliament, had even the remotest ancestral connection with the district he represented: but I think that he had in some slight degree; and we know for certain that a branch of the Harcourt family, of Stanton-Harcourt, in Oxfordshire, settled in Breconshire at the end of the seventeenth century as Stewards of the Earl of Worcester.

A representative of this Breconshire branch, Godfrey Harcourt, lived at Wire-wood's Green, near Tidenham, in the Co. of Gloucester, in 1740, and Mary, one of his three daughters and co-heiresses, married the Revd. Henry Burgh, of Monmouth; and he, on the death of his father, John Burgh, of Troy, succeeded to the Sirhowy lands (with other considerable property), which we are about to describe, and which their only son, Charles Henry Burgh, granted the following lease of.

The connection is, it is true, very remote, as the property was a Burgh and not a Harcourt estate by descent; but still this Charles Henry Burgh was, on his mother's side, a Harcourt.

[The other two Misses Harcourt married Breconshire squires: Amy became the wife of John Powell, of Peterstone Court (family now extinct); and Ann, of Edward Williams, of Llangattock Court, Crickhowell, from whom the Lloyds of Dinas are descended.]

But we must return to our subject.

These, the Sirhowy Iron Works, are situate in the Valley of, and near the river of that name, and a little higher up the stream than the Tredegar Works.

And on February 4, 1778, the following Indenture was made between

Charles Henry Burgh [This Mr. Charles Henry Burgh, last-described, died the same year, 1778, unmarried], of the Town of Monmouth, Esq., of the one part;

and

John Sealy and Bolton Hudson, of Threadneedle Street, in the City of London, Grocers, Teamen, and Copartners;

Thomas Atkinson, late of South Carolina, in North America, and now of Skipton, Yorkshire, Merchant; and

William Barrow, of Newgate Street, in the City of London, Grocer and Teaman, of the other part;

And it was therein witnessed that the said Charles Henry Burgh, in consideration of the rent to be paid and covenants to be observed, did Grant to the said John Sealy and Copartners, their heirs and assigns, All that messuage and lands known as Upper and Lower Sirhowy and Tarren Sirhowy, late in the occupation of Phillip Howell Rees and his assigns.

Also all those Messuages known as Penpont Sirhowy, late in the occupation of William George and his assigns; all which properties are situate in the Parish of Bedvelty, in the County of Monmouth.

With full liberty to the said John Sealy and his Co-partners to build such and so many Furnaces, Forges, Foundries, Mills, Engines, Storehouses, buildings, etc., for the placing and keeping of ore, coal, and charcoal for the making and manufacturing of iron, as the said John Sealy and others may think convenient. And also with full liberty to take out of the said lands and out of all other lands of the said Charles Henry Burgh materials for the erection, etc., of such Furnaces, etc.; and with also full liberty to make weirs and impound water of the Sirhowy stream, or any other brooks where they flow through his lands, for the purpose of carrying the water to the use of such ironworks to be erected; and also with full liberty to bore, search for, and dig all coal and iron ore as may be found on the said lands, and as may be found on the lands held by the Widow of Edmund Lewis, commonly called or known by the name of Sychfoes and Gwayn hellig Llwyna; and also in, upon, and under the waste and commons, now in the occupation of the said Widow Lewis, called Gwainy y Pound, Rhassanyr Mowy, Pen Mark, and Brinore; and also in, upon, and under the lands in the occupation of Evan Thomas Evan, John Rees, and William Lewis, respectively; and the lands in the tenure of Thomas Evans, called Meirdu; and the lands leased to Evan Moses and John Reynold, and now in the possession of John Guest, Gentleman, and his assigns; all which lands are situate in the Parish of Bodvelty (Bedwelty).

Also with full liberty to dig pits for the produce of their Works, provided as little damage as possible was done to the tenants of the said lands. Clay and stone not required for the building of this Works to be excepted, also veins of Tin, and all other Mines (save coal, culm, Iron ore, and iron mine).

Also all trees excepted. And always reserved out of this present demise as much Hearth, or Fire Coal, as Amy Powell, of Peterstone Court, in the County of Brecon, Widow, or Thomas Harcourt Powell, her Son, may want or have occasion for their own use only.

[This Amy Powell was one of the co-heiresses of Godfrey Harcourt, of Wire-Wood's Green, and Aunt to Mr. Burgh, and Sister of my Great-Grandmother, Ann Williams, wife of Edward Williams, Esq,, of Llangattock Court, Co. Brecon.]

To have and to hold from January 1st, 1778, for 40 years, paying yearly the rent of £134 9s. 0d., and paying all rates and charges on the said buildings and on the said coal and iron ore; and also for any damage that may be done by the prosecution of the works to the tenants of the surface lands; Covenants to uphold and repair by Lessee; Covenant by Lessor for quiet enjoyment, and to pay a sum of not exceeding £5 in respect of limestone to be paid for to the Duke of Beaufort, and for water rights.

(Signed) Charles Henry (L. S.) Burgh.
John (L. S.) Sealy.
Bolton (L. S.) Hudson.
Thomas (L. S.) Atkinson.
William (L. S.) Barrow.

Witnesses to the signature of Charles Henry Burgh and Thomas Atkinson—Hen. Phillips, H. Parry.

And to the signature of John Sealy, Bolton Hudson, and William Barrow (being first duly stamped), W. Bullock, Copthall Court, London; Edw. Barrow, Devonshire Square, London.

---

1st November, 1794—The following Articles of Agreement were entered into for a change in the Partnership :—

Between

WILLIAM BARROW, of Sirhowy, in the Parish of Bedwelty, Co. Monmouth, Ironmaster;

REVD. MATTHEW MONKHOUSE, of the same place, Clerk, of the one part;

And

RICHARD FOTHERGILL, of Clapham, in the County of Surrey, Builder, of the other part,

Reciting that the said William Barrow and Matthew Monkhouse were joint proprietors of the Sirhowy Iron Works.

And reciting the Lease of February 16th, 1778, granted by Charles Henry Burgh before-mentioned.

And reciting a Lease of Jany. 1st, 1778, of certain messuages and lands situate in Bedwelty, granted by Thomas Johnes, Esq. (Thomas Johnes married the sister of Mr. Burgh), to Thomas Atkinson and William Barrow, parties to the Leases from Mr. Burgh, for 30 years.

And reciting also a Lease of Jany. 1, 1778, of certain other premises, called New bridge farm, with Mill, etc., there, belonging to Monythers Toyne (Mynyddysllwn), granted by Thomas Johnes, Esq., to the said Thomas Atkinson and William Barrow, for 50 years.

And reciting a lease of certain other land and premises at Sirhowy, in the Parish of Bedwelty, granted to Thomas Atkinson and William Barrow, by Charles Morgan, Esqre., of Tredegar, for 40 years, which will expire about the year 1818.

And reciting that William Barrow and Matthew Monkhouse are also entitled to other premises belonging to the said Iron Works.

And reciting that William Barrow and Matthew Monkhouse have agreed to admit the said Richard Fothergill to be an equal partner with them in the concern.

This Indenture witnessed that The Partnership to commence on January 1st, 1795, and continue for the full term of the Leases; £6,000 additional Capital to be placed in the concern, in equal proportions, by the partners. Richard Fothergill to have equal share with the other partners, also in a certain Agreement with Walter Watkins, Esq., of 1793, And also in certain contracts with the Proprietors of the Llangroyney Forge with Harford, Homfray, etc.

Then follows a provision that a proper Deed of Ptrship. be executed before the 1st January, 1796.

Signed by WILLIAM (L. S.) BARROW,
MATTHEW (L. S.) MONKHOUSE,
RICHARD (L. S.) FOTHERGILL,

And duly Witnessed.

(Certified to be a true copy.)

---

1797.—By an Indenture of this date made between

WILLIAM BARROW, of Trevethin, Co. Monmouth, Gent., one part,

And

RICHARD BRANTHWAITE, of other part,

Reciting the previously-recited Leases and the various changes in the partnership of the Sirhowy Works:

It was witnessed that in consideration (not stated), William Barrow assigned one-eighth Share in the Sirhowy Works to Richard Branthwaite;

And by another Deed of even date, William Barrow entered into a Bond to pay £1,000, in certain claims in Hudson's Bankruptcy (one of the original Partners) being substantiated, to Richard Branthwaite.

1797.—By an Indenture of this date made between William Barrow, of Trevethin, of the one part, and Richard Fothergill, of the other part:

It was witnessed that in consideration of £3,500, paid by Richard Fothergill, in hand, the said William Barrow did grant seven undivided 24th-parts or shares in the Sirhowy Works and the properties held in connection therewith, and in the Llangrwyney Works, to Richard Fothergill.

1st August, 1799.—By an Indenture of this date, made between

Richard Fothergill, of Sirhowy, Ironmaster;

Matthew Monkhouse, Do. Do.;

John Hanscomb, of Clapham, Co. Surrey, Builder; and

Richard Branthwaite, of Llangroiney, Co. Brecon, Irnmstr. (being the Company of Proprietors of certain Iron Works in County of Monmouth, called Sirhowy Furnace), of the one part;

And

James Harford, City of Bristol;

John Partridge, of Town of Monmouth;

Philip Crocker, Samuel Harford, and Richard John Tomlinson, all of Bristol (being the Committee of Tradesmen known by the name or firm of "Harford, Partridge and Co.)," of the other part:

It was witnessed that in consideration of the Agreement, etc., thereinafter entered into by the said James Harford and others, they, the said Richard Fothergill and others, did grant unto said Saml. Harford and others, Certain dwelling-houses and lands in the occupation of Thomas Jones and William Jones, with liberty to dig out, try for coal and iron ore in, upon, or under the same, and also in, upon, or under a certain common, called Gwain y Pound, extending on the north to the Confines of the County of Brecon; on the East to certain enclosed lands called ———; on the south to certain lands, called Sychfoes, on the west to a line passing by a ——— called Sirhowy, such line having been recently marked out, and also under the grounds called Sychfoes and Gwain helig Llwyna, and other lands comprised in the 1778 lease from Mr. Burgh.

Coal to be reserved for the supply of Llangrwyney Forge.

To hold for a term of 18 years.

Rent to be paid, £300 per year first 3 years, and after the first 3 years £500 for the remainder of the term.

Usual conditions for leases, and to pay rates and taxes, and to make good any damage to enclosed ground.

This was merely a lease by the Sirhowy Company for 18 years to the firm of Harford, Partridge and Co., and it is quite consistent with that to find the following letter, written by Mr. Richard Fothergill on behalf of the Sirhowy Company, the owners, with regard to an important action pending with the Union Company.

"Sirhowy, 8th July, 1805.

"Dear Sir—I now have to request your answer respecting the Law Suit with the Union gentlemen, which now presses on all sides. We cannot avoid it, therefore it seems useless delaying it.

"I know well your situation with Mr. Hall, and much lament that in this case it so happens that if you are concerned at all it will be against a friend.

"And believe me no one went to the gallows with more reluctance than I go into this law suit.

"For it seems clear that it will be a complicated and difficult matter, and probably of infinite consequence to the loosers.

"However, if you will be concerned for us I shall save much trouble, and have confidence that the matter will be understood and probably simplified.

"I am, dear Sir, yours truly,
"RICHD. FOTHERGILL,
"Sirhowy, 8th July, 1805. "for Sirhowy Company."

"P.S.—My bro. or some others will be at Brecon on Friday, and will call for a letter in answer to this.

"Mr. Jno. Powell, Attorney-at-Law, Brecon."

---

By the year 1818, when the lease expired, the Messrs. Harford and Co. had acquired by purchase all the ownership rights of the Sirhowy Company (for what sum the papers do not show); and it is similarly consistent with the change of ownership to find the following letter, written by Messrs. Partridge and Co. to Mr. Walter Powell, of Brecon, complaining of Mr. Fothergill's conduct:—

On 15th January, 1818.—Mr. Richard Harford writes to Mr. Walter Powell, of Brecon: "In consequence of the unwarrantable detention of our property at Sirhowy by Richard Fothergill, we are under the unpleasant necessity of resorting to legal measures with a view of compelling him to do us justice.

"(Signed) Thy esteemed friend,
RICHD. S. HARFORD."

---

Our own papers carry us no further, but I am enabled to add the following brief statement by Mr. Powell, of 30, Stow Park Avenue, as to the further history of these Works:—

"HISTORY OF SIRHOWY IRON WORKS.

"I am sorry I have no very reliable information as to these Works. The early name of these Works was Sorwy. The name of Sirhowy came into use after 1800; in 1794 Wm. Barrow and Co. were, I think, the proprietors. The Harfords of Ebbw Vale purchased Sirhowy Iron Works and Collieries in 1818 from Monkhouse and Co., and held them until 1844, when they sold them to the Ebbw Vale Company (Messrs. Darby and others). The Ebbw Vale Company was made into a Limited Company in 1864, and Sirhowy is still their property, 1905. The five furnaces are dismantled."

The Returns of iron sent by the Monmouthshire Company are included with those of Ebbw Vale (Harford and Co.).

---

END OF THE SIRHOWY WORKS.

---

XX.

# Ebbw Vale Iron Works.

In the case of all the South Wales Iron Works, the object kept in view is to ascertain and describe accurately their very earliest history, what were the names of the men who built the first furnaces, and when, and to gain some insight into the transactions of those times. The later and modern developments and history of the various works we leave in the main for others to tell, being content to give them, if possible, a safe groundwork to build upon.

Having now left the Sirhowy Valley, and crossed the low (at one point) mountain ridge that divides the two valleys of the Sirhowy and Ebbw, we come to the Ebbw Vale Iron Works, which are situate on the river Ebwy-fawr (Greater Ebbw). At one time, in the height of their prosperity, these Works were one of the greatest of the South Wales Iron Works, and are so to-day.

In the first main deed, that of the assignment of the Ebbw Vale Works by Jeremiah Homfray to Messrs. Harford, Partridge and Co., dated April, 1796, there are recitals of numerous Deeds and Agreements entered into, commencing with a lease, dated 25 January, 1786, from Edmund James to Walter Watkins of Dan y graig, in the County of Brecon, Esquire, of the farms of Blaeneant and Pentwyn, situate in the Parish of Aberystwith, in the County of Monmouth.

We have looked through this main deed carefully. It is not only lengthy, but so closely packed with references to other documents, the terms of which are interdependent, that we have tried in vain to make any satisfactory abstract.

The document, if quoted at any length, must be given in its entirety, and for such our limits of space do not admit.

And we have thought it advisable—possibly more useful than inserting the document in full—to give in lieu a statement of the general position, and of the transactions and circumstances that placed Mr. Jere. Homfray in 1796 in a position to assign over the completed iron works as a going concern to the Messrs. Harford, Partridge and Co.

This was not a case like that of the Senghenith Manor, which has been alluded to under the head of Dowlais, nor like that of Bedwelty Common at Tredegar, nor of the

*Page* 131.

VIEW OF EBBW VALE IRON WORKS. 1905.

great Manors of the Duke of Beaufort and Earl Abergavenny, next to be alluded to, and where large tracts of land (so far as the minerals were concerned) are leased to individuals or companies for the purpose of working the minerals and forming ironworks thereon; but a case where a large and sufficient tract of mineral ground (excepting a part of the Abercarne Manor) had to be leased from many and different private—and in some cases, small—freeholders.

Between 1786 and 1796 (date of the main deed) the main Ebbw Vale, etc., property, was obtained and consolidated together; and the persons concerned, in more or less degree, in that operation were:

Walter Watkins, of Dan y graig, and Occupier of Llangrwyney Forge;

Charles Cracroft, a capitalist in a small way, living at Sunny Bank, Crickhowell; and

Jere. Homfray, the elder brother of the Homfrays of Penydarran Iron Works.

There is little doubt that Mr. Watkins was first in the field, and that from an early period, in order to supply his Llangrwyney Forge with Pig Iron, he himself erected and worked some small kilns, like limekilns, hardly to be called furnaces, in the Ebbw Valley, where iron ore was abundant; and that it was with that object he took the first lease we hear of, that from Mr. James Lewis, of the Blaeneant and Pentwyn Farms.

Mr. Cracroft was the capitalist who assisted Mr. Watkins with money, either by way of share or loan, in the Llangrwyney Forge business, a necessity of which was the obtaining of pig iron; and it will be seen that Mr. Watkins was familiar with working iron ore, as he subsequently contracted with Mr. Jere. Homfray to supply him with the same for the Ebbw furnace.

In 1789, or a little earlier, Mr. Jeremiah Homfray being dissatisfied with his brother's management of the Penydarran Works, but who undoubtedly was possessed by early training, and after won experience of considerable knowledge of the iron industry, came, shall we say, prospecting along the Hills for a likely venture, and then met Mr. Watkins in the Ebbw Valley, making pig iron in his primitive and crude fashion.

This led on 3rd April, 1789, to the partnership between Watkins, Homfray and Cracroft, as ironmasters, being formed; and in June, 1789, further lands were leased from John Miles for 99 years, with full permission to erect furnaces thereon.

The partnership, however, was of short duration, and on 31st March, 1791, it was dissolved, and Watkins and Cracroft assigned their shares to Jere. Homfray, the latter becoming sole owner, on the condition that Jere. Homfray was to make certain payments to the then outgoing partners, and to supply Watkins with certain quantities of pig iron and iron plates for his Llangrwyney Forge, and Walter Watkins was to supply Jere. Homfray for the Ebbw furnace with certain quantities of iron ore and limestone at an agreed price.

On 30th June, 1791, various deeds were entered into between the old partners, each assigning his own property over to Homfray, and Homfray assigning over his property to them as security for the payments to be made and contracts entered into; and by deed of July 1, 1791, Walter Watkins granted to Jere. Homfray all those forges, mills, buildings and premises, called Llangrwyney Forge, by way of collateral security for payment of the pig iron and plates to be supplied.

It will be readily seen that the affairs had become greatly involved between the three persons named, and Homfray being in sole possession of the Works, sought and found the firm of Harford, Partridge and Co., then starting the Nantyglo Iron Works, to join him as partners.

On the 21st April, 1791, an agreement was entered into of partnership between Jeremiah Homfray of the one part (then of the Parish of Aberystwith, Ironmaster), and

Messrs. Harford, Partridge and Co., of Bristol, Ironmasters, of the other part, whereby it was agreed—

That the Parties should enter into Co-partnership and joint dealings in the making of pig iron at a certain furnace and works, called Ebbw Vale, in the Parish of Aberystwith, and carrying on the business of Ironmasters there, and that Jere. Homfray was to have one-third share, and the Messrs. Harford, Partridge and Co., two-third shares.

That the said Jere. Homfray should, out of his share of the profits, with his present advance, make one-third of the capital of £7,000, and shall not withdraw any sum meantime from the concern, except his salary.

The shares to be as follows:

| | £ | s. | d. |
|---|---|---|---|
| Jere. Homfray ... ... | 2,333 | 6 | 8 |
| Harford, Partridge and Co. ... | 4,666 | 13 | 4 |
| | £7,000 | 0 | 0 |

That Jeremiah Homfray should reside on the premises in the house where he now does, taking upon himself the superintendence of the Works, at a salary of £100 a year, with the privilege of a house and firing, and in lieu of other charges, such as treating people who may come on business, the buying and keeping of horses, cows, and all other charges, a further sum of £50 per annum to continue unless he is sooner called to the management of Penydarran Works by the death of his brother, Mr. Samuel Homfray. If he thinks it prudent at any time to quit the superintendence, the salary as managing partner shall then cease, and that the said Jere. Homfray should be the treasurer and cashier until otherwise agreed.

And on the 6th July, 1792, a deed of partnership to that effect was executed between the parties.

And in April, 1796, by a Deed confirming an Agreement entered into on March 3rd, 1796, Jere. Homfray having previously assigned his interests in freehold and copyhold property, now assigned all his interest in freehold and copyhold property in the Ebbw Vale Works, and in the partnership thereof, to Messrs. Harford, Partridge and Co., for the sum of £500, £100 to be paid on the execution of proper deeds, and £400 in certain proportions and at certain times.

. . . . . . . .

We here think it well to give a summary of this Agreement in relation to these works.

. . . . . . . .

By Memorandum of Agreement, of 3 March, 1796, between

James Harford, of the City of Bristol, Ironmaster, on behalf of himself and Partners, under the firm of Harford, Partridge and Co., one part;

And

Jere. Homfray, of Ebbw Vale, in the Co. of Monmouth, Ironmaster, other part.

Whereby it was agreed that James Harford should purchase all the share and interest of Jere. Homfray in certain Iron Works, called Ebbw Vale, held in conjunction with Harford, Partridge and Co., together with all the Estates, Farms, Leases, Debts, Contracts, Agreements, Stock and Effects, in consideration of said James Harford paying unto said Homfray £500 by instalments of £100 per annum, the first payment on execution of the Deed which was to be prepared by Powells, of Brecon.

| | | | |
|---|---|---|---|
| 2nd payment | on 4th April, | | 1797, |
| 3rd | „ | „ | 1798, |
| 4th | „ | „ | 1799, |
| 5th and last | „ | „ | 1800, |

which Homfray agreed to accept in above mode in satisfaction of his share.

That parties should execute mutual releases and the usual Gazette Notice.

That Harford and Co. would pay all partnership debts, and Homfray would pay all personal debts which did not come under the partnership account.

Signed and Sealed by Jas. Harford and Jers. Homfray,
in the presence of W. Taitt.

In 1802 Mr. Samuel Glover sold the extensive tract of land to Messrs. Harford, Partridge and Co., at Sirhowy and Ebbw Vale, of which the following are particulars :—

Samuel Glover agrees to sell to Harford, Partridge and Co.

All that tract of inclosed and waste land, with the minerals and buildings of every description, and all privileges and appurtenances whatsoever, as well manorial, or otherwise thereto belonging, comprised in a schedule signed by Mr. Glover, Richd. S. Harford, John Harford, and Richd. Blakemore, on the part of Harford, Partridge and Co., bounded on the south side by a line to be drawn from the most southern point of the inclosed farms on the Ebbw Vale side of the mountain, coloured blue on the map, and in the occupation of William Morgan, to the south corner of the rough tract of land called Coed Cae Phillip Lewis on the Sirhowy side of the mountain, to include the whole of those lands or farms, and to comprise all Mr. Glover's property, whether inclosed, or waste, or otherwise, to the north of that line, for the sum of Fifteen thousand pound, viz., on compleating the title (which each party are to use their utmost diligence in doing), the sum of £3,000 by 6 Bills upon London for £500 each, at 2, 4, 6, 8, 10 and 12 months, with interest at 5 per cent. for the same attached to each Bill.

| | | | | |
|---|---|---|---|---|
| The further sum of | £2,000 | to be paid | 16th March, | 1803, |
| „ | £2,000 | „ | 16th Decr., | 1803, |
| „ | £2,000 | „ | 16th „ | 1804, |
| „ | £3,000 | „ | 16th „ | 1805, |
| „ | £3,000 | „ | 16th „ | 1806, |

making together the sum of £15,000, with interest for such remainder as shall from time to time be unpaid at 5 per cent. Mr. Glover to make a good and sufficient title to the satisfaction of Harford, Partridge and Co., and their Solicitor, either by himself or in conjunction with the Mortgagee as speedily as possible.

Dated at Gellywastod, 12th November, 1802.

(Signed) Saml. Glover.
Richd. S. Harford.
John Harford.
Richd. Blakemore.

Witness : John Vaughan, Senr.

. . . . . . . . .

The Ebbw Vale Works seem to have been carried on for a number of years regularly by the firm of Harford, Partridge and Co.

And we append the following letters, which are written from the Works.

. . . . . . . . .

"Ebbw Vale Works,

"WALTER POWELL, Esq. "31st, 7th Month (July), 1819.

"Esteemed Friend—About a week since I did myself the pleasure of writing thee, requesting some information respecting Charles Powell, of Castle Madock, in the County of Brecon, may be sent to our house in Bristol, but no reply being received, I am requested by our friend there to trouble thee with a few lines on the subject again, lest the last letter may not have reached thee. The particulars required were a certificate from a suitable person to show that Catharine Powell was the Administratrix and heiress-at-law of her father, Charles Powell, late of Castle Madock, in the County of Brecon, Esq. And also at what Court the letters of administration were granted.

"The object of this enquiry is this: the late contest with our unworthy neighbour, Fothergill, having given us some trouble respecting our titles, has induced us to have all our deeds looked over to see that all is clear now; in the course of looking over those of the Pen y Cae estate, which we, in the first place, rented of John Miles, and afterwards purchased it, we find there was a mortgage held thereon by Chas. Powell, Esq., which after his decease was conveyed by his daughter, Catharine Powell, to a new Mortgagee; and it seems necessary by the testimony of a suitable person to obtain a proof of her identity, as before mentioned; and conceiving from personal acquaintance that it may be in thy power to give such proof by certificate, was the reason of our thus troubling thee. We are sorry to be thus troublesome to thee, but hope the object will plead our excuse, and hoping for some early information either to Bristol or this place: the former I prefer,

"I remain with respect, thy assured Friend,

"RICHD. S. HARFORD."

---

"Ebbw Vale Works,

"POWELL, JONES and POWELL. "13th, 6th Month (June), 1820.

"Esteemed Friends—By yesterday's post we received your favour of the 8th inst. In reply, we are concerned that our neighbour, Edwd. Kendall, should have troubled you with a subject, that if he had called upon us himself (which he has never yet done) might easily have been settled, particularly after what passed between our neighbour, Wm. Bevan of Beaufort and ourselves sometime since at this place upon the subject.

"The circumstances between us are these: Some years since we had a lot of Lancashire ore at Newport, which we were desirous of removing to this place. In that operation, of course, in following the line of the Monmouthshire Canal, it was necessary to land it on the wharf at Crumlin, belonging to Edward Kendall; and in order to avoid any unpleasant understanding, or charge of thereby hindering the business, we applied to our then neighbour, Joseph Latham, who was at that period acting trustee for Edward Kendall, to fix a place for its deposit; he considering it was likely to remain there some time, said, if we would put it in a place out of the way of the general use of the wharves, and inclose it with a wall, he would point out one, where it might remain until convenient to us to remove; this we consented to do; he accordingly marked out a small spot not exceeding 10 yards long and 4 or 5 yards wide behind the Store House there, which, agreeable to his injunction, we surrounded with a wall. At the end of that quarter he made a charge for the wharfage of the ore, which we paid, and considered we were to be exonerated from any further demand—this was confirmed, by never receiving any from him—during the time he had the care of the property, nor from his successor, Wm. Bevan. As soon as we received notice from Edwd. Kendall to remove it we complied with the requisition.

"After having made this representation, as you have so kindly taken a friendly interest in the affair, we feel no hesitation in stating our readiness, if Edwd. Kendall be really willing, of leaving it to you to decide under all the circumstances of the case, whether we ought to pay more than we have already done—if your opinion should be in the affirmative, then to say the amount, and we will readily comply with your decision. We remain,

"Your assured Friends,

"HARFORDS, CROCKER and Co.

"In the conference we had with Wm. Bevan, he proposed that we should leave the business to the decision of Jos. Latham, which we consented to, but have heard nothing from him since.

"We have heard nothing from our Solicitor, Isaac Cook, respecting the business of Park gras Dew (Parc Grace Dieu) Annuity; nor is it the writer's belief any communication has been received by him from the Council whose opinion was sought."

---

"Ebbw Vale Works,

"POWELL, JONES and POWELL. "27th, 5th Month (May), 1822.

"Esteemed Friends—I have just now received your favour of the 23rd inst., with a cheque annexed for £35, being part of the arrears due to the Society of Friends in Monmouthshire, agreeable to the tenor of my receipt sent you, dated the 21st inst., and for which am obliged, as well as for your kind interference respecting it. I will write to Kingsmill Evans, Esq., of Hill, agreeable to suggestion, and remain,

"Your Friend,

"RICHD. S. HARFORD."

---

And now we append the notes of the more modern history of these works, which Mr. Powell, of 30, Stow Park Avenue, Newport, has most kindly obliged us with.

It will be observed that Mr. Powell makes no allusion to the connection of Mr. Walter Watkins with the Ebbw district, but starts with Mr. Jeremiah Homfray as the builder of the first blast-furnace. In this respect Mr. Powell is at fault, and our old papers give the true early history, we think, beyond a doubt; though the furnace or furnaces built by Mr. Watkins were very small affairs. The blast-furnace Mr. Homfray designed, and with the assistance of his partners built, was, however, probably of a larger and improved type. At any rate, the claim of Walter Watkins, the Welsh yeoman, to be one of the first founders of the Ebbw Vale Iron Works, and one of the pioneers of the South Wales iron industry, is undoubted.

## HISTORY OF EBBW VALE STEEL, IRON, AND COAL COMPANY, LTD.

NOTES ON, BY MR. POWELL, OF 30, STOW PARK AVENUE, NEWPORT.

From 1800 down.

One blast-furnace started between 1780 and '90 by Jeremiah Homfray.

In 1793 Homfray was joined by the Harfords, who were interested in the Nantyglo Works, and other Works near Machen.

In 1796 this partnership was dissolved, and the Ebbw Vale Works were carried on by Harford, Partridge and Co.

Their first coal pit was sunk before 1803.

Sirhowy blast-furnaces and Collieries were purchased in 1818.

Ebbw Vale Forge and Mills were built somewhere near this time.

Between this time and 1830 three blast-furnaces and mills were built, and a large trade was done in bar iron.

In 1829 rails were rolled in these works for the Stockton and Darlington Railway.

In 1842 Messrs. Harford and Co. failed; the works were carried on by Trustees until 1844.

In 1844 the works were bought by Messrs. Darby. The partners were Abraham Darby, Alfred Darby, Hy. Dickenson, Francis Tothill, Thomas Brown, Joseph Robinson, trading as the Ebbw Vale Company. Mr. Thomas Brown, as managing partner. Messrs. Darby were the proprietors of the Coalbrookdale Works in Shropshire, and the partners in Ebbw Vale were all Shropshire men.

In 1848 Victoria Works Collieries, 4 blast-furnaces, forges and mills were bought; this works is some two miles south of Ebbw Vale, and was started in 1836. The proprietors failed.

In 1852 Abersychan Works were bought; they consisted of 6 blast-furnaces, collieries, forges and mills.

In 1855 Pontypool Collieries, 3 blast-furnaces, 3 tin-plate works, bought.

Cwmbran Works were at one time also worked by the Co.

Abercarn Colliery. Abercarn was purchased and worked (somewhat later).

In 1861 Mr. George Parry, Chemist to the Ebbw Vale Co., patented a process for the conversion of wrought scrap iron into material suitable for the Bessemer process. The Ebbw Vale Company sold this and another patent they held (E. P. Martin) to Mr. Bessemer for £30,000, and paid Parry £10,000.

Between the years 1862-3 to 1866-7 steel was made in a fixed converter by the Bessemer process, and was, I think, the first steel made in South Wales.

In 1864 the Ebbw Vale Co. sold the works to the Ebbw Vale Co., Ltd.; the present title is the Ebbw Vale Steel, Iron and Coal Co., Ltd.

Large sums have been spent of late years in renewing the plant, and at the present time, 1905, the blast-furnaces, Bessemer plant, mills, etc., are all in first-rate condition.

---

We now give the Returns of Iron sent by the Ebbw Vale Co. (Harford, Partridge and Co.) by the Monmouthshire Canal to Newport, 1802 to 1830.—*Scrivenor*, p. 126.

| | Tons. | | Tons. |
|---|---|---|---|
| 1802 ... | — | 1817 ... | 3,123 |
| 1803 ... | 1,653 | 1818 ... | 2,476 |
| 1804 ... | 2,890 | 1819 ... | 1,907 |
| 1805 ... | 1,012 | 1820 ... | 3,605 |
| 1806 ... | 3,252 | 1821 ... | 6,041 |
| 1807 ... | 2,209 | 1822 ... | 5,960 |
| 1808 ... | 1,553 | 1823 ... | 8,613 |
| 1809 ... | 786 | 1824 ... | 10,101 |
| 1810 ... | 2,758 | 1825 ... | 10,325 |
| 1811 ... | 2,633 | 1826 ... | 10,297 |
| 1812 ... | 4,648 | 1827 ... | 14,403 |
| 1813 ... | 5,939 | 1828 ... | 15,479 |
| 1814 ... | 4,752 | 1829 ... | 16,959 |
| 1815 ... | 4,953 | 1830 ... | 18,133 |
| 1816 ... | 2,949 | | |

It will be seen that the large increase soon after 1818, when the Sirhowy property was purchased, agrees with Mr. Powell's account of the great development of the joint Works at that period.

---

We now give the Returns, from the same source (*Scrivenor*, p. 294), for the years 1831 to 1840.

Iron carried on the Monmouthshire Canal and Tramroads—

| Year. | Proprietors. | Tons. |
|---|---|---|
| 1831 | Harford and Company (Ebbw Vale and Sirhowy) | 18,778 |
| 1832 | " " | 19,740 |
| 1833 | " " | 19,226 |
| 1834 | " " | 20,228 |
| 1835 | " " | 25,392 |
| 1836 | " " | 23,120 |
| 1837 | " " | 22,475 |
| 1838 | " " | 23,579 |
| 1839 | " " | 25,342 |
| 1840 | " " | 24,199 |

---

END OF EBBW VALE IRON WORKS.

---

# XXI.

# The Abercarne Iron Works.

---

THESE Works consisted of an important Forge for the working up and manufacturing of Iron, and were situate on, or immediately adjacent to, the Ebbw main stream at Abercarne.

Of their formation we have no particulars, but in 1783 we find Messrs. Joshua Glover and Samuel Glover, of Birmingham, carrying on an important business there, and entering into a contract with Anthony Bacon, Senior of Cyfarthfa, for the supply to them at Abercarne of 800 tons of pig iron yearly.

The following is a summary of the Agreement then entered into :—

BY ARTICLES OF AGREEMENT OF THE 22ND AUGUST, 1783,

Between

ANTHONY BACON, of Merther, Co. Glamorgan, Esq., one part ;

and

JOSHUA GLOVER and SAMUEL GLOVER, both of Birmingham, in the Co. of Warwick, Merchants, Co-partners and Joint Proprietors of Abercarne Iron Works, Co. Monmouth, other part.

It was agreed as follows:—That the said Anthony Bacon, his heirs, etc., did agree with the said Glovers, their exors., etc., that the said Bacon, his exors., etc., in consideration of the sums of money, to be paid to him as hereafter mentioned, should from the 25th day of April next, for the term of 50 years, deliver, or cause to be delivered, unto said Glovers, 800 tons of pig iron yearly, and so much more as he could make in each year during the term, to be composed of good dark or bright gray metal, whichever sort they, the said Glovers, should best approve of, and could be made at Hirwain Furnace only, agreeable to directions to be received from the said Glovers, the same to be delivered at Glovers' Forge at Abercarne at the rate of £5 per ton long weight (that was to say), 120 lbs. per hundred weight, and 20 cwt. to the ton (customary breakage to be deducted). But in case of accident, or impediment to the said Furnace, whereby the quantity of 800 tons annually, and such further quantity as aforesaid, should be prevented from being made at the said Furnace, so as to cause a deficiency of delivery of said 800 tons, and further quantity as aforesaid,

Then, in that case, said A. Bacon did agree with Glovers that such impediment should be removed with all despatch, and the Furnace repaired with all speed.

Also that said Bacon should deliver, or cause to be delivered, at said Forge from the said Furnace at Hirwain all such sorts of castings as Glovers should want or require at the same price as the pig iron.

That is to say, £5 per ton long weight, without any allowance for breakage, the said Glovers paying the usual and customary price to the Founder for moulding the said castings, and also paying the difference of extra expense (if any) for carrying such of the castings as might be wanted, and could not be carried on horses' backs. All which pig iron and castings from said Furnace were to be delivered at Glovers' Works aforesaid in 4 parts, and at 4 different times in each year (*i.e.*), the 1st delivery of such goods to commence from 25th April then next, and to continue for and during the said term of 50 years.

And Glovers agreed and covenanted with Bacon as follows: That they, Glovers, would receive all iron so sent from said Furnace to Abercarne as aforesaid.

And Bacon further covenanted and agreed with Glovers that he, Bacon, would deliver or cause to be delivered unto said Glovers on the Bank of said Hirwain Furnace as often as they required during said term of 50 years, all or part of the pig iron and castings thereby contracted for, instead of delivering the same at Abercarne Forge as aforesaid. The said Glovers giving Bacon 4 months' notice of such their intention of receiving the said pig iron or castings, or part thereof, on the Bank of said Hirwain Furnace. That Glovers should pay for same after the rate of £4 2*s*. per ton long weight (the customary breakage deducted as aforesaid).

And also that Bacon would, during this demise, provide all the coal for Glovers for the use of the forges, finerys, chaferys, and air furnaces, together with what workmen's houses they may erect for the purpose of carrying on their said Works at Hirwain aforesaid, for the purpose of melting or refining pig iron, from the collieries that shall be worked by the said Bacon for the use of his said Blast-Furnace at Hirwain aforesaid, so that as such supply of coal can be supplyed from the said collieries that might be then or at any time thereafter opened, and not to the prejudice to the supply of the said Blast-Furnace aforesaid. All which supply of coal as aforesaid the said Bacon engaged to deliver at the Bank upon Glovers' Works at the following prices, viz.:—

First 25 years of said term of 50 years at 5*s*. per ton long weight, and during remainder of said term 6*s*. per ton long weight. Also with liberty to Glovers to take and use at their Works aforesaid, all the brays that shall be thrown away from the coke hearths of the Furnace aforesaid.

And it was mutually agreed between the parties that the accounts for the quantities of pig iron castings and coal delivered should be settled quarterly, on the 25th July,

Glover of the other part or all things according
meaning of the same then this Obligation —
effect or else to remain in full force and virtue

Joshua Glover

Saml. Glover

*Page* 159.

SIGNATURES ON BOND TO ANTHONY BACON I. 1783.

25th October, 25th January, and 25th April, in each year during the 50 years, and from which periods of time they, the said Glovers, should have 14 days extra allowed for settling said accounts.

And Glovers further agreed with Bacon to pay Bacon at end of said 14 days, at the rates and prices aforesaid, for all such pig iron castings and coal as should be delivered, in good notes or bills, payable at some substantial house in London at 6 months.

Proviso, that Bacon should be at liberty to supply Messrs. Maybery and Wilkins, of Brecon, Co. Brecknock, with 200 tons from Bacon's Furnace at Hirwain annually, if Maybery and Wilkins demanded the same.

Proviso, that Glovers should be at liberty to determine and make void this Agreement at end of first 7 years of the term if they wanted to, by giving 12 months' notice in writing to Bacon.

Signed, sealed and delivered, being first duly stamped, by

ANTHO. BACON (L.S.), JOSHUA GLOVER (L.S.), and SAMUEL GLOVER (L.S.)

And attested by Thomas Richardson and Richd. Hill, Clerks to A. Bacon, Esq.

---

## BOND FOR PERFORMANCE OF COVENANTS.—DELIVERY OF PIG-IRON, MERTHYR TO ABERCARNE, 22ND AUGUST, 1783.

MESSRS. GLOVERS TO ANTHONY BACON, ESQ.

Know all men by these presents, that we, Joshua Glover and Samuel Glover, both of Birmingham, in the County of Warwick, Merchants, Co-partners and Joint Proprietors of Abercarne Iron Works, in the County of Monmouth, are held and firmly bound to Anthony Bacon, of Myrther, in the County of Glamorgan, Esquire, in the penal sum of three thousand pounds of good and lawful money of Great Britain, to be paid to the said Anthony Bacon, or his certain attorney, executors, administrators or assigns, for the true payment whereof we bind ourselves, and each of us by himself, our, and each of our heirs, executors and administrators, and every of them, firmly by these presents, sealed with our seals, dated this twenty-second day of August, in the twenty-third year of the reign of our Sovereign Lord George the Third, by the grace of God, of Great Britain, France and Ireland, King, Defender of the Faith, and so forth, and in the year of our Lord, One thousand seven hundred and eighty-three.

The condition of this obligation is such that if the above bounden Joshua Glover and Samuel Glover, their respective heirs, executors, administrators or assigns, do and shall well and truly pay, observe, perform, fulfill and keep all and singular the covenants, conditions and agreements whatsoever, which on the part and behalf of them, the said Joshua Glover and Samuel Glover, their respective heirs, executors, administrators or assigns, are, or ought to be paid, observed, performed, fulfilled, and kept comprised or mentioned in, and by Articles of Agreement, bearing date respectively with these presents, and made, or expressed to be made, between the said Anthony Bacon, of the one part, and the said Joshua Glover and Samuel Glover, of the other part, in all things according to the true intent and meaning of the same, then this obligation to be void and of none effect, or else to remain in full force and virtue.

(Signed) JOSHUA GLOVER.
(Signed) SAML. GLOVER.

Sealed and delivered in the presence of

(Signed) Jn. Anth. Fry.
(Signed) Wm. Smith.

The pig-iron was carried over the hills from Hirwain to Abercarne on the backs of horses and mules, and a solvent buyer of pig-iron on a large scale was a useful friend to the owners of the South Wales furnaces in the period referred to.

Whether the Messrs. Glover erected any forges at Hirwain to work up the pig-iron there, on the same being delivered to them on the bank, our papers do not tell us, but such an arrangement was provided for in the above agreement.

In 1786, on the death of Anthony Bacon, senior, the Messrs. Glover became lessees under the Court of Chancery of the Hirwain Works, and carried these on until bought out by Anthony Bacon, the son, and his brother Thomas, as we have already seen. We next find the Messrs. Glover as purchasers of the Llwydcoed property at Aberdare.

Passing on to 1808, we learn from Mr. Benjamin Hall's letter of December 10th of that year (*ante*, p. 55) that Mr. Glover—presumably the last surviving member of the firm—had shortly before his death agreed to sell the freehold of the Abercarne estate to Mr. Richard Crawshay, of Cyfarthfa. This sale was carried through, though Mr Hall's letter tells us there were many difficulties to be overcome, there being "broils in the family, and two mortgages." On the completion of the purchase, Mr. Richard Crawshay handed the estate over as a gift to his son-in-law, and the property has remained in the hands of the Hall family ever since.

Our old papers carry us no further in the history of these Works.

## THE BLAENAU, VARTEG, ABERSYCHAN, AND PONTYMISTER IRON WORKS.

Although we have a few old papers relating to these Works, they are not sufficient to justify our attempting any description of their early history; and it will be best, we think, to leave that task for another hand.

But, relating to Blaenavon Works, we have several old papers, and to Nantyglo and Beaufort a great many, and these Works will now engage our attention.

## XXII.

# The Blaen Afon Iron Works.

These large iron-works were placed at the head or source (Blaen) of the Afon or Afon Llwyd river, which flows through the Pontypool Valley in its rapid headlong course to the River Usk at Caerleon.

Their origin dates from 1789, when, by a lease of November 30th in that year, Henry, Earl of Abergavenny, granted the royalties, mines and minerals, coal and limestone, with power to work the same and to erect furnaces thereon, in, under, and over a vast tract of mountainous land in the County of Monmouth, to Thomas Hill, of Dennis, in the County of Stafford, Thomas Hopkins and Benjamin Pratt.

Such mineral properties and royalties are described in the lease as being

*Page* 160.

IRON WORKS AT BLAENAFON. 1799.

(*Coxe's "History of Monmouthshire.*")

All the mines, beds, quarries of iron ore, coal, limestone, stone, clay, and marl, in, under, and upon all that tract of mountainous or hilly land, estimated to contain 12,000 acres, commonly called Lord Abergavenny's Hill, and being in the several parishes of

| | |
|---|---|
| Aberystwith, | Goytrey, |
| Trevethin, | Llanover, |
| Llanhilleth, | Llanfoist, and |
| Mamhilad, | Llanwenarth, |

and within the Manors of Abergavenny and Pelleine, in the County of Monmouth (said to be described in a map), with full liberty to erect furnaces, etc.

The lease was to run for twenty-one years only, but the Earl of Abergavenny covenanted to extend it for seven years beyond. An application was also arranged to be made to Parliament for a private Act, enabling longer leases to be granted, and which power was subsequently granted by 30 Geo. III.

The rent stipulated to be paid was £1,300 per annum, but no royalties appear to have been reserved in addition. And, as remarked *passim* previously, we do not find (except in the Duke of Beaufort's lease to Kendall, and that only as regards mine ore—see Beaufort Works—and in that of Walter Wilkins at Abernant), in any of the older leases the reservation of royalty payment per ton, and the general introduction of it, seems to have originated with the lessees, like the Dowlais Co. and Kendall and Co., when granting leases of the minerals of their lands to their sub-lessees. The lords of the manors and freeholders of olden times were, as a rule, content to grant long leases of their mineral rights at low and fixed reserved rents.

True, in this instance, the reserved rent of £1,300 was unusually large, but the mineral rights were enormous ; and by one deed and instrument the whole taking over of a vast tract was placed in the lessees' hands.

Mr. Thomas Hill, who came from Dennis, co. Stafford, must, I think, have been a man of wealth, as he is spoken of in that regard by the firm of Harvey, Partridge and Co., of Bristol, in 1795. Thomas Hopkins was then little known of (at least, we cannot learn much about him) ; but we consider him to have been a man of means at that time, and of good standing, and we know little also about the third partner, Mr. Pratt.

In the formation of the Monmouthshire Canal to Pontnewynydd, and the extension of the tram-road up the Valley to the Works at Blaen Afon, all the partners gave large moneyed help, Mr. Kendall, of Beaufort, being the Chairman of the Canal Company.

Of course, it was essential to get this means of access to the sea at Newport open.

Latterly, when the Company had a forge at Garnddyris, the Blaen Afon Company made a tram-road and inclined plane down the steep side of the Blorenge Mountain, delivering the iron manufactured at this Forge on the Brecon and Abergavenny Canal wharf at Llanfoist.

The elder Mr. Hopkins died about 1791, and Mr. Pratt about the same time ; and in 1792 it was proposed by Mr. Hill, the surviving partner, to detach the Nantyglo portion of the mineral taking, and work that as a separate iron-works, and apart from the Blaen Afon, and for this purpose sought and obtained the co-operation as partners of the old and established firm of Harvey, Partridge and Co., of Bristol. The story of that partnership, ending ultimately in 1811 in the sale of the newly-established Nantyglo Iron-works (of which a fresh lease from the Earl of Abergavenny had been obtained in 1806) by Thomas Hill (the son) and Samuel Hopkins (the son) to Joseph Bailey and Matthew Wayne, will be described under the heading of the Nantyglo Iron-works, next to follow.

The papers I have relative to the Blaen Afon Iron-works are few and unimportant. I have no original letters of either Thomas Hill or Thomas Pratt, his partner ; but I have several of Samuel Hopkins, the son of Thomas Hopkins, one of the lessees of 1789, and the following are copies of two of these :—

"Blaenavan, April 12th, 1805.

"Dear Sir,—Be pleased to draw the Bond for the Award given Mr. Homfray at Cardiff to be paid according to the instalments by Thomas Hill, Senr., of Dennis House, in the County of Stafford, only. I conclude his separate security will be equally satisfactory to Mr. Homfray.

"I remain, Dear Sir,

"Yours very truly,

"John Powell, Esq., Brecon. "SAML. HOPKINS."

---

"Blaenavon, April 23rd, 1805.

"Dear Sir,—On my return from Abe'g Market, after dining with Major Morgan, I found Mr. Williams here, and with some dificulty prevailed on him to stay the night. In reply to your esteemed favor, I will send the Bond and release to Mr. Hill at Cheltenham, where he intended going with his family to-day for a short time; and after getting them properly executed by him and Mr. Griffith, I'll consider if I can send them to you before the 1st of May. Meantime, I will take care of Mr. Homfray's release and the contract untill all is settled to your satisfaction, and you direct me how to dispose of them.

"Yours very sincerely,

"SAML. HOPKINS."

---

It will be now interesting to quote the account given of the Blaenafon Iron Works by the well-known historian of Monmouthshire, Archdeacon Coxe, in 1801, in his book, cap. 24, pp. 200-2.

"In the course of my expeditions, I three times visited the Iron Works of Blaenavon, recently established in the vicinity of Abergavenny, which form a new and interesting object in the tour of Monmouthshire.

"From Abergavenny, in company with Sir Richard Hoare, I passed over the stone bridge of the Usk, along the plain between the river and the Blorenge, and went up the steep sides of the mountain, in a hollow way enclosed between high hedges, with occasional openings, which admit different views of Abergavenny and the circumjacent country. Emerging from the thickets of wood which clothe the lower and middle parts, we ascended a common, strewed with vast masses of rock, from whence a dreary moor leads to the summit overlooking the Works of Blaenavon, situate in the hollow of the mountain, near the source of the Avon Lwyd, from which the place derives its appellation.

"At some distance, the Works have the appearance of a small town, surrounded with heaps of ore, coal, and limestone, and enlivened with all the bustle and activity of an opulent and increasing establishment. The view of the buildings, which are constructed in the excavations of the rocks, is extremely picturesque, and heightened by the volumes of black smoke emitted by the furnaces. While my friend, Sir Richard Hoare, was engaged in sketching a view of this singular scene, of which an engraving is annexed, I employed myself in examining the mines and works.

"This spot and its vicinity produce abundance of iron, with coal and limestone, and every article necessary for smelting the ore; the veins lie in the adjacent rocks, under strata of coal, and are from three and a-half to seven or eight inches in thickness; they differ in richness, but yield, upon an average, not less than forty-four pounds of pig-iron to one hundredweight of ore. The principal part of the iron, after being formed into pigs, is conveyed by means of the railroad and canal to Newport, from whence it is exported.

"The shafts of the mines are horizontal, penetrating one below the other, and under the coal shafts; iron rail roads are constructed to convey the coal and ore, which are pushed as far as the shafts are worked, and gradually carried on as the excavations are extended; the longest of these subterraneous passages penetrates not less than three-quarters of a mile. The coal is so abundant as not only to supply the fuel necessary for the works, but large quantities are sent to Abergavenny, Pont y Pool, and Usk.

"Although these works were only finished in 1789, three hundred and fifty men are employed, and the population of the district exceeds a thousand souls. The hollows of the rocks and sides of the hills are strewed with numerous habitations, and the heathy ground converted into fields of corn and pasture. Such are the wonder-working powers of industry when directed by judgment.

"The want of habitations for the increasing number of families has occasioned an ingenious contrivance: a bridge being thrown across a deep dingle for the support of a rail road leading into a mine, the arches, which are ten in number, have been walled up, and formed into dwellings; the bridge is covered with a penthouse roof, and backed by perpendicular rocks, in which the mines are excavated. Numerous workmen continually pass and repass, and low cars, laden with coal or iron ore, roll along with their broad and grooved wheels; these objects, losing themselves under the roof of the bridge, again emerging, and then disappearing in the subterraneous passages of the rock, form a singular and animated picture, not unlike the moving figures in a camera obscura.

"The mountainous district which contains these mineral treasures is held by the Earl of Abergavenny, under a lease from the Crown. It was formerly let to the family of Hanbury, of Pont y Pool, for less than £100 a year; and as the value of the mines was not sufficiently appreciated, no works were constructed; but the masses of ore found near the surface were conveyed to the forges of Pont y Pool. Soon after the expiration of the term, the district was granted by another lease to Hill and Company, who began these works in 1788, and expended forty thousand pounds before any return was made; this expense, however, has been amply repaid by the produce.

"On considering the rise and rapid progress of the iron manufactories in this district, as well as in the neighbouring mountains of Monmouthshire and Glamorganshire, it is a matter of wonder that these mineral treasures should have been so long neglected. This wonder will increase when it is known that iron was manufactured in this country at a period beyond the reach of tradition or history. Large heaps of slag or cinder have been repeatedly discovered, some of which are evidently the product of bloomeries, the most ancient method of fusing iron; in other places are traced the sites of furnaces long disused, of which no account of their foundation can be collected. The appearance of these iron cinders, and the vestiges of ancient furnaces, indicate that many parts of this mountainous district, now wholly bare, were formerly covered with large tracts of wood, charcoal being the only species of fuel originally used in the operation of smelting, both in the bloomeries and furnaces. This conjecture is corroborated by numerous names, alluding to woods and forests, in places which have never been known to produce trees; and it is still farther ascertained by the discovery of trunks and branches, with their leaves, under the boggy soil in the vicinity of Blaenavon, and on the neighbouring hills. The lands being cleared and the forests neglected, their destruction was hastened by numerous herds of goats, maintained in these mountainous regions; the want of fuel occasioned the gradual decline of the bloomeries and furnaces, and for a considerable period little or no iron was manufactured.

"About forty years ago the iron works suddenly revived, from the beneficial discovery of making pig iron with pit coal, instead of charcoal, which was soon afterwards followed by the improvement of manufacturing even bar iron by means of pit coal: hence a district, which contained such extensive mines of ore and coal, prodigious quantities of limestone, and numerous streams of water, could not fail of becoming the seat of many flourishing establishments. Besides these local advantages, the progress of the manufactories has been powerfully aided by the application of mechanics; particularly by the use of the steam engine, and the great improvement of water machines; but in no instance have they derived more advantage than from the adoption of rollers instead of forge hammers, now used for the formation of bar iron, with a degree of dispatch, as well as exactness, before unknown. From this concurrence of circumstances the success has been no less rapid than extraordinary; fifteen years ago the weekly quantity of pig iron made in this part of Monmouthshire, and in the contiguous district of Glamorganshire, did not exceed 60 tons; at present it scarcely falls short of 600; at that period no bar iron was manufactured, but now the quantity amounts weekly to more than 300 tons.

"The works are still rapidly increasing in extent and importance, and appear likely to surpass the other iron manufactories throughout the Kingdom.

"In the vicinity of Blaenavon we observed the process of making a railroad, so called because it is formed by a kind of frame with iron rails, or bars, laid lengthways, and fastened or cramped by means of cross-bars. The ground being excavated, about 6 ft. in breadth, and 2 ft. in depth, is strewed over with broken pieces of stone, and the frame laid down; it is composed of rails, sleepers, or cross-bars, and under-sleepers. The rail is a bar of cast iron, 4 ft. in length, 3 in. thick, and 1½ in. broad; its extremities are respectively concave and convex, or, in other words, are morticed and tenoned into each other, and fastened at the ends by two wooden pegs to a cross-bar called the sleeper. This sleeper was originally of iron, but experience having shown that iron was liable to snap or bend, it is now made of wood, which is considerably cheaper, and requires less repair. Under each extremity of the sleeper is a square piece of wood, called the under-sleeper, to which it is attached by a peg. The frame being thus laid down and filled with stones, gravel, and earth, the iron rails form a ridge above the surface, over which the wheels of the car glide by means of iron grooved rims, 3½ ins. broad.

"This is the general structure of the road when carried in a straight line; at the junction of two roads, and to facilitate the passage of two cars in opposite directions, moveable rails, called turn rails, are occasionally used, which are fastened with screws instead of pegs, and may be pushed sideways. The level of the ground is taken with great exactness, and the declivity is in general so gentle as to be almost imperceptible: the road, sometime conveyed in a straight line, sometimes winding round the sides of precipices, is a picturesque object, and the cars filled with coal or iron, and gliding along occasionally without horses, impress the traveller, who is unaccustomed to such spectacles, with pleasing astonishment. The expense of forming these roads is very considerable, varying according to the nature of the ground, and the difficulty or facility of procuring proper materials; it is seldom less than a thousand pounds per mile, and sometimes exceeds that sum.

"The cars, from the solidity of their structure, and the quantity of iron used in the axle-tree and wheels when loaded weigh not less than 3½ tons; they are drawn by a single horse, and the driver stands on a kind of footboard behind, and can instantaneously stop the car by means of a lever and a drop, which falls between the wheels, and suspends their motion. In places where the declivity is more rapid than usual the horse is taken out, and the car impelled forward by its own weight."

---

In the course of succeeding years, great changes were made in the management of the concern; and by a printed paper carrying us nearly down to our fixed date of 1840, we find that in 1836-7 a Company of Shareholders was formed, and that the Works were then taken over by them.

---

The following is the return of iron sent to Newport for shipment by the Monmouthshire Canal from Blaen Afon and Garnddyris Iron-works in the following years:—

| Year. | Blaenafon. | Garnddyris. |
|---|---|---|
| 1802 | 1,091 | Nil |
| 1803 | 2,079 | " |
| 1804 | 8,490 | " |
| 1805 | 7,262 | " |
| 1806 | 6,594 | " |
| 1807 | 6,042 | " |
| 1808 | 7,163 | " |
| 1809 | 9,848 | " |
| 1810 | 12,254 | " |
| 1811 | 12,337 | " |
| 1812 | 14,579 | " |
| 1813 | 13,562 | " |
| 1814 | 12,248 | " |
| 1815 | 14,002 | " |
| 1816 | 11,773 | " |
| 1817 | 11,082 | 2,247[1] |
| 1818 | 8,771 | 5,097 |
| 1819 | 6,776 | 4,427 |
| 1820 | 9,423 | 2,769 |
| Total | 176,376 | 14,596 |

| Year. | Blaenafon. | Garnddyris. |
|---|---|---|
| 1821 | 8,973 | 2,838 |
| 1822 | 5,831 | 3,476 |
| 1823 | 10,745 | 4,370 |
| 1824 | 11,265 | 4,517 |
| 1825 | 9,043 | 4,218 |
| 1826 | 8,059 | 2,145 |
| 1827 | 8,255 | 2,446 |
| 1828 | 9,766 | 2,645 |
| Carried forward | 71,937 | 26,655 |

[1] 1817. Garnddyris Works were apparently commenced at this date.

| Year. | | Blaenafon. | | | Garnddyris. |
|---|---|---|---|---|---|
| | Brought forward | 71,937 | ... | ... | 26,655 |
| 1829 | ... ... | 10,124 | ... | ... | 2,242 |
| 1830 | ... ... | 9,397 | ... | ... | 3,654 |
| 1831 | Hills and Wheeley | 9,708 | ... | ... | 4,133 |
| 1832 | Do. | 8,986 | ... | ... | 1,837 |
| 1833 | Do. | 8,285 | ... | ... | 3,600 |
| 1834 | Do. | 8,406 | ... | ... | 2,214 |
| 1835 | Do. | 9,023 | ... | ... | 4,286 |
| 1836 | Do. | 7,606 | ... | ... | 4,257 |
| 1837 | New Company | { 5,058 | ... | ... | { 4,159 |
| | | { 2,699 | ... | ... | { 2,092 |
| 1838 | ... ... | 9,857 | ... | ... | 8,074 |
| 1839 | ... ... | 1,280 | ... | ... | 5,718 |
| 1840 | ... ... | 1,269 | ... | ... | 7,347 |
| | | 166,383 | | | 90,064 |
| | | 176,376 | | | 14,569 |
| | | 342,759 | | | 104,633 |
| | | 104,633 | | | |
| Total No. of Tons of Iron in 40 years | | 447,392 | | | |

[From Scrivenor, *Iron Trade*, pp. 126 and 294.]

[David Mushet (*Iron and Steel*, pp. 68 and 415) writes that there were five Blast-Furnaces at Blaenafon in 1839 (two also in building), and that the coal of that district had fine smelting properties.]

XXIII.

# The Nant y Glo Iron Works.

These works were of the largest of their kind in South Wales, second only in importance and output of iron to the Dowlais Works, and about equal to those of Cyfarthfa. Their situation lay at the very source almost of the little Ebwy river (Ebwy Fach), in the Parish of Aberystwith, in the County of Monmouth, near the outcrop of the coal measures, and near what was then considered rich and abundant veins of iron ore.

Their early origin is as follows:—

On the 30th November, 1789, by an Indenture made between Henry, Earl of Abergavenny, of the one part, and Thomas Hill, Thos. Hopkins, and Benjamin Pratt of the other part,

All the mines, beds, veins, and quarries of iron ore, iron stone, coal, limestone, shale, clay, and marl, lying or being within, under, or upon a very large tract of mountain land in the Parish of Aberystwith, in the Co. of Monmouth, with liberty to search for such minerals, and to erect buildings, forges, and other works thereon,

Were demised by the said Earl of Abergavenny to the said Thos. Hill and others, for the yearly rent of £1,300, with a covenant from the said Earl to renew the lease at the end of the first seven years.

In May, 1791, Mr. Hill, one of the lessees, wrote to Messrs. Harford, Partridge and Co., of Bristol, that the Royalty was more extensive than they could possibly make use of with ironworks, and proposed that a partnership in that line with the Messrs. Harford and Co. should be entered into as to a part of the Royalty.

Mr. Hill, in his letters, described the situation to be the most eligible in the country; and after some interviews it was agreed in July, 1791, to enter upon a partnership, and it was then settled that two blast-furnaces, with all necessary appendages, workmen's houses, etc., should be made with all possible dispatch.

And in the same month Mr. Pratt (one of the partners in the firm of Hill and Co.), and an agent of theirs in another work, and Mr. Partridge, one of the partners in the firm of Harford and Co., met upon the ground to fix the site for building the works; which being done, workmen were immediately employed to cut the foundations, and other necessary preparations were set on foot; and it was arranged that the management of the concern should be left in the hands of Mr. Richard Summers Harford, one of the firm of Harford, Partridge and Co.

On the 30th April, 1792, a formal deed of partnership (dated February preceding) between Messrs. Hill and Co., lessees, of the one part, and Messrs. Partridge and Co., of the other, was entered into.

And after reciting the Lease from the Earl of Abergavenny of 1789, and the Act of Parliament, 30 Geo. III., more fully enabling the said Earl of Abergavenny to grant such lease; and after describing all that tract of mountainous or hilly land, part of the Royalty now intended to become the estate of the proposed partnership,

It was agreed that Messrs. Thomas Hill, Thomas Hopkins, and Benjamin Pratt, under the style of Messrs. Hill and Co., and Messrs. James Harford, John Partridge, and their Co.-partners, under the style of Harford, Partridge and Co., should become partners, for the term of the lease granted to Messrs. Hill and Co., or such as should be hereafter granted: each firm to pay one-half of the renewed rent of £1,300, to share equally in all profits, and to bear in equal moieties the cost of erecting the two blast-furnaces, and other necessary appendages.

Apparently, it was understood by Messrs. Hill and Co., that their share of capital required would not exceed £10,000, but on the sums expended being far in excess, Mr. Hill demurred to paying any amount beyond £10,000, and which (or rather more—£10, 485 17*s.* 3*d.*) he had then advanced (1793).

The Messrs. Harford had always advanced sums more freely than the firm of Hill and Co., and their payment of capital had reached £16,831 4*s.* 11*d.*—making the total expended, with Mr. Hill's payment, £27,316 17*s.* 3*d.*

A long correspondence ensued.

On October 6th, 1794, Messrs. Harford informed Mr. Hill that by advice from Nant y glo the works were ready, and that nothing prevented their being blown in when orders are given, and in order that this long wished-for and desirable event should take place, expressed a hope for immediate settlement.

However, Mr. Hill would not go beyond his £10,000 advanced, and said that Harford and Co. could take their over-payment out of the profits of the concern, until they were paid off.

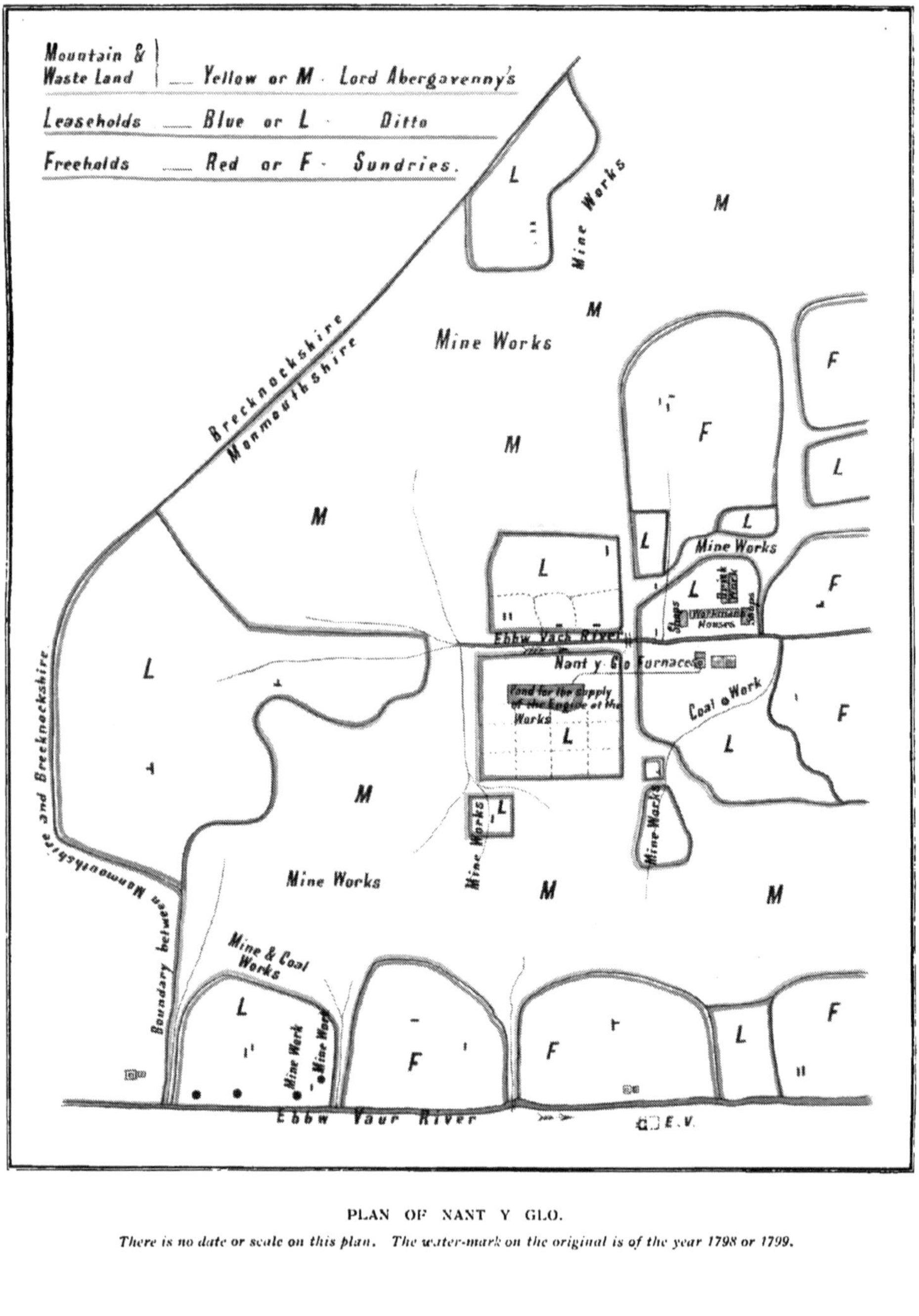


PLAN OF NANT Y GLO.

*There is no date or scale on this plan. The water-mark on the original is of the year 1798 or 1799.*

On the 27th January, 1795, Messrs. Harford and Co., finding Mr. Hill obdurate on the point, resolved to discharge the miners and other workmen, and to put the furnaces (which were then just finished) in blast to work out the stock then in hand, and to place the produce in reduction of the excess of their advances.

And accordingly the miners were discharged, and the furnaces put in blast on the 28th January.

The differences were further aggravated by Mr. Harrison being sent, on the part of Mr. Hill, to claim one-half the pig-iron.

Upon this, a case was submitted to Counsel by Messrs. Harford and Co. (from which we are quoting), whether Messrs. Kinsey and Harrison, on the part of Mr. Hill, could take away one-half of the pig-iron, not only from the furnaces, but from the carriers to various places, as they threatened to do.

The opinions of Robt. Graham, of Lincolns Inn, January 7th, 1796, and of J. Stanley, of Lincolns Inn, of December 30th, 1795, were taken, and both agreed that Messrs. Harford and Co. were justified in applying the proceeds of the pig-iron in diminution of their over-advances; and if any further threats of interference were made, a Bill in Equity to restrain should be applied for.

The miners having, however, been discharged, the using-up of the stock of ore did not take long; and then ensued the ignominous result of these new works coming to a stand-still, and so they remained idle for several years.

It should be mentioned that Mr. Hopkins, one of Mr. Hill's co-lessees, died as far back as March, 1793, and Mr. Pratt soon after; and it was thought that, though nominally Mr. Hill called Kinsey and Harrison partners, he was latterly standing alone in that firm.

A Plan of the Nant y Glo part of the Royalty, leased in 1789 by the Earl of Abergavenny, is before me. There is no date upon it, but the Water Mark denotes the make of the paper to have been 1798 or 1799. The two blast-furnaces, with an engine-house attached, and a row of workmen's cottages, are shown thereon, and the mouth of a coal level or pit is within a very short distance of the Furnaces; and we shall give later a copy of this map on a reduced scale. [The Ebbw Vale Furnace is also shown at the extreme western limit of the map.]

It will be interesting to give a copy of the Agreement for raising iron ore and scouring it clean, entered into between Hill, Harford and Co., and John Morgan, mine worker, on March 31st, 1794.

Memorandum of an Agreement made this Thirty-first day of March, 1794, between Richard and John Harford, of Nant y Glo Works, in the Parish of Aberystwith and County of Monmouth, Iron Masters, for and on behalf of themselves and Partners, under the firm of Hill, Harford and Company, of the one part, and John Morgan, of the same place, Miner, on the other part, Witnesseth That the said Richard and John Harford have and do hereby set out unto the said Jno. Morgan all that scouring Race or Mine Work above Cabbin Gwin and the Pond belonging to it as was let to him last Year, and also a New Work near it now opening, for which a new Pond is making, for the sole purpose of raising Iron Mine for the said Company, and for the considerations under-mentioned for and during the full end and Term of Three Years from the first day of April next ensuing the date hereof, in which said Mine works, the said John Morgan hereby engages to raise during the said Term of Three Years the full Quantity of Three Thousand Two Hundred Dozen (each Dozen to consist of Thirty Six Hundred Weight) of good, clean, and Perfect Iron Mine; and if at any time he shall deliver such as is not so, it shall be clean'd by the Mine Weigher, and the expence of such cleaning, the said John Morgan agrees to allow out of what may be due to him for Mine raised on the next Pay day after such Mine has been cleaned. The said John Morgan agrees to raise the said Quantity of Three Thousand Two Hundred Dozens in the following proportions, viz., One Thousand Dozens during the first Year of the said Term; One Thousand Dozens more during the second Year; and One Thousand Two Hundred Dozens during the Third and last Year; but if from having had a very dry season, or any unavoidable accident, or that it appears he has done his utmost to raise the whole Quantity of Three Thousand Two Hundred Dozens within the time specified, and it should not be quite compleated by the said term, the said John Morgan is to be allowed a further term of Six Weeks over and above the Three Years.

And as it is expected the Mine rais'd by the said John Morgan will not be carried in to the Yard belonging to Nant y Glo Works aforesaid as fast as it will be raised, the said John Morgan hereby engages to put up what shall be remaining in the Mine Works on the Saturday previous to every pay day in tidy heaps to be measured, each heap to consist of as much as will measure whole Dozens of the before-mention'd weight—each Dozen being consider'd to measure Seven feet long, three feet and an Half wide, and Twenty-One Inches high.

The said John Morgan further engages to carry on the said Mine Work in a fair and Workman-like manner, that he will at no time rob the work of the mine unfairly by driving holes in it without the consent of the said Richard or John Harford or the Company's Agent, unless he will scour away all the Rubbish he may bring down by so doing immediately afterwards.

The Ponds and Ditches being delivered to the said John Morgan in good working order, he hereby engages to keep them so during the continuance of this Agreement, and leave them at the expiration of this term in the same state and condition; but if during the present Agreement the Banks of the Ponds should be materially damaged by a sudden Storm, or other unforseen cause, not owing to the neglect or carelessness of the said John Morgan, then, and in that case, the repair is to be made at the Company's expense, but not otherwise.

And in consideration of the said John Morgan performing his part of this Agreement fairly and honestly, or without giving cause for dispute by not cleaning his Mine properly, or any other Act contrary to the true intent and meaning of this Agreement, The said Richard and John Harford hereby engage to allow and pay the said John Morgan Six Shillings and Three Pence for raising each and every Dozen of good, clean, and perfect Mine he shall raise in the course of every Month during the continuance of the said term; and if he raises the full Quantity of One Thousand Dozens during the first Year of the said Term, or by the first day of April One Thousand Seven Hundred and Ninety-five, the said Richard and John Harford agree to Allow and pay the further sum of Sixpence per Dozen for each and every Dozen so deliver'd over and above the Six Shillings and three pence before mention'd; but if he does not compleat the said Quantity of One Thousand Dozens by the time specified the extra allowance is not to be paid him. If that should be the case, and he makes up the Quantity of Two Thousand Dozens by the end of the Second Year, he is then to be paid the Six-pence per dozen for the whole Quantity deliver'd; but if he should not have compleated the Two Thousand Dozens by the end of the Second Year, the extra allowance is still to be withheld from him; but if at the end of the Third Year he shall have compleated the whole Quantity of Three Thousand Two Hundred Dozens, the said Richard and John Harford then agree to allow and pay the said John Morgan the extra Sixpence per dozen on the whole Quantity; but if he does not compleat the said Quantity of Three Thousand Two Hundred Dozens in the time specified no part of the extra allowance is to be paid him.

It is further Agreed between the said Richard and John Harford and John Morgan, that the said John Morgan is to pay for all Wheelbarrows and Tools of every description that may be requisite for raising the said Mine and carrying on the said Mine Work that may be procured for, or deliver'd him by the said Company or their Agents, nothing of which are to be found at the Company's expence but sharpening of the Maundrills and other Tools that may have been worn out in the said Mine work.

If any Slabs, Planks, etc., are deliver'd the said John Morgan for the purpose of wheeling over, an account of them must be taken by the Company's Agent or Stocktaker; and if any of them are missing, and the said John Morgan cannot give a good Account what is become of them, he hereby agrees that the value of them shall be charged in his Account, and he will pay for them the next pay-day after they may have disappeared.

And further, the said John Morgan engaging to carry the aforesaid Mine to the Mine Yard belonging to the said Iron Works, the said Richard and John Harford agree to allow and pay him One Shilling and Nine Pence for each and every Dozen (of the weight aforesaid) he shall deliver on the said Yard.

In Witness whereof the said parties have hereunto set their Hands and Seals the day and year first above written.

Seal'd and deliver'd by the within parties in the presence of — Richard S. Harford.

John Harford.

Joseph Finney.

Thomas Phillips.

the mark of
John X Morgan.

If John Morgan finishes the 3,200 according to agreement, he is to be given a Guinea when the whole is settled for.

---

These Works were, we have seen, stopped in 1796, and though Mr. Richard S. Harford continued to live at Nant y Glo up to the end of 1799, they remained idle, and no attempt was made to re-open them in his time, and for several years they were entered on the parish books as "empty."

However, by February 8th, 1802, a new firm seems to have been formed, called "The Nant y Glo Company," of which Joseph Harrison was one of the partners, and who had been closely identified with Mr. Hill, of Dennis, in previous transactions.

We hear no more of the connection of Harford, Partridge and Co. with these Works, and we may assume that for some money payment, the firm surrendered their moiety to Mr. Hill, or his nominee, probably suffering a considerable capital loss. As to the new arrangements our papers are silent, but we find that by February 8th, 1802, the new firm were able to enter into a contract, through their partner, Joseph Harrison, to supply Mr. Samuel Homfray, of Penydarran Place, with 15 tons of pig-iron weekly for six months, and afterwards for 21 years with 390 tons of pig-iron weekly:—

Memorandum of an Agreement made, entered into, and concluded upon this Feb. 8, 1802, by and between Joseph Harrison on the Behalf of himself and Partners known by the Firm of the Nant y glo Company, in the County of Monmouth, on the One part, and Samuel Homfray, Esqr., of Penydarran Place, in the County of Glamorgan, on the other part, that is to say, The said Joseph Harrison for himself and Nant y glo Company, and his and their Exors., etc., doth hereby covenant and agree to and with the said Samuel Homfray and his Exors., etc., as follows:—

The Nant y Glo Company agree to sell and deliver at Penydarran Iron Works, and the said Samuel Homfray hereby agrees to take Weekly and every Week during the Term, between the Day of the date hereof and June 24 next ensuing, Fifteen Tons Long weight of Pig Iron, or One Hundred and Ninety-five Tons per Quarter, with the usual Breakage, and of the quality hereafter specified. And also to sell and deliver at Penydarran aforesaid Weekly and every Week during the further Term of Twenty-One years to commence from the said June 24th next ensuing the Day of the Date hereof, Thirty Tons Long Weight of Pig Iron, or Three Hundred and Ninety Tons Per Quarter, with the usual Breakage, and of the quality hereafter specified, viz.:—One third part good Dark Grey, One third part Bright Grey, and the remaining Third part Mottle. And for every Ton of Pigs of the weight and description aforesaid, so delivered at Penydarran by the Nant y Glo Company, the said Samuel Homfray hereby agrees to pay the following Prices subject to the alterations hereinafter mentioned, that is to say, when the Price of Assorted Merchantable Bar Iron of Three Quarters of an Inch Square, and upwards, and all flatts of One Inch and a half Broad, and upwards, is sold by the Penydarran Company at Cardiff and Netts on the Average Price, Nineteen Pounds per Ton during One Quarter of a Year, then the Price of such Pig Iron so sold and delivered at Penydarran by the Nant y Glo Company during that Quarter is to be Six Pounds per Ton of the weight aforesaid. And when the Price of Bar Iron is altered and Netts the Penydarran Company at Cardiff more or less than Nineteen Pounds per Ton on the Average, then the Pig Iron is to rise or fall from the Price of Six Pounds proportionably thereto at a Rate of One Third of the rise or fall of such Bar Iron as aforesaid, or in the Ratio of Six Shillings and eight pence in every Ton of Pig Iron for Twenty Shillings in every Ton of Bar Iron of the description before mentioned. And the Sales of such Bar Iron at Cardiff, as aforesaid, shall be kept an Account of in a Book for that purpose at Penydarran, and shall be open for the inspection of the Nant y Glo Company at every Quarter day's Settling, which Quarter Days it is agreed shall be regulated by the Quarterly Meetings at Stourbridge, when so much Pig Iron as shall have been received at Penydarran in the preceding Quarter shall be paid for by Bills for the Amount, One Moiety at Three Months, and the other Moiety at Five Months after Date.

And it is hereby further agreed that if the said Samuel Homfray shall find it his Interest to take all or any part of the aforesaid Quantity of Pig Iron on the Bank at Nanty glo Furnaces, he shall be allowed so to do by giving one Month's Notice in Writing of his intention; and in that Case the Amount of the Carriage from thence to Penydarran, which is at that time paid by the Nanty glo Company shall be deducted from the price to be paid for the Pigs delivered at the end of each Quarter as aforesaid, supposing the same were delivered at Penydarran; and if the same Samuel Homfray has a wish to have all or any part thereof delivered at Newport or elsewhere, the Nant y Glo Company, on receiving One Month's Notice to that effect, shall send the same to such places as he may direct on being paid the extra price of Carriage, if any, between that and Penydarran, or if carried at a less expense, allowing the difference to the said Samuel Homfray out of the Price of the Pigs, supposing the same to have been delivered at Penydarran on the Days of Settlement before-mentioned. And the said Parties do hereby agree that upon either of them giving to the other Twelve Months' Notice in Writing previous to the expiration of the first seven or fourteen Years of this Agreement, the same shall become void. But upon the failure of either to give such Notice, it shall continue in full force and Virtue to the end of the Twenty-One Years herein before mentioned.

It is also agreed that if any Misconstruction or difference of Opinion should arise between the Parties relating to this Agreement, the difference shall be referred to two Arbitrators, who, if they cannot agree, shall chuse an Umpire, and the Determination of any two of them shall be final and Conclusive.

In Witness whereof the said Parties have hereunto set their Hands, the Day and year first before mentioned.

JOSEPH HARRISON,
for Self and Nanty Glo Co.

Witness, W. FOTHERGILL.

SAML. HOMFRAY.

It is further agreed at and before the signing of this Agreement that if the Nanty Glo Company chuse to deliver Sirhowy Pig Iron instead of Nant y Glo Pig Iron, the said Samuel Homfray will, and he hereby engages to, accept it accordingly.

JOSEPH HARRISON,
for Self and Nanty Glo Co.

Witness, W. FOTHERGILL.

SAML. HOMFRAY.

---

A serious dispute arose over this contract, and the Arbitration Clause was brought into operation, and Messrs. Wm. Taitt, of Cardiff, Edward Kendall, of Beaufort, and Richard Hill the younger, of Plymouth Works, were appointed arbitrators.

The partners in the Nant y Glo Company are disclosed in the Arbitration Deed, being Thomas Hill, of Dennis, Joseph Harrison, of Newport, and John Griffiths, of Blaenavon, in the parish of Llanover, innkeeper.

The original Award, signed by Wm. Taitt, Edward Kendall, and Richard Hill, junr., is now before us, and we quote the concluding portion :—

" Now know Ye, that we, the said William Taitt, Edward Kendall, and Richard Hill the Younger, having taken upon us the Charge and Burthen of the said Award, and having deliberately heard, Examined, and Considered the claims, Proofs, and Allegations of the said Parties, Do make, Publish, Declare, and Deliver this, our Award, Arbitrament, and Judgment between them of and concerning the several matters and things mentioned in the Conditions of the said respective Writings Obligatory, and thereby submitted to us as follows, that is to say : We do Order and direct that from and after the Publication of this, our Award, the said Thomas Hill, Joseph Harrison, and John Griffiths, their Heirs, Executors, Administrators and Assigns, shall not, nor shall any or either of them, be required or compelled by the said Samuel Homfray, his Executors, Administrators, or Assigns, or any of them, to deliver or cause to be delivered to the said Samuel Homfray, his Exors., etc., or any of them, any Pig Iron in Pursuance of the said Agreement mentioned and set forth in the conditions of the said several Bonds made and entered into by and between the said Parties; nor shall they, the said Thomas Hill, Joseph Harrison, and John Griffiths, their or either of their Exors., etc., any or either of them, be Subject or liable to Pay any damages to the said Samuel Homfray, his Exors., etc., by reason of the non-delivery of such Pig Iron to the said Samuel Homfray, his Exors., etc., or the non-performance of any other matter or thing contained in the said Agreement, on the part and behalf of the said Thomas Hill, Joseph Harrison, and John Griffiths, their Exors., etc., to be done and performed by them, any or either of them. And we do further Order and Award that at and upon the Execution and delivery of the Bond hereinafter required to be executed and delivered by the said Thomas Hill, Joseph Harrison, and John Griffiths to the said Samuel Homfray, the said Agreement, and every clause, matter, or thing therein contained shall cease, determine, and be utterly void to all intents and purposes, and shall no longer be binding upon the Parties thereto, their any or either of their Exors., etc., but the same and every part thereof shall be delivered up by the said parties respectively each to the other, to be cancelled and shall be cancelled accordingly.

And We do further Order and direct that the said Thomas Hill, Joseph Harrison, and John Griffiths, their Exors., etc., shall and do well and truly Pay or cause to be Paid unto the said Samuel Homfray, his Exors., etc., the Sum of Two Thousand Two Hundred and ffourteen Pounds Thirteen Shillings and ffour Pence of lawful Money of the United Kingdom of Great Britain and Ireland, Current in Great Britain, on the first day of October next after the Publication of this our Award. And that they, the said Thomas Hill,

Joseph Harrison, and John Griffiths, their Exors., etc., shall and do also Yearly, and every Year, during the term of four Years, to commence from the said first day of October next, well and truly Pay, or cause to be Paid, unto the said Samuel Homfray, his Exors., etc., the Sum of One Thousand and two Hundred Pounds of like lawful Money, by four equal Quarterly Payments, that is to say, on the first day of January, the first day of April, the first day of July, and the first day of October in each Year, the first of the said Quarterly Payments to begin and to be made on the first day of January next after the Publication of this our Award.

And for securing the due and Punctual Payment of the said several sums of money to the said Samuel Homfray, his exors., etc., in manner aforesaid, We do further Order and direct that the said Thomas Hill, Joseph Harrison, John Griffiths, their exors., etc., shall and do on or before the first day of May next, after the Publication of this, our Award, execute and deliver their joint and several Bonds or Writing obligatory to the said Samuel Homfray, his exors., etc., in the Penal Sum of ffourteen Thousand Pounds of lawful money of the United Kingdom of Great Britain and Ireland, current in Great Britain. Conditioned for the due and punctual Payment of the said Sum of Two Thousand Two hundred and fourteen Pounds, thirteen Shillings and ffour Pence, and also of the said Yearly Sum of One Thousand and two hundred Pounds to the said Samuel Homfray, his exors., etc., in manner aforesaid.

And We do declare that the said Sum of Two Thousand Two Hundred and ffourteen Pounds thirteen Shillings and ffour Pence, and the said Yearly Sum of One Thousand and Two Hundred Pounds, together with the said writing obligatory, to be executed and delivered as aforesaid, are meant and designed by us as and for full satisfaction to the said Samuel Homfray, his exors., etc., for any Damage the said Samuel Homfray may at any time have sustained by occasion of the non-performance of the said Agreement, or any matter or thing therein contained in lieu of any Right or benefit he has or had under the said Agreement, and as a full compensation to him, the said Samuel Homfray, for his delivering up the said Agreement to be cancelled, and Releasing the said Thomas Hill, Joseph Harrison, and John Griffiths, and each and every of them for the further Performance thereof.

"And We do further declare that the said Thomas Hill, Joseph Harrison, and John Griffiths are not to be liable to the Payment of the said several Sums of Money, or any part thereof, nor are they to be required to make and deliver such security for the Payment thereof, but upon and in consideration of his, the said Samuel Homfray's delivering up the said Agreement to be cancelled, and Releasing the said Thomas Hill, Joseph Harrison, and John Griffiths, as aforesaid, and as hereinafter mentioned, it being our intention that neither of the said Parties shall derive any benefit from this our Award, but as and when he or they shall have performed and fulfilled the same in all things therein directed to be done and suffered by him or them respectively.

"And further We do Order that the Costs and Charges of this Arbitration and of the making this our Award, shall be equally borne and paid by the said Parties, that is to say, one moiety thereof by the said Samuel Homfray, and the other moiety thereof by the said Thomas Hill, Joseph Harrison, and John Griffiths.

"And lastly we do Award that the said Thomas Hill, Joseph Harrison, and John Griffiths, and the said Samuel Homfray, shall and do on or before the said first day of May next respectively in due form of Law execute each to the other, and others of them, mutual and general Releases, sufficient for the releasing by each to the other and others of them, his and their Executors and Administrators, of all Actions, suits, cause and causes of Actions, Debts, Trespasses, Quarrels, Controversies, Costs, Damages, Claims and Demands whatsoever, from the beginning of the World to the day of the date of the Recited Bonds or Obligations aforesaid.

"In Witness whereof we, the said William Taitt, Edward Kendall, and Richard Hill the Younger, have hereunto set our Hands and Seals, this Twenty-seventh day of February, in the Year of Our Lord One Thousand Eight hundred and ffive.

"W. TAITT.
"EDW. KENDALL.
"RICHARD HILL, Junr.

"Sealed and Delivered in the Presence of us,
"Wm. Wood, Agent at Penydarren.
"Jno. Powell, Brecon."

---

The history of "this very unfortunate concern," as Mr. Samuel Hopkins[1] writing from Blaenavon on March 5, 1805, describes it, is not very clear at this period.

"Blaenavon, March 5th, 1805.

"Dear Sir,—By appointment, Mr. Hill and Myself met Mr. Latham and Mr. Harrison at Nant y Glo, but could not proceed with the Closeing of this very unfortunate concern without Mr. Knowls, from whom we received a letter that he could not possibly leave his ingagements at Brecon until he had closed the Coal Cos. account, considdering you as one of the principals, and also fully acquainted with the very unpleasant situation of Mr. Hill's feelings, while anything remains unsettled with such a Man as J. Harrison. I take the liberty of requesting the favor of you, if possible, to permit Mr. Knowls to meet the arbitrators at Nanty Glo, on Monday next, to state to them how far he has proceeded with the accounts, and whether he sees any material reason why they may not be brought to a final conclusion; as farther delays from being connected with a Man of such a Mind as Harrison's may be attended with more mortification to Mr. Hill's feelings than anything that is now past recovery; if you can permit Mr. Knowls to attend, and will have the goodness to recomend him to conclude the business before he leaves it, and favor me with a line by bearer how far we may depend upon him, that I may apprize the arbitrators and Mr. Hill, it will be esteemed a particular favor by

"Dear Sir, yours very Sincerely,
"SAML. HOPKINS.

"P.S.—If Mr. Knowls can be at liberty to leave Brecon on Sunday Morng., Mr. Hill would make a point of Meeting him here in the Evening; he might then sleep here, and go to Nanty Glo early on Monday Morning."

---

And considerable trouble seems to have arisen between Mr. Thomas Hill and his partners, Messrs. Harrison and Griffith, and in 1808, there appears to have been a trial at the Worcester Assizes contemplated to settle their differences.

"Blaenavon, Decr. 10th, 1808.

"Dear Sir,—Mr. Harrison having refused to pay his proportion, Mr. Robins is prepareing to bring the cause on at the next Assizes at Worcester, to prove the Sum paid as damages for the contract entered into by Mr. Harrison.

"The arbitration Bond, signed by Messrs. Harrison and Griffith, Mr. Hill will be much obliged by your sending me by Post, if in your possession, and also the agreement for enlardging the arbitration beyond the time first fix'd upon; if you have them not, be so kind as to inform who has them.

"Dear Sir, yours Sincerely,
"SAML. HOPKINS."

[1] This Mr. Hopkins was probably the son of Mr. Hopkins, one of Mr. Hill's Co-lessees, who died in March, 1793.

[Enclosed.] "Brecon, 13th Dec., 1808.

"Dear Sir,—We received your favor of the 10th, and after some search found the papers relating to the Nant y Glo Contract, and among them the Arbitration Bond, executed by Mr. Hill, Mr. Harrison and Griffith, of which we enclose a Copy, and trust it will ansr. every purpose in the present stage of the proceedgs., but we do not feel justified in parting with the Origl., at least without the express Authority of Mr. S. Homfray, who employed us in the bus's. If you sho'd. find it necessary, and will procure such authority, we will readily send the origl. Bond whenever it may be desired. There is no agreemt. for enlarging the Time, nor does there seem any to have been necessary, as the time originally given by the Bond was to the 18th of Apl., and the Award was made the 27th of Febry.

"I am still weak and confined to my own house, but gradually getting better.

"I am, for Mr. W. P. and self,

"Dear Sir, yours sincerely,

"JNO. POWELL.

"Samuel Hopkins, Esq., Blaenavon Iron Works, near Abergavenny."

---

And we now come to the turning-point in the life of the Nant y Glo Works. Their natural advantages were immense, and only required capital, combined with skilful and united management, to develop the property into a vast profitable concern.

These were found by Joseph Bailey, who, on his uncle Richard Crawshay's death in 1810, left the Cyfarthfa Iron Works, and well-laden with the gold which his uncle had left him, and accompanied by Mr. Matthew Wayne, an old and experienced Cyfarthfa agent, came across the mountains to Nant y Glo, where they arranged for the purchase between them (in certain proportions) of the Iron-works from Messrs. Thomas Hill and Samuel Hopkins, the then sole owners and partners.

What the sum given was, or what share Matthew Wayne bore, our papers do not tell us.

But we must go back a little.

It appears from the recitals in the deed of 25th June, 1821, relating to the Beaufort Iron Works, that Mr. Thomas Hill and Mr. Samuel Hopkins (the son) had been able to take a fresh lease on the 28th September, 1806, of all the minerals and royalties of Henry, Earl of Abergavenny, in the large tract of mountainous land in a number of parishes in the County of Monmouth, including the parish of Aberystwith—said to be 12,000 acres in extent—for sixty-three years, from June 24th, 1806.

And it also there appears that the Messrs. Hill and Company being enabled to sublease,

They then agreed, as from the 25th March, 1811, to demise, and did demise, subject to certain rents and covenants, to Joseph Bailey and Matthew Wayne for a term to end 22nd June, 1869, being fifty-eight years two months and twenty-eight days, the Iron-works called the Nant y Glo Works, with the mountainous land, etc., etc., which are described as follows :—

"And all that part of the said mountainous tract demised to the said Thomas Hill and Samuel Hopkins by the Earl of Abergavenny, together with all mines, etc., in, under, and upon the same, with power to work the same, and which are situate and lying on the Nant y Glo —— on north-west and north east sides of the said mountainous or hilly land, commencing at a place called Pont Lammarch, and running from thence in a direct line to a

Mere Stone placed on a certain Hill, called Mynidd Cwm Cellan, near to and on the north side of an old Tile Stone, called Gray Cluch, and from such Mere Stone in a direct line to a certain barn, formerly occupied by one William Anthony, and then occupied by———, and situate near to the said Cwm Kellan brook.

"And from thence along with the course of the said brook, on the south-west and north-west sides thereof, to its junction with a certain brook called Ebbw Vach, near to Aberystwith Church. And from thence following the course of the said river Ebbw Vach on the south-west and north-west sides to its junction with the Ebbw Fawr, and from thence following the course of the said river Ebbw Fawr to the extent of the said Earl of Abergavenny's estate. And the better to ascertain the boundary from Pont Lammarch to the said Mere Stone placed on Mynydd Cwm Kellan, and from thence to the barn mentioned to have been formerly occupied by Wm. Anthony, a Ditch has been already thrown up; all which hilly land was situate in the parish of Aberystwith, in the manor of Abergavenny, and Pelleine, in the Co. Monmouth."

During the early years of the tenancy, Joseph Bailey took the active personal direction of the Iron-works, assisted by his partner, Matthew Wayne; but whether his brother, Crawshay Bailey, was then at the Works in any capacity our papers do not state. The Works, however, doubtless prospered; and we find that about 1820 Mr. Matthew Wayne transferred all his interest, for certain considerations, in the Nant y Glo Works, with the leases, buildings, materials, etc., mentioned in the Deed of 1811, to Mr. Joseph Bailey to hold the property for the residue of the term.

And we also find that about the same time his brother, Crawshay Bailey, entered into partnership with Joseph Bailey in the Nant y Glo Works, and in the interests in the 1811 lease assigned by Mr. Matthew Wayne.

The two brothers then worked together with one will, and having ample capital, and experience gained by training in their Uncle's works at Cyfarthfa, and being men of no ordinary intelligence, vigour, and careful business habits, soon made the Nant y Glo one of the great Iron Works of the Kingdom, and of the world.

At a later period, in 1830, we find Joseph retired from personal direction of the works, and living at Glanusk Park, but still closely watching every part of the working of the machine. His place at the Works was now taken by his brother, Crawshay; and very soon after, or in 1833, it was arranged by the Nant y Glo Co. to purchase the Beaufort Iron Works, just over the County boundary, in Breconshire, from the firm of Kendall and Co.

To that purchase we shall refer later, when dealing with the Beaufort Works.

From this date on—1833—the two Works, Nant y Glo and Beaufort, were worked as one concern, the latter being mainly employed in supplying pig-iron from its blast-furnaces in addition to that of the Nant y Glo Furnaces, the whole of which was none too much for the large new rolling mills at Nant y Glo to convert into rails for the great Home and American markets.

---

I have been taken through the great Nant y Glo Works at night, when at the zenith of their power and fame, and I knew both of the brothers, when in full vigour of life: Crawshay ruling the Works at Nant y Glo, and Joseph dispensing at times a lavish hospitality at Glanusk. My father was a cotemporary and friend of both, often meeting the elder brother at the Brecon and Abergavenny Canal Meetings, and occasionally over an evening rubber at Glanusk Park.

Both were undoubtedly men of strong character—great men we call them. Of course, they had a bit of luck in finding the Black Band on the Beaufort hills, and probably in other ways, but their large fortunes were acquired mainly by their skill and industry, backed by proper capital to start with, and Nant y Glo and Beaufort Works proved gold mines in their hands.

---

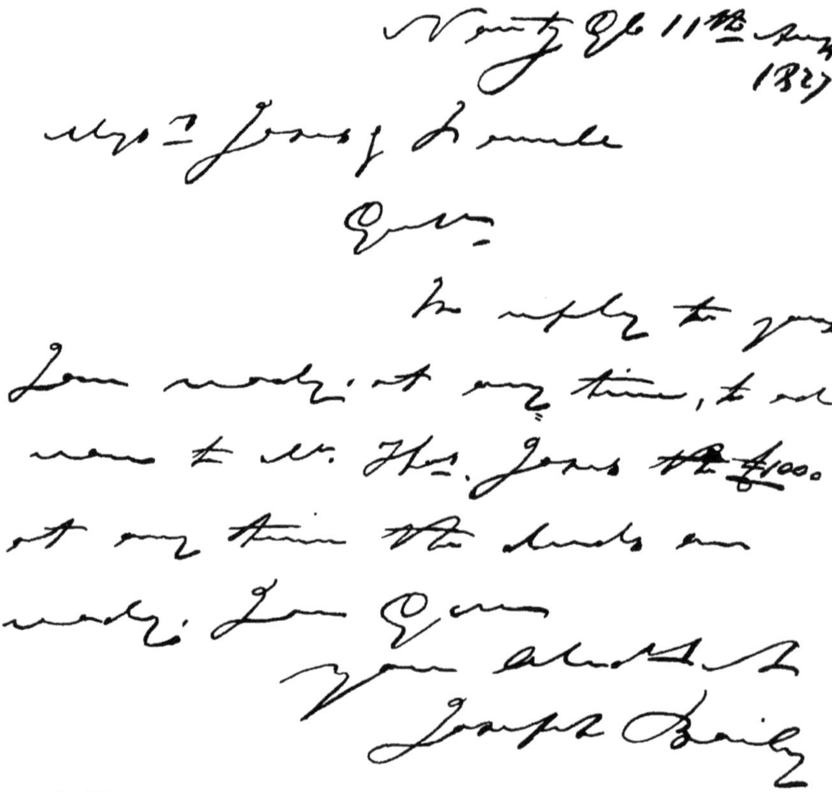

Page 175.

AUTOGRAPH LETTER OF JOSEPH BAILEY.

The following are letters of Joseph and Crawshay Bailey respectively :—

"Nant y Glo, 1st Novr., 1823.

"Dear Sirs—I have yours of yesterday. Mr. Hill and ourselves have determined to advance 2*s.* per ton at Abergavenny.

"I did not know that he was sending any quantity to Brecon. I have not the least doubt but he will do what we do in advancing at Brecon; Mr. Overton will also do the same. I am quite sure the County can well afford 2*s.* [illegible] them, they would pay the present price 3 years ago, and I am strongly of an opinion we ought to advance 2*s.*

"Truly Yours,
JOSEPH BAILEY.

"I do not think a meeting is necessary if you advance 2*s.* I have not the least doubt but Hill and ourselves will do the same.
"John Powell, Esq."

---

"Nant y Glo, 5th March, 1833.

"Dear Sirs—I shall be quite ready to take up Prosser's principal and interest, upon the regular notice being given as expressed in the Mortgage deed, which you are acquainted with.

"I am, Dear Sir, your Obedt.,
"C. BAILEY.

"Messrs. Jones and Powell, Sols., Brecon."

---

## NOTES ON NANT Y GLO.

The following Notice must have been given just previously to the stoppage of the Works in 1796 (see page 167):—

"TO RICHARD HARFORD & CO.

"You are to take notice that we have assessed your Two Furnaces and Mines at Nant y Glo, in the Parish of Aberystwith, to the valuation of £200, and also Richard Edmonds' Lands to the valuation of £10, and also Tir y Gwaun Lwud to the valuation of £10 in the Land Tax Assessment.

"If you think yourself aggrieved by being over-rated, you are to appeal at the 'Crown and Anchor,' in Pontypool, on the 29th day of this Inst.

"As Witness our hands this 5th day of June, 1795.

"JOHN LEWIS AND WILLIAM ROGERS, Assessors."

---

These great Works, like the Cyfarthfa, had a Band, and it will be seen that the Band, consisting of thirteen men and a boy, were employed for five days by Colonel Wood's Election Committee for Breconshire in 1831. It would be an illegal item of expenditure in these days. The signature at foot of the receipt is in Crawshay Bailey's own handwriting.

COLONEL WOOD'S COMMITTEE.

To the Nant y glo Band.

| | £ | s. | d. |
|---|---|---|---|
| May, 1831. | | | |
| To thirteen men, five days at 7s. p. day ... ... ... ... | 22 | 15 | 0 |
| To boy, five days at 5s. p. day ... ... ... ... ... ... | 1 | 5 | 0 |
| | £24 | 0 | 0 |

May 24.
By Cheque on Wilkins & Co. of Mr. Davies, £24 0s. 0d.

CRAWSHAY BAILEY.

## NANT Y GLO SHOP.

When the "Company's Shop" was first established at these Works we have no record, but it may be assumed that it existed during the whole of the ownership of J. and C. Bailey (if not of that preceding of Bailey and Wayne), or say from 1820 downwards.

My own recollection takes me well back to the time when the shop was carried on—from 1850 to 1860—and the well-known Mr. John Jayne, of Pantybailey, was the chief managing partner. I should be untrue to my self-imposed task of an historian, unless I were to mention here that serious faults were found from time to time by the workmen and their wives with the quality of the goods supplied at the Company's shop. The grievance appears to have been, not that of the payments being forced, and of the independence of the workmen and liberty to buy where they liked being sacrificed, but that inferior food and goods were supplied.

The complaints may have been unjustifiable, but that such complaints were constantly being made by the workpeople and their wives is undoubted. My informant, who lived on the spot and who was daily in contact with the workmen's wives, and was to some extent their confidant in little matters, has assured me that such was the true state of the case, and that the "truck," or Company's shop system, as carried on at these great Works, is still remembered, though scores of years have passed since, with a shudder of abhorrence.

---

### Extract from Coxe's "History of Monmouthshire," 1801.

We now give another extract from this valuable work, cap. 26, p. 215:

"Quitting this delightful vale (Ebwy Fach), we gradually advanced into a wild, dreary, and almost uninhabited district, among bleak hills and barren moors. From the top of the rise we looked down on the works of Nant y glo, which once gave activity and life to this solitary region. In our descent we crossed a small but rapid stream, derived from the contiguous hills of Brecknockshire, which, forcing its way through a deep channel worn in the rocks, falls into the Little Ebwy, and gives to the place the appellation of Nant y glo, or the 'Cold Brook.'

"We called upon Mr. Hertford, son of one of the proprietors, whom I had casually met at Pont y Pool, and who is settled with his family in this sequestered spot. After refreshing ourselves with a hearty meal at his hospitable board, which the keenness of the mountain air and a long ride from Pont y Pool made us doubly relish, he kindly accompanied us to the works, consisting of two furnaces, several forges, a steam engine, and the necessary buildings and machinery for smelting and forging the iron ore which abounds in the vicinity.

"They belong to Hill, Hertford & Co., and are held under a long lease from the owners of the Blaenavon Works; they were finished at a vast expense in 1795; after being worked a year were discontinued on account of a misunderstanding between the proprietors, and are hastening to decay. A long range of stone cottages, built against the side of a rock, was constructed for the workmen; each cottage consists of two stories, which form two tenements without communication; the entrance to the lower part is in front, and the doors of the upper tenement open to a ledge behind, which is cut in the rock, and runs the whole length of the range.

"The discontinuance of the Works impressed me with much regret, as they had already given a new life and spirit to these dreary regions, and would soon have fertilised the surrounding district. The residence, however, of Mr. Hertford, is attended with considerable advantage: the adjacent grounds have been cleared and cultivated, and an extensive tract of moor, which formerly produced only heath and fern, has been converted into pasture, and yields excellent hay."

---

It will be interesting to compare this description with that which I have previously given, and with the old Plan of 1798.

We agree, as will be seen, in our particulars, except that Archdeacon Coxe is wrong as to the name of one of the partners. It was Harford, not Hertford.

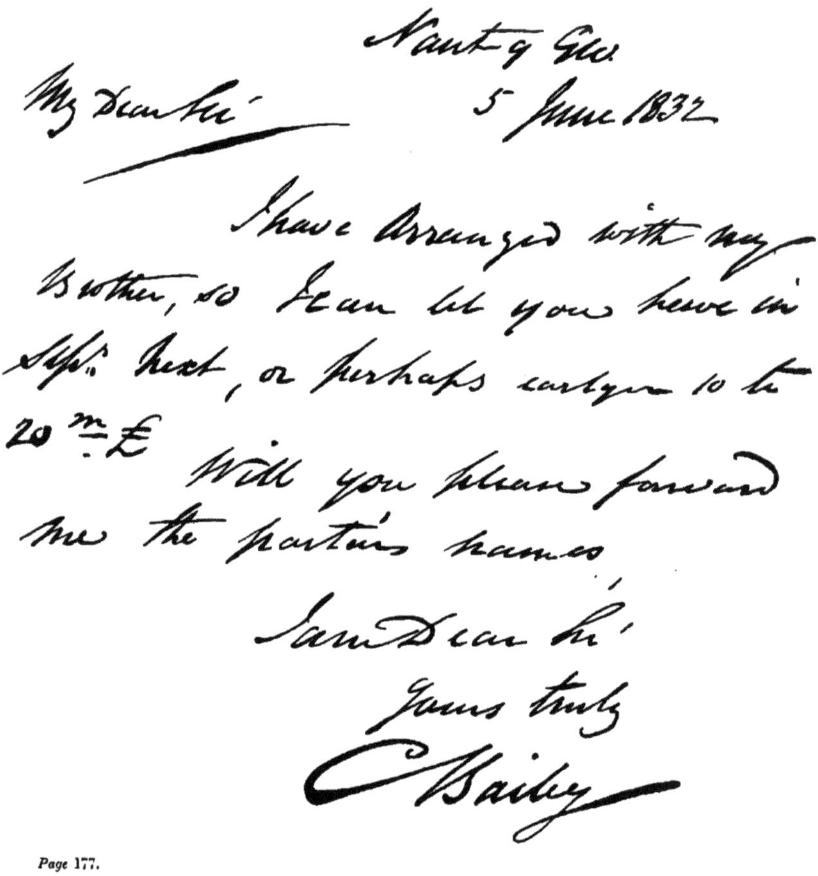
Nant-y-Glo
My Dear Sir 5 June 1832

I have arranged with my Brother, so I can let you have in Sept. next, or perhaps earlier 10 to 20 m/£

Will you please forward me the parties names,

I am Dear Sir

Yours truly

C Bailey

Page 177.

AUTOGRAPH LETTER OF CRAWSHAY BAILEY.

I also think that there is a confusion in the account between the Clydach brook, and the Nant y glo, or Ebwy fach brook. The Clydach tallies more with the description "of the small but rapid stream we crossed on our descent;" but the Clydach, we know, does not fall into the Ebwy Fach.—Ed.]

---

The following are the Returns of Iron sent for shipment at Newport by the Monmouthshire Canal from Nanty Glo Iron Works :—

[Scrivenor, *Iron Trade*, pp. 126, 294.]

| | | Tons | | | Tons. |
|---|---|---|---|---|---|
| 1802 | ... ... | Nil. | 1822 | J. and C. Bailey | 10,906 |
| 1803 | ... ... | " | 1823 | ... ... | 12,723 |
| 1804 | ... ... | " | 1824 | ... ... | 15,134 |
| 1805 | ... ... | " | 1825 | ... ... | 16,536 |
| 1806 | ... ... | " | 1826 | ... ... | 11,512 |
| 1807 | ... ... | " | 1827 | ... ... | 18,059 |
| 1808 | ... ... | " | 1828 | ... ... | 19,032 |
| 1809 | ... ... | " | 1829 | ... ... | 17,433 |
| 1810 | ... ... | " | 1830 | ... ... | 17,115 |
| 1811 | J. Bailey and M. Wayne | .77 | 1831 | ... ... | 17,866 |
| 1812 | ... ... | 1,168 | 1832 | ... ... | 21,333 |
| 1813 | ... ... | 1,855 | 1833 | ... ... | 21,007 |
| 1814 | ... ... | 2,292 | 1834 | ... ... | 22,594 |
| 1815 | ... ... | 4,684 | 1835 | ... ... | 24,597 |
| 1816 | ... ... | 6,160 | 1836 | ... ... | 25,384 |
| 1817 | ... ... | 7,242 | 1837 | ... ... | 23,981 |
| 1818 | ... ... | 7,235 | 1838 | ... ... | 25,263 |
| 1819 | ... ... | 7,934 | 1839 | ... ... | 24,945 |
| 1820 | J. and C. Bailey ... | 8,826 | 1840 | ... ... | 26,662 |
| 1821 | Do. ... | 10,460 | | | |

---

(End of the Nant y Glo Iron Works.)

# XXIV.

# The Beaufort Iron Works.

These Iron Works were of comparatively old date, being established by the Kendall family in 1779 under a lease from the Duke of Beaufort. They were situate on the Ebbw Fawr stream, higher up than the Ebbw Vale Iron Works, and just within the boundary line of the County of Brecon.

The great man who first gave an important development to these Works was Edward Kendall, Senior, Chairman of the Monmouthshire Canal, Justice of the Peace and High Sheriff of Breconshire, and subsequently owner of Dany Park, on the Usk, at Crickhowell. The Kendall family all had money, but Edward was a specially able man; and not only to his own affairs as an ironmaster, but to County (Breconshire) matters he gave close attention, probably more so than any of the other great ironmasters ever did in Breconshire—and naturally, because he resided in the County, and his Works were in the County. And in that he never became a Member of Parliament, which would have taken him to perform duties elsewhere.

We do not, however, see his name among the promoters of the Brecon and Abergavenny Canal; but we find him very active as the Chairman of the Monmouthshire Canal, and strongly supporting the making of it to Crumlin, and of the tramway up to his works at Beaufort, because his iron would go that way to the sea at Newport; and he had secured an important freehold wharf at Crumlin, at the Canal Head, for stocking his iron.

I have several original documents signed by him in his own handwriting as Chairman of the Monmouthshire Canal, in 1792-3, relating to the making of the Brecon Canal, and the supply of water to it, which will be important some day when they see the light, possibly in the High Court of Justice. (*Hist. Mem. of Breconshire*, vol. I., p. 191, and Note *infra*, page 182.)

"Nothing like Iron," he thought, and he fenced the river front land of Dan y Park, soon after the purchase of that estate from Mrs. Skrine in 1804, with a massive Park Deer Fence, which has stood unharmed to this day.

This Mr. Kendall—*the* Edward Kendall—died suddenly almost, in March, 1807, having recently married a widow lady, Mrs. Bevan, of Crickhowell, one of whose sons, William Hibbs Bevan, Mr. Kendall wished to be brought up to the iron business, and to become a Partner, when of age.

Mr. Kendall left only one son, also called Edward, who cared very little about the Iron Works, and was possessed of ample fortune otherwise. During his minority, Mr. Joseph Latham, an old and trusted servant of his father, acted as Manager, if not managing-partner of the works.

But we must return to the point we started at:—

By Deed of this date (Oct. 16th, 1779), between Henry, Duke of Beaufort, of the one part,

And

Jonathan Kendall, of Drayton, Co. of Salop, gentleman;

Henry Kendall, of Alverstone, Co. Lancaster, gentleman;

Edward Kendall, of Worlingham, Co. of Chester, gentleman; and

Jonathan Kendall, of Seaforge, Co. Glo'ster, gentleman, of the other part.

All the waste lands belonging to the said Duke in the Parishes of Llangattock and Llanelly, in the Co. of Brecon (certain lands being excepted during the lease of Joseph Jeffreys at Blaen Ebbw and Gwybedog), were demised to the said Jonathan Kendall and others, with liberty to erect a furnace or furnaces on any part of the Duke's waste lands as they may think proper, and to make ponds and railroads.

Also all waters and streams,

And power to divert and turn the said streams *so far as it was in the Duke's power to grant the same.*

Also all coal and iron ore in, under, and upon the waste lands in the said Parishes, and with liberty to carry away the same, and also under the Freehold land of the said Duke, making compensation to the tenants for damage done.

Also all lime and clay as should be necessary for building furnaces or making iron, called Hearth stone.

To hold the same land, etc. (except as before excepted), for the term of 99 years from 29th Sept. last past,

Paying therefore after the rate of £130 per annum for the first 1½ years, and thereafter the sum of £406 a year, and

Paying the further sum of 2*s*. for every dozen of iron ore and stone used by them in any one year, a quantity of 2,320 doz. to be allowed for the said reserved rent of £406, such dozen to contain 34 cwt. and no more, and each cwt. to contain 6 score, or 120 lbs. to the cwt.

And also paying to the Duke 300 horse loads of coal at the pit's mouth.

Also a heriot of £5 5*s*. on the death of any of the partners, and the like sum of £5 5*s*. on any alienation.

Also yielding and reserving to the Duke's Mill at Crickhowell all corn, malt, and oats to be brought there for grinding and shealing. Also that no mill shall be erected by the said lessees for grinding corn within 2 miles of their premises.

Covenants to pay rent, to keep proper weigh-books, not to permit waste, and to keep and deliver up the Furnaces in good repair at the end of the term.

There is a special covenant on the part of the lessees that they would not advance the price of coal above 3*d*. per bag or horse load at the pit's mouth without the consent of the said Duke.

On February 15th, 1800, the Messrs. Kendall (as we have seen in the case of the Messrs. Hill at Blaenafon), finding the tract of mineral land too large for their own use, agreed with Edward Frere, ironmaster, and Thomas Cooke, of Llanelly, co-partners, to form a partnership for erecting iron-works in the parish of Llanelly, having a certain tract of waste land assigned, and the same denoted by a line drawn along the middle of the Rhassa near Edmund Andrews' house, and continued from the top thereof in a south-west direction to the confines of the County of Monmouth.

To hold for the residue of the term, paying £500 for the first year and £780 a year rent to Messrs. Kendall and Co., subject to a deduction by Messrs. Kendall and Co. of £15 yearly, until the Brecon and Abergavenny Canal should be made and opened to Pontymoile.

And a royalty of 9*d*. per ton for every ton of coal not used by them, and sent away (not to include Country coal) to be paid to Messrs. Kendall and Co.

The Messrs. Kendall and Co. were to be "nominal partners" only, the Messrs. Cooke and Frere being responsible for the finding of capital and the erecting of furnaces, and the management.

This was soon found an unsatisfactory arrangement, and was not concurred in by the Duke of Beaufort; and by a fresh deed the partnership was dissolved, and instead a sub-lease was granted, independently of any partnership, to Messrs. Frere and Cooke, but on the same terms as to the payment of rents to the Messrs. Kendall and Co. by Messrs. Frere and Cooke as were specified in the deed which formed the now dissolved partnership.

Thus was formed the Clydach Iron-works Company, on or about the year 1800.

Further light is thrown on the history of the partnership by the following extract from a Case submitted to Counsel in 1815:—

"7th Novr., 1797.—By an Indenture of this date made between the said EDWARD KENDALL, of the 1st part, the said JONATHAN KENDALL, of the 2nd part, and JOSEPH LATHAM, Ironmaster, of the 3rd part.

"After stating that the said EDWARD and JONATHAN KENDALL were possessed of certain Iron-works called the Beaufort Iron-works, and of a part share of Clydach Furnace, as well as other properties (all of which they enjoyed under the Duke's lease), the said parties

"Agreed to become Partners in such properties for the term of 14 years, commencing 5th of April, 1795,

"The Capital to be £16,000, contributed as under:—

| | | | |
|---|---|---|---|
| E. Kendall, | 17, 32 parts, | amounting to | £8,500. |
| J. Kendall, | 13, do. | " | £6,500. |
| J. Latham, | 2, do. | " | £1,000. |
| | | | £16,000. |

"At the time of making his Will, Edward Kendall was a Widower, with only one child, the Son to whom he gave his property.

"The Partnership between Messrs. Jonathan and Edwd. Kendall and Mr. Latham was extended upon the same terms for 7 years further, so as to continue for 21 years instead of 14.

"In 1801, Mr. Kendall married a Mrs. Elizabeth Bevan (a Widow Lady), who had two children by her former husband, namely, George and William.

"Mr. Kendall died very suddenly on the 7th of March, 1807, leaving his wife and his son Edward, as well as his stepsons before named, surviving him. Mr. Kendall left large property, and his son was not brought up to the iron trade; but his stepson William Hibbs Bevan was placed at the Beaufort Works, under the Instruction of Mr. Latham, the managing Partner. At the age of 24, Mr. W. H. Bevan was admitted into a share of the Profits of the Beaufort Works.

"The Partnership of the Beaufort Company was to cease on the 25th March, 1816, when Mr. Latham would wholly retire."

In 1801, when the Brecon Canal was about to be opened to Brecon, an application was made by certain moneyed and enterprising gentlemen at Brecon, named Jeffrey Wilkins, banker, of Brecon; John Lloyd, of Brecon, gent.; John Powell, solicitor, and John Peirce, accountant, who had formed a partnership, called the Brecon Boat Co., for the purpose of supplying the town and county of Brecon with coal by means of the canal, applied to Messrs. Kendall and Co. to lease to them a colliery on their mineral taking for such purpose, with the consent of their lessor, the Duke of Beaufort. This application was approved of by the Duke of Beaufort and his lessees.

On December 28th, 1801, the Duke of Beaufort granted to Messrs. Kendall and Co. all that messuage called Llwyn y Pwll Farm, and all seams and veins of coal under the same, and in any waste lands adjoining, which are described as follows:—

"Bounded on the North by the River Clydach, and on the South by the Co. of Monmouth, on the East by a line drawn across the Rhassa, near Edmund Andrews' House and continued along the Top of the said Rhassa in a South-West direction to the confines of the Co. of Monmouth, on the West by the fence between Llwyn y Pwll Farm and Gwayn yr Helycon (said to be described on a map).

"To hold for 77 years from the 25th March, paying £12 a year rent, and, in addition, 4d. royalty for every ton of Coal raised, provided that no sub-leases should be granted, except to the persons hereinbefore named, as forming the Brecon Boat Co."

"December 29th, 1801.—On this, the following day, the Messrs. Kendall and Co. granted a lease of all the veins of Coal, except the three-quarter Coal under the Llwyn y Pwll Farm, and other waste lands, particularly described in the Deed of December 28th, 1801, to the Brecon Boat Co. for 70 years from the 25th March last, the said Brecon Boat Co. covenanting to pay the 4d. royalty per ton reserved to the Duke of Beaufort, and an additional royalty of 8d. per ton to the Messrs. Kendall for every ton of Coal raised. [Under this lease, the Brecon Boat Co. carried on a prosperous trade along the Canal and at Brecon (adding to it the lime trade) down to the time of the general introduction of railways in Breconshire in 1860].

When Mr. Edward Kendall died, in 1807, the original taking from the Duke of Beaufort had been thus divided.

Messrs. Kendall and Co. held the Beaufort Iron Works and the mineral district west of the Rhassa.

The Brecon Boat Co. held the Llwyn y Pwll (Farm) coals, subject to royalties.

Messrs. Frere and Cooke, subject to the payment of rents and colliery royalties, held the Clydach Iron Works and minerals east of the Rhassa.

In 1816, when Mr. Edward Kendall, the younger, came of age (24 years), and began to take some slight interest in the Works, and Mr. Joseph Latham having retired, the important question was raised by Mr. Kendall on the part of the Firm as to reducing the cost of conveyance of the make of iron to Newport. Hitherto, the iron had always been taken down the tramway along the Ebbw Valley to the Crumlin Branch of the Monmouthshire Canal; and it will be remembered that Edward Kendall, the father, was Chairman of the Monmouthshire Canal, and had a special wharf at Crumlin.

However, it was now thought that the Tolls charged by that Route were too high, and it was suggested that the Iron could be taken more cheaply *viâ* the Llanelly Tramroad and the Brecon Canal, to the Junction at Pontymoile, and thence by the Monmouthshire Canal to Newport, if the Monmouthshire Co. could be compelled, in accordance with the special provision in the Brecon Canal Act, to lower their rates for carriage of Iron to the same level that the Brecon Canal had done. The Monmouthshire Co. denied their obligation and refused to reduce their tolls, and a great law-suit ensued as to whether they were obliged to or not; and at last they were compelled to concede the point. For a short time, while the dispute lasted, the Beaufort Iron was carried over Beaufort Hill, on horseback, to the terminus of the Llanelly Tramroad at Llwynypwll, and thence by the way of Clydach and Llanfoist to Newport. Years later, the Messrs. J. and C. Bailey improved upon this, and made a new line of Tramway from Beaufort and Nantyglo right to Llanfoist, and used it very largely, until that again was superseded by the opening of the Western Valleys Line to Nantyglo. In 1820, there was a further leasing of Coal veins to the Brecon Boat Co. by the Beaufort Iron Works Co. See letters *infra*.

Mr. Joseph Latham proved an able manager, but he retired in 1816, soon after young Mr. Kendall came of age, and there was a difficulty about young Mr. Bevan, as partner, taking a share of the Clydach rent; and it will be seen that Mr. William Henry West, of the Blaenafon Iron Works, had joined the Beaufort Company, and also Mr. William West Jones, of Crickhowell.

It may be said that the Kendall family had taken for some years very little interest in the business, and when, in 1833, a purchase was proposed by their neighbours, Joseph and Crawshay Bailey, it was readily received. Though there some difficulties as to title, the Baileys were given possession of the Works on the 25th March, 1833, the price paid being £45,000.

The Agreement is dated 17th January, 1833, and made between

EDWARD KENDALL, of Clifton, Gloucester;

WILLIAM HENRY WEST, of Beaufort Iron-works;

WILLIAM WEST JONES, of Crickhowell, Esq.;

WILLIAM HIBBS BEVAN, of Crickhowell, Esq.; and

JOSEPH BAILEY and CRAWSHAY BAILEY, both of Nantyglo Iron-works. Signed by all the parties.

And as regards the Memorandum endorsed on the Agreement, that is signed as follows:—

CRAWSHAY BAILEY, for and on behalf of myself and the above-named JOSEPH BAILEY.

This indorsement is in Mr. Crawshay Bailey's own handwriting.

---

## NOTES ON THE MONMOUTHSHIRE AND BRECON CANAL CASE, AS TO SUPPLY OF WATER TO THE HIGH-LEVEL LENGTH OF CANAL, 1792.

It will be sufficient here to state briefly the position.

The Monmouthshire Canal was the first to be made, and the committee of that undertaking were very anxious that the Brecon Canal, which was projected a year or two after, should be planned to form a junction with their Canal on the High Level at Pontymoile. To this the promoters of the Brecon Canal objected, preferring their own proposed line of Canal, which was to communicate with the tideway of the River Usk at Newbridge. And they further advanced the objection that the High Level line was more expensive to construct, and very difficult to maintain a supply of water for navigation, when constructed.

To overcome these objections the Monmouthshire Company undertook, by formal stamped agreement, signed by their chairman, Mr. Edward Kendall, to contribute £3,000 towards the extra cost of effecting the junction at the High Level; and further to supply in a full and ample manner, sufficient water for the navigation of the said High Level length of the Brecon Canal from their own sources of supply, independent of the Brecon Canal.

These formal Agreements are extant to-day, and valid, and it will be found, as a matter of fact, that what was called the High Level length of the Brecon Canal from Llangynider to Pontymoile Junction was so planned and carried out by their Engineer as to be upon a dead level from end to end, and capable of being supplied with water from the Monmouthshire or Pontymoile end to its full top water level.

These Agreements have only once to be brought forward and explained to upset completely and for ever the claim, which the Monmouthshire Canal Company, now the Great Western Railway Company, are said to make to draw a large supply of water from the Brecon Canal, and even from the Usk, at Brecon. Such a claim, in the light of facts, is quite unfounded. The liability to supply sufficient water for the navigation of the High Level length rests solely to-day on the Monmouthshire Canal Company and their sucessors—the Great Western Railway Company. The original Agreements, or certified copies, to the above effect are among the Maybery Papers in my possession.

---

## THE BEAUFORT BARLEY MEAL CASE—1800.

The following interesting case may be aptly given here. It shows that times were very troublous just then for ironmasters.

This was an Indictment at the Spring Assizes of the Great Sessions for Breconshire in 1800, against William Phillips and three other men, and one woman, for having riotously and routously assembled to the number, with others, of one hundred persons or so, on the highway in the Parish of Llangattock, on the 22nd March, 1800, and did seize and lead away five horses laden with Barley Meal and Bran, and also three mules laden with Barley Meal and Bran, to the Beaufort Works, and keep them one hour, to the great damage of the owner and prosecutor, Evan Evans, and against the Peace.

It appeared from the evidence given that Evan Evans had been employed by the Dowlais Company to supply the workmen with Barley Meal, and had sent his son-in law to Abergavenny to buy forty bushels of Barley, with orders to take the corn to be ground at the Moor Park Mills. One Thomas Morgan of Noyadd Llangattock undertook to supply him with horses and mules for the carriage from the Mills to Dowlais, and the journey was commenced on the 22nd March, and when they reached Cwmgwybedog they met with a number of people who seemed to have been waiting for them; two hundred men, women, and children then ran down a Hill to meet them, and shut a gate on the road to stop them. They said the Barley meal should not be taken out of the country, and some were for taking it before the Mayor at Crickhowell, and others for taking it to Beaufort Works. Some of the men caught hold of the horses' heads. They were told that small quantities would be sold, if they were in want of it, at market price. Mary Morgan said that before the meal should go to Merthyr, she would rip the sacks open, and drive the horses into the Furnace.

This case created great excitement in all the "Hill" district, and was the subject of much anxious thought in the counting-houses of Dowlais and Cyfarthfa, and to the great Breconshire Ironmaster, Mr. Kendall. The times then no doubt were serious; indeed, they must have been so to induce the workmen of Beaufort, with their wives and children, to waylay the carriers of Barley Meal on the highway, and for a short time to impound it. And it will be further seen that it was only barley meal, not wheaten flour, and that it was destined for the Company's shop of the Dowlais Company. We may, I think, learn a a lesson from this to-day, when it is sought to place a tax, however small, on the staple food of the people.

---

The following letters of Mr. Edward Kendall, the father, written in 1800, are of interest. It will be seen that an important Bill was then passing through Parliament touching injury to property, and that the Ironmasters were closely watching the proceedings of the Committee, the recent Barley Meal prosecution at Beaufort giving the Bill additional importance:—

"London, June 10th, 1800.

"Dear Sir,—I thank you for yours of the 4th, and am glad to hear you got safe down; but I dare say you will not easily be prevailed upon again to go into Longfellow's Coach. Yesterday our business came on as proposed; Mr. Estcourt and myself, having previously in the morning waited on Mr. Bragg, and spent near an Hour with him, in altering the Bill, to meet the objections made by Mr. Burdon, etc., etc., the Principal of w'ch were fixing a Time for the commencement of the Act, a Proviso, not to make it Felony Cuting Coal where there is a dispute about ownership, or to Trespass upon boundaries working under Ground, or Cuting Coal, within the Inclosures; adding some words respecting breach of Agreements (proposed by Mr. Harris), in the Stealing Clause, adding Wood, Iron, Ropes and Leather, and the words 'not exceeding the value above mentioned' at the end of the 9th line in that Clause.

"In the form of Conviction after the words 'following the words of the Act' are added whether the same is the first or what other offence. And in the last clause, after the word 'Act' in the fourth Line, save and except any order of Commitment. Lord Worcester took the chair. Mr. Bragg entered into a very full explanation of the objects of the Bill; and was I dare say half an hour upon his legs, Jollif siting opposite to him and following him through the whole of the amendments: not an objection was made; but the Bill is re-committed, and will be considered on Thursday, after being reprinted; and as soon as we have pass'd the Commons I will send you a Copy. I trust we have now only forms to go through in the Commons, and I hope we shall, by Lord Eldon's assistance, and the Duke's Friends, get through the Lords: but I can assure you I am almost tired of the Jobb.

"The Wet Docks Bill will pass the Lords to-day, and the Bill for rebuilding the Albion Mills, and establishing a Baking Company, will be bro't into the Commons. I observe what Davies says, and will talk to you about it when I return.

"I remain, Yours very sincerely,

"EDWD. KENDALL.

"John Powell, Esq., Brecon.

"P.S.—I would have wrote you last night, but the Post Bell rung before our business was over."

---

"London, June 13th, 1800.

"Dear Sir,—I am glad to inform you our Bill was reported Yesterday, order'd to be Engross'd and Read a Third Time To-day. If I can get a Frank I will send you a Copy by this Night's Post.

"It will, if the House of Lords are sitting, be read a first Time To-day, a second Time on Monday, and probably be Committed for Wednesday. I shall go to Lord Moira To-morrow, and Deakin will see Lord Fitzwilliam, so that after Lord Eldon has seen the Bill, I hope we shall get through, and I get home again. You will see there is no material alteration since I wrote you. I saw Bodle Yesterday, who would inform you what has been done in Bills' business.

"I remain in haste, Dear Sir, Yours very sincerely,

"EDWD. KENDALL.

"John Powell, Esq., Brecon."

---

The following letter relates to the purchase by Mr. Edward Kendall, the father (after effected), of the Danypark estate from Mrs. Letitia Harcourt Skrine—the last of the direct line of the Breconshire branch of the Harcourts—in 1804-5. Mrs. Skrine was very reluctant to sell the old property, where her great-grandfather (Godfrey Harcourt), her grandfather and her father, had all lived. But she gave way at last.

"Llangattock, May 28th, 1804.

"Dear Sir,—I recd. your Letter with Mrs. Skrine's proposal for Dan y Park; to put an end one way or other to the treaty, I have wrote to her to say I will not give one Shilling more for the Estate; but if she prefers selling the Estate for £14,720, I will pay Interest for £7,220 till Lady-day next: this you will see, in effect, is the same to me, but falls in with her Idea of receiving Interest. I have requested an early reply.

"I thought this the shortest way of bringing the treaty to an end rather than troubling you with it.

"I remain, Dear Sir, Your obedt. Servant,

"John Powell, Esq., Brecon. "EDWD. KENDALL."

---

Mr. Edward Kendall, the son, was a strong politician, and in the great County Election of 1818 (Breconshire), espoused the cause of Col. Wood, the Sitting Member, as against the representative of the Morgan family of Tredegar. The date of the Election was not until 1818, but an active and exhaustive canvass of the County commenced in 1816, and we give one of his letters to Col. Wood's agents, dated from Danypark, Jany. 24th, 1816:—

"Dan-y-Parc, Wednesday, Jany. 24th, 1816.

"My dear Jones,—I am glad to find you did so much good at the Hundred meeting you speak of. Go on and prosper is my most earnest prayer.

"Besides my wish for the County to assert its independence, my personal regard for the man is so great that if he was my own Brother I could not be more anxious for his success. Pray tell Parry Wilkins if he has any chance or carrying any votes about here, I beg he will make my House his Inn, and I will accompany him. I am sorry to see you complain of a deficiency of activity of Friends—pray stir them into action and rouse the true spirit of British Independence in their Breasts—Do not, tell them, let us be the Dupes of old Houses—all Rottenness and decay—ever since I saw you I have been as active as I could be where I thought I had any influence. On Monday I called on Gott, Prosser, Nant-y-ffin, Herbert, Gilvach, John Saunders, a tenant of mine, John Prosser, Vro, and John Jones of Dan Darren; the former is our Friend, and regrets his indisposition prevented his being at the meeting; the second seems to be with us, as does the third; the fourth with me decidedly, as is the fifth; the sixth I am in hopes will be with us. I yesterday called on old Harris, who says he must go with Mr. Gwynne, of Buckland. John Lewis, I hope, will be with me when once he becomes my tenant; at present he is with Davies, Court-y-gollen. Two labourers of mine are with me, and a promise from another yesterday; so much for my success, besides Burfield, of Crickhowell, who would not like to displease me, at least so he says.

"We must have Wood down without delay. One man told me he will not give his vote to Colonel Wood untill he has seen him. When he has, he cannot, I am sure, refuse him. Last night I sent up to Beaufort, and I shall hear to-day. Depend upon it, I will use my utmost endeavours in Wood's favor.

"I have just heard from Beaufort, and our agent, to whom I wrote about Lewis Harry, says he knows him well; and if has any land in Breconshire I think you may rely on having his vote, but I believe that all his freehold is in Monmouthshire. We want more papers, etc., etc., etc., for they have only told their own story, and I think ours ought to be heard as well. Frere ought to be ascertained which side he will go, as some others look to him for their movements. Evans, of Llanelly, ought to be written to likewise; a great deal might be done by the Boat Company using their influence, so pray stir them up. Let me hear the result of your going to Maeslough. I should have sent this by William Jones, but have only just returned with Gabell from the midst of the enemies' quarters.

"Ever, my dear Jones, Yours sincerely,

"John Jones, Solicitor, Brecon. "(Sd.) Edward Kendall."

---

The following letters relate to the taking of the fresh coal vein in 1820 by the Brecon Boat Co, from the Beaufort Iron-works Co.:—

"Messrs. Pierce, Lloyd, and Powell,

"Gent.,—Having walked over the Coal ground with your Agent, Mr. Elwood, we have now to state our wishes respecting the Leasing it out to you. The extent which we think we can afford to part with will be about fifty acres on this side the Great fault in which our Colly. stands, together with all the Coal ground on the other, or Eastern, side of the said fault, and extending to the Clydach dingle. The ground on this side to be marked out with reference to our mutual convenience.

"The quantity to be worked, say one half that now worked by you, or 6,000 Tons yearly, in default of which we are to have the power of entering on the ground in question, paying you the amount of the expense incurred in opening to the Coal, with an allowance of [blank] per Cent. per Annum on such expense.

"We propose to give up to your use our present Colliery, with its roads, tramplates, etc., you leaving the same in repair, and the Tram-plates in equal weight.

"In case the demand for Coal does not enable you to work a greater quantity than that now afforded by your present Colly., that quantity to be worked as usual from that Colly.

"The Royalty we ask, including Colliery, road, Tramplates, etc., together with that due to the Duke of Beaufort is 1*s.* 3*d*, p. Ton, to be paid half-yearly, as the present Royalty is done.

"You to commence opening to the Coal within six months from the date of the Agreement.

"Beaufort, June 9th, 1820. We rem., Gent., etc.,

"(Sd.) Kendalls and Bevan."

---

"Messrs. Pierce, Lloyd, and Powell.

"Gent.,—We have recd. yr. favr. of the 18th Inst., the terms on which you therein propose to rent our Coal-ground we understand to be these:

"That for the first three years you will undertake to raise 4,000 Tons of Coal yearly from the proposed Colliery, in addition to the average of 12,000 Tons now raised from your present one. In default of your doing this, we are to have the option either of re-entering on the premises on paying a certain proportion of the expense incurred in opening to the Coal, or of accepting such an annual payment, not to exceed £50, as will make up the defcy. of the galeage to the amount to which 4,000 Tons would come at 1*s.* 3*d.* per Ton, or £250 p. annum; and further, that for the remainder of the term you agree to raise at least 6,000 Tons annually at 1*s.* 3*d.* p. Ton galeage, with a similar option of re-entry or payment on our parts.

"The spirit of these proposed terms appears to us to be fair and equable, and we have only to propose a modification of one part and a more detailed explanation of others.

"We propose, then, that you shall engage to open to the Coal within the first year, and shall raise within the first three years a quantity certain, in addition to the average of 12,000 Tons, as one year may make up for the deficiencies of another (should any such take place) we would say 10,000 Tons in the first three years; afterwards, 6,000 Tons p. annum, with the option on our parts as above stated. We hereby place the quantity of the first three years—2,000 Tons— under what you propose.

"In case of re-entry on the premises, we wish to name a sum for the outlay on the Level, above which we are not to be called upon to pay. Perhaps this may be fairly stated at £400, and as in that case we should be entitled to certain allowances thereout for the decreased value of the roads, plates, etc., we should think these should be regulated by the quantity of Coal carried along them.

"We think 1*d.* p. Ton for this allowance might suit the views of both parties, supposing the above sum to be fixed on. Should you approve these proposals we shall be happy to hear from you, and will meet your Agent to mark out the ground, which shall be done with due attention to your wishes and convenience. Mr. Powell will be aware that the consent of the Duke of Beaufort will be necessary to carry the plan into effect.

"We remn., Gent., etc.,

"Beaufort, Sep. 27th, 1820. "(Sd.) Kendalls and Bevan."

---

## THE WATER SUPPLY OF THE BEAUFORT WORKS.

This Company had always largely used the water supply coming down from the head of the Clydach brook in scouring the iron ore, when worked in "patches" on the open mountain land, the rapid fall of the stream favouring this rough-and-ready process of freeing the ore from the soil. [Whether this was a wasteful process as regard the ore I do not know, but having regard to the destruction of the natural soil of the land, it certainly would never have been permitted, except on open common land of very trifling value, and even there it seems to me to have been a bad custom.]

There was also what was known as the "Balance Pit" of early date, when water was largely used in raising the coal on the balance plan from shallow pits to the surface. This, again, the sharp fall of the ground favoured.

But when the Beaufort Works had become, in 1833, one with Nantyglo, and were worked together as a joint concern; arrangements were then made for dealing on a larger scale with the water of the Clydach, both at the Blaenclydach pond, and away up the mountain to the very source of that stream. And though Nanty Glo Works were in a different county, and under a different Manorial Lord from the Beaufort Works, yet the latter were now called upon to give a supply from their sources by a special feeder for Nanty Glo. It took some time to understand the intricacies of the arrangements, and it was only a long training in river lore that would enable anyone to do so, and to cause the defeat of the deceptive proposals of the Ebbw Vale Urban Council, in the Committee Room of the House of Lords, and after these had passed muster and been accepted by the Committee of the House of Commons. It was only what was right and due to the Clydach stream and the Usk to have their waters protected and saved; but, nevertheless, it was a great victory, and one that will be long remembered in the Committee Rooms of Parliament. Even a model—inaccurate in its details, I fear—had been prepared at considerable expense, and brought into the Committee Room, the more certain to enable the promoters to carry their Bill!

These head-waters (Blaen) of the Clydach brook have other features deserving of notice, which have received such recently in the Report of the Geological Survey on that district. [*Geo. Sur.*, Pt. II, "Abergavenny," p. 43, 1900.]

Our readers will remember how the Cynon stream at Penderin, instead of making its way naturally to the west to the Neath valley, turns sharply to the east, and flows down to join the Taff at Abercynon. Probably a fault in the strata of the district was the cause of this.

And the same feature occurs here. The Clydach brook would be expected to join and form part of the Ebwy Fach river; but it does not, and instead it turns sharply to the east, and flows down the ravine, to which it gives the name (the Clydach), to join the Usk at Llangrwyney. Here evidently a great upcast fault in the strata has been the cause of diverting this stream from its natural gravitation course, and it is interesting to find—whether the cause may be the same or not—the Cynon brook at a distant part of the same mountain limestone range indulging in a similar vagary!

And there is another peculiarity about the head-waters of the Clydach, true also of the Ebwy Fawr, Sirhowy, and Rhymney streams, which all take their rise on the millstone grit formation immediately overlaying the mountain limestone. This, the millstone grit, is sandy and porous, and where the layer is only thin over the limestone the rain-water does not freely run off into the tiny streams and brooks, but soaks through to the limestone below, which is, it is well known, highly porous. And in course of ages numerous pit-holes, or swallow-holes, have been thus gradually formed on the surface, some of them 40 ft. deep and only little less wide, and into these in rainy seasons large volumes of water poured, and for the time disappeared to view. When the ironmasters first began to utilise the waters of these uplands, they made gutters to divert the surface water from the old swallow-holes, where they could; and so it is stated in the Geological Survey referred to, they went even the length of filling up one or more of the chief of these pit-holes on the Llangattock mountain.

Of course, the water had made itself seen somewhere formerly, though for the time it had disappeared from sight down the pit-holes, and probably a good deal came out at the foot of the northern outcrop of the limestone escarpment. However, there was no attempt to stop this diversion of the water by the ironmasters; and the millers in the Usk Valley, finding their water failing, put the fact down to dry summers and the act of Providence: never dreaming that the true cause of the water failure was probably the enterprising action of the ironmasters, out of their sight on the other sides of the lofty Darren Limestone rocks!

There is, we know, only the same rainfall and water-supply for the two sets of people, and what the one gains the other loses. And the question is to the fore now, as it was in the Iron age of South Wales, because enterprising public boards have made, and are making their reservoirs and collecting grounds for water to-day along this same millstone grit formation—though unsuitable, they have none else—and have tried, are trying, and will try to intercept every drop of rain-water from penetrating through swallow-holes and otherwise down to the limestone, and so being lost to them. How will fare the Valley of the Usk is another matter; but it is time that the inhabitants, and the authorities representing their interests, should climb up the ascent of Llangynider and Llangattock mountains, and have a look at what is going on over the other side of their hills!

---

And there is need still for those interested in the Clydach and Usk streams to watch the head-waters of the Clydach, so that such may not be tampered with. The Duke of Beaufort, the Lord of the Manor, has no more right to divert the water, or to authorise or allow others to do so, than any riparian owner has; and in the original lease of 1779 it is therein stated that only such rights over the stream are then granted to the lessees as he then was possessed of.

---

## THE BLACK BAND AT BEAUFORT.

Often had I heard of the famous Black Band, the discovery of which at Beaufort is said to have added greatly to the fortunes of the Brothers J. and C. Bailey, but I had never seen it *in situ* until the other day, and my preconceived notion was partly wrong. Traversing the abandoned and desolate shale heaps and mine workings of Beaufort Hill in search for the natural channel of the river Clydach, and of the line of its watershed, we came to a slight rise or bank of ground untouched by pick and shovel, and in the natural state. That, said my companion, is the famous Black Band! It was a thin vein of crumbling grit, partly pulverised coal, and partly fine iron ore intermixed; and it was easy to imagine that by laying this in clamps or beds on the open land, and firing it, a rough sort of iron would be the residuum. There was no need of "scouring" to cleanse the iron ore before taking it to the furnace, and half the work of the furnace itself was even done by this rude preliminary step, possible because the iron ore and coal had been thus blended by nature into one stratum. My companion informed me that he had seen the whole hill-side there alight with the heaps of burning Black Band.

But those horrid, desolate shale heaps up the Clydach Valley! They haunt my memory now as a hideous dream of Nature defaced and dishonoured, like the lava-covered slopes of Vesuvius and Monte Nuovo. Where has all the natural soil gone to? Why, washed away in millions of tons down the precipitous Clydach Valley to the Usk, and thence to the Bristol Channel, forming, probably, there by this time fresh shoals in one or another part of it. For Nature's workings are so arranged that *matter* can never be absolutely destroyed.

Dr. G. P. Bevan, of Beaufort—1840 or so—wrote a clever original paper on the geology of this district, and which appears in the *Geologist*, vol. i, p. 126.

The later history of the Beaufort Works is practically the same as of the Nant y Glo, though under different managers, Mr. Needham taking that position at Beaufort.

---

The following Note, as to the Beaufort Iron Works, by the late Mr. W. H. West, of Gliffaes, one of the partners, has been kindly forwarded to me by Lord Glanusk :

## NOTE AS TO BEAUFORT WORKS.

"Beaufort Iron Works were founded by Jonathan Kendall and his brother Edward in 1779, with a 99 years' lease from the Duke of Beaufort, of all the minerals in the parishes of Llangattock and Llanelly.

They erected a furnace in Llangattock, on the border of Monmouth, and called the place Beaufort. Mr. Joseph Latham joined the Kendalls as partner, with one-sixteenth share of the Works, in 1798. A second furnace was built, and soon after, a forge.

On the death of Edward Kendall, the Works became the property of his son, Edward Kendall, of Danypark. He married the widow of Mr. W. H. Bevan, of Glannant; her son by her first husband succeeded Mr. J. Latham as manager of Beaufort. Mr. (afterwards Sir) Joseph Bailey and Mr. Bevan, the younger, each married daughters of Mr. Joseph Latham. The works at Beaufort were sold to Messrs. J. and C. Bailey (I do not know the date). They remained part of the firm's undertaking until it was sold in 1870.

In 1793, Messrs. Kendall sub-leased the minerals in Llanelly to Messrs. Frere, Cook and Co. The well-known Sir Bartle Frere was of this family, and born at the Great House, Llanelly.

The firm became Frere, Cooke, and Powell, and the Works were carried on by the brothers John and Lancelot Powell, till, in 1861, they met with financial trouble."

---

# THE BRECON BOAT COMPANY.

A few further Notes as to this prosperous little Company. They had under their sub-lease of 1801, from Messrs. Kendall, some good veins of coal, the "Elled" and the "Old Coal," each of 6 feet thickness, and of the finest House Coal and Smith Coal quality, and which were worked with short levels from the crop.

A short but steep railroad of 4 miles (edge rail), with a gradient of 1 in 12 at the Black Rock, took the loaded trams down the Clydach Valley from the mouth of the levels to the wharves at Llanelly, and then a fleet of 16 Canal Boats of 21 tons burden each, conveyed the Coal to Brecon, a distance of 18½ miles, and the Company were able to sell there at 14s. a ton, though the profit was small. All the country-side came for their supply of coal, and in the late Autumn every farmer came and fetched his stock of Coal from the Brecon Boat Company's Wharf. And further afield, to Herefordshire and Radnorshire, coal was delivered from this Wharf to traders like Benjamin Trusted, the Quaker of Hay, and William Bridgwater, of Glasbury, along the Hay and Eardisley Tramroad. In severe frosts there was great interruption to the Canal traffic, but the Yard at Brecon was always well stocked for winter against the chance of severe frosts occurring.

They had also large limestone quarries and limekilns, and supplied a wide district with lime, the farmers in the middle of the last century growing much more corn and using lime in agriculture far more largely then they do at the present time.

At a later period, about 1821, a lease of additional coal was taken from the Messrs. Kendall, the vein being the Bydyllog, about 4 ft. in thickness; but this Coal was much inferior to those of the "Elled" and the "Old Coal," worked under the original lease. As much as 1s. 3d. a ton royalty was paid for some coal to the Messrs. Kendall, but this included a repayment of the cost of a level partly made by them, when the new lease was granted.

The Brecon Boat Company subsequently sunk a pit to the "Old Coal," and there obtained their main supply and of the finest quality, the Old "Elled" Coal at Llwyn y Pwll level being abandoned.

The Brecon Boat Company had two Colliery Agents of note—the first was really a man of mark, Mr. Ellwood, and the early success of the concern is due to him. There is a story told of him, that, one day a collier mentioned that when working in his stall in the "Elled" level, he had heard the sound of a pick near. Mr. Ellwood told him that he must be dreaming, as there were no other coal working of their's near, and it was a long way to the Clydach boundary.

Ellwood, however, resolved to test the statement, when he found it to be correct, and that the Clydach Company had worked some 39,000 tons of their best coal beyond the boundary line. An arrangement was made that when the Brecon Boat Company wanted Coal, they were to be allowed to work a similar quantity in the Clydach taking; but when that day came, in after-years, the Clydach Company had no coal to spare.

Another trusted Colliery Agent was William Morris, and he lived at the Company's Hafod Farm. Many a night have I spent there; and he it was who took me into the Bydyllog 4 ft. level, and set me to cut a ton of coal with my own hands. I did not quite achieve this, cutting and loading into the tram 16 cwt. only, and that at the price of hands raw with blisters from the rough grit of the coal dust, when holding and using the mandril. I was, however, justly proud to see my name in the pay-sheets, and to receive 2*s.* as my payment for cutting 16 cwt. of coal. Mr. Morris and his son also gave me a lesson or two in dialling under ground, and I flattered myself I knew enough to plot correctly on a plan the underground workings, with all their twists and turns, headings and stalls. It is very easy once you know how!

Rees Lloyd, of Brecon, was also a trusted Agent, and another was Mr. Mordecai Jones, the son of their old boat-builder, who introduced many improvements in the conveyance of the coal to Brecon, arranging for the trip of a boat to and from Llanelly to take two days instead of three days as formerly. In after-years he became the enterprising Lessee of valuable Collieries in the Aberdare Valley, and proved himself long-headed and clear-sighted, and a man of no ordinary business ability and capacity.

---

The following are interesting letters of Mr. Ellwood, the Agent referred to:—

"Clydach Colliery, 27th April, 1817.

"Dear Sir,—Last night I received your letter requesting the prices of Limestone.

"The Lowest calculation I can make that Limestone will cost put in the Boat at Llangattock is per Boat Weight of 20 cwt. to the Ton, 2*s.* 0½*d.*

"The price of Limestone above is what I consider is what it will stand the Company at in the Boat.

"I intend being in Brecon on Tuesday evening, when I can give you any further information on the Business.

"I am, &c., THOS. ELLWOOD.

"John Powell, Esq., Solr., Brecon."

---

"Clydach Colliery, 5 Decr., 1823.

"Dear Sir,—Since the conversation yesterday with you and others concerning the arrangement between the Gass Company and the Boat Company, something has forcibly struck my mind (not that I am acquainted with the Manufacture of Gass) that the Gass Company might be suplyd with Gas from the Boat Company's Oven or Ovens by means of conveying pipes to communicate with the Gassometer of the former Company. It may be a case worth so considering for the benefit of both parties. [These ovens were on the Boat Company's yard at Brecon.]

"You observed to me the thoughts of adopting Broke Limestone in the place of pitching the streets of Brecon by way of experiment. I would recommend 20 or 30 yards to be covered with a certain thickness of the offal chips or breakage from the limestone, which can be had on the top of the Watton kilns. [The limestone was burnt at Brecon at this time.]

"The part I should recommend to be tried is from the turnpike gate towards the entrance into Brecon, and let some old man be apointed (the expense would not be great) to use a rake and close up the ruts made by wheels passing till the whole surface became united.

"Seeing the anxiety you have for every publick Improvement, I cannot help offering my Service in anything I can assist you,

And am, &c., THOS. ELLWOOD.

"John Powell, Esq."

---

The following are the returns of Iron sent from Beaufort Iron-works (Breconshire), for shipment at Newport by the Monmouthshire Canal, 1802-1830.

| Year. | Tons. | Year. | Tons. |
|---|---|---|---|
| 1802 | — | 1817 | 2,104 |
| 1803 | 1,612 | 1818 | 2,100 |
| 1804 | 2,950 | 1819 | 2,124 |
| 1805 | 4,605 | 1820 | 3,132 |
| 1806 | 3,989 | 1821 | 2,962 |
| 1807 | 3,947 | 1822 | 3,786 |
| 1808 | 4,004 | 1823 | 4,269 |
| 1809 | 3,566 | 1824 | 5,347 |
| 1810 | 3,948 | 1825 | 7,091 |
| 1811 | 3,910 | 1826 | 6,028 |
| 1812 | 3,995 | 1827 | 5,914 |
| 1813 | 3,204 | 1828 | 5,701 |
| 1814 | 3,146 | 1829 | 6,896 |
| 1815 | 3,767 | 1830 | 5,065 |
| 1816 | 3,164 | | |

(Scrivenor's *Iron Trade*, p. 126.)

---

The following are the returns of Iron carried on the Monmouthshire Canal and Tram-roads, 1831-40.

FROM BEAUFORT IRON-WORKS (CO. BRECONSHIRE).

| | | |
|---|---|---|
| 1831 | (Kendall and Co.) ... ... ... | 5,150 |
| 1832 | ,, ,, ... ... ... | 6,052 |
| 1833 | ,, ,, ... ... ... | 2,257 |
| | (J. and C. Bailey) ... ... ... | 5,255 |
| 1834 | ,, ,, ... ... ... | 9,808 |
| 1835 | ,, ,, ... ... ... | 12,976 |
| 1836 | ,, ,, ... ... ... | 14,567 |
| 1837 | ,, ,, ... ... .. | 11,145 |
| 1838 | ,, ,, ... ... ... | 10,903 |
| 1839 | ,, ,, ... ... ... | 10,505 |
| 1840 | ,, ,, ... ... ... | 10,049 |

(Scrivenor's *Iron Trade*, p. 294).

XXV.

# The Clydach Iron Works.

WE are now nearing the end of our long task. As an offshoot of the Beaufort Works, we have already given the early history of the Clydach Works under the former head.

They date from the sub-lease of February 15, 1800.

In the days of Mr. E. Frere, who was undoubtedly an able man, and subsequently under the management of John Scale, of Aberdare, down to nearly 1830, the Works may have paid more than their way, and yielded a profit for a few years; but it was never for long. They had always been under-capitalized, though the Frere family invested a large sum at the outset; and we find Mr. Richard Crawshay advancing £10,000 as a loan even in Mr. E. Frere's days; and they were always in debt—heavily, sometimes—to their Bankers, Messrs. Wilkins and Co., of Brecon. And it was almost their invariable rule to have their bills discounted; and a bit of bad luck in large customers failing, like the Messrs. Le Bas House of Guernsey, almost spelt ruin. Mr. Walter Powell, the famous member of the firm of Walter and John Powell, from whose papers I am deriving almost every item of information contained in this narrative, advanced the firm £14,000—fortunately as a loan, and not as a partner—and which his daughters were able with some difficulty to recover against the Works. But his partner, John Powell, was not so prudent: he put his money in as a partner, and his son, John Powell, still more money, until he became the sole responsible partner. Ultimately, the crash came. Walter Powell's children called up their father's loan (for it was proved at law to have been only a loan), the Bankers pressed, and Mr. John Powell had to succumb to the pressure of the flood of adversity, and the whole of his not-inconsiderable landed estate, and the old family mansion of Watton Mount in Brecon, had to be parted with.

*Page* 192.

THE CLYDACH IRON WORKS. **1813.**

(*Wood's "Rivers of Wales."*)

The chief cause of want of success from the first was the dependence on borrowed capital; but, apart from that, it seems unlikely that the Works under any circumstances could have proved a great success. True, they had the advantage of great water-power in the Clydach stream, but which, when steam-engines had come into common use, had lost its special value; and even that was far more than counterbalanced by carriage of coal and iron ore down endless and costly (in making and maintenance, not forgetting grease, wire ropes, or chains, and extra trams required, and delay) incline planes from the hill ground high above, to the furnaces and rolling-mill at the bottom of the narrow defile. And when that was reached, there was hardly room to turn, and scarcely tipping space for the *scoria* of these furnaces.

They were very short, too, of the best veins of coal, and their iron ore was poor and difficult to win; and the wonder is, to me, how they managed to carry on the Works as long as they did.

I have a mass of papers connected with these Works, and a hundred or more of John Scale's letters; but nothing of importance and interest, I think, or worth quoting. It was a small Iron Works, with few natural facilities (except water-power), and what might have been a small success in the hands of a strong capitalist could not but prove a failure, when in the hands of, and conducted by men of little capital.

And of later years, of course, the great changes and improvements in the Iron industry, which a Works of this kind could not possibly adopt from want of capital and other reasons, left it hopelessly behind.

Their access to the seaport of Newport for the delivery of manufactured iron was good, a short tramroad of a mile or so leading to their Canal-side wharves, and thence the continuous water route by Canal to their wharves at Newport.

Sir Bartle Frere was one of this family of Freres, and is said to have been born at the Works.

Mr. Edward Frere was a keen politician, and in the family fights for Breconshire between the Morgans of Tredegar and Col. Wood (for both were Tories, though possibly of different shades), he brought up to the Poll at Brecon a boat-load of electors in support of Col. Wood. I cannot fix the date, but it was either that of the 1808 or 1818 Election.

---

The following are letters of more or less interest:—

"Wednesday Evening, 1st Feb., 1797.
"From 'The Lion,' Brecon,

"Mr. E. Frere's compliments to Mr. John Powell, and will be glad to see him at 'The Lion,' or wait on Mr. Powell, if *alone*, Mr. E. F. not being *Dizen'd*" (*i.e.*, in full evening dress.—Ed.).

---

"Messrs. Walter and John Powell.

"Sirs,—Underneath you have a Statement of the Quantity of Iron made at Clydach Furnaces, Week ending 20th May, inst.:

| | | T. | C. | | | | | | |
|---|---|---|---|---|---|---|---|---|---|
| No. 1.—Pigs | ... ... | 32 | 1 | 0 | 0 | | | | |
| Castings | ... ... | 5 | 17 | 3 | 20 | | | | |
| Scraps | ... ... | 1 | 0 | 0 | 0 | | | | |
| | | | | | | 38 | 18 | 3 | 20 |
| No. 2.—Pigs | ... ... | 42 | 1 | 0 | 0 | | | | |
| Scraps | ... ... | 1 | 0 | 0 | 0 | | | | |
| | | | | | | 43 | 1 | 0 | 0 |

"The Iron from both last week was very good; the greatest part of it, I am certain, was as good as any that has ever been made here: as good or better than any that I saw on the Blaenavon Yard last Sunday; but we may thank the Crop Mine for it; we had about $\frac{1}{3}$ of it at work on each Furnace, but I believe that is all over with us at present, as we have had nothing down the Tram Road this two Days. The Colliers brot. in their tools to-day, but I should suppose that they will go to Work again in a day or two, the greatest part of them: for I don't suppose that they can do better any where. There may perhaps be a little secret in it. Or else, why should your Colliery and Mines shew a different conduct to the Blaenavon Colliery and Mines? They—the most part of them—took it very easy, and went to their Work without any bustle.

"I am, Sirs, etc.,

"Clydach Works, 22nd May, 1804. "THO. PHILLIPS.

"Mr. Cooke wrote last Week to several of the old Customers, offering them Iron: but I suppose he has had no answer to it: other People some how do mannage to sell Iron that is not any better than we are at present making. Mr. Leigh, of Pontpool, has had 10 Tons of Forge Pigs upon Trial. I was down at the Bason last Sunday to forward it to him."

---

"Messrs. Walter and John Powell.

"Sirs,—Underneath you have Acco'ts of Iron made at Clydach Furnace. No. 2. Week ending 24 Feby., 1805:

| | | | | | TONS. | C. | | |
|---|---|---|---|---|---|---|---|---|
| Pigs ... ... ... | 46 | 14 | | | | | | |
| Castings ... ... | 3 | 12 | 1 | 28 | | | | |
| Scraps ... ... ... | | 10 | | | | | | |
| | | | | | 50 | 16 | 1 | 28 |

"Week ending March 3rd, 1805:

| | | | | | | | |
|---|---|---|---|---|---|---|---|
| Pigs ... ... ... | 50 | 9 | 0 | 0 | | | |
| Castings ... ... | | 10 | 2 | 0 | | | |
| Scraps... ... ... | 1 | 0 | | | | | |
| | | | | | 51 | 19 | 2 |

"The quality of the above was 1st and 2nd Foundry. The quality at present is just the same; in trying to make it still more Grey—as our Mr. Frere wishes—we make less Quantity than we otherwise should. In another fortnight we shall finish the Dock Company's Pipes, and Tram Plates. Then I don't see that our moulders will have but little to do, except you will get the Tram Plates to make for your Tram Road; or that Mr. Frere will bring an Order with him home from Bristol.

The new Hammer seems to do very well. The bars look extremely well after they are drawn. If you can get Orders enough, you may make a good deal of Iron, Stamped and Puddled.

"I am, Sirs, etc.,

"Clydach Works, 5th March, 1805. "THO. PHILLIPS."

---

"Abbey Tintern Works, Nov. 27th, 1810.

"Dear Sir,—Since I last saw you, I have been in London; and, as I promised you, have had a conversation with Mr. Crawshay respecting Clydach Works, and I have very little doubt of his being a purchaser of them, if the whole were to be disposed off without any Loss to the Parties concerned; whether he would be a Purchaser or not of two-thirds, I could not so well form an opinion.

"If the present Partners should not have it in their power to carry on the Works for want of capital, it may be some consolation to you and your Friends to know that they are considered valuable, and anything I can do to serve you in any way will give me great pleasure, and remain,

"Dear Sir, Very truly yours,

"Mr. Walter Powell, Solicitor, Brecon. "ROBERT THOMPSON.

"P.S.—I have sent Mr. Frere a copy of the above."

On Nov. 10th, 1813, the Clydach Iron Works were offered for Sale by Auction, and were described as consisting of two well-constructed furnaces, capable of making each 70 tons of Iron per week. The blast for these furnaces was supplied by two capital machines worked by water, which is abundant. Also a rolling mill and a forge.

The mineral taking was stated to be 600 acres in extent, held of Messrs. Kendalls and Bevan as lessees of the Duke of Beaufort.

The forge was held of Capel Leigh, Esq., and a capital Trevethick steam engine was used for "occasionally" blowing the same, the chief power being that of water.

The property, however, does not appear to have found a purchaser.

---

In 1823, and about that period, there were rough times with the workmen, and the Assize Calendars at Brecon show many prosecutions for assaults, &c., coming from that district; and there is a record extant of one collier walking stark-naked from his cottage up to Llanelly Church.

At the Clydach Level, in July, 1823, the following notice of intimidation was stuck up. It is a mixture of Welsh and English, of which we give the full English translation:—

"How many times we gave notice to you about going in to work before you settle all together to go on better terms than were before and better than what you ask at present?

"Notice to you David Thomas John, and David Davis, and Andrew Cross, that the Bull and his friends are all alive, and the vale of Llamarch is wide, and woe shall be to you, since death you shall doubtless have all at once, you may depend upon this. It may be that the night you do not expect, we shall come again. We are not afraid were you to go all at once to work."

---

In 1824, Mr. John Scale, from the Aberdare Iron Works, had been appointed manager, and the following is one of his numerous letters:—

"Clydach, 16th Decr., 1824.

"My dear Sir,—I am obliged by your favour of yesterday. I would have sent the plans of the Minerals, but as it is possible Mr. Frere may be here on Saturday, it may perhaps be as well to keep them. I enclose you a Letter received from him, but as this would cross one of mine saying I was going to Bristol on Saturday and would see him on Sunday, it may most likely stop him. This I shall learn by to-morrow's post. I have not heard any thing from Mr. Leigh or Lewillin.

"I am, my dear Sir, etc.,

"John Powell, Esq., Brecon. JOHN SCALE."

---

In 1825, Mr. L. Powell (Lancelot), brother of John Powell, appears to have been acting in some capacity at the Works, and sent the following return of make of Iron to his brother at Brecon:—

"Clydach, Sept. 22, 1825. Week ending Sept. 17, 1825.

| | T. | C. |
|---|---|---|
| No. 1 Furnace made ... ... ... | 40 | 0 |
| No. 2 do. do. ... ... ... | 45 | 0 |
| Mill saleable ... ... ... | 70 | 0 |
| Forge, Char. Blooms .. ... ... | 15 | 17 |
| Pud. do. ... ... ... | 18 | 4 |
| Coal weighed .. ... ... | 311 | 0 |
| Mine do. ... ... ... | 223 | 0 |

Mr. John Scale was, however, the manager, and remained so until 1830.

And by the following agreement, dated 1832, Mr. E. Frere withdrew from the concern, and sold all his interest to Mr. John Powell.

BRECON, 17TH JANUARY, 1832.

An Agreement made this day between Edward Frere of the Clydach Iron Works in the County of Brecon, Esquire, of the one part, and John Powell, of the town of Brecon, Gentleman, of the other part.

The said Edward Frere agrees to withdraw entirely from the controul and management of the Clydach Iron Works, and to give up the entire controul and management thereof to the said John Powell from this time. And also to sell all his interest in such Works (subject to the Interest of the Right Honourable John Hookham Frere therein, but for which the said John Powell is not to be personally liable) to the said John Powell.

In consideration whereof, the said John Powell agrees to pay the said Edward Frere the annual sum of Two hundred pounds by half-yearly payments during his life, or until the said John Powell shall have effected a sale of the said Edward Frere's Interest in the said Works and satisfied the claim of the said John Hookham Frere therein—such annual payment to be considered as commencing on the 25th day of September last.

That the said Edward Frere shall be entitled to the rents of his Manchester Estate from and until the same respective Terms, free from the interest of Mr. Wilkins' Mortgage, which the said John Powell agrees to pay from the 25th day of December last.

The said John Powell to indemnify the said Edward Frere from all partnership debts contracted for or appearing upon the Books of the concern.

(Sgd.) E. FRERE.
JOHN POWELL.

Witness—Wm. Evans, Clerk to Messrs. Jones and Powell, Brecon.

---

Difficulties seemed to continually beset the career of this Company, and

On the 17th July, 1833, the whole of the Clydach Iron Works were put up for sale at the Auction Mart, London, by Messrs. Winstanley.

The following are some of the chief particulars :—

3 Blast-Furnaces, each 44 ft. high and 14 ft. across the Boshes, capable of making 240 Tons of Pig-Iron per week.

26 Coking Ovens for coking small Coal, and producing Coal Tar sufficient for the Works.

3 Running-out Fineries, Foundry Air-Furnace and 2 Cupolas.

A Boulton and Watt Engine for Blast.

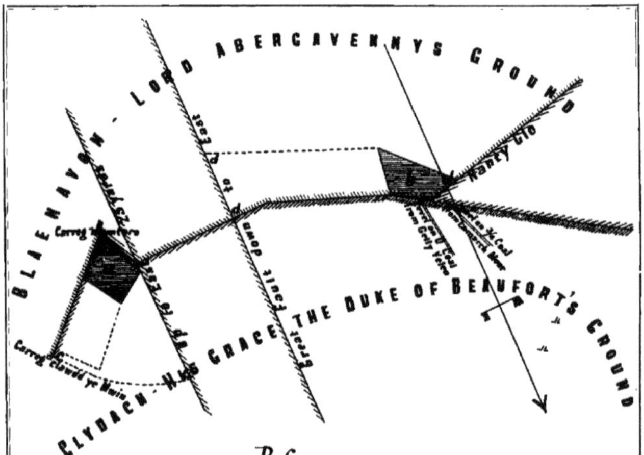


## Reference.

a. 16 Acres of ¾ Coal granted to be laid on Blaen Avon.
b. 16 Acres of ¾ Coal as equivalent laid on Clydach.

c. c. c. 84 Acres of all the other Veins of Coal and Mine granted to be laid on Blaen Avon.

d. d. d. 84 Acres D° as equivalent laid on Clydach.

Plan of exchange of Minerals between Clydach and Blaenavon Companies, also showing Great Fault in Clydach Valley.

PAGE 197

A Blowing Machine, worked by a Water-wheel, 42 ft. high; Coal and Ironstone under 600 acres of land, held of Messrs. Kendalls and Beavan, as lessees of the Duke of Beaufort.

A Rolling Mill, worked by Water-Wheel 42 ft. high, capable of making 120 Tons of Finished Bars per week.

Also a Capital Forge for the manufacture of Charcoal Blooms and Puddled Bars.

---

The property, however, appears again to have found no purchaser, and remained in the hands of Mr. John Powell.

We have to mention one further matter.

The exact date is not stated on the Plan, but an arrangement had been made between the Blaenafon Company and the Clydach Company for an exchange of mineral land convenient to each other, adjacent to the Great Faults which cross the Clydach Valley. Probably it was about the year 1835; but we are unable to fix the date with any certainty

---

The following are the Returns of Iron sent from Clydach Iron Works (Breconshire) for shipment at Newport by the Monmouthshire Canals, 1802 to 1830:—

| | | Tons. | | | Tons. |
|---|---|---|---|---|---|
| 1802 | ... | — | 1817 | ... | 3,162 |
| 1803 | ... | 447 | 1818 | ... | 3,947 |
| 1804 | ... | 1,266 | 1819 | ... | 3,778 |
| 1805 | ... | 1,455 | 1820 | ... | 3,397 |
| 1806 | ... | 1,599 | 1821 | ... | 3,876 |
| 1807 | ... | 1,196 | 1822 | ... | 4,225 |
| 1808 | ... | 963 | 1823 | ... | 3,651 |
| 1809 | ... | 1,336 | 1824 | ... | 3,617 |
| 1810 | ... | 1,372 | 1825 | ... | 3,748 |
| 1811 | ... | 872 | 1826 | ... | 3,660 |
| 1812 | ... | 1,774 | 1827 | ... | 4,107 |
| 1813 | ... | 2,174 | 1828 | ... | 5,183 |
| 1814 | ... | 1,472 | 1829 | ... | 6,967 |
| 1815 | ... | 2,999 | 1830 | ... | 6,771 |
| 1816 | ... | 2,658 | | | |

Also from 1831 to 1840:—

| | | | | | |
|---|---|---|---|---|---|
| 1831 | ... | — | 1836 | ... | 7,640 |
| 1832 | ... | 6,542 | 1837 | ... | 7,081 |
| 1833 | ... | 7,252 | 1838 | ... | 9,283 |
| 1834 | ... | 6,261 | 1839 | ... | 9,606 |
| 1835 | ... | 7,618 | 1840 | ... | 10,038 |

(Scrivenor's *Iron Trade*, pp. 126 and 294.)

---

END OF CLYDACH IRON WORKS.

XXVI.

# The Llanelly (or Clydach) Forge.

THIS very old Forge was situate on the Clydach stream, a little below the Blast-Furnaces and Rolling-Mill of the Clydach Company, and was the private freehold of Mr. Capel Hanbury Leigh, of Pontypool Park. Many years previously, Captain John Hanbury, Mr. Leigh's ancestor, is said to have formed this forge in 1680, being engaged in the iron trade, like several of the Hanbury and Leigh family, and having already two Furnaces at Pontypool.

Of course, that site was chosen to place the Forges there for the sake of the famous almost unfailing water-power of the Clydach stream. And it has often struck me that the Glawcoed farm had been purchased on the Usk at Llangynider by Mr. Leigh, or his ancestors, in order to secure the full water-power of the Usk for works that were contemplated to be, or might be, thereafter put there. If steam-power had not been discovered, there is little doubt the water-force of the Usk at the Glawcoed falls would long ago have been used for manufacturing purposes, if not for iron-making, for some other industry.

Mr. Leigh's ancestor did not purchase the outlying property for the sake of the fishing —good as it is—even though Mr. Leigh himself bought the great Crown fishery at Usk and Newbridge in the same river; but methinks this outlying property in Breconshire was acquired solely on account of the great natural water-power which he saw it possessed.

Up to the time of the advent of the Freres and Cookes, and the formation of the Clydach Iron Works in 1800, the Llanelly Forge had been let independently by Mr. Leigh.

In 1800, Messrs. Frere and Cooke, occupiers of the Iron Works near, became the lessees of the Forge; and in particulars of sale of the whole Iron Works by private Contract, printed in 1813, the Forge Property is thus described :—

"A FORGE,

"Consisting of Two Hammer-Wheels and One Blowing-Machine, Two Fineries, Three Hollow Fires, Capital Trevethick's Steam-Engine for occasionally blowing the same. One Air-Chafery and Three Puddling and Balling Furnaces, capacious Charcoal House, Smiths' Shop, Warehouse, Agent's and 20 Workmen's Houses, situate on the Rail-way, leading from the Canal. About half a mile from each.

"It commands the same stream of water which works the machinery of the Furnace.

"The Neighbourhood abounds in Coppice Wood, and the Vicinity of the Tin Works occasions a constant Demand for Charcoal Iron, for which this Work is in high repute.

"It is held by Lease from Capel Leigh, Esq., for a term of 81 years, from Midsummer, 1797, at a Rent of £235 10*s.* 0*d.* per annum, and the whole of the Works have been substantially rebuilt since that time."

It was at this Forge some of the best merchant iron was made, and large quantities of charcoal were used. A team of mules was employed in bringing the charcoal there from the different woods, which had been purchased by the Company's Agent, Mr. Watkins. I remember selling him several hundred cords from the Ithyn farm at Llangattock.

This Forge shared the adverse fate of the Clydach Iron Works in 1861, and I do not believe that it has been worked as a Forge since that disaster. The property is still held, however, in the Hanbury family; and fortunately so, because Mr. Hanbury was able as a riparian owner of the Clydach, and with very ancient water-rights in that stream to take the praiseworthy and even noble part of defending the water-interests of the river when the Ebbw Vale Urban District Council sought, with the aid of the Duke of Beaufort and his Agents (the Duke receiving the large sum of £10,000), Parliamentary powers to take away all the natural head-waters of that stream into another Valley, without giving any compensation-water whatever to the Clydach brook. Mr. Hanbury, fortunately, had a foothold on this stream; and, by his timely aid and intervention, was the means of stopping this proposed depredation, and saving the interests of the Clydach and of the Usk from injury. . . . . .

The following letter is interesting, showing that Mr. Leigh, of Pontypool, and Mr. George were partners in some Iron Works in 1825. Probably these were situate at or near Pontypool.

"Ponty Pool, March 18, 1825.

"Sir,—We would propose giving you £35 per annum for 13 years for the Coal Allied Mine, which lies under your two upper fields, you allowing us to bring any mine which we may obtain adjoining yours through your land.

"We are, yours, etc.,
"Leigh and George."

---

In 1827 Mr. C. H. Leigh was appointed High Sheriff for Breconshire, and the following letter, in which he requests the services of Messrs. Jones and Powell, of Brecon, as his Under-Sheriffs, contains some interesting details of the High Sheriff's arrangement as to Javelin Men.

"Burrows, Swansea, 10th Feby., 1827.

"Messrs. Jones and Powell, Sol'rs, Brecon.

"Gentlemen,—The *Gazette* of the 5th inst. has moved all uncertainty and suspense as to the appointment of Sheriff for your County, and it now only leaves me to request your services—which I have great pleasure of doing—to officiate as my Under-Sheriffs. I certainly do not feel that I owe any particular attention to the Judge as a personal compliment, and shall therefore only wish to discharge the dutys of the Office with reference only to such respect as I should wish to pay the County; but, as I am ignorant of what is expected to be done, I fear that I must impose on you a greater portion of trouble than would otherwise devolve on you.

"You will have the goodness to inform me the style usually observed in receiving the Judge in the County, which, I believe, is not with equal ceremony as the English Judges. I shall request the favor of your assistance in selecting the proper number of Javelin Men; and if not to be found amongst my Tenants at Llanelly and Llanthetty, you will fix upon others qualified for the purpose, as I wish whatever expense may be incurred should be expended in the County. With respect to their equipment, I had yesterday an application from a Mrs. Elizabeth Ransom, who proffers every accommodation and comfort in her Lodgings, and that she has given much satisfaction to several of my Predecessors (whom she enumerates) in the Articles she has furnished them with. If you approve of this, I can have no objection to take her Lodging, and give her any advantage from the outfit of the men. I will send you the particulars of my Livery, and that it might be as useful to the Men as possible afterwards, I shall dispense with the Crest on the Buttons. I will thank you to give Mrs. Leigh's and my kindest regards to Capel Miers, . . . . . who, we hope, continues well. Mrs. Leigh joins me in best compts. to yourself and Mrs. Powell.

"Believe me, Dr. Sir, yours very faithfully,
"C. H. Leigh.

"Mrs. Hanbury Leigh and myself v'y best comp'ts to Mrs. Jones and Mrs. Powell."

---

# XXVII.

# The Llangrwyney Forge.

THESE Works were of very ancient date, probably contemporaneous with the Llanelly Forge, and even with the Brecon Forge, which we know was built in 1720.

These were situate on the double-headed Grwyney brook, which rising in the Black Mountains on the borders of Herefordshire and Monmouthshire, flows into the Usk on its left bank, a mile or two below Crickhowell. No more bleak, icy-cold, barren hills, where top-coats are never amiss to wear, but in the warm Vale of Tempe, where even the nightingale—and nowhere else in Breconshire—is to be heard.

Of course, the Forge was placed on that stream for its abundant water power, and the store of wood for charcoal in the neighbourhood. These forge-owners were good customers of the country gentlemen for their smaller and otherwise unsaleable wood, like that of Alder swamps (Wern or Gwern). If the Iron trade prospered, the country gentlemen shared the increase in a better price for their cordwood, and both made common cause to keep foreign iron out, by the imposition by Parliament of heavy duties.

Walter Watkins, of Dany Graig, was the man we find mentioned in our papers as being the first to do with this forge; and there is little doubt he was—unlike nearly all the ironmasters we have written of—a pure Welshman. His name "betrayeth him," and we also find him in a quiet way working his forge at Llangrwyney, and forming little kilns in Ebbw Vale, rudely to smelt the iron ore for working up into bar and merchant iron, when brought down to his forge, some years before Mr. Jere. Homfray, or Messrs. Harford, Partridge and Co., came upon the scene. Mr. Watkins was the first pioneer of the iron industry in the district, and he at least of the Welsh had the intelligence and enterprise to take up the trade of an ironmaster of his own accord, and not as the follower or agent of Englishmen—capitalists or prospectors—coming there to introduce the manufacture of iron.

His connection with Mr. Charles Cracroft, of Sunnybank, who was, according to Theo. Jones, his son-in-law, and also it would seem a small capitalist, we have alluded to in previous papers, and also to their partnership with Mr. Jere. Homfray at Ebbw Vale.

Whether that latter partnership proved advantageous to Mr. Watkins I am not certain, but I fear not.

As far back as 1777, we find that Mr. Walter Watkins, of Dany Graig, was High Sheriff for Breconshire.

A very important event happened about 1792, the making of the Brecon and Abergavenny Canal, about which a writer of a letter from the Grwyney Works (Mr. Philip Williams) in 1792, says: "We are all Canal-mad!"

No doubt Mr. Watkins was very anxious to have the bridge made across the Usk at Llangrwyney by the Canal Company, in order by a tramroad to put his Works in easy communication with Ebbw Vale and other Iron Works, and so get his Pig Iron to the forges.

The bridge was built in 1794, and just completed, when, on the melting of the snow in February, 1795, down came an unprecedentedly high flood in the Usk, which destroyed the bridge and the land embankments on either side. That was a well-remembered day, February 11th, 1795. It was said the solid bridge-approach embankments impounded the

*Page 201.*

LLANGRWYNEY FORGE. THE FORD ACROSS THE RIVER USK. 1813.

(Wood's "*Rivers of Wales*.")

flood water, so as to press violently on the piers, and thus caused its destruction. The Builder was under contract to maintain the bridge for three years, and the Canal Company called upon him to reinstate the bridge at his own expense.

This he refused to do, and his non-liability was upheld by a Herefordshire jury at the trial, it being found that he had strictly carried out all the plans, and that this great flood and disaster was an Act of God, for the consequences of which he was in no way responsible.

However, the bridge was never rebuilt, and the Llangrwyney Company were still obliged to cross the Usk to their Works by a dangerous ford.

Mr. Watkins' original letters, of which I have several, are in a bold, clear handwriting, denoting the vigour and determination as well as the intelligence of the man.

The names of Messrs. Harvey, Wason and Co., of The Forge, or Trostre Forge, Ironmasters, are mentioned more than once in relation to the Llangrwyney Works, as if doing business together, possibly at one time partners.

. . . . . . . . . .

---

"Dany Graig, 6th July, 1791.

"Sir,—Having occasion to make a remittance to Mr. Atkinson, I have drawn upon you in his favour for £300 at 90 days, of which I desire your acceptance, by directing the same to be paid at Bristol, or exchange with your Draft to the same amount, which will answer the same purpose, to

"Sir, Your most hble. Servt.,

"Mr. Homfray, at Ebbw Vale Works. "WA. WATKINS."

---

"Dear Sir,—I have sent you up 2 Ladle Moulds, which I think is large enough to contain as much Mettle as any One Person can carry at a time; if they'll do, shall draw you four more after receiving your answer.

"I have sent a Pattern for a Huish Boist, if you'll be pleased to get 2 Cast of 'em I shall be obliged as soon as possible—also if you'll be pleased to cast some Turrons for us as soon as Possible, say Wednesday morning, and you'll oblige,

"Sir, yr. very hble. Servt.,

"Grwny Works, 16th April, 1792. "PH. WILLIAMS.

"P.S.—If the Article had this day from Dany Graig is desirable, the same conveyance is the best; it cannot so well be sent by the Carriers.

"To Jere. Homfray, Esq., Ebbw Vale."

---

"Septr. 15th, 1798.

"Sir,—The Pattern of the Castings for the Bridge will be ready to-morrow morning, and shall be sent to you in the evening or early on Tuesday morning; each of the Sills will weigh 30 hundred, and there will be 12 of them wanting, and the same number of the uprights. I am in great hopes of seeing my Friends in the course of a week, and

"I am, etc.,

"Messrs. Harford, Homfray and Co., at Ebbw Vale. "WALT. WATKINS."

---

"Dany Graig, 29th Septr., 1798.

"Sir,—The inclosed came here this morning, the Drift of which can only be to accommodate the Bridge Builder, that he may gain time. I will send for John Lewis, of Trostrey, to-morrow, and get the Casting tried, and if any alteration will be thought necessary he should come to do it; till then I desire you will cast no more of them.

"I am, Sir, etc.,

"Messrs. Harford, Homfray and Co., at Ebbw Vale. "WAL. WATKINS."

---

It appears that in 1787-1790, Mr. Watkins purchased considerable quantities of what is called "stamped iron" from Mr. Kendall, of Beaufort, and disputes arose between them as to the delivery and the quality.

A formal inquiry seems to have been held at Crickhowell, on April 21st, 1790, when a great deal of evidence was taken, of which we give that of Walter Osland, and some other witnesses. How the dispute terminated, our papers do not tell us.

Walter Osland says that in the stamp'd Iron Mr. Watkins received from Mr. Kendall there was a quantity of small Iron and Cinder, and had not been ridled, and that out of 80 tons of small Iron which was delivered, there were 17 tons of Dirt and Rubbish which they co'd not use, some of which was sent to Danycraig to make the Walks, and some to make Roads, and some now in the forge yard at Llangrwney; he did not weigh it, but guessed by an experiment tried before Mr. Kendall by washing and weighing 1 Cwt. The Forges were at work on Stamp'd Iron 23rd Apl., 1787; co'd have drawn 6 or 7 tons of Bars p. week at the Hammer at that time single handed. A ton of Bars take 2.6 cwt of stamped Iron.

Mr. Watkins made Merch't. Iron of s'd stamp'd Iron which he sold for £18 p. ton sh't w't, delivered at Bristol, Worcester, and paid

| | |
|---|---|
| The Two Hammer Men - - | 1/- each p. Day play wages. |
| Furnace Men - - - | 1/6 p. Do. |
| Do. Assistant - - - | 1/- p. Do. |
| Stock Taker - - - | 1/2 p. Do. |
| Common Charges - - - | — |

When they worked double handed they c'd have drawn 10 tons of Bars p. week on the average, if they had had sufficient supply of stamped Iron for that purpose during the time he continued at Llangrwney, which was from 23rd April, '87, to October, 1788. They did not work more than 3 days a week. He cannot tell what time the Iron was washed in presence of Mr. Kendall, but believes to have been in the summer of 1788. Made a deduction for dirt in August, 1788, of 2 tons 7 cwt. 2 qrs.; for some time after s'd washing the Iron was better, and afterwards was sent as bad as before. Says that Mr. Kendall acknowledged that the Iron was not properly cleaned, and that he w'd take care of it in future. Previous to s'd washing he had often made complaints of the dirtiness of the Iron to Mr. Kendall and his clerk, who said that they had no convenience for keeping the Iron from dirt. Mr. Watkins was often obliged to wash the large Iron. He says the quality of the Iron was very good had it been properly cleaned from dirt. Says that he and Edward Tamplin went to Beaufort in Apl. 1789, to look at stamped Iron, and found it as bad, or rather worse than Mr. Watkins had thentofore been used to receive it. Says that he was at Beaufort some time before, when there was a smaller quantity of Iron in stock, and the quality better than that he saw in April.

Edward Tamplin says he is a hammer man at Llangrwney. He went there, he believes, in Octr., 1786, to work at a common Chaffery. The first week he went there draw'g Blooms, which were sent from Trostrey. Says that the air Furnaces were at work in March or April, 1787. The first stamp'd Iron they had was from Mr. Kendall. Does not know how long the furnace was ready before stamp'd Iron was sent by Mr. Kendall. Could have drawn 6 tons of Barr Iron a week single handed, if they had had a sufficient supply of stamp'd Iron. In consequence of not having a sufficient quantity of stamp'd Iron to work upon, he and his two sons gave notice to quit Mr. Watkins. One of his sons did go: they could not work half their time. He asked Mr. Watkins to let him go away to work elsewhere, and that he wo'd return back whenever Mr. Watkins sho'd have a sufficient supply of stamp'd Iron. He says they made some Mill and some Merch't Iron—most of the latter. Says that there was a great deal of dirt amongst the small Iron, which when riddled out, was about a quarter of the quantity. They left off work a week before Xmas, 1788, for want of stamped Iron, and did not go to work again for a month or 5 or 6 weeks. Says he and Walter Osland went to Beaufort in April, 1789, to inspect Stamped Iron, and found the large iron very bad, worse than usual, being raw and bad. He examined the small Iron; it was full of Dust and Cinder. He told Mr. John Kendall that it was not fit to make a sound Mill bar for want of ridling. Mr. Kendall s'd that it sho'd not be ridled, not being customary to do so. Mr. Watkins never had any stamp'd iron of Mr. Kendall after that Time. Says that they wo'd have used more than all the Quantity which Mr. Kendall was to supply, and what they co'd have from Cyfarthfa also.

Richard Tamplin says he is hammerman at Llangrwney. He went there abo't a Month before Easter. The Air Furnaces were then ready. There was no stamp Iron for 6 weeks after he went there. Says they washed sometimes 4, sometimes 5, sometimes 3 Days a week; on the average worked about half their Time when they had only Mr. Kendall's iron. Drawed some Mill, but mostly Merchant, Iron before they began to riddle the stamped Iron. They did not make the Iron so good as since, but made some Mercht. or Strake Iron.

Joseph Hemus says that he made an agreement which was to begin 25th March, 1787. with Mr. Watkins to supply him with 25 doz. Pots. p. week, but they did not use more than 11 doz. p. week. They did not make more than 3 tons of Iron p. week. Believes that he began to make Pots in 9 days or a fortnight after 25th March, 1787. Says that Mr. Watkins did never advance more money to him than he worked for.

LEWIS MORGAN says he carried the greater part of the stamp'd Iron which Mr. Watkins had from Mr. Kendall. He co'd have carried more Iron if he could have had it. Could have carried 12 tons p. week from Beaufort to Llangrwney. Says that he once was going to Beaufort for iron, but was told by the way that there was none; therefore did not go. He saw the Iron always weighed at Beaufort, and had sufficient weight. There was a great deal of Dirt and Wet in it, of which he complained to Mr. Williams (Clk. to Mr. Kendall), who said he could not help it; he must take it as it was. He says the stamped Iron he carried from Mr. Kendall was more full of Dirt, as it appeared to him, than the Iron he carried from Merthyr. Says he had 21/- per ton for carrying Iron from Merthyr, and had 7/- p. ton for that from Beaufort; that he would not, on any account, carry more from Merthyr.

---

As we are passing by Abergavenny, it may be mentioned that the meetings of the South Wales Ironmasters were held quarterly in this town, for the transaction of business affecting their common interests.

The minute-books are, we believe, still extant, and if of interest, the contents will, we hope, some day be published.

## XXVIII.

# The Forge, or Trostre Forge.

---

THIS is one of the old Forges in Monmouthshire, placed on the Usk at a convenient spot to obtain the water power of the full stream of the Usk. It is part of the family property of the Fludyer family.

In the years 1790 to 1800 the firm of Harvey, Wason and Co. were the occupiers, and carried on the business of forging and manufacturing merchant wrought-iron there, and the name of that firm is mentioned in our Llangrwyney Forge papers as having business relations about that time with the Llangrwyney firm.

Though the old corn mill and weir, lower down the river at Trostre, formerly belonging to the Priory of Usk, and subsequently to the Fludyer family, intercepted with its cruives or boxes most of the salmon ascending the Usk, a good few fish reached the Forge weir, a ro ugh wattled stank extending across the river from island to island.

Tradition relates that this was a fatal spot to the passing fish, especially those descending the river, as a huge walled chamber, with iron bars at the lower end, was used for passing the river water through when the Forge wheel was not working; and that in the spring time a great slaughter of foul fish, and later of the descending salmon fry, took place, and that this fish trap was, in fact, incidentally a source of profit to the occupiers of the Forge and mill.

The deep tail race is famous for the tussle between my old friend—and founder of the Usk as a modern salmon river—James Greenfield, of Brynderwen, and Jim Lucas, the well-known fisherman of Usk. The dispute was over the right of access to the weir, and it ended in both rolling over together into the water of the tail race of the Forge.

The high flood of February 11th, 1795, reached a record point here, some two feet above the doorway of the mill, and a stone niche shows still the level, and in which a recording brass tablet had been placed by Messrs. Harvey, Wason and Co. The tablet is not there now, but I have seen it; and anxious to restore and preserve historical marks like this, I offered—but in vain—£5 to its present possessor to allow me to have it to refix in its proper place. Monmouthshire men should see that this is done.

The Forge pound, as it is called, above the weir forms, I think, the largest pool on the Usk, and the deepest, being probably larger than Newton pool at Brecon, Llanddetty pool at Buckland, or the Bridge pool at Crickhowell.

Complaints are made of this self-same weir hindering the passage of the fish up the Usk to-day, and probably there is good ground to believe that this must be the case on the sudden lowering of a slight rise, or "fresh," in the river. It would be sound policy for the Conservators to acquire this mill and weir, as they acquired the famous Trostre mill and weir lower down many years ago.

---

## EXTRACT FROM

## WILLIAM COXE'S "HISTORICAL TOUR THROUGH MONMOUTHSHIRE."

### Chapter 16, Pages 152, 153. 1801.

In company with Mr. Rickards, proprietor of Llansanfraed, I made an excursion from Clytha House. We walked to the banks of the Usk, nearly opposite to the church of Lanvair Kilgeden, which is singularly picturesque, from its solitary situation in the midst of fields, at a distance from any house, and surrounded by venerable yews. Here the river, which had hitherto flowed in a sinuous course, is interrupted by the Clytha hills, turns at right angles, and runs in a straight direction under the precipitous and woody ridge on which the castle is situated. We descended in a boat to Trostrey Forge, and disembarked at a weir, where I took an opportunity of examining its structure and observed the method of catching salmon.

An embankment of stakes and stones is thrown diagonally across the river, between two and three hundred yards in length. In the middle of the weir is a vacancy, provided with an iron grate, through which a considerable body of the river rushes with great impetuosity. At the lower part of the weir, on one side of this stream, is a large wooden box, perforated with holes, to admit the water and air, with an aperture, to which is affixed a long, round, wicker basket, resembling a tunnel. This aperture is closed with a small iron grate, which opens within the box, like a trap door, and falls to its original position by its own weight. A square wooden frame, similar to those used at mills for the purpose of catching eels, extends nearly across the whole of the stream, below the large iron grate, leaving only sufficient room for the salmon. The fish in his migration, is obliged to ascend this narrow opening, and having passed the wooden frame, is stopped by the grate. Instead of retreating down the narrow pass by which he ascended, he turns sideways, is hurried by the rapidity of the stream along a narrow current, leading through the tunnel, forces up the trap door, which immediately falls down behind him, and is thus secured in the box. The box contained several salmon, one of which did not weigh less than thirty pounds.

Trostrey Forge is rented by Harvey, Wason, and Company, from Sir Samuel Fludyer. The place contains little worthy of observation, except an inscription over the door, which marks the extraordinary height of the Usk :—

"FLOOD, FEBRUARY 11TH, 1795. HARVEY, WASON, AND COMPANY, BRISTOL."

This memorial will convey some idea of the dreadful inundations to which the country, in the vicinity of the river, is subject. The inscription is fourteen feet above the ground, and twenty-two above the ordinary level of the river. The water rose to this uncommon height in the space of twelve hours. Several of the workmen witnessed the inundation, and Mr. Wason, one of the proprietors, confirmed to me the truth of the memorial. Fortunately, however, the river subsided almost as rapidly as it had increased.

The bar-iron manufactured at this forge is sent to Tredonnoc bridge by land; from thence conveyed down the Usk to Newport, and exported to Bristol. A little beyond the forge the river is no longer navigable, even for small vessels. It flows in a deep abyss amid hills and woods, until it emerges near the town of Usk.

---

It is on record that in 1782 a salmon of the monster weight of 68½ lbs. was caught in the Usk, somewhere near Trostre. A painted drawing of it was made at the time, and long hung in Mr. Nicholls' arbour in his garden at Usk. Mr. Rees, the Postmaster, had a similar drawing made. Some forty years ago I had a facsimile painted of the latter, which has hung in my hall ever since.

---

There is a famous inn at Usk called "The Three Salmons," and here tradition has it some of the Welsh ironmasters used to meet occasionally to eat an Usk salmon : it being the opinion of such epicures that the fish was at its best when caught after twelve hours in the fresh water.

## XXIX.

# Abbey Tintern Iron Works.

WE have left the Usk, and are now on the Wye, but still in Monmouthshire. In the olden time every little stream was utilised as water power to turn the wheels of the iron industry, if otherwise conveniently placed, as these Works were, for shipping on the tideway of a great river.

What precise description of Iron Works these at Tintern Abbey were, I do not know, but they were certainly of ancient date.

As far back as 1753, we find in an inventory of New Wear Forge, also on the Wye, but some miles higher up its course, there were then in stock 35 tons and 15 cwt. of "Tinterne Pigs" (valued at £6 15*s*. per ton), which would point to the existence of a Furnace there at that period.

On July 15th, 1805, the following letter was written from the Abbey Tintern Works to our old friends, Walter and John Powell, of Brecon, by Mr. Robert Thompson, presumably then the owner, or part owner, of these Works.

"Abbey Tintern Works, July 15th, 1805.

"Dear Sir,—As I shall not receive the Draft you are to send me before Wednesday. I shall not have time to peruse it with the parties before I see you at Quarter-day.

"You must, therefore, if possible, go with me to Chepstow on Tuesday next, and I will get them to meet you there. I must meet the Gloucester Bank People this day week, and enter into some engagement with them to pay the money.

"I, therefore, much wish to have the Articles agreed before I do so, and am

"Dear Sir, yours most sincerely,

"Messrs. Walter and John Powell, Brecon. "ROBERT THOMPSON."

## XXX.

# Monmouth Forge.

THIS Forge is undoubtedly one of the oldest in South Wales (and Monmouthshire), and I am inclined to think that it was built even before New Wear Forge, which we know was erected as far back as 1684.

The great suitability of the Monnow river, both in its volume of water and in the ease with which its stream could be impounded, would be likely to induce the early ironmasters to place one of their Forges there ; and I have seen somewhere among our family papers that our ancestor, the George White there referred to, once occupied the Monmouth Forge, and entrusted it to one of his brothers on taking up himself the new and bigger venture at New Wear.

We shall see presently how Messrs. Partridge—father and son—became lessees under Mr. George White, the son, of New Wear Forge, in 1753, and we now find that in 1795 Mr. John Partridge (the son, I think) writes to our old friends, Walter and John Powell, of Brecon, from "Monmouth Forges," for Harford, Partridge and Co. Apparently, the John Partridge (father and son, or son only) did not now stand alone, but in becoming the occupiers of the Monmouth Forge had entered into partnership with the great Bristol firm of Harford.

And at that very time this firm of Harford, Partridge and Co. held the Nantyglo Works, the Ebbw Vale Works, and those at Melin Griffith.

"Monm'h Forges, October 11th, 1795.

"Dear Sirs,—Your favor of the Ult'o was duly received. David Jones's conduct does not merit any indulgence from us. However, if you can have a security for the Balance, in case of his failure or decease, I shall leave you to settle it with him. I shall have occasion to pay to the Brecon Bank a Call for the Aberdare Canal some time this month. I will send them an Order upon you for the am't in your Hands. I think David Jones ought to pay your Charges, as we took a considerable deal of trouble and expense to settle with him without effect.

"I was in great hopes I sho'd have heard of your having taken the opinion of Counsel upon Nant y glo affairs long since. I don't see that delaying it can answer any good purpose.

"I am, for Harford, Self and Co., etc.,

"Messrs. Walter and John Powell, Att'ys, Brecon. "JNO. PARTRIDGE."

---

And probably, though in a little way, these Monmouth Forges were the safest and best-paying of the concerns.

In 1821 they were called the Monmouth Iron Works, and we find one of the well-known Staffordshire name of Whitehouse as manager there in 1821.

"Monm'h Forges, Octr. 11, 1821.

"Dear Sirs,—I saw Mr. White, of Afon, yesterday, who informed me that you had told him that you were giving eleven shillings per Cord for Charcoal wood at your work near Abergavenny. If so, you must mean the long and not the short cord, and which I hope you will have the goodness to explain by return, as I may set Mr. White right in his opinion as respects the price of Cordwood for this season. Waiting your reply.

"I am, Dear Sir, etc.,

"John Powell, Esq., "BENJ'N WHITEHOUSE.

"Messrs. Powell, Jones, and Powell, Atty's, Brecon."

---

Mr. Richard Blakemore, of the Melin Griffith Works, and afterwards of the Leys, Monmouth, was Mr. Partridge's nephew, and it is probable that he at one time or another was a partner in the Monmouth Works.

I can well remember, as late as 1856, the sound of the ponderous hammers going thump, thump! in the night time; but even a Works of this kind had at last to give way before the advent of new and more improved modes of iron manufacture.

*Page* 207.

NEW WEAR FORGE. 1797.

*(Ireland's "River Wye.")*

XXXI.

# The New Wear Forge.

There had been a wear across the Wye at this point, it was said, time out of mind, and also an Iron Forge standing near the same, but that the wear had been thrown down by rioters, coming from Herefordshire and the Forest of Dean, in 1587 or 1588, as stated in "Bamforth's Old Account Book." The wear was also again destroyed by ice in 1683-84, and it cost the owner, Anthony, Earl of Kent, who was the Lord of the Manor of Goodrich, and possessed of the royalties of fishing in the Wye thereabouts in Herefordshire, upwards of fourscore pounds to repair the damage, and which repairs were done by Mr. Thomas Fletcher, of Monmouth.

Upon this happening, and the wear being made good, Mr. George White, then of Monmouth Forge, gentleman, having obtained a lease for ninety-nine years, or for the lives of himself and his sons, George and John, and twenty-one years after of the wear and lands and adjacent fishery from the Earl of Kent, proceeded, in conjunction with one Anthony Grub, in 1684, to erect a forge or iron mill there on the old foundation.

The Works were erected and successfully carried on for many years by Mr. George White—Father White, he was known as.

In 1695, when the Wye and Luggs Navigation Act was passed, the Works are thus described in an old paper.

> "The Earl of Kent, upon an old Foundation, has lately built his Forge, which is one of the best in England, having two Hammers, and three Chaferies or Fineries, which can work in the driest time of summer. There were, besides, a dwelling-house for a Tenant, Stables, Warehouses, and outhouses, and several Dwelling-houses lately built for above 30 families, costing together about £4000."

A daughter of the old George White married a Mr. Jordan, ironmaster, of Tinterne, in 1690, or so.

George White, the son, succeeded George White the father, and the Works still prospering, the son had built himself, in 1739, a comfortable mansion at Goodrich, of the native Old Red Sandstone, with pretty grounds and a rich garden attached.

In 1753 George White, now living in his new mansion at Goodrich, and his only child, Elizabeth, having married previously, in 1746, John Osborne, the wealthy clothier of Monksmill, at Wotton-under-Edge, Gloucestershire, he resolved to retire from the business of an ironmaster.

Accordingly, in this year he granted a lease (by permission of the trustees of the Duke of Kent's will) for fourteen years of

> "The Wear, Lock, Forge, fishing, Dwelling-house, Slitting Mill, Storehouses, and including the royalty of fishing, at the yearly rent of £270, and £10 to be paid to the Lock-keeper, to Mr. John Partridge, Ironmonger, of Ross."

There is a further special covenant as to the fishery to this effect :—

> "If, after paying all expenses of managing the fishery, the neat produce should exceed £30, then of all such excess one-third was to be paid annually to Mr. White, and Mr. Partridge undertook to send him annually 'a true and just account.'"

Mr. Partridge purchased the stock contained in the following inventory, amounting in value to £1,175 9*s.* 4*d.*

INVENTORY.—FORGE.

Lidbrook Coale for the Slitting Mill ... 13 tons 10 cwt., at 10/- per ton.
46 loads of Coales in Stock at 36/- per load (noe brasses).
Tinterne Pigs - - - 35 tons 15 cwt., at £6 15*s*. per ton.
Carmarthen Pigs - - 9 tons at £6 5*s*. per ton.
3 large Sledges for the use of the Wear.
German Steel—3 qrs. 18 lbs., at 6½*d*. per lb. - £2 15*s*. 3*d*.

| ALSO FOR THE RIVER AND FISHERY. | £ | s. | d. |
|---|---|---|---|
| For the Barge, 14 Tons Burden, with saile, mast, and other riggin | 20 | 0 | 0 |
| For the horse Boat - - - - - | 12 | 0 | 0 |
| For a large Stock Boat - - - - | 2 | 15 | 0 |
| For netts, coracle, fishing boat, drag, with other implements at the fish-house (with two hogsheads, belonging to the Fishery) - - - - - | 17 | 0 | 0 |

The horse boat was built by William Hudson in 1747. The nets included "a new long nett."

The Works seem to have consisted solely of fineries and puddling mills for turning out manufactured iron in the state of sheet and rod iron. The pigs were brought from Tinterne by the river, and from Carmarthen by vessel to Llandogo, and thence by barge.

The coal was brought down the river from Lydbrook by barge, being obtained in the Forest of Dean levels.

Charcoal was greatly used there, and Mr. White was a large buyer of the woods round, and especially of the Scudamore family, of Kentchurch Court.

A prodigious quantity of salmon was caught some years, of which I have some of the returns; and Mr. Partridge is reported to have said: "The fishery paid better than the Forge;" but that was, of course, an ironmaster's bit of fun.

I am thinking that, probably through Mr. Partridge being initiated into the mysteries of ironmaking by the old George White, either at Monmouth Forge or at New Wear, it first came about that the Partridge family entered into the business, where they so largely figured after as partners in the Bristol firm of Harford, Partridge and Co, of Nant y Glo, Ebbw Vale, and elsewhere in South Wales.

And now to a finish of our tour round the old South Wales Iron Works. We began with the 1720 Forge at Brecon, and we leave off with one still older, that of New Wear, dating, beyond a doubt, from 1684; and in respect of its antiquity, and of the curious admixture of the iron and salmon fishery industries in the same concern—not forgetting its uninterrupted prosperity for one hundred years—this old Forge on the Wye, once owned and worked by our family, is a fitting one to close the roll of fame.

---

END.

# Annex.

## MR. WILLIAM CRAWSHAY II. ON THE HISTORY OF THE CRAWSHAY FAMILY, 1847.

At an entertainment given to the inhabitants of Merthyr and Dowlais, at the "Bush Hotel," in October, 1847, in response to the toast of his health, Mr. Crawshay referred to the part his family had taken in founding the Cyfarthfa Works, with special reference to his grandfather Richard :—

"I ask not," said he, "for public life; I never did, my whole object being to enjoy the esteem of those I see before me, and of the men whom I employ; to know that I enjoy their goodwill is my greatest satisfaction. God grant that my sons, at sixty years of age, may receive the same compliment from your successors. My connection with the place is so well understood, that little remains for me to tell you; but if I do describe to you the first part of my grandfather's life, I trust you will receive it in the way in which I intend it. I mean, that it should be heard not by setting suns, but by rising suns. And think not, gentlemen, that I am proud to make a boast of my origin. Although I tell these things, and am in one sense proud of them, yet I do not boast of them. My grandfather was the son of a respectable farmer at Normanton, in the County of York. At the age of sixteen, father and son differed. My grandfather could not agree with his father—the reasons are unknown to me—and my grandfather, an enterprising boy, left Normanton for London, and rode his own pony up. When he got to London, which, in those days, was an arduous task of some sixteen or twenty days' travelling, he found himself as destitute of friends as he possibly could be. He sold his pony for £15, and, during the time that the proceeds of the pony kept him, he found employment at an iron warehouse, kept by Mr. Bicklewith; he hired himself for three years for the price of his pony. His occupation was to clean the counting-house, to put the desks in order for his master and the clerks, and to do anything else that he was told to do. By industry, integrity, and perseverance, he gained his master's favour, and, in the course of a few months, he was considered decidedly better than the boy who had been there before him. He was termed the Yorkshire Boy; and the Yorkshire Boy, gentlemen, progressed in his master's favour, by his activity, integrity, and perseverance. He had a very amiable and good master, and, at the end of a very short period, before he had been two years in his place, he stood high in his master's confidence. The trade in which he was engaged was only a cast-iron warehouse, and his master assigned to him, the Yorkshire Boy, the privilege of selling flat-irons, the things with which our shirts are flattened. The washerwomen of London were sharp folks, and when they bought one flat-iron they stole two. Mr. Bicklewith thought the best person to cope with them would be a person working for his own interests, and a Yorkshire man at the same time. My grandfather sold these articles, and that was the first matter of trading that ever he embarked in in his life. By honesty and perseverance he continued to grow in his master's favour, who, being an indolent man, in a few years retired, and left my grandfather in possession of this cast-iron business in London. That business was carried on on the very site where I now spend my days, in York Yard, London. In the course of time my grandfather left his business there, and came down here; and my father, who carried it on, supplied him with money almost as fast as he spent it here, but not quite so fast; and it is there I spend the produce of this county. And you know to what an extent the iron produce of this county has risen up. My grandfather established the iron works at Merthyr and Cyfarthfa. My father was only left 3-8ths of it: but by purchase he obtained the whole of it, and by his benevolence I have succeeded to it. During my time, the concern has not diminished, and I pray God it never may diminish; and I hope the rising generation will see that, by industry, integrity, and perseverance, wealth and rank in life in the position they have chosen are attainable by everybody who started with humbler prospects than my grandfather. No man in the room is so poor that he cannot command £15. I have told you this before, and I am proud of it. Depend on it, any young man who is industrious, honest, and persevering will be respected in any class of life he may move in; and do you think, gentlemen, that there is a man in England prouder than I am at this moment? What is all the world to me, unless they know me? And you would not be here to-night, unless you thought me entitled to your good will."

---

## MR. WILLIAM CRAWSHAY II. AND THE BANK OF ENGLAND, 1848.

The following letter, protesting against the Governors of the Bank engaging directly in business as an ironmaster, appeared in *The Times* of December 6th, 1848:—

"Sir,—As neither your time nor your columns are of so little value as to warrant unnecessary words being addressed to you, I beg to trouble you with the following simple facts only; and, if you are pleased to insert this communication in your all-powerful paper, it may elicit attention in the quarter from which a redress of the grievance of which I complain may be derived. I am an ironmaster, carrying on, through the superintendence of my sons, the several Works of Cyfarthfa, Hirwain, Newbridge, and the Forest of Dean, and am the vendor of the produce of these Works myself, as an iron merchant in Upper Thames Street. Owing to the falling-off in the demand for rails, the iron trade is in a sad state of depression, and the competition is such that bar iron and rails may now be purchased at or about the rate of £5 per ton at the several ports of shipment in Wales—a price which is below the present actual cost of production. I have met with the most cutting competition from a Company of ironmasters entitled in the iron trade 'The Bank of England,' and in Liverpool and London, almost every quotation which I make to enquiries of the price of iron for export, is met with the reply, 'The Bank of England will sell considerably lower.' To a quotation which I made to a metal-broker for only 50 tons of sheet iron for shipment in India, of £9 per ton free on board in the docks here, I received the answer, 'I can buy it from the Bank of England at £7 10*s.* free on board here,' and I have since been informed by the same party that he so bought the said 50 tons of sheet iron, the total amount being £375. In consequence of this very low, and to the makers, ruinous sale of sheet iron, I deputed the same broker to purchase of the Bank of England, for me, 100 tons of the same description; but, after a delay in the acceptance of my order of three days, I was informed that the Bank of England had been deceived in the quantity of sheet iron which they could manufacture, and, having already sold several other parcels, could not enter into further engagements at present.

"Now, sir, it appears to me that, however unwillingly or unpremeditatingly the Bank of England may have been drawn into the manufacture and sale of iron, it cannot be within their own province, even 'as mortgagees in possession of iron works,' to carry on, as the Bank of England, a trade or manufacture beyond what is contemplated and warranted by their charter; and as an individual ironmaster and iron merchant, I can but feel deeply aggrieved by such a competitor as I met with in the Company. The wages which I individually am compelled to pay my men weekly, and at the end of each month, amount to not less than £25,000, the whole of which I am bound to find in cash, and no part of my Works (unlike those of my competitor) afford me the advantage of making my own bank notes. Were such convenience attached to my Works I could sell bar iron 20*s.*

and sheet iron 30*s.* per ton below the market price, and yet be enabled to pay my workmen on Saturday night; and surely, sir, if a charter to the Bank of England for note-making be construed to extend to making iron, a privilege ought to be allowed to us depressed ironmasters, in addition to the manufacture of iron, to make our own notes, and then we might by possibility exist under competition with the Bank of England. How long this new trade of iron-making is to be carried on by the Governor and Company of the Bank of England, in addition to their grand monopoly of paper, will, in my humble opinion, much depend upon the notice which you may be pleased to take of this matter; and, powerful as you are in abating other grievances and improprieties, I trust this may not be considered unworthy of being taken up by you with your usual extraordinary ability and acumen.

"I am, Sir,

"Your very obedient Servant,

"London, December 6th, 1848. "WILLIAM CRAWSHAY."

---

## MR. WILLIAM CRAWSHAY II. AND THE "TRUCK" SYSTEM, 1860.

The following important letter was addressed to Mr. Charles Wilkins, F.G.S., then the Editor of the Merthyr *Telegraph*, which he has kindly allowed me to reproduce:—

"Sir,—In your paper of the 7th instant, you have paid me a compliment which I cannot but acknowledge as publicly as you have made it, and I thus do so direct to yourself, in the expectation that this my letter will also appear in your paper.

"I thank you sincerely for your flattering expressions as to myself, and could have wished, that through a long life, I had merited all you say of me, more particularly in the one point, 'Never hasty in decision.' I have, however, no cause myself to complain of the result of a rather hasty temperament, for I have been blessed, as a manufacturer and tradesman, with unusual and ample success, and I hope that no man has at any time been injured by my quick determinations.

"Your highly complimentary article, and this my acknowledgment of it, arise from the early termination of my present lease of the Cyfarthfa Iron Works, and the negotiation which has been so nearly broken off, for its renewal; I say nearly, for since my letter of the 28th of March to Mr. Jacob Jones, I have received an invitation to meet a gentleman, on the part of my landlords, again upon the question of renewal; and I now again say, that I will not fail to give the earliest information in my power of any alteration which may affect the welfare of my workmen and others interested in the continuance of the Cyfarthfa Works.

"There is much to be said, and felt, as to what you write of the "Decline of Merthyr!" I am willing and ready to devote my few remaining years, under the aid of my son, to stave off this, some day, inevitable event. But instead of being baffled upon superficial trifles, after having agreed as to the mineral rents and royalties, I have a right to look to the most liberal encouragement in such minor matters, rather than stringent extortion, from those who are so deeply interested in the carrying on and success of the Cyfarthfa Iron Works, for the welfare of their large house and other property in the neighbourhood, and which are wholly dependent upon the continuance of the iron trade of Merthyr Tydfil, and of which Cyfarthfa forms so large a part. I have to labour, however, henceforth under many disadvantages in carrying on the Works at Cyfarthfa, in opposition to those of Scotland, Lancashire, and the East Coast, where newly discovered iron ore is used, and to contend with which I am obliged to convey the same ore to my Works, at a cost much aggravated by long carriage, and mineral profit (of course) to those who raise it, and this to a greater extent than two-thirds of all I use in my furnaces at Cyfarthfa!

"But I feel, Sir, that I am digressing from my intended simple acknowledgment of your article, so complimentary to me, and I will only further allude to one other disadvantage under which I am compelled to labour at Cyfarthfa, though I will never, by availing myself of similar injustice to my workmen, take that advantage which is enjoyed by many of my brother competitors in the manufacture of iron, over me—"The Truck System!" I wholly and utterly disapprove it, and will while I live, pay my men for hard work in hard money, and money only; and I feel that I should be justified in joining any league to put an end to a system which I have no doubt gives to those who practise it a clear advantage over me of 10 per cent., or 2*s.* in the pound, upon all amounts incurred for labour, and which Truck System, although attempted and intended to be suppressed by the Legislature, is openly and notoriously carried on, under masked declarations and provisions, to the contrary.

"I am, Sir,

"Your obliged and obedient Servant,

"Caversham Park, April 9th, 1860. "WILLIAM CRAWSHAY."

---

## MEMBERS OF THE FIRM OF J. AND C. BAILEY, OF NANT Y GLO AND BEAUFORT IRON-WORKS, IN PARLIAMENT.

| | JOSEPH BAILEY. | | Seat. |
|---|---|---|---|
| 1835. Jan. 8 | ... Joseph Bailey (father)... | ... Glanusk Park | ... City of Worcester. |
| 1837. July 22 | ... Joseph Bailey (father) | ... Do. | ... City of Worcester. |
| 1837. Dec. 12 | ... Joseph Bailey (son) ... | ... Do. | ... Sudbury, Suffolk. |
| 1841. June 29 | ... Joseph Bailey (father)... | ... Do. | ... City of Worcester. |
| 1841. July 5 | ... Joseph Bailey (son) ... | ... Easton Court | ... County of Hereford. |
| 1847. Aug. 2 | ... Joseph Bailey (father)... | ... Glanusk Park | ... County of Brecon. |
| 1847. Aug. 4 | ... Joseph Bailey (son) ... | .. Easton Court | ... County of Hereford. |
| 1852. July 14 | ... Joseph Bailey (father), Sir, Bart., | Glanusk Park | ... County of Brecon. |
| 1857. March 3 | ... Joseph Bailey (father), Sir, Bart., | Glanusk Park | ... County of Brecon. |

(Died in 1858. Succeeded as Member by Godfrey Morgan.)

| | CRAWSHAY BAILEY. | | Seat. |
|---|---|---|---|
| 1852. April 3 | ... Crawshay Bailey | ... Nant y Glo | ... Monmouth Boroughs. |
| 1852. July 6 ... | Do. | ... Do. | ... Do. do |
| 1857. March 27 .. | Do. | ... Do. | ... Do. do. |
| 1859. April 30 ... | Do. | ... ... Do. | ... Do. do. |
| 1865. July 11 ... | Do. | ... ... Do. | ... Do. do. |

(Defeated by Sir John W. Ramsden at the Election of 1868.)

∴ The late Lord Glanusk, of Glanusk Park, who was one of the Members for the County of Hereford in 1865, and subsequent Parliaments, was the grandson of Joseph Bailey, M.P., 1835, as above.

# Index.

## A.—GENERAL.

## B.—IRON MASTERS.

## C.—IRON WORKS.

## D.—MINERAL LANDLORDS, ETC.



PRINTED AT THE BEDFORD PRESS, 20 AND 21, BEDFORDBURY, STRAND, LONDON, W.C.

www.ingramcontent.com/pod-product-compliance
Ingram Content Group UK Ltd.
Pitfield, Milton Keynes, MK11 3LW, UK
UKHW031350140325
5004UKWH00041B/491

9 781015 857049